Inside Babylon

Inside Babylon

The Caribbean Diaspora in Britain

Edited by

WINSTON JAMES
and
CLIVE HARRIS

VERSO
London · New York

First published by Verso 1993
© Verso 1993
All rights reserved

Verso
UK: 6 Meard Street, London W1V 3HR
USA: 29 West 35th Street, New York, NY 10001–2291

Verso is the imprint of New Left Books

ISBN 0–86091–471–2
ISBN 0–86091–636–7 (pbk)

British Library Cataloguing in Publication Data
A catalogue record for this book is available from the British Library

Library of Congress Cataloging-in-Publication Data
A catalogue record for this book is available from the Library of Congress

Typeset by York House Typographic, London W13
Printed and bound in Great Britain by
Biddles Ltd, Guildford and King's Lynn

This book is dedicated to the memory of

KELSO COCHRANE
Antiguan carpenter, killed by racists in the
streets of Notting Hill, 16 May 1959, aged 33

and

CLAUDIA JONES
(21 February 1915 to 25 December 1964)
who fought oppression and exploitation
on both sides of the Atlantic

Contents

Acknowledgements

My receipt of an Arturo Schomburg fellowship, 1991–92, in the Faculty of Humanities at the City College, City University of New York, enabled me to carry out important revisions and editorial work on *Inside Babylon*. And for this I would like to thank Dean Paul Sherwin and Elizabeth Starcevicz for their support.

WJ.

We refuse to be what you wanted us to be;
We are what we are, that's the way it's going to be . . .
We've been trodden on your wine press *much* too long . . .
And we've been taken for granted, *much* too long . . .
De Babylon System is a vampire,
Sucking the children day by day.
De Babylon System is a vampire,
Sucking the blood of the sufferers . . .

BOB MARLEY

What happens to a dream deferred?

Does it dry up
like a raisin in the sun?
Or fester like a sore –
And then run?
Does it stink like rotten meat?
Or crust and sugar over –
like a syrupy sweet?

Maybe it just sags
like a heavy load.

Or does it explode?

LANGSTON HUGHES

Introduction

Clive Harris and Winston James

This book spans the whole post-war period and offers a scholarship on a range of themes reflecting the varied experience of the Caribbean diaspora in Britain. What makes this collection distinctive is its attempt to give voice to the fractured narratives of this diaspora from within. It attempts to speak the real histories in which diasporic groups become inscribed and position themselves despite displacement and ruptures. In standard texts, these histories have often been subverted by those who have perceived them through ideological prisms, most commonly that of the 'politics of race'. Invariably, the outcome is a peroxided and pomaded view of British history in which issues of 'race' are portrayed as absent from the British political scene until the 'nigger hunts' of 1958 (Katznelson 1976). In a like vein, others, in the manner of Park, have tried to subsume the experience of black people under a 'race relations' rubric which perceives relations between groups as moving from competition → conflict → accommodation → assimilation/ integration. In Britain, an early exponent of this tradition was Ken Little's *Negroes in Britain*. The classic example, however, is Sheila Patterson's *Dark Strangers*, whose over-arching analytical framework is the host/immigration situation, albeit 'complicated by colour'. For writers such as Patterson (1965), what determined the position of migrants, and the 'antipathy' they experienced was their 'strangeness' and 'outmoded' form of social behaviour.

This study was to spawn a whole new slide-rule scholarship determined to assess how far along the 'race relations' continuum 'immigrants' had come, i.e. the degree of 'strangeness' that still obtained and the extent of adaptation that still has to be achieved. Even when they purport to draw on more radical, class-based sociological traditions, writers such as Rex and Tomlinson (1979), despite their protestations, hardly managed to escape from the narrow confine of 'race relations' assimilationism. The integration into class-based structures and institutions is now substituted for the assimilation into 'the English way of life'. Such empiricism is elevated to the status of theory in *Race Relations in Sociological Theory* where Rex sought to map out what he terms the

1

possible 'race relations situations' (Rex 1983: 159–60) between what are
described unproblematically as 'groups with distinct identities and recognis-
able characteristics'. With few exceptions, a whole scholarship has been dyed
not only in the colour of the researcher's skin, but in the colour of their
imagination.

The solution quite often proposed hinges on the need for government,
schools and other institutions to take steps to break down the barriers of
difference. On this premiss has flourished the whole new mythology of 'multi-
culturalism'. Ironically, even when 'multi-culturalism' is preached in the
name of anti-racism, cultural belonging becomes fetishized in some quarters
to the point of creating a real cultural nature. Difference is not merely
celebrated, it is absolutized.

This absolutization is evident in many discussions of ethnicity. The most
apparent change that occurs is that researchers substitute the signifier
'culture/ethnicity' for the signifier 'race'. But no sooner is this done than they
proceed to attach to culture a 'heritage', a 'lineage', a set of 'roots' which
naturalize 'cultural difference'. Take, for example, the way in which notions
of 'ethnicity' are yoked to biological notions of 'race'/colour in Brown (1984)
such that only through 'race'/colour does the respondent arrive at his/her
ethnicity. It is the story of genesis all over: on the first day black and white
people were created; on the second day black people, and only black people,
were then differentiated into their various ethnicities. 'True nationals' –
'whites' – remain indivisible. But if only OTHERS have ethnicity, what do
'whites' have? Well, they have . . . they have . . . 'whiteness'. 'Whiteness' is
deemed to confer not only an essential unity and homogeneity but a mono-
thetic sense of identity which posits a 'one true self' held in common by
people of a specific skin colour.[1]

In naturalizing ethnicity and culture, 'ethnic relations' researchers are
assured of ever-present, always-will-be ethnic habitats on which to practise
their craft. Such habitats can thence be colonized and entire ethnic groups
metamorphosed into 'my Pakistanis', 'my black youths', 'my Asian women' or,
simply, 'my minority ethnics'.

In their role as consultants who enlighten neophytes about the essential
qualities of these ethnic groups – the presumption being that the would-be
bearers of ethnicity are incapable of describing what we are told has always
been theirs, will always be theirs – researchers now become part of the system
of power which blocks, prohibits and invalidates that knowledge and
responsibility for consciousness. Once ethnic habitats are exhausted or
become tiresome and unrewarding for the pursuit of career, they are then
jettisoned in favour of more lucrative haunts for which a research grant might
be procured. In the process the real study of racism is transmogrified into a
study of difference.

* * *

What has been central to the experience of black people in Britain has been neither the 'idea' nor the 'politics' of 'race' as the 'idea' or the politics of 'racial difference'. Rather, it has been racism and other forms of oppression. It is racism that has determined the manner in which their labour-power has been utilized; it is racism that has determined the manner in which their 'communities' have been policed; it is racism which assaults their humanity in psychiatric hospitals; and it is the effects of racism, too, that have been internalized. In short, it is racism against which the struggle has to be fought. Not difference.

Since the 1960s Marxists/neo-Marxists have offered different conceptual frameworks for understanding racism. The most crude version has portrayed racism as a ruling class ideology which secures and justifies the 'heightened' or 'super'-exploitation of black and other migrant workers (Castles and Kosack 1973; Sivanandan 1982; Castells 1975; Nikolinakos 1975; Aptheker 1971; Perlo 1975). The consequent divisions thereby created within the 'working class' are perceived as blurring the boundaries of class and inhibiting the common *class* struggle against capital. With primacy given to 'class', 'racial' exploitation becomes merely one aspect of proletarianization. In *Racism and Migrant Labour* (1982), Bob Miles sought to offer a more sophisticated treatment which prioritized 'class' over 'race' on the ground that the concept of 'race' is unanalytical and reactionary since 'races' as such do not exist. Rather, they are social constructions. This process of social construction is grasped by the notion of *racialization* which, by and large, has its provenance in the economic dynamic. The real object of study therefore is 'racism' and not 'race'; and here Miles acknowledges that racism can assume independent forms at the ideological and political levels.

Questioning the economism, reductionism and apriorism of much of this analysis, writers such as Hall (1980); Centre for Contemporary Cultural Studies (1982) and Gilroy (1987) have argued for the 'relative autonomy' of the ideology of racism from class-based social relations. Gilroy, for example, argues for the 'opening up' of class analysis to incorporate 'other' histories of subordination (1987: 18–19). The notion of 'race' for Gilroy, however, is not simply an ideological category; it is, above all, a political category which provides the basis for solidarity and action. As such it is as analytically significant as class. Yet other writers such as Ben-Tovim and Gabriel have gone even further in arguing for a complete break with reductionism and, in so doing, undercut the reformulation offered by 'relative autonomy' approaches. 'Race' and 'racism' are described as products of ideological and political practices and struggles 'with their own theoretical/ideological conditions of existence' and, as such, are irreducible to class. It is only *after* racist ideologies have been produced that they have the capacity to intervene at the level of the economy (Ben-Tovim and Gabriel 1979).

The key lacuna of most Marxist analyses is that they remain imprisoned within the Althusserian/Poulantzian separation of 'economic' from 'political' and 'ideological'. In effect, they hold to a formalist separation between base and superstructure which itself rests on a reductionist concept of 'economy' that excludes 'politics' and 'ideology'. As a result, the critique of the exploitative relationship between a *concrete* labour and a *concrete* capital as a basis for analysis of the position of the black diaspora in Britain tends to be no more than a critique of technicist and labourist notions of class. What has never been fully developed is Hall's interesting, if somewhat elliptical, statement that 'race' is a 'modality in which class is "lived", the medium through which class relations are experienced, the form in which it is appropriated and "fought through" ' (Hall 1980: 341). Hall could perhaps go one step further here: 'race' enters not only in the determination of how class is 'lived', 'experienced' or 'fought through', but in how 'class' itself is constituted. The same can be said for 'gender', 'age', 'ethnicity' and 'national identity' and 'sexuality'. By the same token, 'black people' are never simply *black* people; they are men and women, old and young, Afro-Caribbean and 'Asian', and so on.

Via the conventionally treated notion of the *industrial reserve army of labour*, Chapters 1 and 3, by Clive Harris and Gail Lewis respectively, attempt to understand the way in which politics and ideology have been internal to the very constitution of the economic and thereby to the complex position occupied by black workers in the British economy. The aim is to examine the way in which 'race', 'gender' and 'ethnicity' combine and intersect internally, rather than being added on to class, to produce and reproduce 'white' privilege, to produce and reproduce 'occupational ghettos', to produce and reproduce black people as 'racially, a sort of proletariat' (Wyndham Lewis).

By locating black migration to Britain against a background of 'labour shortage' and Keynesian 'full employment', it questions that 'tunnel history' which deploys the explanatory dyad of push and pull or a replacement population thesis (Peach 1968). What these two positions have in common is the notion that there was 'room at the bottom' of the British occupational structure which sucked in the relative surplus population of the Caribbean and Indian sub-continent. The presumption is that there was no room at the top or in the middle. This thesis is a product of a crass empiricism which presumes that because black workers obtained by and large only semi- and unskilled jobs in specific branches of production, that this was where the 'labour shortage' occurred. Research has now shown that there was also 'room at the top' and 'room in the middle'. The question is why did black workers become trapped in the 'room at the bottom' such that these jobs became identified as 'black jobs'.

More than this, the aim is to question the simple equation of the use of migrant labour with declining profitability or with simple notions of availability and disposability. Against a background of recession and the consequent restructuring of British capital, the very concept of the industrial reserve army has to be rethought to address the position of young blacks who, in many areas, have become bystanders to the process of accumulation, i.e. become a permanent part of the relative surplus-population. This position has been reinforced not only by disproportionately high levels of unemployment but by the experience of the early Youth Opportunities Programme and its successor, the Youth Training Scheme.

An emergent feature of the way in which the industrial reserve army has been used, which takes us beyond disposability, is the development of casualized, part-time, flexible, subcontracting labour. In other words, we have a system of 'contingent work' where risk is transmitted downwards through a process of vertical disintegration (Singleman and Tienda 1985).

For many contributors to the book, the state is central to the production and reproduction of racism. In Chapter 2, Carter, Harris and Joshi explore the little-acknowledged role of government and the administrative apparatuses of state in the racialization of black people. They show that there was never a 'liberal hour', never a 'laissez-faire' period, when black people were not subject to racist immigration control.

In Chapter 3 Gail Lewis returns to the theme of black people and the British economy by examining the position of black women. This is an important contribution which challenges the conventional view that all migrants were men. The key aim is to show how black women's employment experiences have been shaped not only by economic factors and racism but by sexism and the sexual division of labour. It is the intersection between these elements that defines the distinct position of black women in the labour market as akin neither to that of white women nor to that of black men.

Lewis charts particularly the way in which this position has been negatively affected by attempts to arrest the post-war decline of British capitalism by strategies such as monetarism, and consequent public sector cuts. Even as black women move into non-manual occupations these areas are being subject to increasing proletarianization. Thus new conditions experienced may not be much different from conditions left behind.

The restructuring of the workplace has been extended into the community; and Lewis draws attention to community struggles over health cuts, inner-city policies and social security. It is the duality of both restructurings that must be grasped if we are to understand the position of black women.

Lewis too picks up the same theme as Harris, namely, the increasing transformation of the way in which the industrial reserve army has been used as a new lever for accumulation by the move towards casualization, flexible specialization, subcontracting, home-working and sweat-shops. A feature of the latter is the use of patriarchal relations as a mode of control.

The two pieces by Amina Mama, like Lewis's, exhort us not to allow the struggle against racism to blur the need to address simultaneously the way in which sexism and the sexual division of labour powerfully shape the lives of black women, particularly when they manifest themselves in extreme forms such as domestic violence. In short, racism is gendered; or sexism is racialized. And they are here explored without fear or favour.

The idea that identity is constructed across difference and gives rise to multiple politics is further pursued by Claudette Williams in Chapter 6. Here she examines the implications of recognizing the specificity of oppression experienced by black women both vis-à-vis black men and vis-à-vis white women, and the consequent need for autonomous self-organization to combat sexism without subsuming this struggle under the struggle against racist oppression or under a struggle against sexism by an undifferentiated sisterhood.

If the term Caribbean has been masculinized in some quarters, Steve Vertovec in Chapter 7 shows how it, like the term West Indian before it, has become also a homogenizing category that is synonymous with people of African heritage and thereby excluding Indo-Caribbeans. The social construction of the notion of 'Asian' has likewise tended to exclude this group. A brief history of Indo-Caribbeans within the Caribbean is therefore a necessary preface to an elaboration of their experiences in post-war Britain. Vertovec highlights the way in which they have managed to remain a distinct social, cultural and religious community, and suggests implications that exclusion from other groups has had for the formation of British Indo-Caribbean collective identity and community organizations.

In Chapter 8 Errol Francis looks at the repressive apparatus of the 'social police' of psychiatry which, with the increasing medicalization of crime, has assumed a more central role in establishing the boundaries of the 'rational and sane'. The courts now have to be advised of the appropriate means for the disposition of convicted criminals.

Drawing critically upon the work of Michel Foucault, Francis singles out for particular scrutiny the act of diagnosis and the procedures of admission as the loci where psychiatric racism is interpolated as a problem of culture and anthropological knowledge, as the loci where the imagery of the 'insane-as-violent' is fused with racialized stereotypes of the black criminal and mugger: 'All I knew was that he was big and coloured!' said the policeman to the coroner. Once admitted under the various sections of the 1983 Mental Health Act, black patients become further subjected to a medical treatment regime bordering on torture, with rampant over-use of medication and numerous instances of physical abuse. The presumption is that the 'irrationality of black madness' is not susceptible to therapy. This chapter challenges the whole reductionist scholarship which seeks to explain the way in which blacks are disproportionately decanted in mental institutions in terms of the trauma of migration or cultural misdiagnosis.

Francis's examination of the 'social police' is complemented by Cecil Gutzmore's little-known but classic piece which has lost none of its cutting edge since it first appeared in the *Black Liberator* over a decade ago. Gutzmore takes as his focus the intersection between central and local state and how these interact with the 'sub-state' agencies of civil society. He attempts to give some history to the policing of black people through the lens of what is often perceived as the foremost expression of black culture in Britain: *Carnival*. Given as it was as a talk, this is a piece with a very direct style which argues trenchantly against 'isn't-it-quaint' anthropological travelogue notions of 'culture'.

For Gutzmore, culture is not the expression of some essentialist selfhood but a vehicle through which people struggle against oppression. Culture is literally the way we make our living – what we do to obtain food, clothing, shelter, and protection – the projects that we construct for ourselves, the practices in which we become engaged. Culture then, as the *Black Liberator* observed, is not just high writing, high music, and high ballet. Culture is also 'rasta', 'rudie', 'reggae' and 'rap'. In the words of Amilcar Cabral, 'Culture is simultaneously the fruit of a people's history and a determinant of history.' Culture is Carnival.

A people's culture is the basis of their independence; and when a dominant group attempts to stamp out the culture of oppressed groups, every mani-festation of this culture becomes a political act – an act of insurgency – for the dominant group. This is particularly so in periods of economic, political and ideological crises.

With a combination of grassroots knowledge and a sharp and clear political sense, Gutzmore's piece describes the Carnival events of the mid 1970s when the police, employing an extraordinary 'high profile', snuffed out both days of the 1976 Notting Hill Carnival with an overwhelming show of urban mass-control tactics and technology. We are presented not merely with the story of the Carnival but the lesson, the political lesson, of the Carnival. How we organize in response to the state and its agencies depends on this lesson. It ceases to be adequate to be simply *for* the Carnival; it is important to know why and how we defend the Carnival.

Finally, in Chapter 10, Winston James addresses a grossly neglected theme, namely, the process of *racialized subjectification*. He explores the way in which social agents are defined or define themselves as racialized subjects quite often with damaging consequences for identity or notions of 'who we really are' or 'what we have become' as a result of the process of migration. Out of this process of migration to a society in which 'race' and racism are salient features, have emerged new identities which are significantly different from those found in the Caribbean historically. Identities which are both pan-Caribbean and black, in which blackness is positively affirmed with an even greater vehemence on the part of people of the Caribbean diaspora than in the Caribbean itself. The varied and painful processes through which such new identities have been created in the metropolis are for the first time analysed in their full complexity. Moreover, the political implications of these processes – including relations between people of Caribbean and Asian descent – are frankly addressed with an eye to the continued need for the struggle against racism in Britain. As Stuart Hall (1990: 225) argues, cultural identities come from somewhere, have histories, and, like everything else that is historical, they undergo transformation and are subject to ruptures and discontinuities. It is the entrails of these ruptures and discontinuities which form the subject-matter of Chapter 10.

Clearly, there are major omissions in this book despite its breadth. In the areas covered, there is no attempt to offer a uniform 'line'. What unites all contributions is a desire to explore the sites and structures which produce and reproduce racism and sexism, and a clear understanding that the deep wounds of racism cannot be dressed by the loose bandages of 'race relations'. But most of all, this book hopes to bear witness to the painful sojourn of the Caribbean diaspora in Britain. *Inside Babylon* also hopes to give voice to the specificities of the diaspora's experience, to help give vent to the unabated yearning and struggles of Caribbean people for their unjustly and long-deferred liberation from racist oppression in Britain. We make no secret of the fact that our undertaking of this project was not solely or simply motivated by academic or even scholarly intent. May the analyses contained herein contribute, however modestly, to the forging of weapons by the children of the Caribbean diaspora and their allies in Britain in their prolonged, necessary and justified struggle against Babylon.

Notes

1. The deconstruction of 'whiteness' has not been taken on board much by academics. Some noteworthy exceptions are Richard Dyer (1988), bell hooks (1991), bell hooks (1992) and Toni Morrison (1992).

Post-war Migration and the Industrial Reserve Army

Clive Harris

Introduction

There is much that is unclear in the use of the concept of reserve army of labour or industrial reserve army (IRA). For most writers, the very concept itself, embodying as it does the word 'reserve', seems to evoke the idea of something lying *outside* production, outside the active labour force, but which can be later incorporated. Reserve here has the same connotation of 'reservation', reservoir, 'homelands', 'available pool', unemployed etc. This is a highly misleading usage which fails to distinguish adequately between two apparently interchangeable Marxian concepts: industrial reserve army and relative surplus-population (Marx 1974). In elaborating the distinction between these two concepts, this chapter will argue that the formation of the industrial reserve army cannot be read off from any analysis presented by Marx. Even in sections where Marx descends to a very concrete level, it is a concreteness that does not rise much above the economic in the sense that it omits any clear elaboration of the way in which politics and ideology exert their reciprocal influence.

In the immediate post-war years, it appeared as though British capitalism had come up against the barrier of 'labour shortage'. Conventional wisdom would explain this 'shortage' in terms of demography and posit as explanatory variables such factors as war deaths, fertility, birth and death rates. Such explanations are inherently limiting and fail signally to understand the manner in which the process of combined and uneven development on a national and international scale creates 'shortage' at one pole and 'surfeit' at another. The relative surplus-population or 'surfeit' drawn on from the Caribbean and Indian sub-continent to fuel post-war British capitalist expansion was both a product of an over-accumulation of capital in Britain fostered by imperial protection as well a product of the specific forms of capital accumulation in the colonies.

A second major limitation of simplistic explanations of 'labour shortage' is their failure to grasp the specific role that the post-war state was to play in securing the conditions of capital accumulation by the adoption of Keynesian policies. Of crucial importance for us was the way in which the 'social wage' curtailed the ability of capital to transform the indigenous relative surplus-population into an industrial reserve army as a lever of post-war accumulation.[1]

The key focus of this chapter, however, will be the manner in which the industrial reserve army recruited from the Caribbean and the Indian sub-continent was to be threaded through the labour process of spheres such as textiles, the National Health Service (NHS), London Transport and so on such that it emerged again in the 1970s, as superfluous, as unemployed. Central here were the policies pursued by labour exchanges, employers and trade unions. No less important was the manner in which the post-war state systematically racialized black labour and constructed it as an 'OTHER' that had to be excluded from the post-war British industrial reserve army. (See also Chapter 2 which deals with the 1951–55 Conservative government.)

The outcome of such practices was a vertical differentiation of branches of production with black workers confined to particular sectors, and a horizontal differentiation between various levels of the occupational hierarchy with black workers confined to semi- and unskilled jobs. In short, racism and discrimination were to intersect with class to produce segmentation and fractionalization, i.e. 'occupational ghettoes'. Such ghettoes represent 'occupations which are arduous, repetitive, often dangerous and unsocial, and more often than not relatively ill-paid. Second, they are traps from which movement to other, more varied, better paid occupations is difficult' (Feuchtwang 1982: 251).

Industrial Reserve Army and Relative Surplus-population

The relative surplus-population, Marx tells us, is the 'necessary product' of accumulation while the industrial reserve army is the 'lever' of accumulation. Product and lever: these are two very distinct functions (Behar 1974). Only at a highly abstract level of analysis can we assume that the mass which composes the 'product' is identical to the mass which composes the 'lever'.

Stating that the relative surplus-population is a 'necessary product' of capitalist accumulation is to say that it cannot be explained by reference to demography. Rather, one must examine the way in which the movement of capital necessarily produces a tendency to exclude from its productive apparatus part of the labour force. The size of this excluded element expands and contracts according to the phases of boom and slump in the capitalist cycle. In this sense it is a surplus that belongs to capital 'quite as absolutely as if the latter had bred it at its own cost'. Marx also demonstrates that, as the spiral of capital accumulation develops, and the use of machinery becomes more commonplace, the inactive part of the labour force is rendered relatively superfluous to the needs of capital accumulation. Indeed, there is even the possibility that this surplus-population will not remain relative but become *consolidated*, i.e. be a constant surplus with regard to the needs of capitalist accumulation.[2]

Clearly the composition of the relative surplus-population will vary from cycle to cycle in concrete capitalist social formations contaminated by the residues of other modes of production, and with the seminal role that politics and ideology play in producing gendered and racialized subjects. Much of Marx's discussion is taken up with the *latent* surplus-population that has been set free by the increasing penetration of agriculture by capital. If this latent element was not a significant feature of the post-1945 British social structure, it was a prominent element of Caribbean and Asian societies. The composition of the relative surplus-population too, Marx notes, may result from the destruction of existing branches and spheres of industrial production or from the further decomposition of artisanal classes. Many of the latter group may already have intermittently been part of the active wage labour army. By and large, however, they remain *stagnant*. Not least of all, the composition of the relative surplus-population may be determined by the concentration and centralization of capital which makes more and more workers redundant. Insofar as some of this repelled mass is again incorporated, it exists only in a *floating* form. Below these groups, Marx mentions the lumpenproletariat and paupers.[3] Which element(s), and to what extent, is later incorporated into the industrial reserve army *in production* as a *lever* for further accumulation cannot be determined *a priori* by a simplistic reference to 'theorized divisions'. Of course, and this may help us to understand the apparent interchangeability of the concepts, at the level of analysis generally presented in *Capital*, it can be presupposed that the whole relative surplus-population is drawn on to compose the industrial reserve army.

In turning our attention to the industrial reserve army we encounter immediately the ubiquitous tautology of the literature, namely, that the industrial reserve army – itself described as a 'reserve' – supplies a reserve for production. It is not the industrial reserve army which supplies a 'reserve' but the relative surplus-population. The industrial reserve army is not something that lies outside production; it is something that is inserted into production as a 'lever' of accumulation. It relates to and regulates the specific phases of the economic cycle of capital: heightened activity, over-production, crises and so on. What is always critical is its function *in* production: the manner in which it can be suddenly thrown 'on the decisive points without injury to the scale of production in other spheres' (Marx 1974). As the needs of the self-expansion of capital change with each cycle of restructuring and each phase of the cycle, so too is this mass constantly recomposed. This should alert us to the fact that the 'labour shortage' met by the industrial reserve army at the beginning of the cycle may be completely different from that which it fulfils midway through the cycle because of the continual transformation of the labour process. It is on this ground that the notion of West Indian migrants to Britain as a 'replacement population' comes to grief since we cannot even be sure – without concrete analysis – that the productive functions that black workers took on were the same as those of their forerunners, European Volunteer Workers, let alone those formerly held by natives.

When we take into account the ways in which politics and ideology structure the very constitution of *the* economic, then it is clear that there can be no attempt to 'read off' a theoretical conceptualization of the industrial reserve army into the concrete world. Hartmann (1979) recognizes this well when she notes that: 'Marxist categories, like capital, itself, are sex blind. The categories of Marx cannot tell us who will fill the empty places.' The same too can be said of individuals who are socially defined as belonging to different 'races' or 'colours'. What has rarely been analysed properly is the way in which 'gender', 'race' and 'ethnicity' combine and intersect internally – i.e. rather than being merely added on – with class to produce 'fractions' or 'segments' within the proletariat. What we have here is nothing less than a process in which ideological, political and economic factors thread the industrial reserve army through the labour process with an assurance that certain elements will re-emerge again to join the relative surplus-population.

Creating an Industrial Reserve Army in Britain

Keynesianism, 'labour shortage' and textiles

To understand the way in which politics, economics and ideology were to intersect to thread the industrial reserve army through the labour process requires a very clear grasp of Labour's 'full employment' solution to the deep crisis of British capitalism. By a policy of 'full employment', explained the Working Party on the Cotton Industry[4] in its 1946 report, a number of issues were put on the agenda:

> The problem of the future years will be . . . how to find enough workers willing to do the tasks to which the British nation has committed itself or which have been loaded on its shoulders by the war . . . We see our commitment to much higher standards for our people at home in wages, holidays with pay, children's allow-ances, and social security; to much heavier expenditure on non-productive services such as education and defence; to a greater housing programme. We see the immense arrears of maintenance and renewal of industrial plant to be made good

as well as war destruction to factories and houses and vast external debts on current account to be settled. Above all we see the urgent problems of exports, needed to pay for imports without which we cannot live . . . There is only one way to get through these difficulties and to make the national income large enough to meet our commitments. This is by hard work, well-planned work, making the most of every modern improvement of science and technology to improve production. British industry needs a great spurt in efficiency and flexibility as well as a transformation in many of its old activities. Above all manpower must be used to best advantage.[5]

Labour's social-democratic answer was the adoption of state interventionist Keynesian strategies[6] which sought to manage capitalism more efficiently in order to avoid periods of stagnation and inflation. When aggregate demand was too low to attract private investment, government would then intervene to stimulate demand through borrowing and public expenditure; when demand was too high government would intervene to deflate demand by increased taxation or public expenditure cuts.

A key aspect of this management of capital was the nationalization of unprofitable sectors of the economy such as coalmining and railways. Another plank of this 'command economy' was the regulation of industrial development by encouraging industries to move to designated Development Areas where a relative surplus-population was available. The hope was that by extending the range of industries in areas such as the North East there would be no recurrence of mass regional unemployment on the scale of the 1930s. In the Labour government's 1945 White Paper on Employment, cotton – with its 'dismal past and uncertain future' – was singled out as an index of the unfortunate domination of one industry: in some areas, for example, as much as 44 per cent of the labour force depended on this single industry. It is for this reason that mills were encouraged to move to other areas though with little success. A more radical and long-term strategy was to encourage firms to modernize. The centrality of textiles to the post-war 'export drive' ensured that it would become a key target for such a strategy. It is worth while pausing to examine in some detail why the scheme failed in textiles since light would thus be shed on the wider difficulties and contradictions facing Labour's attempt to 'modernize' British capitalism.

For an industry which was accorded a privileged position in post-war capitalist reconstruction, textiles had had a rather chequered history. It was a backward sphere of production suffering from the handicap of a 'bad history' of poor working conditions, under-investment and low wages during the inter-war years. High unemployment during this period enabled employers to rely on an over-abundant, cheap, skilled labour force composed largely of women (an average of 65 per cent, and as much as 75 per cent in the spinning branch of production) and juveniles. Thus the low wages offered by the industry. With the exception of a few firms of outstanding ability which maintained their position by specializing in certain lines, the sphere as a whole 'was working with a margin of profit which left it no adequate capital to devote to re-equipment, and was too low to attract new capital. Accordingly it stood still just at a time when new industries were growing up elsewhere, with the result that it has become in some respects out of date in comparison with the industries of other countries.'[7]

Increasing difficulties in recruiting labour – juvenile recruitment between 1936 and 1939 was already down some 80 per cent – had seen the average age of the labour force increase from twenty-nine in 1911 to thirty-seven in 1944. By 1945, 45 per cent of female cotton operatives were over the age of forty. This was exacerbated by the wartime 'concentration' of the textile industry (i.e. the mothballing of mills[8] and the closure of looms in others) and a concomitant concentration of the labour force in a nucleus of mills. More telling was the redistribution of the cream of the textile female labour force – young, mobile women generally under the age of thirty – away from the textile regions to serve in munitions and so on. In 1945 spinning and weaving alone were some 50,000–100,000 labourers short.

As mills came back into production a first priority was to secure a labour force. Where looms were closed it was a question of 'womanning up' to reduce the cost of production. With the demobilization of labour after the war, however, the return of ex-operatives to the critical areas of spinning and doubling – now no longer subject to direction under wartime regulations (effective for a few months after the war too) – hardly kept pace with the 'wastage' caused by retired operatives leaving the industry for a second time after special wartime duty. Moreover, many workers who had experienced high wages and better working conditions elsewhere remained reluctant to return to a textile industry minus canteens, rest rooms, proper toilets, and so on. This was particularly true for the mothballed mills on which no capital had been spent during their closure, and whose constant capital had thereby undergone a moral depreciation. The industry, the working party on the cotton industry advised, would have to prepare itself for the use of male labour in place of female along the lines recommended by the Evershed Report on the spinning branch.

It was the recognition that the labour problems of the textile industry were intractable that prompted the Labour government to address the more fundamental issue of increasing productivity by a 'complete revolution in mechanical equipment' especially for mothballed mills. A state levy of 25 per cent of the capital cost was proposed as an aid to secure the centralization of textile capital by the amalgamation of up to six mills to form a new enterprise. The scheme collapsed for several reasons. Past conditions had circumscribed the industry's ability to mechanize, whilst there was a fear among textile moghuls that the state levy would increase costs of production, lead to product inflexibility and impose an inequitable burden on progressive firms which had already mechanized.[9] Furthermore, in an industry in which women workers were so central but were considered unsuitable for night shift working, new machinery could not be fully exploited without an alternative labour force that could work twenty-four hours a day. Many capitalists, too, saw in Labour's plan to modernize the textile industry a 'creeping socialism' that would further strengthen an already entrenched and well-organized workforce in its resistance to deskilling and redundancy. Last, but not least, the restructuring of capital was a long-term process. More urgent remedies were required and the Labour government therefore turned its attention to strategies which would resolve what became perceived as a 'labour shortage'.

It has become a common orthodoxy to state that in the post-war period Britain experienced a severe 'labour shortage'. Within this orthodoxy 'labour shortage' is often presented as a natural phenomenon grounded in levels of fertility, birth and death rate, war deaths, the raising of the school leaving age, the age structure of the male and female population, and so on.

The logic of this line of reasoning is to counterpose population to accumulation and thereby to metamorphose the social basis of capitalist production into a law of nature. What is required is an analysis which connects population/demography to the global logic of reproduction of the capitalist mode of production (cf. Jimenez 1987).

An examination of the strategies adopted by the Labour government would lead us to reject the equation of the 'labour shortage' with the difference between the number of jobs available and the number of workers ready to fill the vacancies. Neither could it be reduced to a simple demographic equation which perceived the boundaries of the labour force or working population as being fixed in some absolute manner by factors such as war deaths and age structure of the male and female population.

The labour force – working population – is not only demographically constituted but politically determined. Its boundaries are not fixed and finite but socially constructed. There are two aspects to this social construction. In absolute terms, it is possible to increase the labour force by altering the age structure of the working population. For example, by lowering the school leaving age more workers could be brought into the labour force. (To redeem its social-democratic pledge of equal opportunity, the Labour government in 1947 however chose to raise the school leaving age to fifteen.) Similarly, while not formally raising the retirement age, the government encouraged older workers to stay on and retired workers to return.

In the post-war period, too, the Labour government adopted a number of policies designed to increase the labour force by altering the definition of the 'worker' to include groups such as women and the disabled who had been excluded (except for the war years) or confined to certain branches of industry. This is what the 1944 Disabled Persons (Employment) Act was designed to achieve. After the war, however, employers tended to regard

people with disabilities as 'bad placing positions'. Women received contradictory messages from the government. On the one hand they were encouraged to remain in the labour force though in different occupations from those
that they had been engaged in during the war. On the other hand, they were
instructed to 'get back into the home'. Many chose to stay on though their
ability to do so was greatly hampered by the reluctance of the government to
maintain the war-time level of creche provision. In staying on, however, many
women who had moved away from textiles into, say, munitions during the war,
were unwilling to return to a textile industry which, perhaps because of
wartime closure, was bereft of creches, or toilet facilities, etc.

An adequate understanding of the 'labour shortage' would also require us
to examine the issue of mobility. In the closing months of the war the Ministry
of Labour (MOL), through a number of regional offices, had undertaken a
mobility survey to convince ministers 'who find it hard to appreciate that
labour is not infinitely mobile'. Even at a time when 'full employment' was at
its highest, this survey showed that labour was 'badly distributed and lacks
mobility'. The principal reasons cited for male immobility – the question of
female immobility was not examined on the grounds that, given the age
structure of the female population, the central issue here would be the
domestic environment – were old age, industrial diseases, mental subnormality, undernourishment and demoralization resulting from prolonged periods of unemployment. The report recommended that counter measures
should be taken to 'make sure that as far as humanly possible obstacles to
mobility were removed'. Immobility, it stressed, would get worse after the war
as employers sought to get rid of their 'bad placing positions'. There would be
a need, the report concluded, to 'educate' employers about the 'economics of
Full Employment' such that even those 'below normal standards' could form
part of the industrial reserve army. The problem was not an absent relative
surplus-population *in* Britain but an *immobile* relative surplus-population.

On the principle of 'equality of sacrifice' successive governments from the
late 1940s onwards were to introduce measures to get at this immobile
relative surplus-population as well as to 'shake out' from 'unproductive'
sectors of the economy individuals who could be more 'usefully engaged' in
'productive' sectors. A key weapon in Labour's armoury to secure the
direction of labour was the continuation of Aneurin Bevin's war-time Essential Orders in the form of successive Controls of Engagement Orders. These
required employers to use approved labour exchanges to fill their vacancies
and workers to do likewise to find work. The employment exchange, the radio
commentator Douglas Houghton informed his audience, became

> a kind of signal box putting up the red light against man-power running away, and
> giving a green card to those of us on the right lines.

In the signal box, out of sight, but there all the time, is the power of direction, of compulsion if we say no; the power to say, 'Oh yes, you must.'[10]

An example of how this worked was the October 1947 Control of Engagement Order – euphemistically renamed the 'Spivs and Drones' Order – whose aim was to 'round up' those who were not 'gainfully occupied or employed', and to 'comb out' those engaged in 'unproductive functions'. To make this order more effective, MOL issued an 'England Expects' New Year greeting to 'social limpets': the January 1948 Registration of Employment Order. Under this Order, an 'At-Home'-at-the-local-Labour-Exchange-from-9 a.m.-to-5 p.m.-every-day-from-Monday-to-Friday invitation was posted to secure the registration of street-traders (barrow-boys, match sellers, newspaper sellers, buskers, Punch-and-Judy men, shoe-blacks, etc.), 'unproductive' workers (of bookmakers, football pools, night clubs, skittle-alleys and pin-tables), and those who were 'not gainfully employed or occupied'. In his popular radio programme, *Can I Help You?*, Douglas Houghton tried to remove the veil of confusion posed by the Registration Order:

> Mr. Isaacs proposes to begin his expedition in search of miscellaneous fauna by calling on men between eighteen and fifty-one and women between eighteen and forty-one, *doing no work*, to register at the Employment Exchange – to register for employment.
>
> To add to the catch, Mr. Isaacs also proposes to order street-traders and barrow-boys to register themselves. Of those, some will be taken and some put back into the sea.
>
> Casting the net still wider he is going to require employers in the pool and betting business to send in particulars of their employees. And the proprietors of fun fares, amusement arcades, night clubs and such like will be asked to do the same.
>
> This is not being done because the Government wish these pin-table saloons, betting firms, football pools and night clubs any harm, still less to close them down. These flourishing industries will be free to set on new workers, if they can find them who, by reason of age, or something else don't come under control of labour at all.
>
> Nor is it intended to drive street-traders or bookmakers out of business. After all there is such a thing as live and let live even in a crisis.
>
> The hope is rather to comb out from plainly unessential occupations people who could be better employed; and to get the genuine drones in all classes to earn their keep . . . [11]

By these two measures the Prime Minister informed the House of Commons, the alleged 'missing million' within the labour force would be industrially conscripted and transferred to areas of 'essential and undermanned industries'. Despite the threat of prosecution, and despite the incentives of MOL hostels and training, only 95,900 people had responded within six months to Mr. Isaacs's RSVP invitation.

To a greater or lesser extent, all of these strategies were hampered by the way in which Labour's own Keynesian policies circumscribed the key tools of capitalist discipline: poverty and unemployment. Via the 'social wage' the state undertook nothing less than the reproduction of the relative surplus-population as part of the working population. While such policies may have been consistent with the universal subjectivity and citizenship conceded/extended to the working class, employed and unemployed, especially through its trade union movement, they blurred the boundary between the objective necessity and compulsion to engage in wage labour that capital imposes upon all labourers and the subjective 'right to work'/right to subsistence.[12] By the policy of social insurance, note Geoffrey Kay and James Mott (1982: 149), 'the state placed the whole of the proletariat on a continuum, and shouldered an obligation it could not meet without regulating the labour market'.

What can be said more generally about strategies to restructure capital is that they take time. Moreover, they may involve bitter conflicts with entrenched and well-organized workers who benefit from the existing 'labour shortage' and who therefore resist the deskilling, loss of control, redundancy and other associated features of working life that are often implied. As trade unions moved from Trafalgar Square to the committee rooms, too, there was little likelihood that strategies to depress wages would be successful.

It is in the face of such difficulties that the recruitment of workers from outside the national boundaries of the UK became an economic necessity.

The endorsement of the 'labour shortage' orthodoxy by trade unions (Dickson 1983: 2), however, was – as the following section shows – to condition their response to migrant labour.[13] In the textile industry, for example, trade unions were able to insist that migrant workers engaged to replace women should not be paid less than the minimum male rate of £4 per week, that they should not be employed where suitable British labour was available, that foreign workers should be discharged first were redundancies to become necessary. They also rejected the trade union reforms demanded – 'one central body for all negotiating purposes' – and supported by the TUC in its 1945 document *Trade Union Structure and Closer Unity*. Furthermore, while the unions had already made the historic concession of *double-shifting*, they baulked at the idea that such concessions should become substitutes for mechanization.

What we have before us is nothing less than the historical tendency of trade unionism towards exclusivity and sectionalism. In the 1950s onwards such sectionalism and exclusivity were to lead to the marginalization of a particular group of workers. A bargain was struck where migrant labour came to be perceived as so much ballast that could be jettisoned when the slump came.

European volunteer workers: 'Operation Westward Ho'

The solution we know today as the European Volunteer Worker (EVW) scheme was first mooted by Arthur Greenwood in his memorandum to the Cabinet Foreign Labour Committee in March 1946:

> There are a number of factors, both economic and social, operating to reduce the labour force, of which perhaps the most important is the rise in the working age of the population; the effect of which is reinforced at the other end of the scale by the higher school leaving age. A further factor will be the tendency for married women, on whom some industries, particularly cotton spinning, have depended in the past, to remain at home, as better wages and regular employment for their husbands reduce the economic strain on the household. We should also bear in mind that our Social Insurance Schemes will operate in the same direction . . .
>
> I suggest that we should first turn our attention to the possibility of utilizing the services of bodies of foreign labour which are already in this country . . . secondly we should consider the desirability of increasing further our resources of man-power by permitting and if necessary encouraging the entry of special categories of workers. Our primary need is no doubt for unskilled workers for the unattractive industries, but there may also be a case to be made for a certain intake of skilled labour.[14]

In order to stimulate public and parliamentary interest in the matter, prepared questions were asked at question time in the House of Commons in order to prompt 'inspired' ministerial responses. By January 1947, Greenwood's proposal had become 'Operation Westward Ho' recruiting labour from three sources: first, members of the Polish Resettlement Corps in camps throughout Britain numbering some 142,000; second, 'displaced persons' in Germany, Austria and Italy numbering some 720,000, the vast majority being Polish peasants conscripted as forced labour by the Nazis (and returning home in droves), Balts who had fled the Russian occupation of their countries and Jugoslavs; and third, the unemployed of European countries. The recruitment of this 'new blood into our economic system' (Greenwood) was supervised by a team of MOL officials carefully 'chosen for their experience of placing workers in the principal undermanned industries', and 'briefed as to the labour needs of these industries'.[15]

Equally well 'handpicked' were the labourers themselves, with preference given to 'men of the labouring type who are hardy and of good physical standard' – confirmed by a medical examination – and those prepared to leave behind their dependants until further arrangements could be made. There was a limited extent, however, it was admitted, to which 'the British Government can attempt to separate women from their husbands, brothers, etc.' By the middle of 1948, i.e. after eighteen months' activity, 'Operation Westward Ho' had netted 80,000 EVWs in addition to recruiting 80,000 members of the Polish Resettlement Corps, and another 23,000 German and Ukrainian prisoners of war. Attention was particularly devoted to recruiting from among EVW group workers whose contribution to British capitalist reconstruction would be specifically linked to accumulation in new spheres of production, i.e. 'by starting and manning new industries for which there is little or no tradition here'. This is an important function the industrial reserve army always performs in every cycle of capital though rarely in such a circumscribed manner. Such workers, it was argued, would provide 'a leaven of trained workers from countries where these industries have long been established'.[16] More generally, the industries in which female EVWs tended to be located were cotton and wool manufacture, the National Health Service (NHS) and so on. For male EVWs, the major industries were agriculture and coalmining.

If free will is the essential element in the formal exchange between labour and capital, then the employment relation through which the migrant worker confronted capital was a singular for its many external determinations which ensured that the foreign worker 'once guided into productive industry in the first instance . . . does not thereafter drift away into less useful occupations'.[17] As was pointed out by the interdepartmental working party established in 1948 to review the possibility of utilizing 'surplus colonial manpower' in British industry:

> The 'Westward Ho' scheme enables the Department [of Labour] both to put these foreign workers into specific jobs and to keep them in those jobs. The sanction that lies at hand to guard against non-compliance with these landing conditions is deportation of the workers concerned to the 'Displaced Persons' camps in Europe, and this sanction has from the beginning proved to be an extremely effective one. Beside being kept out of the 'inessential' industries, European Volunteer Workers who have been brought into this country could not for any length of time remain unemployed and live at the public expense . . . Unlike British citizens, European Volunteer Workers must not only accept whatever job is selected for them, but approved employment. If their employment record in this country is unsatisfactory in any respect, the sanction of deportation lies at hand.[18]

In sum, the formalized employment contract for EVWs was significant for its undermining of the episodic nature of the transaction between labour and capital, which is essential to the preservation of the illusion that workers remain in ultimate possession of themselves and are therefore in a position to alienate their labour-power. This feature of migrant labour is critical too since it represents one way in which the industrial reserve army was to be politically reproduced consistent with the subjective 'right to work' embodied in the Keynesian ethos of 'full employment'. Here the political marginaliza-tion of EVWs as well as the later ideological marginalization of West Indians and Asians through racism and discrimination represented the manner in which the industrial reserve army was created as part of the working population but apart from it such that the labour market could be regulated and competition between workers for specific productive functions minimized. With respect to the EVWs MOL went so far as to reassure the white English worker in its *Economic Survey* of 1947 that:

> There is no danger for years to come that foreign labour will rob British workers of their jobs . . . The government is prepared to ensure that foreign labour will not be introduced into specific employment while British labour is available.[19]

When placed into the 'bottleneck operations' of the textile industry, EVWs immediately proved their worth with 'an additional output out of proportion to their numbers'. Productivity was being made to 'bubble up' from the shop floor without any fundamental reorganization of the labour process. Constant capital was merely being used more intensively, and wages kept to the minimum agreed with the trade unions. One hundred additional workers of such type in the cotton industry, the Minister of Labour assured us, 'can be regarded as the addition of over 100,000 of dollar-earning or dollar-saving exports or the equivalent'.[20] Any political difficulty in recruiting such labourers had to be measured against such facts. It was against such facts too that Asian and West Indian labour was to be judged.

Caribbean Migration and the Ideology of Racism

Preventing Caribbean labour from becoming a UK IRA

One of the least documented chapters of British political and labour history is the resistance to the use of Caribbean labour to resolve Britain's 'labour shortage'. Such a resistance went far beyond the defensive struggles of white workers to retain their hard-won, more secure position within the labour process. Within the post-war state – indeed within the pre-war state (Harris 1988) – there was tremendous opposition to the use of black labour.

'As regards the possible importation of West Indian labour,' argued M. A. Bevan of the Ministry of Labour in April 1948, 'I suggest that we must dismiss the idea from the start.'[21] Two years earlier the idea had also been emphatically rejected by the Minister of Labour, George Isaacs, in response to a parliamentary question. On that occasion the reasons given were 'problems of shipping and accommodation'. This parliamentary response was contradicted in early 1947 by the arrival of the *Ormonde* with 110 Jamaican workers (including ten stowaways) on board. The arrival of the *Ormonde* proved that neither was shipping the insurmountable problem nor accommodation the deterrent that George Isaacs had hoped. 'It may become extremely embarrassing,' observed one civil servant, 'if at a time of labour shortage there should be nothing but discouragement for British subjects from the West

Indies while we go to great trouble to get foreign workers.'[22] This was all the more true, Colonial Secretary Creech-Jones warned George Isaacs, since

> West Indians are well aware of the labour shortage in Great Britain, and it is known to them that it is proposed to employ thousands of Displaced Persons . . . In these circumstances there has been a natural and immediate demand for the employment of British West Indians, who are British subjects and many of whom have had experience of work in Britain during the war years, to relieve the labour shortage in Britain.[23]

Against a background of local labour unrest, the Jamaican governor added his weight to this demand by explaining in May 1947 that the *Ormonde* migrants were only the 'first columns' of a rush for passport applications numbering some 8,000 in the last six weeks. Like other Caribbean governors, Governor Huggins requested the extension of the EVW scheme to the Caribbean. With this pressure from the colonies the CO added its voice to the chorus by approaching MOL with a formal proposal to recruit black labour.

At a meeting between the two departments, MOL stressed that it did not wish to recruit West Indian labour. It tried to soften the blow by suggesting that a decision should be deferred until the Evans Commission on Caribbean 'over-population' had reported. In the meantime, it got the CO to agree that one of its officials should visit the Caribbean to explain the labour position in Britain. In addition, it undertook to prepare a detailed 'appreciation' of the possibilities of employing 'surplus male West Indians'.

To the local governors, and particularly to the listening Caribbean press, the visiting CO official explained that the 'paper vacancies' people had seen advertised in England were not real jobs at all but merely the temporary vacancies of individuals changing jobs.

The MOL 'appreciation' was unsurprisingly and uncompromisingly negative. It alluded to the 'overwhelming difficulties' of employing black workers and cited accommodation as the main obstacle. Other excuses were advanced. Firstly, Caribbean workers 'were unsuitable for outdoor work in winter owing to their susceptibility to colds and the more serious chest and lung ailments'. In the same climatic metaphor labour conditions underground in the coalmines were described as 'too hot'. Secondly, 'many of the coloured men are unreliable and lazy, quarrels among them are not infrequent'.[24]

Neither the 'appreciation' nor the CO official's visit to the Caribbean prevented the 'bombshell' arrival of the *Empire Windrush* in June 1948 with 492 Jamaicans aboard, half of whom had served in Britain during the war years in the air force, army and munitions. In a letter to the Barbadian-born secretary to the Labour Party's Advisory Committee on Imperial Questions, one correspondent saw in this influx the hidden hand of 'Uncle Joe' Stalin. 'Do you think,' he confided to Greenidge, 'this sudden influx of 400 West Indians is a subtle move of Russia to create for us in another twenty years time a "Colour Question" here?'[25] This was not as farfetched as it might seem since – against the background of the Cold War – elements in the Home Office were already persuaded that there was 'a large Communist element among the coloured population here and the Communists would no doubt not be slow to make trouble if they could'.[26]

Within the Labour cabinet the response to the *Windrush* was equally negative. Even before it docked the *Windrush* had been the subject of intense inter-departmental wrangling over whose responsibility it was to receive the migrants. MOL initially took the line that 'coloured colonial' migration was a CO issue and therefore required no special action on their part beyond directing the migrants to local employment exchanges.

In addition MOL was of the conviction that intervention on their part would only serve to encourage other black migrants. As Ness Edwards, George Isaacs's parliamentary secretary, expressed privately: 'We do not want to take any actions with this ship load of Jamaicans which will encourage others.'[27]

The impending arrival of the *Empire Windrush* was the subject of extensive press and parliamentary comment. The unwelcome comparison drawn between the considerable effort that had been lavished on the recruitment of EVWs and inactivity in the case of Caribbean migrants forced MOL to alter its stance. A more fundamental reason for the change of heart, however, was the alleged 'grave danger that these people may be walking the streets in London and stirring up a great deal of trouble'.

Unable to persuade the owners of the *Empire Windrush* to delay its docking, MOL hastily launched Operation 'Wind-Up' and sent a number of ministry officials to Tilbury to interview the migrants before they disembarked. The aim was to register the latter for employment in areas of 'undermanned and essential industries', i.e. the industries that were perceived as having the most acute demand for an industrial reserve army, rather than have them congregate at labour exchanges in London.

Most of the *Empire Windrush* shipload were placed in iron foundries, agriculture, railways and bricklaying as far apart as Scotland, Gloucester, the Midlands and South Wales. By July only twelve members of the party remained unplaced in jobs.

Creech-Jones found himself carpeted by the cabinet for not 'having kept the lid on things' sufficiently in the colonies to prevent this exodus of Jamaicans and was asked to shed some light on this 'argosy' or 'invasion' (Dunkirk in reverse) to 'ensure that further similar movements either from Jamaica or elsewhere in the colonial empire are detected and checked before they can reach such an embarrassing stage'.[28] Attlee asked for a report and reiterated the query of the Economic Policy Committee about the possibility of diverting the *Windrush* party to ground nut projects in East Africa.

In the memorandum prepared in his defence, Creech-Jones again reiterated that neither the Jamaican nor the British government had any legal power in peace-time to prevent the landing of the *Empire Windrush* party. Secondly, this migration of Jamaicans was a 'spontaneous movement' of people which was not likely to occur again, and was certainly 'not organised or encouraged by the Colonial Office or the Jamaican government. On the contrary, every possible step had been taken by the Colonial Office and by the Jamaican government to discourage these influxes.'[29] The Welfare Officer had visited Jamaica and the Governor had done what little he could on passports. Moreover, before the party of 492 had left Jamaica, 'they were warned by the Jamaican government about the difficulties which would beset them on arrival in this country, but they decided, as they were free to decide, to take the risk'.[30] On this point, Creech-Jones received unexpected support from the Ministry of Health which attributed the influx to the penny-pinching of the Treasury:

> The RAF were repatriating a number of demobilized Jamaican servicemen and the Treasury had insisted that the ship chartered to take them back to Jamaica should try and recoup as much money as possible by carrying passengers on return. The master of the vessel accordingly offered cheap rates on the return journey and a number of Jamaicans who were not finding life in Jamaica very pleasant seized the opportunity to *return* to Britain.[31]

Thirdly, the threat of Caribbean migration would only recede by removing the underlying cause, namely the underdevelopment of Jamaica. Such under-development, he explained, was hardly touched by the projects being undertaken at present since they were 'mainly agricultural'. In other words, the projects did not offer the kind of industrial employment the men wanted and for which many had undergone training after being demobilized from the armed forces. 'These men,' he concluded tetchily, 'want work in *England*. We [the colonial office] shall try to open out possibilities in British Honduras.'[32]

Underlying the concern of the socialist Attlee government was an unmis-takable anxiety about the challenges posed by black immigration to a racial-ized conception of national identity. In a letter sent by eleven Labour MPs to Clement Attlee on 22 June 1948 we find attempts to redraw the boundaries of this racialized identity:

> This country may become an open reception centre for immigrants not selected in respect to health, education, training, character, customs and above all, whether assimilation is possible or not.
>
> The British people fortunately enjoy a profound unity without uniformity in their way of life, and are blest by the absence of a colour racial problem. An influx of coloured people domiciled here is likely to impair the harmony, strength and cohesion of our public and social life and to cause discord and unhappiness among all concerned.
>
> In our opinion colonial governments are responsible for the welfare of their peoples and Britain is giving these governments great financial assistance to enable

them to solve their population problems. We venture to suggest that the British
Government should, like foreign countries, the dominions and even some of the
colonies, by legislation if necessary, control immigration in the political, social,
economic and fiscal interests of our people.

In our opinion such legislation or administrative action would be almost
universally approved by our people.[33]

In this letter, 'our people' in the UK are distinguished from 'other people' in
the colonies despite centuries of colonialism and despite recent war-time
service by 'colonials'. The construction of 'other people' is meant to throw
into sharp relief what 'we' are. The 'other' is the polar opposite of a highly
valorized Britisher with their allegedly distinctive, superior, national sensib-
ility and physiognomy. 'Our people' are signified implicitly by their 'whiteness' and are thus a separate and distinct 'race'. 'Our people' – the 'real'
British people – share a 'way of life' characterized by homogeneity, tolerance,
cohesion, unity without uniformity, and harmony. In sum, immobile, 'other
people' could wave their Union Jacks 'out there' and be British; mobile, they
were an unassimilable alien presence which would irreparably damage 'our
way of life' and create a 'colour racial problem'.

In this portrayal we are presented with a nationalism deeply attached to
'spirit of place'; but it was a national epic that was now being transposed from
the battlefields of Dunkirk and Arnhem to the ports and airports where 'other
people' were now 'invading'. In this portrayal, too, we see the extent to which
notions of a [black] empire and of 'race' had become profoundly constitutive
of 'Britishness' and Britain's sense of selfhood. In the mirror of empire
Britain found its identity reflected back twice as large . . . as *Great* Britain.

This racialized notion of identity was to pervade the deliberations of the
inter-departmental working party set up after the arrival of the *Empire
Windrush* in 1948 to 'explore the possibilities of using the surplus manpower
of certain colonies to assist in manpower situations here'. In his opening
address at the first meeting of the working party, the Home Office chair-
person outlined the substantive issue to be deliberated on:

> Suggestions had naturally arisen in some of the colonies that the two problems –
> unemployment in the Colonies and shortage of manpower in the United Kingdom –
> should be considered together and that each might provide opportunities for
> helping with the other.[34]

The response of the MOL official, M. A. Bevan, made clear what the findings
of the working party would be. Caribbean unemployment, he argued, could
not be elided with the 'quite separate' issue of manpower 'shortage' in
Britain. All that this displayed, he added, was a fallacy of misplaced connect-
edness. The study of colonial unemployment figures contributed nothing 'as
it would not be possible in any case to take sufficient workers to eliminate the
unemployment in the Colonies'.[35]

When all the fudging was over, there were four fundamental reasons why, in Bevan's words, 'the labour available in the colonies would not be of the type required in the United Kingdom'. These four reasons were clearly spelled out in the WP's report.

Firstly, if Afro-Caribbeans elected to leave the 'undermanned and essential industries' with their low wages and poor working conditions into which EVWs had already been channelled, nothing could be done about it. Unlike EVWs, explained the Report, 'Colonial workers, being British subjects, are free from the labour controls imposed under the Aliens Order, and could not be sent out of the country if they elected to leave the "essential" jobs to which they had been sent.'[36]

Secondly, there was the fear that if Afro-Caribbean labourers left the 'undermanned and essential industries' they would gravitate to seaport towns such as Liverpool with what the working party called their long-established 'coloured ghettoes' and thereby exacerbate the conditions under which racism had been flourishing since the 1919 'race' riots.

A third factor which applied equally to EVWs was the lack of accommodation. Despite the prevalence of racist discrimination in housing, MOL pressed that its system of state-run hostels should not become a substitute on the grounds that experience has shown that 'the presence in any hostels of coloured workers in appreciable numbers invariably leads to trouble'. It was only on 'political grounds' that MOL had refused to accede to the request for a rule stipulating that 'no more than three coloured workers should simultaneously be resident in any one hostel'.[37] In any event, the hostel scheme was so vital to the 'maintenance of the necessary labour forces in many highly important industrial areas' that it could not be 'imperilled'.

The fourth, and undoubtedly the most important, factor, was the 'inescapable conclusion' that racism was already an important feature of British industrial and political life with many prominent unions declaring that they did not want 'coloured' workers. It was the 'social implications' of introducing 'other races', asserted one official, which 'is the real answer to the question . . . and no amount of fencing will in the end lead the working party to any other conclusion'.[38] Many on the *Empire Windrush* had already had first-hand experience of racist discrimination during their war-time service in Britain (Sherwood 1985; Smith 1987; Bousquet and Douglas 1991, Carter, Harris and Joshi 1994). The existence of racism, noted Bevan, made organized schemes on the lines of 'Operation Westward Ho' fraught with danger:

> It is to be clearly understood that as soon as any government-sponsored scheme
> was organized it would then have to accept responsibility for every aspect of the
> colonial workers' existence here from arrival to final absorption in industry. It was
> highly undesirable that workers should be brought to the United Kingdom who
> could not be absorbed into industry.[39]

In the 1949 factsheet of the CO's advisory committee, attention was drawn to racist disturbances in places such as Liverpool, Birmingham and Deptford in 1948–49. In the latter place, the factsheet explained, 'There is a good deal of racial antagonism.'[40]

It was thus that at 'an early stage in our enquiries' the WP came to the conclusion that no state-sponsored schemes should be implemented to import male colonial workers. However, given the acute 'labour shortage' of female labour in textiles and the NHS, the working party recommended that recruitment in these areas should be reviewed.

To discourage black workers, particularly black male workers, from coming to Britain a number of administrative devices were resorted to (see pp.57–8). The trickle, however, continued; and in 1950 a cabinet committee meeting was called to consider the possibility of introducing legislative control on immigration. The idea of repealing rights of entry affirmed by the 1948 Nationality Act was peddled but quickly discarded as too controversial. Only stowaways could be dealt with. In any case, the scale of migration was considered as not yet 'such as to justify legislation to control the immigration of British subjects'. Nevertheless, it was thought 'necessary to reconsider the question if there were signs that such immigration was starting on a considerable scale'.[41] In 1950 ministers were still sensitive to the charge of racist discrimination 'as powers taken would almost certainly be applied to coloured persons . . . [and] any solution depending on an apparent or concealed colour test would be so invidious as to make it impossible of adoption'.[42]

In Chapter 2 we detail the efforts of the incoming Churchill government to grasp the legislative nettle that Labour dared not clutch. What we see is nothing less than a dress rehearsal of the hypocritical and tortuous, if not tortured pettifoggery that was to be advanced at the time of the 1961 Commonwealth Immigrants Bill to keep blacks out as well as to define 'Britishness' and 'belonging' in increasingly racist terms.

'Signal boxes' and colour discrimination

In this section we wish to look at how, despite the relaxation in the 1950s of many of the measures introduced by the 1945–50 government to conscript labour, the light in the signal box of the employment exchange remained a racist red for black workers and a racist green for white workers. With the lights on red, black workers found themselves channelled into semi- and unskilled labouring jobs.

In an early survey of regional controllers in 1949, the northern region representative explained that black workers in his area had been placed in the 'hot working conditions' of the iron and steel industry 'unpopular with British workers'; in the 'dirty work' of the graphite industry deserted by white workers; or as rivet catchers 'which is normally looked upon as a job for youths but which youths are now forsaking for more attractive work'. In the Birmingham area, explained the Midland region representative, Mr McCahey, male workers were placed 'in firms like Lucas, BSA, and Singers on dirty and rough finishing work . . . As regards vacancies in building, Post Office, transport, coalmining, railways, clerical, and draughtsmen's work, coloured labour would not be accepted.'[43] As in other regions particular care was taken to ensure that male black workers were not placed in firms where white women were present. In Cardiff with its long-standing seafaring black community, the Welsh regional officer reported that the only kind of work available to black men – against a background of increasing contraction of British merchant shipping – was on foreign-owned ships which did not come under the aegis of the Establishment Office responsible for recruiting labour for British-owned ships. In 1953, the Wales Office was still reporting on the 'deep prejudice about employing them outside the dock and sea area'. For black women in Cardiff, explained the regional officer, the prospects were even bleaker: 'They are not employed among the white population of Cardiff such as domestics and shop assistants; they are confined to undertakings (mainly rag and bone merchants) in the docklands area.'[44] In the south, the occupation of domestic in hospitals and private institutions was to be the mainstay for female migrants in the early 1950s.

As the 'labour shortage' worsened this picture was to change with black workers being recruited by branches of production such as transport and the post office. In the Midlands, explained the regional officer in 1953, black workers were 'only suitable for unskilled work' in the foundries and heavy engineering sectors. This placing policy was supported by the memorandum presented to the Trades Union Congress by the Ministry of Labour Staff Association (representing employment exchange workers) in 1954. The document observed that: 'When the announcements are made after the landing of boat loads of West Indians that many of them have been found work, it really means that many of them have been found work of an uncongenial kind and that they will not stay in it.' Of the 152,000 vacancies available to men eighteen and over in August 1954, the association went on to add, only about half would have been open to male black workers. The employment exchange workers association offered the following explanations:

> Employers do not seem to like to employ coloured workers in work which is done by both sexes, for they can foresee trouble arising out of the intermingling. Nor do they like the proportion of coloured workers in a particular shop, for instance, to rise too high in relation to the white workers . . . [45]

In this quotation we have allusion to some common reasons offered: the presence of white women, the objection of employers, quotas. Others were the type of work, the 'lack of skill', location, racist stereotypes of the fitness of different black groups for different kinds of work, attitudes of TUs.

As in the case of EVWs and Poles, employment exchanges were to encounter tremendous resistance from trade unions and employers in the placing of black workers. TUs in particular sought to limit the occupations for which black workers could be recruited to ensure that they were not placed in authority over white workers, to negotiate 'last-in-first-out' policies with employers to ensure that workers were not paid below the minimum rate, and to impose a quota which remained within the 'threshold of tolerance'. In like manner, commented one exchange official, employers sought to explain away their reluctance to engage black workers in the following terms:

'They've been a failure in the past', 'We have our share', 'We employ too many girls', 'The union objects', frequently prefaced by 'Of course, I've got no objection myself, but . . . .'[46]

An analysis undertaken by a London branch of the National Assistance Board at the time of the 1958 'riots' portrays a labour situation little changed:

The type of work obtained by the better educated includes, for men, skilled or semi-skilled factory work, drivers, conductors, guards and porters, etc., for London Passenger Transport, clerical and other semi-skilled work on British Railways and for women, nursing and typing. The less well educated and the illiterate have usually been absorbed into unskilled labouring, kitchen and restaurant work and various jobs in the clothing trade . . . [47]

In an article published in *Minlabour* – a Ministry of Labour staff magazine – an Edgware Road employment exchange official reiterated this point:

Bus conducting or railway porting can be regarded as practically their pinnacle of achievement, except for the minority who obtain experience in their own trade in this country. Clerical work is particularly difficult to obtain. The individual with education but without experience is often forced into manual work.[48]

As more and more black workers became trapped in labouring jobs so too did these jobs become identified as 'black jobs'. In a brief prepared by MOL for a 1958 House of Commons debate, the MP Miss Hornsby-Smith was informed that white unemployed people are 'not suitable for the kind of jobs held by the coloured people'.[49]

Since Peach (1968), a whole 'tunnel history' has been constructed around the theme of black workers forming a 'replacement population'. This is offered as an explanation of the structural and occupational location of black workers and corresponds to the dictum of 'room at the bottom'. What is astonishing is that exponents of this thesis do not even ask the simple question: Why were not the 'skilled' jobs that *unskilled* and *semi-skilled* white workers moved into equally available to black workers? By definition, the areas into which white workers were moving must have been areas of 'shortage' too; in short, there must have been room not only at the bottom but at the top and in the middle. Given the recognized chronic skilled labour 'shortage' why were not proportionately more blacks recruited into skilled manual occupations? A common answer is to focus on the alleged low skill background of migrants. Yet, extensive evidence on the downgrading experienced by black workers casts serious doubt on this argument. A corollary of this argument is to focus on the unwillingness of unions and employers to recognize apprenticeship credentials earned in the Caribbean and elsewhere. A second response popularized by employment exchanges was to assert that black workers:

> change their jobs frequently and therefore are not worth training and therefore have to be employed on unskilled work. . . . On the other hand, many white workers change their jobs frequently, the main reason being, of course, that all are looking for better pay.

If both black and white workers changed jobs frequently in a context of 'labour shortage', why should this disadvantage black workers? One factor must certainly have been the racist and paternalistic attitudes of exchange officials disgruntled by the fact that black workers did not express gratitude for the efforts made on their behalf by employment exchanges to secure them employment with racist employers and in the face of racist trade unions.

A key explanation for the occupational distribution of black workers has to do with their pervasive exclusion from the training programmes that unskilled and semi-skilled white workers used as avenues into skilled occupations. It was not only private employers – sanctioned by trade unions – who were reluctant to provide places for black workers on training programmes; labour exchanges too discriminated against black workers on government-sponsored training programmes in areas such as London and the south east region where it was admitted there was a 'heavy unskilled persons placing problem'. So perturbed was the Ministry of Labour headquarters in late 1953 by the 'politically dangerous' nature of this exclusionary practice in the London and South-East region that it wrote in the following terms:

> I find this difficult to believe and in fact it would mean that training was not practicable for any coloured worker. As soon as this became known, we could hardly escape the accusation that the Employment Service is itself exercising a discrimination on grounds of colour. . . . I wonder whether we are not merely adding to our difficulties if we refuse to train those coloured workers who are in themselves able to absorb the training given, while at the same pleading that we cannot find work for coloured persons because they are unskilled.[50]

The Midland region, too, commented upon the inability of black workers to obtain employment in skilled occupations or to get places on training programmes and attributed this less to an 'exaggerated idea of their own ability, but more frequently it represents a genuine grievance which has some substance'.[51] The explanation offered by the London and South-East Region was that it would be difficult to place skilled black workers. In other words, they were not prepared to challenge discrimination.

If labour market mobility held out the possibility of higher wages in other branches of production, it did not necessarily improve the ability of black workers to get into skilled manual jobs and white-collar occupations. By 1954, it was reported by the Ministry of Labour that, 'Jamaicans in particular have gained the reputation of being steady and reliable workers.' Such a reputation was equally built on levels of productivity, low rate of absenteeism, and on a willingness to stay put in jobs when the lack of accommodation as well as racism by landlords made it difficult to be mobile. An inquiry undertaken in 1956 by the Assistance Board in London concluded:

> It is the unanimous opinion of the area officers that nearly all the coloured immigrants are keen to obtain work and to keep it once they have started and this is particularly true of the West Indians. The Indians and Pakistanis are inclined to be more selective . . . [52]

In the area of white-collar work, noted Senior and Manley (1956: 14), black migrants had to live up to the additional requirements of proper clothing, proper accent, and proper interpersonal relations. Added to this was the unwillingness of employment exchanges to place black men in offices where white women were present. In a peculiar way, racism in white-collar work in the civil service – where the recruitment of women was well represented – was to reinforce gender segregation. In 1952 the signal box of the Civil Service Commission flashed a red light to the recruitment of male typists as soon as qualified black men responded to advertisements. The explanation offered was that 'mothers of young girls' would object to having their daughters work in close proximity with black men. The real reason, however, was that the civil service found it quite difficult to devise administrative measures to exclude black men without laying themselves open to charges of discrimination (Harris 1991a).

Discrimination in white-collar work was underlined when Prime Minister Winston Churchill, at a cabinet meeting in December 1952, instructed the Chancellor of the Exchequer to 'arrange for the examination of the possibility of restricting the number of coloured people obtaining admission to the Civil Service'.[53] The initial problem for the Treasury working party which examined the problem was to define who was a 'coloured' person:

> Would the phrase cover people who are coal black, or would it also cover people who are slightly 'off-white'? How should we pick out without seeing him the really

black man born in this country of pure British parentage with a hundred per cent.
English name? Should we exclude him without seeing him the Jamaican with an
African sounding name who might be slightly off-white, born of English parents
resident in Jamaica? The innumerable difficulties are obvious.[54]

An alternative suggestion was to phrase regulations in an inclusionary, rather
than exclusionary, manner by requesting candidates to prove that they were
of 'pure European descent'. Such a regulation, too, would have had the added
advantage of permitting the recruitment of 'genuine whites' born in countries
such as Jamaica and India.[55] The real difficulty of a 'pure European descent'
clause, noted the working party in its report, was its resemblance to Hitler's
'final solution':

> The discussions which arose around the Nazi theory of race suggested that there
> was no such thing as pure European descent; and the medical evidence is that, even
> if there were, there is no possibility of determining on purely medical grounds
> whether a man is of European or non-European origin.[56]

After searching through its records for the number of candidates 'who might
be "coloured" in the sense of being both dark and foreign, i.e. noticeably un-
English', the Civil Service Commission informed the working party that of the
23,000 candidates qualifying for interview in 1951–52, only twenty were
'visibly un-English'; and of these only six were successful. The working party
therefore decided to recommend that any alteration of regulations would be
tantamount to applying a sledgehammer to crack a very small nut.

That the number of successful candidates was so small can be attributed to
the covert administrative measures implemented after the return to open
competition in 1948 to keep blacks out of the civil service, particularly at the
level of the administrative classes (Harris 1991a). For such posts which
required an interview a policy of marking down the interview score of black
candidates by the selection panel was adopted. A typical example was the
Afro-Caribbean candidate who applied for an engineer officer post in the
Ministries of War or Air in 1949 and was marked down because of his colour:

> His qualifications were all right; his English was quite good; he answered pretty
> well; and although he wasn't a strong candidate, he would have been passed as he
> was. But both departments represented that it was out of the question to appoint
> him, and Major Sumner [chairperson of the selection panel] felt bound to
> acquiesce. They gave him a border-line mark, but he won't get in.[57]

For a body which prided itself on its impartiality, this exclusion of black
candidates posed a severe moral dilemma since they were in effect 'accepting
the candidature (and entry fees) of competitors whom they had no intention of
passing'. A new policy was developed of not marking down the candidate but
giving a provisional mark pending a further consultation with the department

concerned. The aim was to throw the onus of refusal on to the shoulder of the minister concerned. Alternatively, there was the hope was that even if the minister still refused to accept the successful black candidate assigned to the department, there was the possibility of placing him/her with a more 'tolerant' department such as the CO. More significantly, after the Nationality Rules were revised in 1951, racism was bureaucratically rationalized by making 'lack of knowledge of English life and customs' a basis for rejecting a candidate. Such a ruling was to mean the exclusion of black workers from a whole range of civil service posts: Inspector of Mines, Ministry of Health Inspector, National Assistance Board officers, Customs and Excise officers, fuel engineers, mechanical, civil and electrical engineers, chemists. This exclusion was to be applied rigorously in government departments which brought blacks into contact with the 'public', placed them in positions of authority over white people, or brought black men into contact with white women. Even GCHQ in 1956 were to send instructions to the Civil Service Commission stating that 'where there is a suspicion either from the candidate's appearance or from the material about parentage normally available to the Commissioners, that he may be a "coloured person" . . . he should not be assigned to GCHQ'.[58]

What we have seen in this section is that, in the same way that the politics of aliens control was to condition the essential freedom of the relationship wherein EVWs disposed of their capacity to labour, so too was the activity of the black worker to be mediated by ideological processes which themselves became, or were reformulated as, conditions of production circumscribing his/her activity. In the following section we shall look in greater depth at how this reformulation was to take place in textile production.

Asian Labour in Textiles

From the 1950s onwards textiles was to experience a severe drift of female workers away from the industry enticed by employment opportunities elsewhere with cleaner, better-paid jobs. Quite often such opportunities arose from the diversification of industries which the Labour government had initiated through its Development Areas scheme. It was to combat this drift that Poles and EVWs had been recruited by an immobile capital. By the mid-1950s EVWs had followed the pattern of white English women and left the industry in which they had been located. In resorting to West Indians and Hungarians in the late 1950s, and to Asians in the 1960s and 1970s, textile employers were preserving the long historical tradition of using successive waves of migrant labour. With respect to the movement of skilled, male English workers away from the industry, employers were generally able to muddle through with the pool of labour generated by the contraction of the industry. Between 1951 and 1959, wool textile employment fell some 14 per cent, and continued to fall at an accelerated rate throughout the 1960s and 1970s.

The recruitment of male Asian workers as direct production operatives, initially on an 'experimental' basis, on the dirty, poorly-paid jobs such as wire-pulling and scouring in woolcombing rejected by white women was to expand even more to counter the drift of women away from the industry in the 1960s and 1970s. Quite often Asians gained access to new areas of work by working night shifts, a necessity given the legal and social barriers to the employment of women on night shifts. The combination of youth plus the fact that most Asian workers were single or separated from families imposed no such restrictions on the development of night shifts. In many firms Asian men were performing functions carried out by women during the day. And despite the increasing representation of Asians on day shifts in the 1960s and 1970s they remained over-represented on night shifts and, indeed, tended to compose all the permanent night shifts (Fevre 1984; Pulle 1972; Clark 1982; Thakur 1970). In some firms they were employed only on night shifts. In all of the cases examined by Ralph Fevre (1984) the proportion of night shift workers who were Asians exceeded 59 per cent, and rose to over 90 per cent in some Bradford woolcombing firms (Fevre 1984: 104). 'I would not think of starting a night-shift,' declared one manager of a Bradford textile firm, 'without thirty or forty Pakistanis' (Allen 1970: 125). More graphically, a CIS report claimed: *The Blacker the Sky, the Darker the Faces*. The extent to which male Asian workers replaced white female workers in Bradford wool textiles is illustrated in Table 1.1. This table should not lead us to assume that Asian workers merely inherited the employment distribution of white English women and EVWs. The opportunities for Asian workers were even more limited:

> Throughout the 1960s and 1970s white women retained better access to the more skilled operative jobs, live weaving, and a monopoly of the relatively well paid occupation of burling and mending. Burling and mending, together with some processes intermediate between spinning and weaving, provided access to non-mechanised work. By way of contrast, where Asians were employed in jobs from which white women were absent their work was of the least desirable kind. Thus Asians found work as machine minders in combined mills (where very few women were employed) and in the least attractive of the non-mechanised occupations, for example woolpulling and general labouring in spinning mills (where no women were employed). It is therefore clear that the extant, sexual division of labour between white women and white men was not simply replicated in the division of labour between Asian men and white men. Instead, the division of labour was established on a three cornered basis with white men retaining the best jobs but with white women and Asian men working separately in the remainder. While the

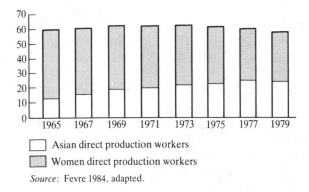

Table 1.1 Percentages of Direct Production Workers in Wool (1,000s)

sexual division of labour remained, an additional element became apparent with
the recruitment of Asians: the division of labour now had a racial basis . . . (Fevre
1984: 80–81)

Secondly, the nature of many occupations was to be altered by the increased
mechanization that the use of male Asian workers now made possible.
Throughout the 1960s and 1970s many textile employers sought to restructure their labour processes both by mechanization and a more general
transformation of other class features of work such as control. The general
deskilling of white workers by the introduction of new mechanical productive
functions such as French combing, ring spinning, and automatic winding
tended to provide interstices for Asian labour that were not available in out-
of-date mills. The widespread adoption of night work to augment the level of
productivity and to lower the cost of production underlined this movement
towards Asian labour in Bradford mills. In the 1970s, 30 per cent of the wool
textile labour force was Asian.

Deskilling was widespread. Whereas traditional female jobs on the old
technology may have been regarded as skilled and responsible, 'Asian' jobs
were redefined as 'minding' not merely because the skilled element had been
degraded by mechanization but because it was now unacknowledged. The
fundamental aim was to secure a greater degree of control over, and
exploitation of, labour. In the old labour process women were expected to
'take an interest in the job', to exhibit 'good housekeeping', and to preserve an
element of flexibility in their working hours so long as the piecework rate was
maintained. Such customs and practices were soon discarded. The watch-
word became flexibility of job content.

It is ironic that strategies designed to restructure capital in this way should
have had an adverse effect on the so-called 'labour shortage' by hastening the
exit of more white workers unwilling to tolerate the degradation and deskilling involved. Quitting was the most common mode of registering resistance.

However as the proportion of Asian workers steadily increased, they were rarely recruited into productive positions formerly occupied by white men. Only in the worst jobs or on night shifts did such a replacement occur. Crucial here was the fact that well into the 1970s skilled male occupations were not subjected to the transformations undergone by female productive occupations.

Of course, not all textile capitalists restructured their labour processes. Many employers, including small worsted spinners, preserved the old technology and working practices. In such cases, there were few openings for Asians. Recruits could always be found among white female workers who had quit other transformed mills.

A general argument which has normally been advanced to explain the use of migrant labour as an industrial reserve army is that it represents cheap labour, understood in the commonsense way of undercutting prevailing wage rates. Textiles present a somewhat complex picture if only for the reason that male labour and shift work are considerably more expensive than female labour. Moreover, within textiles, Asian workers by and large tended to be found in firms with *higher* than average wage levels. Yet, having said this, the evidence does show that average hourly earnings of male migrant workers – given their distribution in machine minding and labouring manual occupations (and their coterminous absence from supervisory positions and even ancillary manual work) – were, and still are, relatively low in comparison to other industries (Fevre 1984; Allen 1970; Pulle 1972). In woollen and worsted mills in April 1975, for example, average hourly earnings were 99.3p as compared with 123.1p in all manufacturing industries. This disparity was also reflected in the West Riding of Yorkshire: wage rates in the wool industry generally compared unfavourably with rates in other industries, especially engineering which was a big competitor for labour in the area. Discrimination and other factors, however, limited the opportunities of Asians in engineering. It is perhaps for this reason that Fevre (1984: 161–2) observed:

> The jobs which blacks do are peculiar in that their pay seems to be unrelated to the level of labour demand in these occupations. Excess demand is not translated into higher pay. Thus black workers sell their labour *as if the labour market did not exist; indeed it does not exist for black workers since they suffer discrimination.*

With what was in effect a captive labour force employers did not have to offer higher wages to attract white workers for the dirty, unattractive jobs done by Asians. In so doing they were able to preserve the equilibrium of differentials that skilled white workers would certainly have wished to restore. In a highly competitive market, and against a background of a high level of bankruptcy, too, there was a tremendous pressure on employers to keep production costs as low as possible.

The debate about 'cheapness' would be further refined by examining shift premium. Until recently the textile night shift premium of 20 per cent was lower than, for example, in engineering where it was a third. Given what has been said about the concentration of Asian workers on shifts, levels of premiums are not without significance in the debate about 'cheapness'. However, there are spheres and branches of production with concentrations of migrant workers such as foundries and fletton brick manufacture in which earnings appear relatively good. Clearly, what is needed is a fuller under-standing of the concept of cheap labour. If Asian textile labour was cheap, it was so because employers did not have to raise wages in order to hang on to their white workers for the extant dirty, dead-end, low-paid jobs given the presence of Asian workers in sufficient numbers willing to undertake such work.

What we have just described is clearly a complex social process of power relationship between capital and labour and between fractions of labour. In this context the issue of racism and discrimination has a role to play insofar as it compels Asians to engage in specific forms of wage labour and thereby circumscribe their ability to alienate their labour-power. It is not that Asian workers had certain characteristics, cultural or otherwise, which particularly fitted them for the deskilled 'dirty jobs' created in wool textiles but, rather, that they were unable to reject these jobs, for instance, in local engineering firms, which were now recruiting a white industrial reserve army from textiles. As Fevre (1984: 161) writes:

> Black workers find that discrimination leaves no alternative but to sell their labour to those employers who cannot recruit whites.

What does the discussion so far tell us about the manner in which Asians as an element of the industrial reserve army were reproduced as part of the active textile labour force? In the first instance, it tells us that they were concentrated in unskilled and semi-skilled operative and labouring productive functions some of which were the product of the process of mechanization. Secondly, it was this very concentration of Asian workers which made them vulnerable to changes in the economic climate such as recessions. There is some evidence, for example, that falling order books in the 1970s may have adversely affected Asian jobs particularly in the case of firms which reorganized or dispensed entirely with night shifts as a means of curtailing production. One worsted spinner kept his Asian employees on only so long as he needed night shift work, i.e. from 1964 to 1976. According to Fevre (1984), however, the effects of the recession were not the primary cause of the higher redundancy among Asian wool textile workers. The answer, he argues, lies in the further trans-formation of the labour process which not only mechanized many of the 'dirty jobs' in areas such as scouring and carding but took them out of the province of Asians. Where the recession may have had an added effect on Asians in wool textile occupations was by making such jobs more attractive to whites. It is worth noting though that unemployed textile workers are more likely to be Asian than white. Formerly white English women and EVWs may have left textiles for better jobs but discrimination and the general lack of opportunities elsewhere ensured that Asians left for the dole.

We can therefore sum up by quoting Fevre (1984: 89–90):

> It is clear that Asian workers were not used as an *alternative* to modernisation by wool textile employers. The only firms which did not employ Asians were the most backward in the industry, nevertheless the employment of Asians may have represented a transitional stage in the industry's development. In the 1960s and 1970s wool textile employers were able to remove obstacles to increased output per head without increased wages. By the end of this period 'custom and practice' over workloads and responsibilities had been successfully challenged and the worker autonomy symbolised by piecework replaced by increased accountability. Furthermore, the workforce had in large part been converted to shifts and low premiums and to work on new machinery. It may be that these changes prepared the way for a more lasting solution to the employers' problems. In other words, the recruitment of Asian workers allowed employers to overcome worker resistance and to make changes which would later allow them to dispense with the *need* for Asian labour.

Embodied in this extensive quotation is a clear plea for us to transcend sociological analyses which interpret class relations and the class feature of work solely in terms of financial rewards. By so doing, we omit associated inequalities of work life such as loss of control, deskilling, redundancy, exposure to health risks and so on which are equally part of what is meant by class structure. An analysis of migrant labour necessarily requires us to analyse all of these factors. Such inequalities, writes Salaman (1984: 15):

> are not haphazard or random. They are themselves the consequences of differences in interest between managers and managed . . . They are not, in other words, simply additional to the distinction, they are *part of the distinction itself*. The considerable inequalities that exist between controllers and controlled reflect the conflict of interest between these two camps and the differential power of each camp – and its external allies – to achieve its interest in the face of the others' opposition or resistance.

Black Labour in the National Health Service

As an employer in its own right, MOL lost no time in setting about meeting the acute demand for nurses which in 1949 had reached 54,000. As before, attempts were initially made to secure white workers as nurses and domestics. Though some EVWs had been recruited in 1946 for domestic work in TB sanatoria, the scheme was by and large unsuccessful. The solution was to hijack the scheme run by MOL on behalf of the CO to train nurses who, on returning to the colonies, were to form the cadre of a Colonial Nursing Service 'based upon the high standard, traditions and practices of the British nursing profession'. The CO was left to demur at the fact that their nurses were being more and more 'regarded as a pair of hands to fill vacancies which cannot otherwise be filled' and 'sent exclusively to "shortage" hospitals rather than to hospitals offering specialized training in tropical medicine'.[59]

An analysis of the use of migrant labour in the NHS should warn us that such workers cannot be correlated simplistically with unskilled labour. British immigration legislation, especially after 1962, has been selectively operated to secure the recruitment of particular types of skilled labour; and doctors and nurses were among the few categories able to obtain vouchers when other categories were being squeezed. It was the student permit system which, by restricting the mobility of recruits out of nursing and thereby circumscribing their ability to alienate their labour-power, forcibly expressed the manner in which the formalization of the employment contract was secured. At the same time too it expressed the manner in which the industrial reserve army was to be threaded through the active labour army given the fact that most nurses were encouraged to qualify as state enrolled nurses (SEN) rather than state registered nurses (SRN). Not only did this limit the avenues for promotion but it posed special problems for nurses from countries such as the Philippines and Singapore where the SEN qualification is not recognized. On converting their student permits into normal work permits many therefore remained in the lower-paid positions of the NHS.

In the 1950s and 1960s the number of overseas-born student and pupil nurses expanded rapidly, reaching a peak in 1970. In 1975 20.5 per cent of all student and pupil nurses were born overseas, half of these being recruited in the countries of birth. Recruitment from the West Indies also exhibited a similar pattern, the peak coming earlier, in 1968. Between 1968 and 1975 the number of West Indian student and pupil nurses declined from 6,500 to under 2,800. Contrary to the belief that many came to train and then return home, one finds that the percentage of overseas nurses among qualified staff remains quite high (83 per cent in some cases). If the percentage of overseas-recruited pupil nurses has declined in recent years, this is partly a reflection of the shift in DHSS policy to a more active recruitment from among the 'ethnic minorities' in this country or from among overseas-born nurses already resident in this country.

The effects of the recession and Thatcherite policies on the NHS should also be mentioned since the high level of unemployment among British nurses has led to permits not being renewed for overseas nurses. For this category of nurses whose labour-power has made a significant contribution to keeping down the cost of medical care in Britain, the loss of job means inability to stay in this country to become part of a floating relative surplus-population.

An uneven 'labour shortage' has ensured that recruits are not evenly spread throughout the health regions, with the greatest concentrations being found in the four Thames regions. Racist discrimination, too, ensures that overseas-born nurses are over-represented in the less glamorous areas of nursing: mental illness, mental handicap and geriatrics. Relatively few, noted the Unit for Manpower Studies, are employed in prestige hospitals.

Domestic work, too, was one of the few occupations to which the Labour government's 1948 working party on surplus colonial manpower considered colonial labour could make a contribution. The reason went beyond a simple 'shortage': 'It was attractive from the administrative angle since the women involved would be living a regulated life and subject to supervision[!]'[60] As in the case of nurses the employment contract was formalized as a means of securing the control and exploitation of labour-power. By 1949 recruitment of domestic workers from Barbados and St. Helena, particularly for hospitals outside London, had been started on an ad hoc basis by the Ministry of Health in conjunction with colonial governments. In the case of Barbados, for example, the government paid the $96 passage money which the girls were to pay back at the rate of 25p per week for the duration of their three-year contract. Incidentally, such arrangements were in contravention of the ILO convention which stipulated that contracts should not be negotiated for more than *two* years for any individual not accompanied by her family. When the Barbadian government encouraged (pressurised in some cases) the girls to renew their contract in 1952 – again in contravention of the ILO convention – other islands such as Jamaica asked to be incorporated into the scheme 'to mitigate the severe unemployment among women in the colony'.

Today, the proportion of immigrants among the ancillary (domestic and catering) staff remains relatively high. A 1968 study revealed that in the hospitals examined 11 per cent of domestic staff were of new commonwealth origin, 3.4 per cent Irish and 7.8 per cent from foreign countries. As in the cases of nurses, notes the Unit for Manpower Studies, 'There is some evidence of a relationship between concentrations of immigrants and labour supply difficulties' (DE/UMS 1977: 63).

Afro-Caribbean Labour and London Transport

For black workers entry into London Transport was entry into an industry – nationalized in 1948 – whose conditions of labour had deteriorated and continued to deteriorate rapidly. In pre-war years, against a background of high unemployment and job insecurity, employment in London Transport had generally been perceived as desirable. Wages and conditions of labour were comparable to those encountered in other branches and spheres of production. After the defeat of the 1937 Coronation strike and the war-time constraints which increased the intensity of labour this favourable position was to be somewhat eroded (Fuller 1985).

A decade of 'full employment' was to devalue the last attractive element: job security. Henceforth, employment in London Transport, particularly as busworker, began to appear as just another semi-skilled opening and not a very attractive one at that.

An examination of wage levels reveals that the favourable position of the London bus driver lost during the war years was never regained. The occupation of the busworker was now no longer one of the most highly paid. Average earnings for drivers in comparison to other branches of production continued to decline in the 1950s and 1960s. In 1954 this percentage was already down to 79.6 per cent and was to fall to 75 per cent by 1960. Only the substantial pay rise offered by the Phelps Brown Committee[61] ensured that this percentage had increased to 75.6 per cent in 1963. The story was the same for conductors. Their percentage had fallen from 77.6 per cent in 1954 to 73.3 per cent in 1960, and remained the same in 1963 (Ministry of Labour 1964). The basic rate of pay for both occupations was indeed among the very few which had risen less than retail prices since the war. If the factory operative had to work at the same times as the busworker, observed the Phelps Brown Committee, the former's earnings would have been significantly greater.

Bearing in mind what we have said about the class nature of work, equal attention should be paid to the conditions of labour for London Transport workers. By and large such conditions retained features which many other workers found unattractive. In comparison to factory operatives and office workers, the passenger worker laboured a longer working week, worked irregular hours, enjoyed a working day of eight hours spread over a thirteen-hour period, had fewer days off per year, started earlier in the morning, had no fixed meal times and no tea breaks, worked public holidays, and had a more restricted social life.

It was the concomitant feature of a branch of production which had 'come to rank too low in the structure' of the London area both in terms of wages and conditions of labour, that London Transport throughout the 1950s and 1960s was unable to attract and retain the labour force required to meet the demands upon it. 'As other groups of workers improved their conditions of employment,' comments Fuller (1985: 204), 'the negative aspects of buswork, especially the shift and weekend-work, became barriers to the retention of staff.'

The high rate of staff turnover speaks for itself. For a public undertaking where long-term employment had always been the norm, 40 per cent of drivers and conductors tended to quit after only two years' service. In other words, this constituted some 4,000–5,000 drivers and conductors per year, or one in five of Central Bus Staff. A similar pattern was exhibited by the Railways and Permanent Ways Department (track construction and maintenance) of London Transport.

The difficulties of London Transport, too, were aggravated by competition from private transport. In the London Transport area alone, private licensed cars increased by 400 per cent between 1948 and 1965 (Fuller 1985: 201). More seriously for the conditions of the busworker, consumerism was to encourage the Ministry of Transport to shift resources away from public transport into road-building for private cars. An immediate outcome was an increase in traffic congestion in London and a decline in the demand for bus services. No less important was the devaluation of the driving skill which had been a symbol of the London busdriver's pre-war high status. Critical here was the experience of the war which had trained thousands of working-class men and women as drivers, and the post-war proliferation of the private car.

However, the continued reduction in services consequent on passenger loss did nothing to resolve the chronic staff 'shortage'. Levels of wastage always exceeded levels of recruitment. It was to overcome this severe 'labour shortage' in most operating grades brought about by the functioning of London Transport as a branch of production which was expected by statute to 'pay its way' while providing an 'adequate service' ('adequate' remaining undefined), that London Transport turned both to female and to migrant labour.

As in other spheres of production women had been employed in considerable numbers during both world wars as station staff and gate operators on the railways, and as conductresses on Central Buses. In the latter position they were often perceived as a temporary expedient for the 'duration of the emergency': London Transport supposedly returning after the war to its pre-war all-male operating staff. It soon became apparent this was not going to be the case at existing wages and conditions of labour. After a 1950 agreement female workers came to be regarded as an indispensable feature of the labour force in the less important grades. The resistance of trade unions ensured that their employment did not spread beyond these restricted grades. As in the case of the textile industry, London Transport was to experience severe competition for female labour from other spheres of production. London Transport experimented similarly with EVWs and Polish Resettlement Corps workers. 'Linguistic demands' however ensured that such workers were initially placed on the outer fringes of the organization. For many the acceptance of such positions meant a certain downgrading or 'declassing' especially since non-British staff before 1955 were ineligible for promotion.

Likewise, London Transport operated a recruitment drive in Northern Ireland (1950), Eire (1952–53), Barbados (1956) and finally Jamaica and

Trinidad in the early 1960s. By and large, black labour did not become a feature of London Transport until after 1954. This was quite often perceived as preferable to recruitment in London since recruits taken on directly from islands such as Barbados were not only young but could be subject to more stringent health examinations than English recruits.

In London Transport as well as in the provinces, the rapid build-up of black workers from the 1950s onwards was to encounter trade union resistance and outrage. Quite deep-seated was the fear that already uncompetitive wages and conditions of labour would be undermined by 'cheap labour', and the fear that black workers would prove unreliable in times of organized industrial conflict. For white operatives continuing to work the buses purely for the overtime – which constituted some 13 per cent of total hours worked and which London Transport had fostered as an alternative to demands for increased wage rates – there was a corresponding unwillingness to lose it. In Birmingham the leaders of the white workers asserted that parents and husbands of conductresses objected to their working late nights with black workers, that black workers were too stupid to issue tickets properly (*Observer* 21.2.1954; Gunter 1955: 6). In the Midlands in 1955, white workers were to go on strike several times in protest at the use of black labour on public transport. In most areas, such protests were defused only by the imposition of a quota on the number of black workers taken on, their confinement to specific duties and agreements about redundancy.

On Central Buses early black operatives were all conductors. The railway department exhibited a similar pattern of concentration with the first recruits being confined to the position of station staff. The prevailing view among English train operatives was that the blacks would 'never get off the platform'. Early recruits to the Permanent Ways Department were initially dispersed at two per work group. Within two or three years this practice was soon overlooked as the 'labour shortage' became more acute. As in the case of textile workers, *quitting* became an important mode by which white workers expressed their resistance to the labour process. Were it not for the contraction in the industry, which had seen employment decline from its peak of 100,000 in 1948 to 73,000 in 1966 and 60,000 in 1970, the 'labour shortage' would have appeared even more chronic.

By 1966 blacks constituted 7.4 per cent of the 13,000 drivers and 29 per cent of the 9,815 male conductors on the Central Buses (West Indian Standing Conference/WISC 1967:1). In some garages, the percentages were even higher.

While the 1958 bus strike disproved fears about disloyal black labour, it did not deter the London Bus Conference in 1961 from passing a resolution opposing immigration and the use of black workers on London Transport. In 1963 white staff went as far as to pass a further resolution that they would not work with more blacks until pay and conditions were improved. Such resolutions clearly reflected the constant fear that the market position of the indigenous worker who chose to stay rather than quit would be undermined.

As with Asian textile workers, discrimination also had a crucial role to play in the occupational opportunities available to black London Transport workers. Brooks's analysis of the early recruits to London Transport reveals the extent to which discrimination by other employers may have served to keep black workers in London Transport while their white counterparts came and went:

> Clearly, job discrimination at that time was widespread . . . What is clear is that most of those who applied for skilled or white-collar employment were given no opportunity to *prove* their abilities: they were turned away at the door (Brooks 1975: 41).

This was all the more relevant given the occupational background of the early recruits to London Transport. Few of them, Brooks informs us, had been 'amongst the most economically oppressed in their home countries' (Brooks 1975: 48). In fact, he adds, 'many were in sought-after occupations . . . The West Indian recruits were more likely to have been carpenters, mechanics, clerks, or policemen than cane cutters. In these terms, they were in the upper strata of the working class and the lower strata of the middle class in their home countries' (Brooks 1975: 48). In short, few had been unemployed (only 6 per cent) or in insecure jobs.

In the 1960s attention was to turn to the way in which black recruits experienced difficulties of promotion to the level of inspector despite the perpetual shortage of inspectors. In a study carried out by the West Indian Standing Conference (1967), it was observed that since recruitment had started in 1956, no black applicant had been promoted to the level of inspector. This lack of promotion was attributed to the discrimination of garage and divisional managers as well as inspectors who, 'under the guise of doing their job efficiently . . . book black crews for every offence they committed, no matter how trivial, as against turning a blind eye to the same offences committed by white crews' (WISC 1967: 5). Such bookings ruined an applicant's promotional chances. The concern for white workers at one North London garage was: 'What's going to happen when the monkeys start wearing the cap?'

Before the fullest sense can be made of issues such as 'labour shortage', 'cheap labour', and so on, one would have to examine the precise role of branches of production such as London Transport and the NHS in the overall process of capital accumulation. We shall conclude this section by turning our attention to the latter issue.

It is something of a truism to state that capital cannot of itself, through its own actions, produce the social conditions of its own existence. At the level of total capital, Keynes's major concern, the process of capital accumulation necessitates the organization of a segment of the working population on a social, non-profit-making, non-commodity basis. This is the essence of a London Transport which is required by statute to pay its way while providing an adequate service. It is the essence too of the NHS.

What this means is that in such branches labour-power is utilized in the form of use-value rather than for exchange-value/profit-making as in the case of the textile industry. In the latter branch the use-value content of the product is merely a by-product. By contrast, for London Transport and the NHS, the conditions under which labour-power was socially put to use were not governed by the criterion of the production and realization of surplus-value, of profit-making on an expanded scale. Labour-power was here deployed with regard to its socially useful content: providing a service to the public. Exchange-value was the by-product at least until the advent of Wilsonian prices and incomes policy and Thatcherite monetarism. Even when required to 'pay its way' this quite often meant the acceptance of a rate of profit below the average for capital as a whole throughout the economy. In this way the production that went on in such spheres did not enter into the equalization of the rate of profit that the law of value imposes upon every individual capital. (With privatization this will no longer be the case.)

Nevertheless, as the Phelps Brown Report of 1964 observed, there were limitations imposed by the framework of national economic growth. Wages, stated the report, must be considered in conjunction with the rise in money incomes for the economy as a whole to ensure that they did not exceed the wider level of productivity. Otherwise, 'the consequent rise of costs and prices not only moves up a spiral of inflation at home, but threatens our trade abroad; and that renewed trouble with the balance of payments will renew the checks to economic growth' (Phelps Brown Report: 55). Two years after Phelps Brown, against a background of a policy of wage restraint, Labour's Prices and Incomes Board was to go even further and argue that levels of wages could be used to resolve the labour shortage. Shortage, it stated, should be resolved by 'making better use of existing labour', i.e. by increased productivity. The main thrust of London Transport's 'productivity' proposals concerned the introduction of more one-person operations. It is with a similar foresight that James Callaghan had pugnaciously observed in 1946:

> Who is going to pay for the old age pensions and social services we are rightly distributing now, unless we have an addition to our population, which only immigrants will provide in the days to come?[62]

Taken together, these different observations signal an extremely important point, namely, the danger that labour organized for the purpose of producing use-values directly, may produce use-values other than those that are required by and aid the expansion of capitalism that is foundering. The consequence is quite often an expansion of those intermediate strata which no longer produce surplus-value. Insofar as surplus-value production is no longer contributed to, they violate the essence of capitalist accumulation by eroding the legitimating scheme of equal exchange. It is in this context that migrant labour has a seminal role to play insofar as such labour is more easily induced to obey the needs of accumulation and thereby made to accept these needs as premises for decision-making whether of pay and conditions, the concentration of immigrant workers in specific areas of the NHS, and so on. To the extent that such areas of employment begin to operate under criteria outside the accumulation process, calculation may become political rather than monetary. The present struggle that is raging in the NHS has everything to do with this. If in textiles wages were to be determined by the level of competition between different spheres of production and by discrimination, here, wages were to be determined less by competition and more by extra-economic, political and ideological criteria.

Unemployment and Developments in the Concept of the Industrial Reserve Army (IRA)

The racialized distribution of black workers into semi- and unskilled jobs in textiles, metal manufacture, vehicles, transport and communications in specific regions was to have important bearing on their experience of unemployment. In the 1950s and 1960s periods of recession brought about by stop-go economic policies of successive governments always led to higher levels of unemployment than were explicable by reference solely to the volume of migration and the difficulties experienced by new migrants in finding employment. From the 1970s onwards, too, there is more than ample evidence to show that black men and women have been disproportionately affected by the rise in unemployment brought about by long-term structural recession (Smith 1981; Brown 1984; Runnymede Trust 1980; Newnham 1986). Not only have unemployment levels been higher but unemployment has increased at a faster rate. Between 1972 and 1981 black unemployment increased 325 per cent in comparison to 138 per cent for all workers. Labour Force Surveys for 1984 reveal an unemployment level for black workers (20.4 per cent) that was almost double that for white workers (10.6 per cent). This pattern still prevailed in 1988 when employment levels had fallen (see Table 1.2). Such a level of unemployment too has also been reflected in the greater tendency to be among the long-term unemployed.

For black workers, the pattern of distribution has not been uniform. As in the late 1950s and early 1960s (Davison 1963) Pakistanis and Bangladeshis have experienced the highest levels of unemployment (34.6 per cent in 1984). Throughout the country, too, this pattern is uneven. For Afro-Caribbean

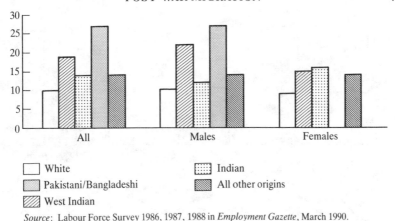

White
Pakistani/Bangladeshi
West Indian
Indian
All other origins

Source: Labour Force Survey 1986, 1987, 1988 in *Employment Gazette*, March 1990.

Table 1.2 Percentages of Unemployment Rates by Ethnic Origin and Gender

workers the areas of highest unemployment in 1984 were the North-West (41 per cent) and West Midlands (32 per cent); while for Asians the areas of highest unemployment were Scotland (30 per cent) and the West Midlands (28 per cent) (Newnham 1986). Evidence for the inner cities reveals even more marked disparities between black and white unemployment rates (Brown 1984).

If one examines the levels of unemployment for young people under twenty-five the picture is even grimmer, as Table 1.3 indicates. What is not highlighted is the desperate position of young black men. In 1985 41 per cent of Afro-Caribbean youths were unemployed, in comparison to 26 per cent of Asian males and 19 per cent of white males (Newnham 1986: 17). Clough and Drew (1985) have shown that this picture cannot be explained by levels of qualifications. Indeed, while qualifications increase the chances of finding a job, the survey found that those with higher qualifications experienced more discrimination than lesser-qualified youngsters.

Increasingly, concern has shifted to the failure of the Youth Training Scheme to provide an avenue into paid employment for black youth. Success-ive surveys (Banks 1981; Fenton et al. 1984; Cross and Smith 1987) have examined the way in which racist discrimination shunts them into the dead-end sectors of work-preparation schemes on the early Youth Opportunities Programme and mode B courses on Youth Training Schemes which are less likely to lead to jobs. Young black people are thus being made increasingly a permanent feature of the relative surplus-population, i.e. a feature which is rendered relatively superfluous to the accumulation process.

It is not enough however to rest the case for or against the concept of the industrial reserve army on the basis of disposability or availability as most writers have sought to do (Milkman 1975; Simeral 1978; Breugal 1979). What is missing from accounts which reduce the concept of industrial reserve

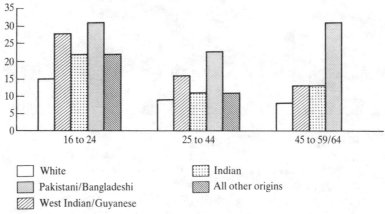

Source: Labour Force Survey 1986, 1987, 1988 in *Employment Gazette*, March 1990.

Table 1.3 % Unemployment Rates by Ethnic Origin and Age

army to disposability or availability is the ability to analyse capital as a constant process of reconstruction and expansion in which the very nature of the industrial reserve army is consequently altered. Disposability is part of the wider process of risk and security to which all workers are subjected to a greater or lesser degree. For example, what the present recession has shown is not so much that women constitute the majority of part-time workers, but that part-time work may have become an intrinsic feature of contemporary capitalism.

It is this feature that is captured by Christopherson (1986) in her concept of 'contingency work' which includes not only part-time employment but independent contracting and temporary help. In recent years, as a result of the reconstruction of capital that has taken place, the phenomenon of permanent part-time workers in banks, retailing, and the wholesale trade has become even more marked.

In her study of female Asian homeworkers in the clothing industry in areas such as East London, Swasti Mitter (1986) too highlights the connection between flexibility/casualization, subcontracting, sexism/patriarchy and eth-nicity. In the face of severe competition margins of profitability are preserved not by the investment of new technology but by the shifting of employment from the official to the hidden economy. Work that once took place within a large firm (or within the public sector) may now be subcontracted to small firms or individuals who provide goods and services across industries. These subcontractors, in turn, may employ a number of people 'on call' in order to remain flexible with respect to the market. Risk is thus transmitted down-wards to the worker or subcontractor who must adapt. We thus have developing the process that Singleman and Tienda (1985) term vertical disintegration. What firms in the clothing industry, for example, have learned is that it is highly unprofitable, indeed disastrous, to hoard labour on the main factory floor (for productive functions such as machining – 80 per cent of the cost of production in the garment industry and for which there is no accompanying technological innovation such as computerized 'cutting') for long run production (and presumed economies of scale) in a volatile, fashion-conscious market. The situation may thus develop where one has a core labour force protected from the vagaries of the market by subcontracting the same product during high transaction periods. What we have here is not some sort of labour market segmentation, i.e. inter-occupational distribution of work, but an intra-occupational segmentation based on the allocation of work time.

The study by Swasti Mitter (1986) has focused on this process of vertical disintegration at the level of subcontracting and homework. The ethnic minority entrepreneur is described as having an edge in the cut-throat competition because of his access to a cheap, captive labour force provided and solidified by the extended family structure organized around notions of patriarchy. Employment comes to be regarded as an obligation rather than a pure labour contract. Ethnic and familial links serve to keep wages low, and it is an uphill task to unionize. Mitter writes:

> In an economy where employee–employer relationship is underpinned by the ethnic and familial network, a woman may find it difficult to get work if she is identified as 'disruptive' or 'unionized' elements. The servility, subservience and passivity that the communities expect of wives towards their husbands, daughters-in-law towards fathers-in-law in the home, were reproduced to an important extent in the factory. For a woman recruited through friends and relations, a direct telephone-call to a father, husband or uncle is often enough to suppress rebels.

Conclusion

An exploration of the concept of industrial reserve army in this chapter forced us to interrogate the notion of the 'labour shortage, that crops up ubiquitously in discussions of the post-war period. We saw that rather than being a simple product of demography and population, the 'labour shortage' was equally the outcome of the policies pursued by the Keynesian welfare state in relation to the process of accumulation – noteworthy was the way in which the system of welfare benefits forced it to adopt measures to regulate the labour market – and the outcome of the struggles fought by a very well-entrenched and organized white working class against deskilling, redundancy and subordination to capital. It is not accidental that the 'labour shortage' was most acute in industries such as textiles and transport which white workers were leaving in droves in response to transformations in the labour processes and the relative decline in conditions of labour.

It is in these two processes – the role of the state and the struggles of organized white labour – that one should look for explanations about the manner in which migrant workers were to become a new lever of accumulation, an industrial reserve army. It was a lever though that was to be economically, politically and ideologically reproduced as part of the active labour force but apart from it by its concentration on night shifts, and by its confinement to semi- and unskilled work which, in areas such as textiles, were later mechanized and taken out of the province of black workers. For black workers, it seemed that their very activity was mediated by ideological processes that themselves became, or were reformulated as, conditions of production. The result has been the perpetuation of a racialized hierarchy in which claims to skill status have come to rely more on skin colour and less on the technical content of the job. In short, definitions of skill are saturated with a credo of racialized meanings such that certain types of work are deemed to be unsuitable for some workers and unskilled by virtue of the occupants who perform them.

Stuart Hall (1991) has rightly criticized that prevailing Eurocentric orthodoxy which views capital as singular and unitary in its effects. In other words, capital is perceived as a rationalizing, all-absorbent juggernaut which obliterates difference and particularity in its onward march to commodify everything, in its relentless search for profit. Such a 'logic of capital' is contradicted by the evidence that we have presented. The advance of British capital nationally and globally occurs through a process of uneven and combined development working in and through specificity, or as Hall (1991: 29) puts it, working 'between the different ethnically and racially inflected labour forces'.

Our interest has been not only in the vertical differentiation of production and the horizontal differentiation between different levels of occupations but in the way in which the industrial reserve army has been threaded through the labour process to re-emerge again as superfluous, and jettisoned as so much ballast to form part of an increasingly *consolidated* relative surplus-population. For black youngsters the scenario remains grim: levels of unemployment remain high and youth training (YOP, YTS and YT) have turned out to be cul-de-sacs rather than avenues into paid employment. Those who remain within employment have found that disposability is no longer the only hallmark of the industrial reserve army. Other features such as subcontracting, flexibility and casualization have come more and more to the fore. And as the vertical disintegration of firms has become more common so too has risk grown apace.

What we have detailed here is nothing less than a process of racialization in which complex significations and signifying practices have been articulated around notions of 'race' and a regime of visibility constructed around colour. Via the imperializing and hegemonizing palimpsest of the 'immigrant', black workers found themselves positioned within new discourses of differentiation, hierarchization and fixity which were to have a profound impact on notions of 'Britishness' and black identity (see Chapter 10 below).

On the former point we see the way in which 'race' and 'colour' were to be reworked once more as powerful signifiers of belongingness, of determining 'us' and 'them', 'British' and 'not-British', 'the British way of life' and 'how the Other half lives'. Worse, relations between social groups were presented as though constituted in and ordained by nature, and therefore not subject to human agency or historical processes. What we have here is the exposition of racism not simply as an ideological chiaroscuro for the legitimation of domination but as a philosophy of history in which history is portrayed as inscribed in the hidden biological nature of human subjects and consequently as no more than a process of 'race struggle' between 'stronger' and 'weaker' races. If identities were to be placed outside historical processes, so too was social behaviour. And in this we have the birth of the new disciplinary knowledge of 'race relations' which perniciously renders relations grounded in social inequality and oppression as the product of difference.

Superficially, the 1948 Nationality Act appeared to cut across this process by offering two apparently ex-centric, supranational notions of 'Britishness': subjecthood (British subject) and citizenship (UK and Colonies citizenship): one embracing the whole Empire (subjecthood) and grounded in a notion of allegiance to the monarch, the other, UK and Colonies citizenship, based on the notion of rights. Indeed, by an extraordinary tour de force, the latter version appears to unify what had formerly been present as binary opposites: colonizer and colonized, 'dominant race' and 'inferior race', 'District Commissioner' and 'native'. Citizenship as a right, however, existed only to be surrendered when colonials sought to celebrate their 'Britishness' not by waving their Union Jacks 'out there' in the colonies but in the 'Mother Country'. Then, a third notion of British identity reared its head, namely, the Anglo-centric, racialized conception of *jus sanguinis* which had permeated the 1948 Nationality Act in a subterranean way. In later years this version was to become a full-blown attempt to patriarchally annex 'kith and kin' throughout the Commonwealth to create a *pan*-ic solidarity. Racism then was to universalize British identity by giving it a specificity which it did not possess hitherto.

Notes

1. The reduction in over-manning would have had a similar effect.
2. This suggestion by Marx has become the basis of the concept of 'marginality' and

'marginal mass' developed by a number of Latin American scholars. For these scholars it is not a mere extension of an earlier modality but an expression of underdevelopment in the third world.

3. These distinctions are well known. There are two important points, however, that should be made about these categories over and above the fact that they relate to the rate of surplus value (RSP) and not the industrial reserve army (IRA). First, they conflate different levels of analysis. Secondly they cannot *a priori* be posited as the basis of the IRA. On the first point, it should be noted that only the *floating* element of the RSP corresponds to the theoretically abstract analysis of the pure capitalist mode of production (CMP) that Marx generally offers in *Capital*. The *stagnant* element represents an analysis which presupposes the existence of residues of other modes of production which capital has not yet abolished. Similarly, the allusion to paupers and a lumpenproletariat introduces a concreteness that is only really found in *The Eighteenth Brumaire of Louis Bonaparte*. The reference to a *latent* RSP similarly represents an analysis of the CMP which is more concrete insofar as it introduces a discussion of agriculture and the ancillary problem of ground rent treated in volume 3 of *Capital*.

What can be gathered therefore from these observations is that the categories do not represent – and this cannot be overstated since it is precisely an application of these distinctions with which many writers have unnecessarily preoccupied themselves (Lever-Tracy 1983, Simeral 1978) – different *theorized* divisions into which the RSP decomposes.

4. The Working Party was appointed in 1945 by Sir Stafford Cripps at the instigation of the Cotton Boards 'to examine and inquire into the various schemes and suggestions put forward for improvement of organization, production and distribution methods and process in the Cotton Industry and to report as to steps which should be adopted in the national interest to strengthen the industry and to render it more stable and more capable of meeting competition in the home and foreign markets' (LAB 8/1250, Report of the Working Party on the Cotton Industry).

5. Cotton Industry Report.

6. Another answer which we cannot pursue here is the manner in which it sought to strengthen the exploitative links with the Commonwealth as a counter to increasing US hegemony. What this meant in reality were issues such as the pooling of sterling balances, trade agreements, loans to colonies channelled through the Colonial Development Corporation or Crown Agents to ensure the loans were used 'to buy British', the investment of colonial capital in British securities, the use of the colonies as a source of cheap raw material and as a market for uncompetitive British products. It was to cement these relationships that the 1948 Nationality Act was passed.

7. Cotton Industry Report.

8. In its interim report, the Working Party gave the following figures:

Total labour actually at work (in October)	1939	1942	1944
Spinning & Doubling	158,640	103,505	92,706
Weaving	163,560	103,410	96,880
Total mills in operation			
Spinning & Weaving	932	626	633
Weaving	1,051	674	683

Source: LAB 8/1106, Interim Report, 16 February 1945.

9. Cotton Industry Report.

10. LAB 8/1362, Douglas Houghton, *Can I Help You?*, 22 November 1947.

11. LAB 8/1362, Douglas Houghton, *Can I Help You?*, 10 January 1948.

12. The strategies were also politically hampered by the perceived need to maintain and increase the size of the armed forces in order to meet the government's Cold War and Imperial commitments. In effect, this meant that members of the armed forces could not be released to provide an IRA in industry.

13. Within the trade union movement there was a historical tendency to perceive areas like the Caribbean and the peoples of those areas as 'backward'. Underdeveloped economics became underdeveloped people. It was an element of the 'white man's burden' that the TUC has sought to

fulfil in the late 1930s by allowing itself to be co-opted as trade union advisers in the colonial administration. The aim was to assist in the 'development' of a 'modern' system of labour relations in colonial territories. In his detailed study of the labour movement and imperialism, Partha Gupta (1975) has shown how such experiences were to lead to the racialization of black labour within the British labour movement even before black migrant labour had become significant in the post-war period.

14. Ibid.

15. CAB 124/874, Progress Report of the Minister of Labour, George Isaacs, 8 May 1947, Cabinet Foreign Labour Committee (CFLC).

16. CAB 14/872, Memorandum to the CFLC by A. Greenwood, 1 March 1946.

17. LAB 8/1670, minute, A. Maxwell, 23 January 1947.

18. CO 886/6, Working Party on the Employment in the United Kingdom of Surplus Colonial Labour. Report: The Possibilities of Employing Colonial Labour in the United Kingdom, October 1948.

19. LAB 37/17, Economic Survey for 1947, Cmd.7046.

20. LAB 8/1273, Report of the Working Party on the Increase in Textile Exports, December 1947.

21. LAB 13/42, minute, M. A. Bevan, 15 April 1948.

22. LAB 8/1499, minute, W. Hardman, 11 June 1947.

23. LAB 8/1499, Colonial Office Memorandum to the MOL, 28 May 1947.

24. LAB 13/42, Memorandum, Recruitment of Colonial Subjects for Employment in Great Britain, May 1948.

25. Greenidge Papers 21/9, f.6, E. Tonge to C. Greenidge, 23 June 1948.

26. HO 213/869, Memorandum, Influx of Persons from the Colonies and British Protectorates, J. B. Howard, 15 February 1949.

27. CO 876/88, f.11030/26, Ness Edwards to Earl of Listowel, 9 June 1948.

28. CO 876/88, f.11030/26, Privy Council Office to CO, 15 June 1948.

29. CO 537/2583, f.11030/26/1, Memorandum, SS *Empire Windrush* – Jamaica Unemployed, S of S Creech-Jones, 1948.

30. CO 537/2583, f.11030/26/1, Memorandum, SS *Empire Windrush* – Jamaica Unemployed, Creech-Jones, 1948.

31. Influx of Persons.

32. Influx of Persons.

33. HO 213/244, J. Murray et al. to Prime Minister, 22 June 1948.

34. Working Party on the Employment in the United Kingdom, first meeting, 6 October 1948.

35. Ibid., first meeting, 6 October 1948.

36. LAB 13/42, Report of the Working Party on . . . Surplus Colonial Manpower, July 1949.

37. CO 886/6, Working Party on the Employment . . . of Surplus Colonial Manpower, October 1948.

38. LAB 13/42, P. Goldberg to C. MacMullan, 8 October 1948.

39. CO 1006/1, Working Party on the Employment . . . of Surplus Colonial Manpower, minute of meeting, 10 November 1948.

40. CO 537/5130, f.96038/1(X), Advisory Committee on Welfare of Colonial People in the United Kingdom, 12 September 1949.

41. CAB 130/61, Cabinet Committee on Immigration of British Subjects into the United Kingdom, second meeting, 10 January 1951.

42. Ibid., first meeting, 24 July 1950.

43. LAB 9/202, Conference of Regional Controllers, 20 January 1949.

44. LAB 8/1902, Wales Office, G. Pigott to Majorie Hayward, 2 July 1953.

45. *Venture*, vol. 7(4), September 1955.

46. *Minlabour*, May 1959, R. Woodcock.

47. AST 7/1535, Report, Coloured Applicants, 29 October 1958.

48. *Minlabour*, May 1959, R. Woodcock.

49. AST 7/1535, Brief prepared for Miss Hornsby-Smith, 3 April 1958.

50. LAB 8/2289, M. Yates to E. Eves (Regional Controller), 2 November 1953.

51. LAB 8/1898, Midland Region to W. Hardman, 22 August 1953.

52. AST 7/1535, Report, Coloured Applicants, 29 October 1958.

53. CAB 128/25, C.C.(52)106, 18 December 1952.

54. CSC 5/919, W. Fisher to A. Parnis, 8 January 1953.

55. Indian independence in 1947 was to lead to an exodus of whites seeking employment in the Home Civil Service.

56. CO 866/82, Treasury Working Party, Draft Report.

57. CSC 5/918, Memorandum, unsigned, 24 November 1949.

58. CSC 5/1139, J. Somerville to C. Hayes, 27 February 1956.

59. LAB 8/968, Memorandum, Training of Colonial Students in the United Kingdom.

60. Working Party on the Employment . . . of Surplus Colonial Manpower, minutes of meeting, 10 November 1948, Cummings. loc. cit.

61. The committee was set up in November 1963 to resolve the overtime ban instituted by garages in protest of service cuts. This ban was particularly effective given the level of overtime working encouraged by London Transport to deflect attention away from pressures over basic rates of pay. According to Fuller (1985: 233), there was even the suspicion that levels of recruitment had been held down in order to create overtime.

62. Hansard, fifth series, vol. 4124 (1945–46), 19 June 1946, cc. 344b–345b.

The 1951–55 Conservative Government and the Racialization of Black Immigration

Bob Carter, Clive Harris and Shirley Joshi

Introduction

The problem of colonial immigration has not yet aroused public anxiety, although there was some concern, mainly due to the housing difficulties in a few localities where most of the immigrants were concentrated. On the other hand, if immigration from the colonies, and, for that matter, from India and Pakistan, were allowed to continue unchecked, there was a real danger that over the years there would be a significant change in the racial character of the English people.[1]

In the discussion of post-war racism the role of the state is often ignored or treated as insignificant. Katznelson, Glass, Hiro and Foot for example have all argued that the state played a negligible role in the development of post-war racism until the 1958 'riots' (Katznelson 1976: 129–31; Glass 1960: 127–46; Foot 1965: 233; Hiro 1973). Katznelson's account is one of the most influential. He sees the 1958 'riots' as representing the demise of a 'pre-political' period during which 'race only touched the periphery of political debate'. This chapter will show that, on the contrary, the state took a major role in constructing black immigration as a 'problem' and in so doing reinforced a conception of Britishness grounded in colour and culture (as expressive of colour). Racist policies and practices were an integral part of this construction; the right of black people to freely enter and settle in the United Kingdom was circumscribed by government actions.

Another recurring theme of the literature is the portrayal of the 1940s and 1950s as an era of laissez-faire immigration when unfettered market forces determined the movement of people from the periphery to the centre 'as and when the need arose' (Sivanandan 1982: 106; Freeman 1975; Foot 1965;

Hiro 1973). For most writers laissez-faire came to an end with the introduction of the first Commonwealth Immigrants Bill:

> The period 1961–65 saw the collapse of laissez-faire policies regarding coloured
> immigration and the settlement of coloured immigrants. A laissez-faire policy is
> very comfortable to follow: it meant doing nothing. And this is exactly what the
> Tory Government did regarding coloured immigration until popular anxiety forced
> its hand in 1961 (Hiro 1973: 201).

Against this we will show that the state went to great lengths to restrict and
control on racist grounds black immigration to the United Kingdom despite a
demand for labour by fractions of private and public capital. This points to a
further weakness in the laissez-faire argument, namely the portrayal of the
state as homogeneous, as reflecting in a direct and unmediated way the
interests of an equally homogeneous capital.

In short we wish to argue that well before 1955 the state had developed a
clear policy towards black immigration.[2] This policy involved direct intervention on some issues and an apparent inactivity on others. For example, while
the government was systematically collecting information about black people
to support a draft immigration bill prepared in 1954 it was also opposing
measures such as Fenner Brockway's bill prohibiting racist discrimination,
despite growing evidence that discrimination was widespread. Successive
governments not only constructed an ideological framework in which black
people were to be seen as threatening, alien and unassimilable but also
developed policies to discourage and control black immigration.

For many senior Conservative politicians in the Churchill government
black immigration raised the prospect of a permanent black presence whose
allegedly 'deleterious effects' on the 'racial character of the English people'
were regarded as a cause for concern.

Similar sentiments were expressed under Attlee's Labour government.
Two days after the arrival of the *Empire Windrush* in June 1948 a letter was
sent to Clement Attlee by eleven Labour MPs calling for the control of black
immigration, since:

> An influx of coloured people domiciled here is likely to impair the harmony,
> strength and cohesion of our public and social life and to cause discord and
> unhappiness among all concerned.[3]

The Labour government set up a Cabinet Committee in 1950 to review 'the
further means which might be adopted to check the immigration into this
country of coloured people from the British Colonial Territories'. On
grounds of expediency rather than principle, the introduction of legislative
control was shelved; it was felt that the administrative measures already in
operation were a sufficient safeguard of 'racial character' (see Carter and
Joshi 1984; Harris 1987).

These administrative measures were inherited by the Conservative government elected in 1951. As the failure of such measures to curtail fare-paying
black 'Citizens of the United Kingdom and Colonies' became apparent, the
Conservative government returned to the possibility of legislative control.
However the absence of an articulated public anxiety about black immigration, and a continuing demand for labour, made more acute by the petering
out of the European Volunteer Worker scheme, required the government to
build a 'strong case' for legislation. This 'strong case' was built around a
racialized reconstruction of 'Britishness' in which to be 'white' was to 'belong'
and to be 'black' was to be excluded. This chapter will examine the early
stages of this reconstruction in the policies of the 1951–55 Conservative
government first to discourage and then to control black immigration.

'Holding the Tide'

It is commonly argued that the 1948 Nationality Act conferred on colonial
subjects rights of entry and settlement that did not previously exist. Those
who expound the laissez-faire argument present the Act as a device to
facilitate the free movement of labour from the Caribbean and the Indian
sub-continent to meet Britain's 'labour shortage'. (For a discussion of the
concept of 'labour shortage', see Harris 1987.)

This interpretation needs to be viewed critically. The Act's intention was to
restructure in Britain's interests the empire as an economic and political
force. The concept of a 'United Kingdom and Colonies' citizenship – as
opposed to a separate citizenship for each territory – enshrined in the Act was
meant to curb colonial nationalism rather than to concede rights of entry and
settlement into Britain. This chapter makes it clear that the principle of free
entry was not something over which the Cabinet agonized, and relinquished
only with great reluctance. Indeed, when the lone voice of the Student Officer
at the Colonial Office, J. Keith, sought unwisely in 1955 to reopen the debate
about this principle[4] he was told that:

> the time for review of the question of principle has now passed. There is indeed . . . no
> real question of principle involved, or if there is, the principle is that it is open to
> any country to take steps to control the composition of its own population.[5]

By 1952 Labour and Conservative governments had instituted a number of
covert, and sometimes illegal, administrative measures designed to discourage the 1,000–2,000 black immigrants who came annually. These measures
varied from territory to territory. In the case of West Africa, for example, they
involved the 'laundering' from 1951 onwards of the British Travel Certificate
issued for travel between the French and British colonies along the West
African coast. This document, by confirming that the holder was a British

subject, could be used to enter the United Kingdom legally. 'Most men now realize,' despaired one Colonial Office official, 'that a British Travel Certificate is the minimum document on which they can expect to be landed in this country.'[6] Accordingly arrangements were made in the latter half of 1951 – with the full agreement of the French government – to omit from the documents any reference to British subject status. A holder arriving in the United Kingdom could then be sent back as an alien, despite the fact that 'all concerned, including the Immigration Officer, know perfectly well that they almost certainly are British subjects'.[7]

In the West Indies, where local politics made the refusal of passports impolitic, other measures were required. Governors were asked to tamper with shipping lists and schedules to place migrant workers at the end of the queue; to cordon off ports to prevent passport-holding stowaways from boarding ships; and to delay the issue of passports to migrants. The last measure was adopted by Indian and Pakistani governments who also refused passports to the United Kingdom if migrants had no firm prospect of a job or accommodation. Police checks were carried out at the request of the Home Office to establish the basis of these prospects. Finally shipping companies were instructed by the Ministry of Transport to take steps to deal with 'one-trip seamen' who terminated work agreements on arriving in the United Kingdom. Henceforth, contracts would require companies to disengage workers at their 'home' ports.

These ad hoc administrative measures had their limitations; some were of questionable legality. Above all they failed to prevent black British subjects coming to the United Kingdom. By the early 1950s therefore some government departments had come to favour restrictive legislation. The Welfare Department of the Colonial Office, for example, felt that 'it would be far better to have an openly avowed policy of restricted immigration than fall back on rather devious little devices'.[8] Such a move would also go some way to calm ministerial anxieties about dubious methods being exposed in Parliament. Legislation, however, required a convincing case to be made.

Building a Strong Case from Broken Reeds

Early in 1953 a confidential meeting of ministers took place at the Colonial Office. The case for legislative control, it was stressed, needed empirical demonstration. This meant gathering information about unemployment and National Assistance, 'numbers', housing, health, criminality, and miscegenation, which it was hoped would confirm that black immigrants posed insoluble problems of social, economic and political assimilation. The already widespread surveillance of black communities by the police was supplemented by surveys undertaken by the Ministry of Labour, the National Assistance Board, the Welfare Department of the Colonial Office, the Home Office, the Commonwealth Relations Office, the Departments of Health, Housing and Transport as well as voluntary organizations. A working party on 'The Employment of Coloured People in the UK',[9] set up by the cabinet in 1953, used the findings to produce a report which assessed the strengths and weaknesses of the 'strong case'. This report formed a central part of cabinet discussion in 1954–55 concerning the need to control black immigration and was to be regularly updated throughout the 1950s.

Numbers

Early attempts to build a case which would be strong enough to focus public anxiety deployed the issue of *numbers*. Two concerns were prominent: the accelerating rate of black immigration and the size of the black population. Ministers were particularly alarmed that West Indian migration for 1954 was running at the level of 10,000 compared to 2,000 in previous years. However, an examination of these figures by Betty Boothroyd at the Board of Trade revealed that while West Indian migration was 'going up pretty fast, the overall immigration from coloured empire countries has not increased in any dramatic way in the last few years'.[10] Nevertheless, in addition to the reports provided by the Ministry of Transport and Civil Aviation for arrivals at ports and airports, ministers and civil servants continued assiduously to collect newspaper clippings which suggested that Britain would have to brace itself for an influx of black immigrants who came in 'leaps from the islands and bounds to the UK without let or hindrance'.[11] Even the judicious *New Statesman* was of the opinion that, 'we must prepare ourselves either to accept no fewer than 200,000 immigrants in the next ten years – and possibly many more – or to face a political explosion in the Caribbean'.[12] The problem for ministers, however, was how to defend their inordinate interest in the 36,000 black immigrants who came between 1950–55 when nothing whatsoever was being done about the 250,000 Southern Irish who arrived in the same period or the thousands of Italian and other European workers who were specifically recruited by the Ministry of Labour.

In 1953 too there was some uncertainty about the size of the black population, with figures of 60,000 and 70,000 being bandied about. These estimates were contradicted by figures from the police and the Ministry of Labour. 'It is interesting,' noted one civil servant wryly, 'that the police estimate of the number of coloured people now in the United Kingdom gives a total of less than 25,000 colonials, as against our unofficial estimate of 50,000 to 60,000.'[13] Whatever the figure, it had to be admitted in late 1955 that, 'Colonial immigration was not an acute problem at the moment.'[14] In conceding that 'the "coloured" problem in the United Kingdom remains a small one, e.g. in Lambeth there are said to be 650 coloured persons among a population of 230,105', Keith significantly went on to add that 'it would be better to stop the influx now to forestall future difficulties'.[15]

Such figures revealed the problems facing the cabinet in building a strong case solely around numbers. They therefore sought to extend the argument for legislative control by looking at employment, housing and crime.

Employment

Even before black workers had had an opportunity to respond to job advertisements in the United Kingdom, a propaganda campaign was launched in 1947 in the Caribbean to persuade them that these were not 'real jobs' but 'paper vacancies' and it was 'not in their interests' to migrate to the United Kingdom. In building its 'strong case' in 1953 the working party sought to show that those black migrants who did come were unemployable and represented a burden on public funds and to this end collected evidence from the Ministry of Labour and National Service and from the Ministry of Pensions and National Assistance.

In undertaking its survey the Ministry of Labour was careful to avoid the 'considerable risk of the enquiry becoming public knowledge and a smaller but still calculable risk of a violent reaction among coloured people against our Offices at certain Exchanges'.[16] Rather than adopt the 'dangerous procedure' of asking registrants questions 'which could arouse their suspicion', box clerks used 'visual methods' to spot the 'racial types'. To aid the Home Office to 'interpret' the findings of the survey a questionnaire was sent to area officers inviting their comments despite misgivings that they could 'only be based on hearsay, isolated incidents, or press reports'.[17] In the questionnaire and the responses one finds all those stereotypes which have since become part of popular commonsense:

> *Question*: Is it true that coloured people, or certain classes of coloured people, are work-shy?
> *Answer*: They cannot be said to be more work-shy than white people.
> *Question*: Is it true that they are poor workmen?
> *Answer*: Dutifully some responses alluded to the 'lack of stamina' of black migrants which made the latter 'unsuited for heavy manual work, particularly outdoor work in winter or in hot conditions underground'. Another allusion was to their 'inability to concentrate for long duration'. In the case of women, these images were particularly sharp. They were reported as being 'mentally slow' and ill-adapted to 'the speed of work in modern factories'. Curiously, if factory work was described as 'quite beyond their capacity', it was considered that such women were capable of giving 'fairly reliable service as domestics in hospitals and private domestic employment'.

Question: Is it true that they are unsuited by temperament to the kind of work available?

Answer: Despite the caveat that the evidence was 'not conclusive', reference was occasionally made to their inability to accept discipline, their volatility of temperament, easy provocation to violence, and quarrelsomeness.

Question: Can distinctions be drawn in this respect between particular races?

Answer: West Indians, particularly those from Trinidad and Guyana, were described as more 'stable' than West Africans. Unlike West Indians and West Africans, Indians and Pakistanis were said to be physically unsuited for medium and heavy work, but were reported to do well in light industry and capable of being trained to at least semi-skilled engineering standards. In contrast to Pakistanis who were said to be well-built, diligent and reliable workers – though with a slower tempo than their white workmates – Bangladeshis were described as 'of poor physique' and not well suited to industrial work.

Such stereotypes were to become the basis on which black workers were to be placed in jobs, denied promotion and kept off training schemes both by employers and labour exchanges. The attempt to portray higher levels of black unemployment as evidence of welfare 'scrounging' was scotched by the National Assistance Board Working Party representative. She pointed out that though some recent Caribbean migrants were, like 60,000 Irish workers, in receipt of national assistance this was because of their ineligibility for unemployment benefits. In a joint report prepared by the Ministry of Labour and Ministry of Pensions and National Assistance for a major debate on black immigration in the House of Lords in November 1956, it was categorically stated that:

> Reference is made from time to time to the abuse of public funds by coloured people. It has no real foundation. West Indians cannot be said to be making undue demands on National Assistance and although an occasional rogue or workshy person is unmasked, this is no more frequent among West Indians than among other sections of the population.[18]

From the evidence of these surveys it was clear that Caribbean immigrants – the main focus of the survey – were not unemployable; neither were they 'scroungers'. The surveys did indicate however the extent to which racist discrimination channelled blacks into occupational ghettoes and the extent to which labour exchanges colluded in this practice.

Housing

Prospective migrants to the United Kingdom were issued with a document entitled 'Warnings to Intending Migrants' in which the problems of accommodation featured prominently. Undoubtedly there was an acute housing shortage in Britain during the 1950s but it was a product of government

policies and market forces, not of levels of immigration. Many local authorities 'on a variety of pretexts but mostly via residence requirements' refused
to house black people yet were not penalized by the minister of housing
(Smith 1989: 53). Rather Macmillan, as housing minister in 1954,
announced a reduction in council-house building for the following year from
235,000 to 160,000.

For black people the alternative to council housing was the private sector
and here discrimination, made easier by the relaxation of rent controls in
1954, ensured that only areas designated for slum clearance and/or areas
with short-lease properties were generally available. The difficulties of
finding accommodation were underscored by the reluctance of local authorities to implement redevelopment programmes which might involve rehousing black tenants for fear of antagonizing white tenants who were on long
waiting lists. This was made clear by the Birmingham City Council town clerk
who was part of the deputation which met ministers at Westminster in early
1955:

> One of the areas scheduled for redevelopment happened to be where a section of
> the immigrant population had settled. Although there was very serious overcrowd-
> ing in this area it was virtually impossible to proceed with redevelopment plans
> because of the difficulty of finding alternative accommodation. There was the
> additional risk that if alternative accommodation was found, ill feeling might be
> engendered among the white population at this apparent preferential treatment of
> coloured people while there were still 'local' inhabitants waiting for houses.[19]

For the same reasons they were reluctant to discharge their legal responsibilities under the 1954 Housing and Rent Act which obliged them to rehouse
tenants living in overcrowded and insanitary conditions. As *The Times* bluntly
put it:

> What are likely to be the feelings of more than 50,000 white would-be tenants in
> Birmingham, who have waited years for a decent house, when they see newcomers,
> no matter what their colour, taking over whole streets of properties?[20]

The failure of local and national governments to address the problems of
housing reinforced the emerging 'commonsense' correlation between housing shortage, slums and black immigration. This 'commonsense' was luridly
depicted by the concept of 'new Harlem' deployed by the Liverpool group of
the Conservative Commonwealth Association in their 1954 pamphlet *The
Problem of Colonial Immigrants*:

> Liverpool is admittedly one of the chief centres of coloured settlement and a new
> Harlem is being created in a decayed residential quarter of the city, where rooms
> in large and dilapidated houses are sub let at high rentals to coloured immigrants
> who exist in conditions of the utmost squalor. Vice and crime are rampant and

social responsibilities are largely ignored. Hundreds of children of negroid or mixed parentage eventually find their way to the various homes to be maintained by the corporation, to be reared to unhappy maturity at great public expense. Large numbers of the adults are in receipt of unemployment benefit or National Assistance and many are engaged in the drug traffic or supplement their incomes by running illicit drinking dens or by prostitution.[21]

This document was circulated widely within the Conservative Party despite the feeling of some officials that the facts were 'overstated and had the worst construction placed upon them'.[22] Landlordism, declining property values, spiralling rents, overcrowding, dilapidation and decay were cited as the inevitable consequences of black settlement. Black people not only created slums, it was argued, but these 'new Harlems' had their provenance in the 'racial character' of the inhabitants. Indeed, their very way of life was deemed to pose a fundamental threat to social order.

This racialized view that housing shortage and urban decay were a product of a black presence encouraged the cabinet to consider making adequate housing accommodation a condition of permanent settlement for black immigrants in its 1954 draft immigration bill. If the cabinet seized on the housing crisis as the 'easiest way' to build a strong case for immigration control, the Birmingham City Council deputation made it clear that control through certificates of accommodation would not be easy for local authorities to police. Within the Ministry of Housing and Local Government, too, there was lukewarm sympathy for assuming the role of social police:

> Clearly local authorities cannot go about looking for stray West Indians who have left their first lodgings, nor can they question them about their identity or the date of their arrival in this country and any other particulars that the Home Secretary thinks relevant.[23]

Despite their lack of enthusiasm, the Ministry of Housing and Local Government decided to invite local authority associations to a meeting in March 1955. At this meeting the latter expressed a willingness to cooperate with the home secretary's plan to control immigration but registered the reservation that the certificate of accommodation embodied in the draft bill could not be considered as a permanent solution.

Criminality

The undesirability of black migrants on grounds of a 'racial' predisposition to criminality had been a longstanding concern of government departments and Parliament (Harris 1988). In the House of Commons in November 1954, secretary of state for the colonies Alex Lennox-Boyd was asked by Sir Jocelyn Lucas 'what machinery exists to ascertain the proportion of Jamaican immigrants who have police or criminal records'.[24] Hansard is studded with questions of this nature. Likewise in the questionnaire sent to Ministry of Labour regional offices area officers were asked: 'Can any distinction be drawn between the coloured workers who come here as fare-paying passengers and those who come as stowaways or deserters?' The general tenor of responses was: Not enough evidence to make a judgment.

Behind this question lies a clear assumption that the manner in which the stowaway came to Britain was a confirmation of a criminal proclivity. No attention was given to the way in which increasingly stringent administrative measures introduced by Labour and Conservative governments criminalized the stowaway.

In an earlier survey of the black population of Stepney, Downing Street was informed thus:

> The police reports which we have had from time to time do not indicate that the incidence of crime amongst coloured people is abnormally high, but *it is known that these people's background renders them specially liable to temptation in these directions.* The police, who are already fully aware of this, are being informed of the contents of the memorandum.[25]

It is the reports of this self-same 'aware' and 'informed' police in London and the provinces on which the working party was to draw heavily for its 1953 report. The police reports dwelt upon the size of the black population, the degree to which it had been assimilated and the extent to which it was involved in criminal activity. In Sheffield, for example, the chief constable had deputed two police officers to 'observe, visit and report on' the black population.[26] A card index was compiled, listing the names, addresses, nationalities and places of employment of the city's 534 black inhabitants.

This concern with criminality emphasized certain types of deviance, preeminently drug trafficking and living on immoral earnings, and the ways in which these endangered the social and moral fabric of British society. In its evidence to the working party the police claimed that there had been 'a marked number of convictions of coloured men for living on the immoral earnings of white women'.[27] The working party's own report hinted darkly that 'this practice is far more widespread than the few prosecutions indicate'.[28]

Such alleged criminality merged into a general condemnation of 'the associations formed between coloured men and white women of the lowest type'. Such associations were seen to violate the sanctity of a white British womanhood, the bearer of national culture.

Drug trafficking completed the picture of an alien wedge whose exotic features were graphically presented by Sheffield's chief constable:

> The West Africans are all out for a good time, spending money on quaint suits and flashy ornaments and visiting dance halls at every opportunity. The Jamaicans are

somewhat similar, but they have a more sensible outlook and rarely get into trouble. They take great pains with their appearance and use face cream, perfume etc., to make themselves attractive to the females they meet at dances, cafés etc. One feels, however, that they only attract a certain type of female by reason of the fact that they have more money to spend than the average young Englishman.[29]

These stereotypes were not supported by any evidence that black people were involved in disproportionate amounts of crime. In his report to the working party, the chief constable of Middlesbrough noted that 'on the whole the coloured population are as well behaved as many local citizens'.[30] *The Times* similarly observed: 'Everywhere they have appeared the police and magistrates are ready to say that the West Indians make no trouble, which is more than some are ready to say of Irish workers.'[31] Despite this, such images continued to be used to justify discriminatory policing.

Summary

In struggling to impose some coherence on the information submitted to it, the working party found its report deprecated as 'unnecessarily negative' by the Lord President of the Council, the Marquis of Salisbury. The report, he complained bitterly, did not appear to recognize 'the dangers of the increasing immigration of coloured people into this country'.[32]

These alleged dangers coalesced around the fear that the 'gathering momentum' of black immigration would bring about 'a significant change in the racial character of the English people'. The working party had failed to appreciate that the real issue for the cabinet was not merely unemployment, poor housing or levels of crime but the very presence of black people in Britain. This is the message that the Marquis of Salisbury tried to impress upon the cabinet:

> it is not for me merely a question of whether criminal negroes should be allowed in or not; it is a question of whether great quantities of negroes, criminal or not, should be allowed to come.[33]

On the evidence of the working party report, however, the home secretary was forced to admit to the cabinet that 'a case has not been made out' for legislation.

'The Idea, I Take It, is to Conceal the Purpose of Legislation'[34]

The failure of the Conservative cabinet to garner empirical support for their 'strong case' did not deflect them from the conviction that a black presence could not be contained by administrative measures. Legislative action still needed to be pursued. In the absence of any evidence connecting black people with intractable social problems a different kind of case had to be made which would convey to the public the deep anxieties felt by the cabinet about the threat to the 'racial character of the English'.

To this end home secretary Gwilym Lloyd-George proposed a committee of enquiry in November 1954. The colonial secretary supported the idea. He felt that 'although there are many signs that responsible public opinion is moving in the direction of favouring immigration control', there was still 'a good deal to be done before it is more solidly in favour of it'. A committee would have the double advantage

> of enabling us to postpone an announcement of our policy until nearer the time when the necessary legislation would be put in hand, and of enabling public opinion to develop futher and be crystallized.[35]

The nature of the committee was explained to the prime minister by the cabinet secretary, Norman Brook, in a briefing note:

> Its purpose would be, *not to find a solution* (for it is evident what form control must take), *but to enlist a sufficient body of public support* for the legislation that would be needed.[36]

This purpose would only be fulfilled if the committee's terms of reference left no doubt that black immigration was the proper object of enquiry and if its report was unanimous. However, an invitation to consider discriminatory proposals had the disadvantage of leaving the committee open to charges of racism. The colonial secretary, Lennox-Boyd, met this criticism by proposing to widen the committee's terms of reference to include all immigrants. This

> would not by any means prevent the committee from proposing discriminatory measures, if they saw fit to do so; and if they did, *without a virtual invitation*, we should be in a very good position to measure public opinion and parliamentary reactions to such proposals, *without the government having been in any way implicated in them*.[37]

There was no certainty, though, that a committee which would have to include opposition members and trade union representatives would unanimously support legislation. It was also clear that 'some of those who might acquiesce in such action might find it less easy to give public evidence in support of it before a committee'.[38] Consequently the idea of a committee was abandoned, in June 1955.

As 'a better basis for action', the cabinet instructed a working party to produce an 'authoritative statement of the increasing volume of immigration, and of the social and economic problems to which it was likely to give rise'.[39]

This was intended for publication but was never released because, in the absence of firm evidence, it 'would not have the effect of guiding public opinion in any definite direction'.[40] Moreover, to issue such a statement 'with no indication of the government's intentions would be merely embarrassing'. Some ministers also felt that its release should be prefaced by a white paper giving details of controls on British subjects in the dominions and colonies. This would imply that the introduction of controls by Britain was merely a quid pro quo. A Commonwealth Relations official was more honest:

> It was apparently considered that by publicising the restrictions applicable to the entry of British subjects in other countries, public opinion might be influenced in favour of the introduction of restriction here.[41]

A Colonial Office official was even blunter: the white paper was an attempt to '"cook" public opinion'.[42]

The white paper, like the 'statement', was never published. This was partly because it would have shown that India and Pakistan did not have restrictive controls on British subjects, but principally because it would have been embarrassing to reveal that '"old" commonwealth countries are . . . operating immigration controls which discriminate against British subjects who are not of European race . . . Some of them might well prefer that the attention of the parliament at Westminster should not be directed in this way.'[43] Though this weakened the cabinet's position, it is doubtful, anyway, whether the growing momentum of the cabinet's case would have overcome in 1955 the political and economic reservations that were brought to the fore in the discussions surrounding Cyril Osborne's attempt in January of that year to introduce a private member's bill to regulate black immigration.

In discussions before the Commonwealth Affairs Committee it was pointed out that the measures proposed in the bill were difficult to reconcile with Britain's position as head of the commonwealth and empire. As the chief whip summarized:

> Why should mainly loyal and hard-working Jamaicans be discriminated against when ten times that quantity of disloyal [sic] Southern Irish (some of them Sinn Feiners) come and go as they please?[44]

The timing, too, created difficulties. With the forthcoming general election, there was a desire to avoid controversial issues which might improve the chances of a Labour victory. The celebration of Jamaica's three hundredth anniversary of British rule in 1955 also made it inopportune to present what would have appeared as an 'anti-Jamaican Bill'.[45] This was underlined by the feeling in some quarters that colonial development and not legislation was the solution to immigration. More importantly, the home secretary had prepared his own draft bill in November 1954 which awaited the outcome of cabinet discussion on the committee of enquiry. Osborne's bill was therefore rejected.

It was not until the beginning of the next parliamentary session in October 1955 that this draft was presented to the cabinet. The objections to Osborne's bill still applied. In the cabinet meeting of November 3, other difficulties were noted. There was a recognition by the cabinet that despite the fact that the House of Commons showed itself to be increasingly sympathetic to the idea of control public opinion had not 'matured sufficiently'. Public consent could only be assured if the racist intent of the bill were concealed behind a cloak of universalism which applied restrictions equally to all British subjects.

A further difficulty was that: 'On economic grounds immigration, including colonial immigration, was a welcome means of augmenting our labour resources.'[46] This was the first time that arguments about the economic benefits of colonial immigration had figured in cabinet discussions despite the 'labour shortage' and the labour requirements of specific sectors of public and private capital. Black labour, the cabinet felt, by its 'racial' nature was unsuitable.[47] Some ministers too were of the opinion that full employment would not last and grave problems would be created by the presence of an 'unassimilable', black unemployed and unemployable population. These views provided a sharp contrast with the efforts that were made in the late 1940s to demonstrate the invaluable contribution that European Volunteer Workers could make to the British economy.

These objections compelled the cabinet to postpone the presentation of a bill to Parliament; the strong case required firmer support. A ministerial committee chaired by the Lord Chancellor was appointed to examine the obstacles to be overcome if legislation were to be introduced. In addition, a new interdepartmental working party was convened to provide the committee with bi-annual reports on the 'social and economic problems arising from the growing influx . . . of coloured workers'.

Conclusion

The evidence we have drawn on suggests that the common interpretation of the role of the state in the 1940s and 1950s needs to be revised. Specific measures to discourage and restrict black immigration rested firmly on a policy of preserving the homogeneous 'racial character' of British society. The passing of the 1948 Nationality Act intensified the contradiction between a formal definition of 'Britishness' which embraced black British subjects abroad and an increasingly racialized notion of belonging in which 'racial types' were constructed around colour. Even as the Act entered the statute books it was qualified by a series of 'devious little devices' designed to 'hold the tide' of black immigration. When these proved insufficient, legislative control increasingly became a favoured option among ministers and senior civil servants. For public consent to be won for legislation, however, a 'strong case' had to be built. A consequence of this was an extension of the control and surveillance of the black population in the UK.

Black immigration, it was alleged, would create problems which were insoluble precisely because their provenance was 'racial' and not political. Black people were unemployed not because of discrimination, but because of their 'irresponsibility, quarrelsomeness and lack of discipline'. Black people lived in slums not because of discrimination and the unwillingness of government and local authorities to tackle the housing shortage but because they knew no better. Indeed, their very 'nature' was held to predispose them towards criminality. All of these stereotypes were evoked vividly in the concept of 'new Harlem', an alien wedge posing an unprecedented threat to the 'British way of life'. So powerful was this racialized construction that anti-discrimination legislation was seen as irrelevant to the 'social problems' of housing and employment. This was evident from the consistent opposition to Fenner Brockway's bill seeking to outlaw discrimination and the failure to heed the (Caribbean Migrant Services Division) Welfare Liaison Officer's warning that:

> A freedom of entry to the United Kingdom . . . is nevertheless an empty and vicious one as long as the right to equal employment, accommodation and social intercourse does not exist in practice.[48]

In building its 'strong case' for immigration control the state undertook nothing less than a populist political project which both reconstructed an image of a national community that was homogeneous in its 'whiteness' and racialized culture and defended it from the allegedly corrosive influence of groups whose skin colour and culture debarred them from belonging. This reconstruction simultaneously involved an attempt to de-racialize the Irish who 'are not – whether they like it or not – a different race from the ordinary inhabitants of Great Britain'.[49] Only by arguing 'boldly along such lines' could Irish exclusion from the 1955 draft bill avoid political censure. This line was not without its inconsistencies. As one CRO official minuted: 'This is poor stuff after Irish behaviour in the war and their departure from the common-wealth.' Moreover it ignored the contribution to the Allied war effort of black service personnel like those who had returned on the *Empire Windrush*.

The racialized reconstruction of Britishness also posed problems for Britain's image as the 'Mother Country' of a 'multiracial commonwealth':

> it may well be argued that a large coloured community as a noticeable feature of our social life would weaken the sentimental attachment of the older self-governing countries to the UK. Such a community is certainly no part of the concept of

England or Britain to which people of British stock throughout the commonwealth are attached.[50]

While wishing to prevent black British subjects from entering the UK, the cabinet was concerned to preserve the right of white 'kith and kin' in the dominions to free entry.

Our argument clearly points to the need to recover the history of the state's central role in the construction of post-war British racism. This racism was not simply the product of an imperial legacy, even less the consequence of a popular concern in the 1960s about numbers. Before black workers had begun to arrive here in significant numbers, black immigration was already being racialized. 'Race' was becoming a lens through which people experienced and made sense of their everyday lives. Black people came to be defined as 'a problem' whose solution lay in further and more restrictive control and surveillance. As the state's role in the racialization of black immigration intensified, so the repeated signification of black people's 'presence' and 'difference' as the 'problem' rendered the hand of the state yet more invisible. Any political strategy to combat racism must make the state a central focus of its analysis and campaigns.

Notes

1. CAB 128/29, CM 39(55), minute 7, Cabinet Meeting, 3 November 1955.
2. In Harris (1988), Carter, Harris and Joshi (forthcoming 1993) we show quite clearly that such a policy had been elaborated during the 1930s and 1940s.
3. HO 213/244, J. Murray et al. to Prime Minister, 22 June 1948.
4. Keith's concern in raising the subject of the principle of free entry was based on the fear of many CO officials that the Colonial Office would be railroaded into agreeing to controls which singled out – and therefore discriminated against – in an obvious way the [black] colonies. Controls, it was argued, should in principle be general, i.e. they should appear to apply equally to white and black territories.
5. CO 1032/121, minute, Carstairs 21 October 1955. Emphasis added.
6. CO 537/5219, minute, J. G. Thomas, 23 March 1950.
7. Ibid., minute, J. Williams, 27 June 1950.
8. CO 537/5219, minute, J. Williams, 27 June 1950.
9. The working party was also reconvened to examine the feasibility of introducing (a) a £25 deposit on migrants, and (b) powers to deport 'criminals' as a deterrent to migration.
10. CAB 124/1191, memorandum, Quirk to Marquis of Salisbury (Lord President of the Council), 29 October 1954.
11. CO 1032/119, Lord Glyn to Earl of Munster (Minister of State), 30 April 1954.
12. *The New Statesman*, 17 September 1955.
13. CO 1028/22, STU 91/143/01, minute, B. G. Stone, 9 December 1953.
14. CAB 129/29, CM 31(55), minute 4, meeting 15 September 1955.
15. CO 1028/23, STU 106/03, minute, J. Keith, 5 December 1952.
16. LAB 8/1898, minute, Majorie Hayward, 24 March 1953.
17. LAB 8/1898, ibid.
18. CO 1031/122, memorandum by Mr Hardman and Miss Hope-Wallace, November 1956.
19. DO 35/5217, Deputation from Birmingham City Council, Report of Meeting, 19 January 1955.

20. *The Times*, 8 November 1954.

21. CAB 124/1191, Conservative Commonwealth Association, Liverpool Group, *The Problem of Colonial Immigrants*, January 1954.

22. CO 1032/119, minute, B. G. Stone, 13 March 1954.

23. HLG 117/10, minute, Ryan, 22 February 1955.

24. Hansard, vol. 532, 3 November 1954.

25. CO 876/231, J. Nunn to E. Cass, 23 January 1950.

26. CO 1028/25, Police Report upon the Coloured Population in Sheffield, 3 October 1952, enclosed in Town Clerk (Sheffield), John Heys to V. Harris, 8 October 1952.

27. CO 1028/22, STU 91/143/01, CWP (53) 10, ll July 1953.

28. Ibid., Draft Report of Working Party on Coloured People Seeking Employment in the United Kingdom, 17 December 1953.

29. Sheffield Police Report.

30. CO 1025/25, Town Clerk (Middlesbrough), E. Parr to V. Harris, 14 October 1952.

31. *The Times*, 9 November 1954.

32. CAB 124/1191, minute, Marquis of Salisbury, 8 August 1954.

33. CAB 124/1191, Marquis of Salisbury to Viscount Swinton, 19 November 1954.

34. CAB 124/1191, Philip Swinton (Commonwealth Relations Secretary) to Gwilym Lloyd-George (Home Secretary), 16 November 1954.

35. PREM 11/824, C.(54) 354, Memorandum, Colonial Immigrants, Colonial Secretary, 6 December 1954.

36. PREM 11/824, Norman Brook (Cabinet Secretary) to Prime Minister, 14 June 1955. Emphasis added.

37. CAB 124/1191, Alan Lennox-Boyd to Gwilym Lloyd-George, 26 November 1954. Emphasis added.

38. CAB 128/27, CC 78(54), meeting 6 December 1954.

39. CAB 128/29, CM 14(55), minute 4, meeting 14 June 1955.

40. PREM 11/824, I. W. Hooper to Prime Minister, 14 September 1955.

41. DO 35/5220, minute, Morley, 24 January 1955.

42. CO 1032/83, minute, Carstairs, 12 February 1955.

43. Ibid., Norman Brook to Prime Minister, Colonial Immigrants, 17 February 1955.

44. Ibid., Summary of Commonwealth Affairs Committee meeting by Chief Whip, 27 January 1955, enclosed in Patrick Buchanan-Hepburn to Prime Minister, 27 January 1955.

45. There was a further irony here. Norman Manley, the Jamaican prime minister, had already conveyed to a visiting parliamentary delegation that his government would not object to restrictions on entry which 'were genuinely applied to the whole commonwealth' (Memorandum by Nigel Fisher, West Indian Migration to UK, PREM 11/824). So concerned was the British government to introduce discriminatory controls that this offer was not considered seriously.

46. CAB 128/29, CM 39(55), minute 7, meeting 3 November 1955.

47. If this view seems surprising given the 'labour shortage', it would be important to ask the question about which fraction of the capitalist class did the government represent. The suggestion is that it represented finance capital rather than industrial capital.

48. CO 1028/36, Interim Report of Conditions of Jamaicans in the United Kingdom, 1 January to 31 March 1954, Welfare Liaison Officer, Ivo de Souza.

49. CAB 129/77, CP (55) 102, Report of the Committee on the Social and Economic Problems Arising from the Growing Influx into the United Kingdom of Coloured Workers from Other Commonwealth Countries, 3 August 1955.

50. CO 1028/22, CWP (53), 6 August 1953.

=====================3=====================

Black Women's Employment and the British Economy

Gail Lewis

Introduction

In recent years it has become a commonplace (at least among black activists) to accept that it is black people[1] in general, and black women in particular, who have borne the brunt of the effects of the economic crisis. More particularly, the factors which give rise to this condition are said to be the interlocking of massive unemployment, government legislation and growing racialism in local areas. For black women the added burden of domestic work combined with long hours of paid employment is also alluded to as is the fact that racist government legislation is often predicated on, and reinforces sexist divisions and stereotypes. A strong case in point is the Nationality Act of 1981. In this Act not only is the citizenship status of much of the population redefined, but the ability of black female citizens to confer entry and residency rights on their husbands is denied.[2]

Certainly these are important observations and they point to some of the processes which need to be analysed if we are to move towards a deeper understanding not only of the determinants of black women's employment patterns to date, but also of our future prospects and the political opportunities which these determinants may give rise to in a time of massive restructuring of production and the black population.

In my view the context in which to view black women's employment patterns and prospects is the sexual division of labour (in relation to both the private market economy and domestic production), the long-term relative decline of the British economy: the present recession and government policy as it relates to: first monetarism and public sector cuts; and secondly, control of the black communities at central and local government level.

A third mediating category is 'racism', which we can define as the organization of society on the basis of an ideology of inferiority grounded in 'race' or colour (i.e. biological differences) and/or ethnic (i.e. cultural) differences, which then gives rise to a distribution of the labour force in certain ways. However we cannot analyse the role and experiences of black women in the British economy in ideological terms alone and it becomes necessary to examine the ways in which these factors, including the practice of racialism, connect with underlying economic factors. In other words we begin from an analysis of the workings of the British capitalist economy in general and move, more specifically, to the ways in which the sexual division of labour, racialism and government policy intersect with the economic factors against a background of relative decline and cyclical crisis. However, before we go on to look at these features let us outline the broad contours of black women's employment patterns.

Patterns of Black Women's Employment

One of the characteristics of the British economy in the immediate post-war period was the mobilization of two sources of relative surplus-population: the mass of workers in the Caribbean and Indian sub-continent,[3] and indigenous women workers. By drawing on these pools of labour British capital was in fact attempting to overcome the effects of its long-term comparative decline by intensifying the rate of exploitation.[4] Therefore cheap labour was substituted for capital investment in Britain. This approach was to have the effect of determining the sectors into which the two pools of workers were to be concentrated. For women workers (undifferentiated in terms of 'race') there was the added dimension of the sexual division of labour whose operation was to determine the occupations into which they were absorbed. For black women the ideology of racism and the practice of racialism were to intertwine with the ideology and practice of sexism, both of which were to impact on the structural characteristics of the British economy to determine the industrial and occupational location of black women workers.

As one would expect from the foregoing, the geographical distribution of Britain's black population mirrors that of the traditional industries into which they were recruited. Thus 40 per cent of black people live in the Greater London area, though for Afro-Caribbeans this is 59 per cent, and a substantial number of the remainder live in the major conurbations of the Midlands and North East. Tables 3.1, 3.2 and 3.3 show the industrial distribution of black and women workers nationally and in the Greater London area at the end of the 1970s. Tables 3.1 and 3.2 are not directly comparable because the one for women amalgamates some of the Standard Industrial Classification groupings. However since we also know that black women display a similar concentration into what is considered 'women's work', these tables do reflect the general shape of the industrial location of black women workers.

Table 3.1 Industrial Analysis of West Indian/African and Asian Employment (%) in
Greater London (1979)

	West Indian/ African	Indian Sub- continent	Total
Agriculture, forestry & fishing	5.9	–	5.9
Food, drink & tobacco	4.3	9.4	13.7
Coal & petroleum products	4.4	2.9	7.3
Chemicals & allied industries	4.3	3.1	7.4
Metal manufacture	2.5	7.5	10.0
Mechanical engineering	3.7	2.2	5.9
Instrument engineering	4.5	2.9	7.4
Electrical engineering	5.8	9.9	15.7
Shipbuilding & marine engineering vehicles	9.7	9.4	19.1
Metal goods not elsewhere specified	8.3	7.7	16.0
Textiles	–	4.0	4.0
Leather, leather goods & fur	4.2	5.7	9.9
Clothing & footwear	8.2	7.9	16.1
Bricks, pottery, glass, cement	2.6	2.7	5.3
Timber, furniture etc.	5.7	5.3	11.0
Paper, printing & publishing	0.5	2.0	2.5
Other manufacturing	11.0	8.7	19.7
Construction	3.0	2.1	5.1
Gas, electricity & water	–	0.7	0.7
Transport & communications	5.2	5.4	10.6
Distributive trades	2.7	5.7	8.4
Insurance, banking & finance	1.5	2.4	3.9
Prof. & sci. services	4.7	3.4	8.1
Miscellaneous services	4.0	4.0	8.0
Public admin. & defence	2.4	2.4	4.8
All industries	4.0	4.3	8.3

Source: DE Statistics, 1979.

Within these industries black women tend to be concentrated in the lowest-paid, least skilled jobs with bad conditions of work. Furthermore, as Tables 3.4 and 3.5 indicate, they have very high economic activity rates and a large majority work full-time as will be discussed below. It is however important to note that the contrast between black and white women workers in terms of type and conditions of work is less than that which exists between black and white men. In part this is due to the low employment status of women generally and because of the high incidence of white women who are in unskilled jobs because they work part-time.

More generally this less wide discrepancy is due to the fact that women as a category were themselves brought into the labour market on conditions similar to those of black people, i.e. as cheap labour. Having said this Brown (1984) shows that when we compare Afro-Caribbean women with white women the former are still concentrated in the lowest status positions in both manual and non-manual occupations. This is so despite a slight increase in

Table 3.2 Industrial Distribution of Women Workers in Greater London, 1979
and 1976

	Women as % of industry workforce (1976)	as % of female workforce (1979)		
		F/T	P/T	All
Agriculture, forestry & fishing	44.8	0.0	0.3	0.1
Food, drink & tobacco	33.8	2.2	2.0	2.1
Coal, petroleum, chemicals	35.8	2.8	1.6	2.4
Metal manufacturing, metal goods & vehicles, engineering	29.1	6.2	4.2	5.5
Textiles, leather, clothing & footwear	57.8	3.7	3.2	3.5
Bricks, pottery, glass, timber, furniture, etc.	19.5	0.9	0.7	0.8
Paper, printing & publishing	29.2	2.6	1.9	2.3
Other manufacturing	41.2	1.3	0.3	1.0
All manufacturing & power industries	27.1	24.9	19.7	23.0
Transport & communications	18.5	7.0	2.3	5.4
Distributive trades	50.0	11.5	20.7	14.7
Insurance, banking, finance & business	47.0	12.6	6.4	10.4
Professional & scientific services	64.2	23.6	29.6	25.7
Miscellaneous services	48.3	10.7	16.5	12.7
Public administration	36.6	8.8	4.2	7.2
All service industries	46.0	74.1	79.7	76.1
Not stated, no reply	N/A	1.0	0.7	0.9
All	40.8	100.0	100.0	100.0

NB. The percentages in the first column represent the number of women as a proportion of all the workers in that industry. The figures in the last three columns represent the number of women in that industry as a proportion of all women workers in London.

Source: *Economic Status of Women in London*, GLC Statistical series no.16, Table 9.

the numbers of black women in non-manual occupations between 1974 and 1982. Figure 3.2 shows this.

The sexual division of labour was also to determine the ways in which women in general were to match their domestic responsibilities with their participation in paid employment. However the ways in which women combined these dual responsibilities were subject to 'racial' differentiation. For many white women the way to do this was to do part-time work. For example, 36 per cent of white women in the London area were engaged in part-time work in the late 1970s (NDHS 1977–78). This compares to a national average of 43 per cent for all women. By contrast the same NDHS survey showed that only 19 per cent of West Indian women worked part-time, and only 12 per cent of Asian women. (In 1988, when the national average was 40 per cent, the figure for West Indian women was 25 and 23 for Indian women.) This means that for black women the worrying task of combining domestic responsibilities with paid employment had to be done within the constraints imposed by full-time paid employment. One way out has been to do full-time hours on a regular shift basis. Brown (1984) shows that 18 per

Table 3.3 Women aged Sixteen and Over by Ethnic Origin, Industry Division, Great Britain 1981 (%)

| | Ethnic Origin | | | | | | |
	White	West Indian/ Guyanese	Indian	Pakistani/ Bangladeshi	Chinese/ African/ Arab/Mixed	Not Stated	All
Agriculture/forestry fishing	1.1	0.0	0.5	0.0	0.0	0.2	1.1
Energy/water	1.1	0.5	0.2	2.4	1.2	0.0	1.1
Mining	2.3	0.7	3.2	4.4	1.5	0.7	2.3
Metal goods engineering & vehicles	6.6	7.8	12.0	12.0	5.6	2.1	6.6
Other manufacturing	11.4	8.4	28.7	29.5	11.7	1.9	11.5
Construction	1.3	0.5	1.0	0.0	1.3	0.0	1.2
Distribution, hotels, catering, repairs	24.6	10.2	20.9	11.7	26.7	7.2	24.4
Transport and communications	2.8	5.7	4.2	0.0	2.9	0.5	2.9
Banking, finance, insurance	8.9	6.3	7.7	10.7	3.7	2.5	8.8
Other services	38.4	57.7	21.8	29.2	38.9	15.1	38.2
No reply/working abroad	1.5	2.2	0.0	0.0	1.5	69.8	2.2
All industries	100	100	100	100	100	100	100
Total (1,000s)	n= 8,945	107	93	10	70	102	9,328

Source: Labour Force Survey 1981 (Table 4.24).

Table 3.4 Numbers of Women Economically Active Aged Sixteen and Over by Ethnic Origin, Great Britain 1981

	Population (1,000s)	*Number of economically active (1,000s)*	*% (i.e. % of pop. who are in or want work)*
White	20,773	9,799	47.2
Black	676	334	49.4
which subdivides as:			
West Indian/Guyanese	186	126	67.6
African	23	10	40.5
Indian	236	113	48.1
Pakistani/Bangladeshi	82	13	15.5
Other (mixed etc.)	149	72	48.5
No reply	230	104	45.0
All ethnic categories	21,679	10,237	47.2

Source: *Labour Force Survey* 1981 (Table 4.21).

Table 3.5 Numbers of Employed and Unemployed Women Aged Sixteen and Over by Ethnic Origin, Great Britain 1988

	Number of economically active (1,000s)	*Number in employment (1,000s)*	*Number unemployed (1,000s)*	*Unemployed as % of economically active*
White	10,494	9,487	1,007	9.6
Black	426	358	68	15.9
which subdivides as:				
West Indian/Guyanese	130	110	20	15.3
Indian	147	124	23	15.6
Pakistani/Bangladeshi	27	20	7	25.9
Other	121	104	17	14.0
All ethnic categories	11,008	9,923	1,085	9.8

Source: *Labour Force Survey* 1986, 1987, 1988 (Table 3).

cent of West Indian women work shifts regularly, compared to 11 per cent for white women.

As a result of these differences wage levels are different, although once again the discrepancy between black and white men is much greater than that between black and white women. In the PSI study the average for Caribbean women was slightly higher than that for white women, though that of Asian women was slightly lower, albeit only slightly. This is in part caused by the age composition of the workforce: 47 per cent of white women workers are in the under twenty-five and over fifty-four age groups compared to 28 per cent of

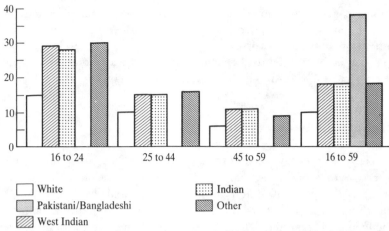

White

Pakistani/Bangladeshi

West Indian

Indian

Other

Source: 1984, 1985 and 1986 Labour Force Survey in *Employment Gazette*. March 1988.

Figure 3.1 Unemployment Rates of Women by Ethnic Origin and Age %

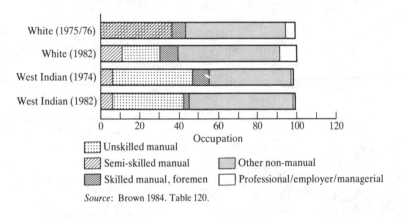

Unskilled manual

Semi-skilled manual

Skilled manual, foremen

Other non-manual

Professional/employer/managerial

Source: Brown 1984. Table 120.

Figure 3.2 Occupational Distribution of Whites and West Indians

black women workers. This difference has the effect of deflating average earnings of white women workers because it is these age groups which have the worst pay rates. Thus if these two age groups are excluded from the calculations we get a reversal of the differential 'from £1.50 in favour of black women to £10.40 in favour of white women' (Brown 1984: 168). However even with this adjustment white women do not tend to have higher wages within employment categories.

Overall therefore white women have better wages because there are more of them in better-paid jobs. Thus black women's earnings are the result partly of their concentration in particular occupations and partly because their concentration in large, better-unionized work-places and the public sector cushions them from the worst levels of pay.

Having outlined the broad characteristics of black women's employment patterns let us now turn to the context in which to consider them.

The Sexual Division of Labour

The concentration of women workers in particular occupations and sectors of the economy is one manifestation of the sexual division of labour which pervades all aspects of society. Primarily the sexual division of labour in British society is based on the ideological separation of the spheres of production and reproduction into 'work' and 'home/family'. The former is considered the sphere of men and the latter that of women, with the wage acting as the mediating factor between the two spheres. Moreover the assumed 'naturalness' and desirability of this ideological division is presented as though it were a historical constant which matched contemporary social reality.

In fact the development of the concept of the ideal family type, desirable and attainable for people of all classes in Britain, itself grew out of the changes which accompanied the development of capitalism (MacKenzie and Rose 1983: 155–200; Wilson 1977; Barrett 1981). A full discussion of the processes which gave rise to the articulation between the extension of capitalist social relations and the ideology of 'separate spheres' is beyond the scope of this chapter. However for our purposes it is important to note two points. The first is that the idea of separate spheres accompanied that of the single family wage which was earned by the 'male breadwinner'. This means that while the preservation and reproduction of the household was more firmly wedded to market relations as articulated by the wage, women were less able to directly influence developments in the wage labour or production sphere (MacKenzie and Rose 1983: 172). Meanwhile men were tied more deeply to the necessity to earn a wage and an ideology of masculinity, and as a result they were expected to be able to provide singlehandedly the ever-expanding supply of household commodities which the expansion of productive capacity and the changing domestic economy gave rise to.

The inadequacy of many individual 'family' wage rates for these purposes was to act as a contributory factor in the demand for state-provided welfare services, since these were essential if women were to be freed for the labour market and new standards for the reproduction of labour were to be met. The possibility of the state providing some level of welfare services was increased by the expansion of the domestic productive base from which some surplus could be redirected for these purposes, together with that portion of surplus which came from the extraction of super-profits in the colonial world.

However a second consequence of the increase in the production of consumer goods and the provision of welfare services was an increase in the demand for labour in the immediate post-Second World War period. This increase was partly the result of the tensions between production and reproduction which were generated by the ideology of separate spheres for men and women. Importantly this was one contributory factor in the expansion of the demand for labour in those manufacturing and service sectors into which black workers were recruited in the 1950s and early 1960s. Examples are the transport, construction, food and drink manufacture (particularly of convenience and snack foods) and the NHS.

For women as a whole however this tension led to a redefinition of their role as wives and mothers so that it could now include the possibility of their participation in the world of 'work'. Thus the second point to note is that by the 1950s the ideology of separate spheres included the notion and fact of 'dual roles' for women. At one level this was a representational shift based on the need to incorporate women into the labour force which the expansion of productive capacity and the requirement of an increased number of commodities for the domestic economy gave rise to. Women became wage workers in both intensive production processes and the expansion of office work. At another level however the concept of the dual role was itself related to the continuation of the idea that women's primary responsibility was that of the home and the family. This was itself to give rise to another contradiction.

On the one hand women who were engaged in paid labour were regarded as acting responsibly in that this second wage[5] enabled the provision of consumer durables for the household, and even the house itself, which had escalated in cost yet were increasingly becoming essential requirements for the 'efficient' running of the modern household. Despite this however women were still regarded as working for 'pin money'. The notion that the wage earned by married women is secondary to that of husbands is one factor in determining that all women's pay (married or not) is lower than men's. For example, the *Employment Gazette* (November 1989) showed that in 1989 the earnings (excluding overtime) of women in full-time paid employment averaged 76.4 per cent of men's. Taken as a total ideological construct then the notion of 'separate spheres' serves to reinforce a sexual division of labour both within and outside the household and acts to determine which occupations women are most commonly found in as well as preserving their position within the industrial reserve army of labour. Moreover changes within the ideology of the sexual division of labour not only mirrored developments within the accumulation of capital but also had material repercussions which were to partially determine the industrial location of black workers in the

British economy. This is an important point which is more often than not overlooked by writers concerned with the position of black people in Britain because they fail to see the relevance of gender divisions within society as a whole and between men and women.

From the foregoing it is clear that an analysis of the role of black women workers in the British economy must be contextualized within an understanding of the dynamic and impact of the sexual division of labour. This is so not just because such an understanding helps to explain the occupational and sectoral concentration of all women workers but also because it helps us to understand the forces which give rise to the expansion of these occupations and sectors themselves.

This is not to presume that the effects of the sexual division of labour on women's employment experience is uniform. Gender categories need to be disaggregated by 'race'; and when this is done disparities emerge.

Two further points need to be mentioned. On the one hand whatever the wider 'economic' effects of the ideology of separate spheres, this notion gave rise to an additional assumption that all migrants who came to Britain with the primary purpose of finding paid work were men, since it is men who are universally deemed to be the main breadwinners. On the other hand to the extent that it was recognized that black women came seeking work in their own right, it was assumed that these women had no family/domestic responsibilities whose fulfilment required an 'adequate' wage. Their very migrant status was assumed to mean that the problems associated with the 'dual role' were absent as far as these women were concerned. Of course in the 1950s and early 1960s this was to some extent partly true and was reflected in the overconcentration of black women workers in occupations where part-time work is less common, for example in manufacturing as opposed to office work.

Moreover, whether or not the assumption about the lack of domestic responsibilities within Britain was true at that time, it was more often than not the case that early black women migrants had financial responsibilities for dependants in the Caribbean or elsewhere. The number of Caribbean-born young women and men who remember the departure of their mothers for England while they were left with a grandmother or aunt, is eloquent testimony to this. Consequently the low wage rates paid here often acted as a fetter on her ability to fulfil these commitments, particularly given the relatively high cost of living in Britain. It is not therefore surprising that the burden of dual responsibilities together with low wages acted as a compulsion to work overtime and shifts to maximize the weekly pay packet. Indeed such is often the case in the 1980s. Black women workers are thus caught by the low wages associated with the assumption that women work for 'pin money', the effects of racialism as practised by employers (and in some cases unions), and the downward pressure on wages that the physical separation of black workers' productive capacity from the previous site of their reproduction (i.e. home) gave rise to.

By the mid-1960s the situation was changing as it became clear that black people were here as settlers and it was increasingly impossible to assume that black women workers did not have 'dual role' functions to perform at home and 'work'. Indeed in some measure this fact was itself the outcome of government attempts to restrict the size of the black population by the introduction of immigrant controls. The change in the status of black workers was itself accompanied by the development of a different kind of racism which was directed at the level of reproduction (e.g. concerns over housing, community facilities, education etc.) and the so-called 'problems' which it was anticipated would arise within this sphere because of the presence of black families in Britain. This new racism covered all aspects of social life and included hysterical 'rivers of blood' type speeches by leading politicians and alarming developments in the policing of inner city areas where the majority of the black population lives. An important additional element from the point of view of black women was the rise of the notion of the 'pathological' black family, a notion which is nothing other than a racially specific ideological assault on the black population in general and black women in particular. Its roots lay, at least in part, in the tensions associated with the particular way in which black women are forced to bridge the 'separate spheres' (e.g. full-time hours in shifts) and, importantly, the community-based struggles in which these women are engaged in the attempt to alter the terms on which they performed their dual roles. Consequently the ideological assault has been accompanied by a host of institutional practices by 'welfare' agencies. Indeed it is the struggle within this arena which has been the sharp edge of black people's political action for some time and it is often even at the core of many of the industrial struggles that black women have engaged in over the years. Hence the common scenario of a mobilization of the community behind strikes, Grunwick being a classic example.

Taken as a whole then, developments within the sexual division of labour have acted in concert with developments within the wider economy, which together with the ideology of racism and the practice of racialism have etermined the place of black women workers in the British economy. Moreover the effects of the cyclical crisis have led to a period of major restructuring in all spheres of social life which will have material affects on black women's employment prospects.

The Crisis in the British Economy

The continuation of the capitalist mode of production depends on the constant accumulation of capital and on the reproduction of the conditions, within and outside of production, which facilitate that accumulation. This includes the continual accumulation of labour itself, employed or unemployed and categorized according to different skill levels. It has meant that periodically the spheres of production and reproduction have had to be restructured, as has the relationship between these two spheres. It goes without saying that this restructuring is itself the subject of struggle in which the working class, defined in its different categories, i.e. as women, black, youth etc., attempts to ensure that the process occurs in their interests and not those of capital. This in part is what 'community' struggles are about.[6] Indeed such a process of restructuring is occurring during the present crisis. However within this general picture of periodic crisis it is arguable that in terms of international comparison the British economy has been in one form of crisis since the end of the last century (Gutzmore 1975–76). For example Britain remained the world's leading country in terms of international trade until well into this century (not least because of the 'captive' markets which the colonies represented), accounting for 25 per cent of the world manufactured exports in 1950. However, in production terms Britain was overtaken as early as the 1880s by the USA and the 1890s by Germany. As one would expect this situation has continued into the present so that by 1978 Britain's Gross Domestic Product was less than half that of Germany's while in terms of output per person of goods and services, only Italy, Greece and Ireland were lower. This is a function of low investment levels: a 93 per cent fall (in constant 1975 prices) in net investment in Britain between 1970 and 1981 illustrates the point.

Within this more long-term relative decline however the British economy (like all capitalist economies) has been subject to long cycles of boom and slump in tandem with, but more pronounced than, the international economy as a whole. More particularly for our purposes we need to note that these distinct but inter-related forms of crisis have given rise to two factors. Firstly Britain's long-term relative decline has led to structural features which have determined the conditions under which black workers in general, and black women workers in particular, were brought into the labour force. Since these conditions were also to affect the relationship between production and reproduction they were to give rise to additional tensions which were gender-specific. I will return to this point below. Secondly the more medium-term, but nevertheless endemic, structural crises such as those of 1974 and 1978–79 onwards, have meant a more pronounced period of restructuring which has heavily impinged on the pattern and prospects of black women's employment.

This restructuring, itself a response to a crisis of profitability (for example as a percentage of income gross profit rates fell from 20 per cent in 1966 to below 4 per cent in 1974–Anderson et al. 1983: 5), has involved widespread bankruptcies and voluntary closure of plants, massive unemployment and a switch to new branches of production. The figure of 5,500 bankruptcies in the first half of 1982, a 75 per cent increase on 1981, is illustrative of the extent of the problem. Moreover Table 3.6 for Greater London shows the extent to which employment loss is particularly severe in those sectors of the economy in which black women are concentrated. It has also meant a cut in wage levels and a reduction in the social wage. A few simple facts illustrate these trends.

Table 3.6 Decline of Employment in Greater London 1973–83

	Numbers employed		% change
	1973	1983	
Manufacturing			
Food, drink, tobacco	99,766	61,000	−39
Coal, petroleum, chemical			
products	60,860	44,000	−28
Metal manufacture	19,911	10,000	−50
Engineering and allied industries	404,871	266,000	−34
Textiles, leather, clothing	88,670	40,000	−55
Other manufacturing	250,008	173,000	−31
All manufacturing	924,086	594,000	−36
Infrastructure			
Construction	197,073	144,000	−27
Gas, electricity, water	56,156	41,000	−27
Transport and communications	419,627	340,000	−19
Distribution			
Distributive trades	528,939	459,000	−17
Other services			
Financial, professional,			
miscellaneous services	1,397,716	1,468,000	+5
Public administration and defence	344,700	313,000	−9
All industries	3,872,739	3,366,000	−13

Source: London Industrial Strategy from Census of Employment.

Britain's long-term decline as a producer of manufactured goods has continued so that by the end of the 1970s Britain's share of world manufactured exports was below 10 per cent and by 1982 Britain was a net importer of manufactures. Moreover manufactured output had declined even in absolute terms so that by 1981 it was below its 1967 level. As one would expect this has been matched by a decline in the numbers employed in manufacturing in both absolute and proportionate terms. Thus while 8.8 million people were employed in manufacturing in 1951 this figure had dropped to 5.8 million by 1981. In percentage terms this represented 45 per cent and 27.5 per cent respectively (Anderson et al. 1983).

While this decline in manufacturing has been accompanied by an expansion in the service sector of the economy – especially during the 1960s – it was not enough to compensate for the loss of employment in the manufacturing sector. Notwithstanding this there is some evidence to suggest that until recently the growth in certain parts of the service sector has helped to cushion women as a whole from the worst effects of employment loss (Breugal 1979). Thus for example growth in the professional and scientific, and miscellaneous services categories has helped to offset the loss of women's jobs in manufacturing, which, between 1974 and 1977, fell by 9 per cent. Factors such as these are attributable to the sexual division of labour in employment whereby certain sectors and occupations are almost exclusively defined as 'women's jobs' (e.g. 70 per cent of all women wage workers are employed in service industries, while in manufacturing they account for 76 per cent, 46 per cent and 40 per cent of the work force in clothing and footwear, textiles and food and drink).

However there is also some evidence to suggest that this cushioning effect was not proportionately shared by black women workers. This is because of the higher concentration of black women in semi- and unskilled manual work, together with their under-representation in routine white-collar work such as clerical work. Annie Phizacklea (1982: 104) for example has concluded that the comparative figures for 'all women' (including all migrant women workers) and 'Caribbean women' in four occupational categories are as shown in Table 3.7. Such discrepancies might be analysed within a 'racialized' sexual division of labour, the effects of which are more fundamental than is conveyed by a simple notion of discrimination, as I have attempted to show.

Table 3.7 Occupational Distribution of Women by Ethnic Origin (%)

	All women	Caribbean women
Clerical workers	27.2	11.0
Sales workers	11.6	1.3
Service, sports and recreation	22.3	21.0
Professional and technical (incl. nurses)	11.7	25.0
Total	72.8	58.3

Source: Phizacklea 1982.

More recently the service sector as a whole has also begun to decline. Between 1979 and 1982 well over half a million jobs were lost in the service sector. In addition during the last decade the main inner city areas where black people are concentrated have experienced an increase in the rate of loss of service sector jobs (Cambridge Economic Policy Review 1982).

Added to this the loss in total employment has declined faster than registered unemployment has increased. Nearly 2.5 million jobs have been lost between mid 1979 and mid 1982, compared to a 1.9 million increase in the numbers of people registered as unemployed during the same period.[7] This is in part due to the fact that even in those industries where there has been increased investment in plant during the recession, employment levels have often declined. For example in the chemical industry investment increased by 70 per cent between 1964 and 1973 yet employment declined by 8 per cent. Overall then the restructuring associated with the recession has meant 'changes in where people work, how they work and if they work' (Byrne and Parson 1983: 128) and the process of shedding the number of workers it requires to produce an expanded amount of goods will only increase unless action by workers stops it.

To approach the question of employment in this way suggests that the concept of 'crisis' implies more than a restructuring of relations at the workplace and of how things are produced. It also suggests that 'crisis' implies a necessity to try and restructure relations within production as well, as was suggested in the section dealing with the sexual division of labour. In other words the struggles of working-class people in general and black workers in particular that take place in the community (over home, policing, education, immigration, health, social security benefit) are as much a problem for capital as it tries to overcome the crisis in its own favour, as are strikes over pay or the length of the working day. Indeed it is only by adopting an integrated approach such as this that we will be able to understand the impact on black women's employment of the recession and the interventionist strategies of the state on behalf of capital. Similarly and more importantly only by adopting this approach will we be able to develop the appropriate strategies by which to defeat the attacks being made on us as black people.

Let us now look at government policy.

Monetarism

Against the picture of the crisis painted above it becomes clear that the Thatcher government's economic strategy has been a radical intervention aimed at hastening the process of restructuring which is required if profitability is to be restored to acceptable levels for British capital as a whole.

At one level crises within capitalism are an inevitable consequence of the pursuit for continued and expanded accumulation on the one hand, and the attempt by workers to subvert this process in their own interests on the other. Thus while investment in more plant as against labour may improve productivity and profit levels for individual capitals by increasing the extraction of relative surplus-value,[8] at the level of collective capital it only serves to eliminate the source of profit, i.e. the workers themselves. Therefore for capital as a whole the effect of an increase in the proportion of machines to workers[9] is that too many firms chase too little profit. Moreover with a strong, well-organized labour force, itself partly the result of full employment during

the boom period, the easy reorganization of production by the introduction of
new technology or different working hours etc. is prohibitive as is a decline in
real wage rates. However as the effects of long-term relative decline and
cyclical structural crisis take hold weaker (and usually, though not always,
smaller) firms begin to go broke. At this point the emergence of a full-blown
crisis acts as a means to re-establish the basis of a renewed cycle of
accumulation. This process if successful is inevitably at the cost to workers
who are themselves engaged in a struggle to force the terms of restructuring
in their favour. There are however also casualties among capital, i.e. those
weaker firms that are driven out of production.

In this context monetarism is a way of hastening the process by which
weaker, i.e. less competitive and profitable, firms go bust, thereby reducing
the total number chasing profits. It is important to note that the strategy does
not cause the recession but it does quite deliberately exacerbate it by
manipulating fiscal and monetary policies in order to bring to bear the sharp
point of competition and to blunt the edge of working-class struggle for its
own interests. Moreover this process not only affects different sections of the
workforce in different ways (e.g. higher levels of unemployment among some
groups, changes in which sections of the workforce work where, etc.), but also
divisions within the workforce are often manipulated in order to hasten and
ease (for capital) the process of restructuring. For example the introduction of
new methods of production may be done by employing more vulnerable
sections of labour for these tasks, as happened at Ford's or as is happening
with the increased employment of black women workers in offices at the time
that new technology is being introduced.

Monetarism is also a cheap labour strategy. Therefore an additional effect
of tightening the supply of money is that those firms that do survive must both
shed labour, thereby increasing unemployment, and lower average wage
levels for those still employed. Given that black women workers are over-
concentrated in those backward, declining sectors most affected by the crisis
it is not surprising that the employment effects of the recession are being
disproportionately felt by black women workers.

The monetarist cheap labour strategy also has additional prongs which
impact still further on black women workers. These include the attempt, in
the main via the MSC (now Employment Department), to restructure the level
and type of skill training available, as well as the sections of the workforce who
have access to such training. For example, the abolition of sixteen of the
twenty-three Industrial Training Boards, the herding of young black people
on to mode B schemes of YTS with the result that their 'training' is worse than
no training at all, and the longer-term demise of any high-quality apprenticeship are all indicators of the attempt to restructure what training exists and for
whom.

At one level this is related to the long-term relative decline of the British economy which was to predetermine that the daughters and sons of those who migrated as workers from the 1950s onwards were never to have access to plentiful and highly skilled occupations. At another level the restrictions and transformations in skill training are related to developments in the technology of production. Such developments have made it possible to deskill larger and larger numbers of workers. This has the effect of both lowering average wage levels and subordinating the worker to the machine (lathe or work-processor) and to further fragment the production process. Both of these impinge on the ability of the workforce to control the production process by collective action.

Important from the point of view of women's employment is the fact that technological developments in the processing and storing of information are rapidly changing the nature of work in the office, making conditions more like those in the factory which had already undergone 'rationalization' with the application of Fordist and Taylorist production methods.[10] For black women who have recently gained any noticeable degree of entry into office work (the 1984 PSI study shows a 10 per cent shift from manual to non-manual occupations for black women) this means that entry into these jobs does not necessarily represent an escape from the bad, hazardous and low-paid conditions of manufacturing, but simply their resurfacing at new sites of employment.

Another effect of the monetarist strategy with potentially dire effects for black women is its impact on the growth of homeworking and sweatshops. Homeworkers are perhaps the least documented sector of workers since by the very nature of their work they tend to be excluded from government and trade union statistics. Despite this the CIS report on *Women in the '80s* (Counter Information Services 1981) estimated that in 1980 there were between 200,000–400,000 homeworkers. Such workers are predominantly women and many are employed in those manufacturing industries in which black women workers are concentrated, such as clothing. Consequently it is not surprising to find that clothing manufacturers in the East End of London themselves estimate that 30–50 per cent of all homeworkers engaged by them are black women (this figure includes Cypriot women).[11]

These workers are employed on low wages, usually piece rate, with 85 per cent earning less than £1.06 per hour in 1979 (CIS 1981). Engaged in homeworking largely because of their geographical immobility, which is itself the result of dual roles, racism in the streets and sometimes additional cultural or linguistic factors, homeworkers often find it difficult to organize either within or outside of the trade union movement. As such this section of cheap female labour may well prove increasingly attractive to employers. This is particularly true at a time of recession and when technological developments make it at least theoretically possible to put out more and more office or manufacturing tasks to homeworkers. Thus for example developments in

information technology are opening up new avenues for homeworking as
when visual display units or micro-computers are installed in a home and
linked to a main-frame at the regional or head office of the employing firm
wherever in the world that may be. Yet clearly this type of homeworking is at
present both spatially and qualitatively removed from the domestic manufacture of the clothing industry. The middle-class, university-trained housewife,
expert in computer programming and based in her Berkshire detached, is far
removed from her homeworking counterpart in the inner city ghettoes of
London or Bradford. Yet the political link lies in the fact that both these
sources of labour have been sought by capital in the attempt to recruit what it
assumes to be a docile or passive labour force in the hope that its (capital's)
interests can be pursued unhindered by the collective action of sections of the
working class. In this sense therefore the widening use of homeworkers and
the development of the technology which facilitates it is an outcome of the
continuing dynamic of the class struggle to control production.

The other side of the homeworking coin often tends to be the sweatshop,
an expansion of which can be expected as the inevitable outcome of successful
monetarist intervention in the process of recession and the process of
restructuring. Once again black women workers can be expected to be
disproportionately affected by this development since it is in some of the
manufacturing sectors where black women are concentrated that sweatshops
predominate, for example in clothing and footwear. Moreover such sweatshops are not the exclusive preserve of the white petty bourgeois super-
exploiting black women's labour. It is often the case that such sweatshops are
themselves black-owned businesses utilizing family and community labour.
George Ward's Grunwick is a classic case in point, while Barbara Hoel (West
1982) has documented the experience of Asian women workers in sweatshops
in Coventry. In both these cases the conditions and level of exploitation were
appalling and there is no prior reason, theoretical or otherwise, to assume that
such conditions are not or would not be duplicated in existing or developing
Caribbean-owned and -run businesses. Indeed it is factors such as these
which demand an organized political response by black progressives against
the current ideological promotion of the development of an Afro-Caribbean
small business sector.[12]

The Re-creation of a Surplus Population within the Black Communities

If industrial restructuring is indicative of a crisis in the economic sense, the
need for restructuring is also indicative of a crisis in the political sense in that
there is a crisis in the power of relations between classes. Thus the need for

economic restructuring to restore the basis for a renewed cycle of accumulation and valorization also includes a need to restructure the working class and in particular divisions between workers.

Restructuring also means then the way in which capital as a whole attempts to create new forms of accumulation in which the needs of the working classes, as expressed through their economic/political demands, are either incorporated into the new dynamic of accumulation or completely marginalized. An essential element in this process is the attempt by capital to restructure the various elements within the working class, thereby reproducing the divisions within the class. Necessarily therefore the struggle of capital to restore its domination is not confined to the site of production alone but is carried out in the sites of reproduction, i.e. those of the home and 'community' together with parts of the 'welfare' state. Thus the struggles of black women workers against the conditions of their exploitation in the workplace and their conditions of oppression in the community, are manifestations of a political crisis (for capital) acted out within the locus of 'racialized gender/ class relations'. Moreover it is struggles such as these which have contributed to the very onset of crisis and demanded a response from capital. This was particularly true because such struggles represented a rebellion of a section of the 'working class' considered the most docile and marginal (by employers and trade unions alike). The consequence of this was that internal divisions within the class themselves threatened to become undermined, suggesting at least the potential for harmonization and greater unity of working-class struggles. Indeed it was this fact, together with struggles elsewhere and the increasing severity of the economic crisis, that was to provide the impetus for the state to introduce a plethora of measures designed to control the black communities.

These measures included the integration of various government departments in the policing of inner city communities. Under the guise of tackling 'crime', state agencies were to co-ordinate and share information on local populations. The Home Office, responsible for the police and immigration, was to work in conjunction with the DHSS, the DES, and the DOE in order to develop so-called crime prevention strategies at the local level. In other words information passed on by the public at the dole office, in the hospital, at the school or in the housing office was to become readily available to the police on request. Integrated surveillance brought 'big brother' into the heart of the community via these state agencies and it did so precisely at a time when the relationship of the working class as a whole to these welfare agencies was itself being changed as a result of public expenditure cuts. Increasing queues at the dole and social security office; destruction of services provided by welfare agencies; and the increasing corporatization of delivery and administration of state services were further tools in the armoury of restructuring (Cockburn 1977). The agencies of welfare and coercion were coming together to attack the working class at the level of the community, but they were doing so by targeting specific fragments of the working class in specific localities.

In short the process is one in which capital is attempting to recreate a relative surplus population, with large chunks of the black population being assigned to this category of people.

Friend and Metcalfe (1981) identify this surplus population as a group more extensive than the unemployed. As a category it also includes temporary and casual workers; those working on the margins outside the tax system; the low paid, especially in the state service sector and the sweated industries; and those dependent on state benefits. The importance of this definition lies precisely in the fact that it embraces those employed in sectors of the economy where the wages and overall condition are well below the average endured by the bulk of the working class. Examples of such sectors are homeworking, the sweated industries, cleaning, or some of the worst part of the catering industry or the fast food trade. As we already know it is precisely these areas where many black women work.[13]

The creation of surplus population is a necessary outcome of changes in the process of production caused by technological developments and the resultant changes in the way work is carried out and products are made. But if the creation of surplus population is located in the sphere of production, its shape and the terrain of its political control occur within the 'community'. In other words when women do battle over the level or form of payment of welfare benefit or the quality of service from a council department, and when black youths opt for unemployment rather than be herded into the worst jobs on offer, they are both engaged in more than a form of protest over conditions of working-class life outside of work. They are also engaged in struggles which affect the potential of capital to transform segments of the relative surplus population into a reserve army of labour which, by competing for jobs, will act as a downward pressure on wages. Additionally such struggles are also indicative of their refusal to accept incorporation into the more highly exploited occupations.

This can be seen more clearly when considering the effects of cuts on welfare and other public expenditure. Such cuts are aimed at lowering the amount the government needs to raise in order to carry out its redistributive functions. They also serve to entrench the sexual division of labour in the home by making women assume greater responsibility for domestic duties and dependants.[14] (This is what the current debate about 'Community Care' is all about.) However precisely by lowering or removing some of the 'social' wage, these cuts force more and more people to seek some form of paid employment and therefore compete for jobs that are scarce. In all probability the sectors where these people will compete for jobs will be those where the process of deskilling and the erosion of pay and conditions, including unionization, have been carried to the furthest extent.

Such competition only serves to entrench divisions between sections of employed and unemployed workers even though the levels of income between them may be extremely slight. Indeed it is precisely where the margins are narrow that the desire to maintain the distinction between employment and unemployment is most keenly felt by those employed in low-paid work.

This highlights the relationship between the re-creation of a surplus population and the trend towards the peripheralization of major areas of work. Peripheralization of the economy simply means that the conditions which prevail in the most highly exploited and worst-organized sectors of the economy (see note 14) become more and more widespread. This development can be seen in the growing trend towards casualization and part-time employment, abolition of wages councils, anti-trade union legislation, and decentralization, by which industries are removed from the orbit of legal control so that forms of employment protection are relaxed. Consequently larger and larger numbers of people will become part of a surplus population as a result of the conscious intervention on the part of capital and the state into the internal dynamics of capitalist production.

From this perspective we can see that just as the success of working-class struggles within the factory, office or shop influence the levels, distribution and conditions of employment, so too the success of struggles within the 'community' will have an impact on who gets work, where and under what circumstances. Consequently the struggles of black women outside of the workplace are an important influence on their future role in the British economy.[15]

Prospects

Taken as a whole the employment effects of the recession and the associated restructuring of both the economy and class relations paint a rather gloomy picture for the employment prospects of black women in the immediate future. On the one hand plant closure, rationalization and relocation, together with cuts and restructuring in the public sector, mean that unofficial unemployment levels will at best remain at the three million mark. On the other hand for those who continue to be engaged in waged employment, the conditions of service will continue to deteriorate as the introduction of new technology serves to deskill, fragment and control the worker. This is true in both manufacturing and office work in both the public and private sectors. Moreover as we have already seen, for those employed in the public sector, the development of multi-agency policing will mean that black people, mostly women, employed by the 'welfare' services will be expected to carry out surveillance tasks on other black people. Conditions will therefore worsen in both the traditional sense of pay and terms and in the political sense of being stooges in the process of policing the black communities, and creating divisions between working-class people as capital attempts to reassert its control.

In short, the economic and political processes by which the black population is being restructured, if successful, will mean that an ever-growing proportion will become part of the relative surplus population; a prospect which was in many senses predetermined by the specific form of capital accumulation within an economy which was both growing but in long-term relative decline, the contradictions of which were exacerbated by the political struggles of black workers in the 1960s and 1970s.

This place within the surplus population is true for both those outside of and within waged labour as we have seen in the case of homeworkers, a form of waged work which may well expand as technological developments and relocation of production facilitate it. Similarly the expansion of this and similar forms of employment is very likely to be predicated on the sexual division of labour since it gives rise to a cheap and relatively immobile female labour force. In addition then to new types of homeworking other occupations may well become 'feminized' as employers relocate to cheaper, more flexible (for capital) sources of labour. Thus restructuring involves not only changes in the amount and value of the wage, in the occupational and sectoral composition of employment, it also involves changes in the racial and sexual composition of employment. Indeed changes in the sexual composition of employment (undifferentiated in terms of race) associated with economic restructuring have already been documented (Massey 1985: especially Chapter 5).

However an increase in women's employment in some regions does not necessarily mean that all women workers gain access to these new employment opportunities. The spatial unevenness of the process inevitably means that the employment impact is regionally specific and reflects the contours of classes in struggle. When analysing black women's employment prospects this is of particular importance since the ruralization of production which is occurring at present means that these new avenues of employment are precisely not in the inner cities where the bulk of the black population lives.

Thus even where restructuring throughout the economy is leading to the proliferation of working conditions familiar to many black women, the spatial and political aspects of restructuring may well serve to limit the employment opportunities of black working-class women, confined as they are to the inner cities which were the industrial centres of another era of accumulation.

Thus the present situation is one in which a number of trends are occurring. Whilst many existing areas of employment for black women are closing altogether or experiencing major decline, others are opening up (e.g. fast food, some office work, especially in 'equal opportunity establishments').

However the extent to which these potential opportunities can be turned into real jobs, which show some movement towards qualitatively better jobs for black women, is less sure.

One thing is clear, however, and that is that is that the outcome will depend, at least in part, on the success of black women's autonomous organization both on the shop floor and outside, in the 'community'. The sooner this lesson is learnt by all sections of the black population and indeed all sectors of the working class as a whole the better.

Notes

1. Note that throughout this paper the term 'black' will be used to refer to women and men who have immigrant or refugee status (and their descendants) and who are from the New Commonwealth or other parts of the 'Third World', unless otherwise stated.

2. Recently this aspect of the Act was ruled as sexually discriminatory by the European Court of Human Rights. The British government's response has been to bring women's status in line with that of men, thereby eliminating sexual discrimination but reinforcing racism.

3. Together with workers from the underdeveloped southern Mediterranean.

4. That is, it was at least in part an attempt to increase the extraction of absolute surplus value. This is not to say that no increase in the extraction of relative surplus value occurred, but that in comparison to its international competitors the rate of increase of absolute surplus value was higher. Hence the continued use of outmoded equipment and the high degree of mobility of British capital overseas.

5. The idea of the women's wage as the second wage is indicative of the fact that the ideology of separate spheres has only been modified and not abandoned.

6. This is not to suggest the a priori existence of a 'community'. Indeed, it is often the case that such struggles reflect the common aspirations of a collectivity and are the process by which that is formed into a 'community'.

7. Anderson et al. (1983). The changes in the way in which government departments classified people as active or inactive are shown here.

8. Relative surplus-value is the production of a greater amount of value created by the worker without extending the length of the working day or the number of workers employed to produce the same amount of goods. In the main, technological developments and/or the reorganization of the work process are the means by which this increase in the extraction of surplus-value is achieved.

9. This is sometimes called an increase in the organic composition of capital. This term refers to a technical relation in that it means the amount of machinery to the number of workers. It is also a value relation in that it refers to the ratio between the value of the machinery and the value of the worker as measured by the cost of the average bundle of goods which workers buy to keep themselves going (i.e. reproduce themselves), i.e. the wage.

10. See for example Jane Barker and Hazel Downing (1980). Fordist production methods refer to the application of conveyor belt or 'line' production as existed in car production, biscuit manufacture or the production of in-flight meals at British Airways. Taylorist methods refer to the application of 'scientific' methods to production, as for example the breaking down of the different aspects of producing a commodity into discrete operations.

11. Quoted in GLC Committee Report, IEC 1011, 1983.

12. There is a whole plethora of schemes aimed at encouraging black people to solve their unemployment problem by going into business. Central and local government schemes for advice and/or financial assistance exist as do private sector ones. There is also a vociferous lobby from some sections of the black community: Business in the Community or The First Partnership Bank being two examples. An important and revealing aspect of all the rhetoric surrounding these schemes is the emphasis placed by all concerned on the supposed relationship between the

development of a thriving black business sector and the cessation of inner city uprisings. The argument is that if young black people (and note here that the emphasis is on Caribbean youth) see some evidence of black investment in the country they won't protest at police harassment and brutality!

13. Marx included these workers in his discussion of the Reserve Army of Labour and described it in this way: 'The third category of the relative surplus population, the stagnant, forms a part of the active army, but with extremely irregular employment . . . Its conditions of life sink below the average normal level of the working class; this makes it at once the broad basis of special branches of capitalist exploitation. It is characterised by a maximum of working time and a minimum of wages' (Marx 1974: 602).

14. Cuts in public expenditure are also accompanied by the construction of more and more people as 'scroungers'. Simultaneously it undermines or removes the notion of people's 'rights' to state-provided welfare and redefines who is entitled to these rights.

15. For example the extent to which black women were successful in gaining improvements in the education received by their children (as measured by formal academic qualifications) affected the type of jobs these black children would then expect or demand.

4

Woman Abuse in London's Black Communities

Amina Mama

Introduction

This chapter examines the form, severity and extent of domestic violence experienced by black[1] women, and the time over which they are subjected to violence before seeking to escape it. The research covered several ethnic communities – loosely divided into women of Caribbean, Asian and African origin. Of these, only domestic violence in the South East Asian communities has received any attention in the mainstream and ethnic media and in the black feminist press (cf. Grewal 1988 and back issues of *Outwrite*), and this has not been substantial. With respect to women of African and Caribbean origin in Britain, no literature was found which addressed domestic violence. Regarding violence against African and Caribbean women only police brutality appears to have been mentioned at all.

In the area of 'race', the existing research is contradictory, focusing on the non-issue of whether black and minority families are more or less violent than white ones with reasons being adduced for each side of the argument (Bolton and Bolton 1987). Staples's work (1982) is perhaps the most interesting here; he utilizes Frantz Fanon's (1967) thesis on violence in colonial contexts to analyse black male violence.

The variable of culture does not appear to have been part of existing research on domestic violence, although it is another recurring theme in women's accounts. For example, it manifests itself most commonly in terms of husbands invoking 'tradition' or 'religion' to justify their expectations of and demands for subservient or obedient behaviour from their womenfolk. None of the world's major religious texts condones (or actively challenges) the abuse of women. Rather the issue is more about men appropriating religion in their own exercise of power over the women with whom they live. There is certainly no justification for tolerating woman-abuse in black communities on the basis of it being 'their culture', as appears to occur in racist and colonial contexts.

The Women Who Participated in the Study

It is these lacunae which the research sought to address, by looking at the strategies employed by the women in the study to reduce or otherwise cope with repeated physical assault or mental cruelty. The study is based on the results of in-depth interviews with over 100 women, conducted in London over a period of twelve months (November 1987– October 1988). This makes it the first detailed investigation of domestic violence in Britain's black communities.

Contact with a range of community and voluntary sector organizations in the preliminary stages did not yield many interviews except in the case of Chinese and Filipino women who were contacted solely through their own community organizations. Contacts through social networks (e.g. through friends or relatives of community, health or social workers who responded to publicity about the project) likewise only yielded a small number (in fact, just five!) of Asian and Caribbean women.

Contact with Asian women was facilitated by the existence of Asian Women's Resource Centres and the six Asian refuges in London, all of which were full throughout the research period. The network of other Asian women's groups was not in a position to offer much assistance, although several were visited.

Caribbean women were contacted through mainstream refuges (within which they are very unevenly distributed), and the single black women's refuge. Black women's centres and groups were also contacted, but again did not result in any direct contacts with women for interview.

African women's organizations and hostels in London were contacted, but did not yield interviews, although discussions were held with those that responded positively. There is no African refuge in London, and the few African women's groups were too under-resourced to offer much support to individual cases (e.g. Akina Mama Wa Afrika, based in Camden), although FORWARD (based at the Africa Centre, also in Camden) does some counselling and has worked on circumcision. Some African women are involved in black women's organizations with Caribbean women of African descent (e.g. Camden Black Sisters, East London Black Women's Organization) and Asian women (e.g. Southall Black Women's Centre).

It can be seen therefore that the sample was predominantly obtained through the Women's Aid network. This meant that the vast numbers of women experiencing domestic violence but not contacting Women's Aid were excluded.

No black lesbian women were encountered in the process of contacting people to interview. The problems faced by black women in violent lesbian relationships are not therefore addressed in this study, although it is apparent that lesbian relationships are not free from abuse and violence, and may well be treated even less sympathetically.

Many of the sample characteristics may be related to the mode of contact: in particular most of the women had left their homes, or were otherwise seeking to terminate relationships with violent partners. In this sense, the sample must be regarded as a highly selective tip of the iceberg. Consultations with community organizations indicated that large numbers of women in all the communities addressed here are forced to tolerate quite high levels of domestic violence without ever contacting Women's Aid or, for that matter, any outside agency. Even within the subject group, many had tolerated violence for quite long periods of time (ranging from a few months to thirty years) before hearing of and contacting outside agencies. Some, particularly older women in the sample, had repeatedly sought help and found none. Similar observations were made by the Select Committee's Report to Parliament in 1975 regarding the population in general. It is particularly likely that violence will be hidden in the more isolated and marginalized black communities.

The fact that all were resident in London at the time of interview was the main unifying factor in this ethnically diverse sample of abused women. Many had been born in Britain, and most of the remainder had lived here for many years. As such all were assumed to be entitled to protection under British law and to the basic human rights set out in the UN Charter. These include the right to shelter, food and to lead productive lives. It was shocking to find that several women were threatened with deportation at the time of the research, as a direct result of having left their violent spouses. Several were not sure of their status at the time of interview, since their spouses kept their papers. None in our sample had or was applying for refugee status. All were resident by birth, residence or (least securely) by marriage to British citizens.

The respondents were all volunteers and were assured of complete confidentiality. Interviews were conducted in an empathic and supportive style, with priority attached to building a good rapport with each woman. The degree of rapport obtained varied widely within the research group. Women were encouraged to articulate their own experience for themselves as much as possible and to indicate any areas they preferred not to discuss. In this free-flowing discussion leading questions were avoided. For example, the researcher sought not to impose a working definition of domestic violence on the women. Instead, the women were allowed to self-define their relational experience as one of domestic violence.

What was embraced by the term 'domestic violence' was no less problematic given that the researchers did not wish to prioritize any particular form of experience. As it turned out, the vast majority of women had experienced high degrees of physical abuse as well as considerable mental and emotional cruelty. Only two were subjected to emotional cruelty without physical violence. (In both cases emotional suffering drove them from their marital homes.) This rendered the definitional problems around more borderline cases irrelevant.

In some respects, however, this process of self-definition was undercut by the reliance on agencies (women's refuges and community groups) to gain access to women since such agencies tended, informally or not, to opera-tionalize in their caseloads a definition of domestic violence through the filtering process by which the women were dealt with.

Marital Status, Class and Ethnicity

Whereas much research has focused on violence against wives – 'wife-battering' – it soon became clear in the course of this research that a significant proportion of the women we interviewed at refuges had not been legally married. Furthermore, a significant proportion had not been cohabit-ing on a full-time basis with their partners during the period of violence, and some of the women never had. It was therefore decided to include these two latter groups in this study, in contrast to existing research on domestic violence, because growing numbers of women (and in this study, women of Caribbean descent in particular) had what we refer to as 'visiting relation-ships' with the men who assaulted them. Their assailants stayed with them on a part-time basis, while also retaining residential rights with their mothers, or with other women. Domestic violence is not restricted to any particular family form or structure. Some women, too, were escaping violent assaults by ex-partners.

Within each of these three relationship categories – married, cohabiting, and visiting – numerous variations existed in terms of roles and expectations, duties and responsibilities. It was not possible to go into any finer analysis in this project, but this variation should be borne in mind.

The three relationship categories identified for the research purposes were not independent of ethnic background. In this sample, the women of Asian and African descent were all legal and/or traditional wives, while more than half of the women of Caribbean origin were cohabitees or were engaged in visiting relationships. This may bear some relation to the fact that the Caribbean sample were predominantly born and raised in Britain where a growing proportion of the population cohabit at some stage in their relation-ship (Barrett and MacIntosh 1982). It may also be strongly related to the material circumstances of the working-class Caribbean communities of Britain. The economic and power relations are very different when one is considering domestic violence against a middle-class but financially depend-ent wife, as compared to domestic violence against a single mother of three in a local authority flat, or violence against a professional working woman.

Assailants fell into a number of categories:

(a) husbands;
(b) cohabitees;
(c) men with whom the woman had a visiting relationship;
(d) ex-husbands, cohabitees or visiting partners.[2]

Men who were violent to the women in this study came from all socio-economic classes, ranging from businessmen rich enough to keep several homes (and women), to working-class men who had never been afforded the dignity of earning a decent wage. What was most striking is that women across a very diverse range of domestic economic relationships and situations can be forced to flee their homes to escape violence from their partners.

This fact raises a major theoretical question about previous research on domestic violence, which has often tended to regard it as part and parcel of male power and women's economic dependence on the men battering them. While this may be true for 'housewives' in a traditional white middle-class nuclear family, it was clearly not the case for a significant proportion of the black women in this study. Many were in fact being beaten by men who were dependent on them, regardless of marital status. This and other issues raised by the research findings are taken up in the discussion at the end of this chapter.

The Violence

The material is of a highly disturbing nature and, because of biases such as sample size or the unrepresentative nature of the sample, should NOT be used as a basis for constructing new, or supporting old, stereotypes about the Caribbean, Asian or African communities, about gender relations, or about the treatment of women by men in those communities.

While certain themes occur frequently in the data, others are more idiosyncratic. This is not the place to attempt a detailed study of the causes of domestic violence, or to go into the detail that an individual psychological understanding would require. Rather the case material is presented to highlight some of the ways in which violence has been manifested, as recounted by women who have been subjected to assaults by their male partners. These highly disturbing accounts are treated and discussed as authentic descriptive data. They are presented to illustrate the circumstances which lead women to approach existing statutory and voluntary agencies, or to desist from, or delay in approaching outside agencies, even when they are being subjected to extreme and often life-threatening behaviour. Within each unhappy tapestry there also lies a rich undercurrent of courage which testifies to the resilience and resistance these women have shown, often without any of the support that one might expect a humane society to offer, in the face of the most extreme degradation and brutality.

Domestic Violence Against Women of Caribbean Descent

Case 1: Sukie   Sukie was staying at a women's refuge with her two young sons (aged six and three) when we spoke. When she was eighteen she moved into a council flat with the tenancy in her name. Eugene, a casual painter decorator, came to help with the decorating. They related to each other quite well, and a few weeks later he arrived at Sukie's flat with his baggage and moved in. Things went well until after the birth of their first son, when Eugene started to feel bitterly jealous of the young infant, and Sukie became pregnant and had their second son. Arguments began and continued, with Eugene forbidding Sukie to have her brother visit, and accusing her of having affairs with other men. When she went to visit her aunt, she would return to find her clothes and pictures hidden and clear evidence that he had entertained other women in their bedroom:

> 'These things were going on because he used to take the children's toys and hide them in the cupboard; take all my things off the dressing table and put them inside the drawer, and once he pretended that I was his sister. When I used to go down to my auntie's he sort of gave this as an excuse for bringing the women there because I wasn't there, which I thought was wrong. If he wanted to do anything I thought he should go outside of the house to do it, not do it inside my house – I've got the children staying there as well. So from there we started fighting every day. One night I had to run out and he came looking for me. While he was looking he got this knife from my cousin's kitchen drawer and slashed me across the face and tore Neville [son] away from me. I've got the scar here [Sukie still bore a number of scars].'

The violence got worse, as did her partner's extreme jealousy, with him waiting outside her workplace and deploying other people to trail her and monitor her movements.

> 'He was possessive and the fact that I was working and saving my money really got to him because he's self-employed and every time he wants anything he wants me to help, so I was not getting any benefit out of working. He said that I was working and hiding my money from him, and that I bring up my kids too fancy – I shouldn't dress them up like that. Every time I visit my friends he said they were a bad influence on me, and he banned me from walking down that particular road. If I took the kids to my friend's house he would sort of trail me, and he got people to spy on me after work.
> 'The thing is he wanted to be the ruler of the house. He said there can't be two kings in one house, and on one occasion he said that I mustn't cook for the kids and

don't cook for him, that he would buy separate shopping and sort of ban me from using the cooker. When we're fighting I wasn't to sleep on my bed, I wasn't to sleep on the kids' bed and I wasn't to sleep on the settee. One night he locked me in the toilet – sort of nailed it down.

'When I was pregnant one time he said that he would see that Neville was born crippled.'

Sukie's workmates observed what was happening through the heavy bruising to her face and arms, and she saw the doctor on several occasions with her injuries. She suffered from frequent nose bleeds, headaches and high blood pressure as a result of frequent blows to the head. She also called the police on several occasions and obtained ouster injunctions from the courts. Her reason for not leaving before this stage: 'I've always said because of the kids – because of the kids I'll stay with him, so the kids can have a father.'

She had left after Eugene had wrapped a cord round her throat in a strangle grip until she almost blacked out. She still bore the scars of that assault on her neck at the time of interview. After that episode, Eugene was convicted of GBH and bound over for a year, but it was not safe for her to go near her flat, so she fled. Her local authority acknowledged she was homeless as a result of domestic violence and placed her in a Bayswater bed and breakfast hotel where she bore filth, cockroaches and no cooking facilities for eight months in one room with her two sons, who repeatedly became ill. Eventually she moved into the women's refuge. A year later I met her again at a different refuge, still awaiting rehousing, thinner and even more worn-looking.

Case 2: Charlotte   Charlotte is a thirty-three-year-old London-born woman who has lived with the father of her two young children for four and a half years. When they established their relationship she put all her own resources into a business with him, which failed – due to his gambling habits. He became increasingly abusive towards her over a two-year period, subjecting her to constant criticism and derision day and night, and then becoming sexually and physically abusive.

'There was mental abuse as well. There were a lot of bad vibes generally. Bad communication, lots of complaints about everything – he would keep me awake all night going on and on criticizing everything about me, my family, what I did, how I spoke, how I reacted to everything. That created a sexual problem which would bring out the violence as well . . . he would – you know – rip off my clothes and . . . ' [in a lowered voice she explained that she was raped].

During her pregnancy with the youngest child she was subjected to extreme emotional and financial neglect. Another woman became pregnant by him at this point. His cruelty and neglect had deep effects on her during her pregnancy:

'It was very depressing. It leaves you inert and with no energy left to do anything. It took me a long time to realize the actual seriousness of the situation. That I was actually in that situation. Might sound funny but it took a long time for me to admit that it actually was a real nightmare.'

In retrospect Charlotte describes her partner as suffering from insecurity, and burdened with debts he had incurred. Their flat was in her name, and she also owned the car (which he prevented her from using).

'I think basically his problem is chronic insecurity, which is something I hadn't realized before . . . he comes over as quite arrogant and pushy actually. But he finds any type of rejection totally unacceptable.'

She left on two occasions, but returned, having nowhere else to go. Eventually she had to call the police for the second time to escort her to a women's refuge when he became frighteningly irrational one night. One of the reasons she gave for leaving were his threats to kill their children.

Case 3: Zoey   Zoey was twenty-three years old and struggling to start a different life for herself after spending six abusive years with a man much older than her, who operated as a pimp. She spoke clearly and insightfully about her life. Zoey had been raised by an English family in the country and came to London at the age of sixteen 'in search of the bright lights'. She started working as a hostess in Soho clubs, where she met her partner – an influential man, quite different from anyone she had ever met, and who gradually took over control of her life.

'I thought I was in control of the relationship. He never worked – has never worked, so it was a completely different way of life. And I thought it was exciting, free – he showed me all different things, all the runnings[3] and everything. He was willing to show me how I'm supposed to be, and where I come from, my roots. I was to stop putting on makeup. I had been very into myself – into makeup and clothes. He was nothing like that. I never thought I would go for a guy like him. I was looking for something different I must admit. But I thought he was sort of soft when I first met him, cuz that style I had never come across – the black man's style. I think I came unstuck because he was so smart. He really worked his brain on me. He was very patient, so he got what he wanted. Everywhere he went everybody just hails him up – he's very popular. That's what attracted me to him. When I first looked at him I thought No, I was just looking into his wrinkled old face. I don't know what it was – it was his style, and after a while . . . '

Zoey had never experienced abuse prior to this relationship:

'The first time he hit me I left him. That's the kind of person I was. I was so shocked and appalled. But in the end I thought, well this is it. I'm in the bottom of hell, I can't get out of it. Now I'm the kind of person who gets beaten consistently and doesn't go, so I've gone mad between then and now. I'd gone mental, lost all contacts, and I had his child. And he knew all those things. He knew what he was doing.'

She concealed the reality of her situation from her parents and sister:

'To my parents I was playing happy families. They never knew the truth at all. Oh no. It would have been too appalling, it would be like a horror movie to them. That's unreal.'

Her partner was also violent to other women, and invoked the Old Testament in his general misogyny:

'He had no respect for women at all. He'd say that over and over again. Women is Delilah, Satan. Woman is man's downfall and all this all the time. Woman is down there. He used to go on about Margaret Thatcher running the country – all these women running the country. When I took him to court I won an injunction. So he had twenty-eight days to get out, and all these things just confirmed that it was a woman's country . . . He's got to have somebody to belittle all the time.'

The frequency of physical abuse varied:

'Sometimes it would be morning and night, morning and night every night for a week. If we was really at each other's throats, really arguing, and then he might not beat me for six months.'

She suffered extensive bruising and cuts from punches, kicks and being hit with furniture and other objects that came to hand. On one occasion he broke his toe kicking her. On another she was hospitalized with her head split open, and had to go to casualty on yet another. The police were called approximately thirty times in five years. Most of their fights centred around money:

'He wanted money from me, from my work. He said he wasn't interested in the house because he was a Rasta and he was going to Africa. But he'd be willing to sit down and let me do everything financially – the food, housekeeping, bills and everything. He used to get me to give him money in the beginning, he said he would pay me back because I loaned him some. But then it got out of hand. For years and years – I can't begin to weigh up how much – thousands and thousands.'

She had a friend who was in a similar relationship:

'Me and my friend used to laugh; for about three years we'd come down and laugh at ourselves. In the end that was our only pleasure. To run ourselves down. When we face them we'd know that we'd been cursing them stupid – it was like that.'

Her friend left the scene and started a new life for herself some time before Zoey did.

'His word was God's to me and he knew best. He knew, you see? He was never supposed to be wrong. Whatever he'd encourage me in, I would have done. That's why I'm here now. Because of sheer disgust in myself. Disgust. That's all I can say, in the end. Absolute disgust.'

Case 4: Elsie Elsie is a twenty-five-year-old woman of Caribbean and European mixed parentage who grew up in a northern English town. She has a particularly extrovert and dynamic character. The violence she was subjected to in her relationship was so bad that it drove her to attempt suicide. She had been in a relationship with Mike, the father of her child, for eighteen months at the time of interview. They had been living with his mother and his sister at his mother's small (two-bed) council flat for the period of their cohabitation. They attempted to get council accommodation of their own on numerous occasions, to no avail.

Elsie has held a wide range of domestic catering and sales jobs, while her partner is a musician who goes for long periods without work, but felt that Elsie should stay at home and be a full-time housewife.

'He wanted me to be a housey woman and I ain't housey at all. I'd rather be out working – not barefoot and pregnant over the stove . . . He used to go out for days on end, yet if I go out for an hour, he used to say: "Where have you been?" I'd be wanting to ask him questions anyway, but alright. And when he comes in it's "Where's my dinner, why aren't my slippers being warmed by the fire?" and all that bit. While I would tend to go about my business. It's a double standard that's been in force since Adam and Eve. I joke about it, but at the time it's not funny at all.'

Most of their fights began with verbal disagreements which escalated into him being violent towards her: kicking her in the legs and chest and punching her to the face and head. He fractured her nose twice and she has a number of scars rendered with an iron bar on her arms and legs. At other times he would strike out suddenly over minor issues. Despite the severity of her injuries, Elsie partly blamed herself:

'I'm a very stubborn person, even now. I was partly to blame. But I don't think it was worth getting slapped in the mouth for it. I mean if it was that I'd done something wrong he could have said – "Elsie you shouldn't have done that," and that would have been it, I would have just said, "Yeah, alright then I'll do it different next time," you know? It could be that I'd put too much salt in the dinner. That to him was a major mistake and I got a punch in the mouth for it. Such little things – okay, I was wrong about it, you know, but I'm not a cook, and I don't think that not being able to cook should get you a slap in the mouth . . . I'm stubborn and he's stubborn, so I wouldn't give in, because I've been a single woman a long time before I met him, and like I moulded myself the way I like myself and I knew that. I told him before I moved in together that he was not going to like living with me.'

The situation got worse after the birth of their daughter, ostensibly because he was jealous of her. When asked what used to spark off these fights, Elsie responded:

> 'Money and sex. I mean I think he expected it to be like it was when we first met. Even though we were going through a bad patch. He still – he would like hit me at half past nine and at half past eleven when we were in bed he be all lovey and "Come on let's do it now", and I'd say "No", and he'd wonder – but why? What have I done? . . . He wasn't sorry for what he'd done, because he didn't believe he'd done anything.'

Elsie explained her suicide attempt as being due to her partner's violence:

> 'It was hurting me that much. I didn't want to give him the satisfaction of killing me, so I thought – well, I'd top myself. But it didn't work – I was unconscious and they tried to put this tube down my throat and I thought, "Oh God, I'm going to die here".'

On one occasion when he was trying to force her over the balcony, the neighbours heard Elsie's screams of 'Help – he's killing me' and called the police. While she did not have any family support, she had met a number of Mike's friends; indeed he had introduced her to a particular woman friend of his who he had hoped would teach her the runnings, as he put it. As his violence became more and more extreme, his friends attempted to intervene, expressing strong disapproval of his behaviour towards Elsie, so that he refused to have anything more to do with them. Eventually, despite repeated visits and appeals to the council, unable to find anywhere else to live and trapped in a clearly life-threatening situation, Elsie grew desperate and contacted the Samaritans for help. She was eventually referred to Women's Aid.

Case 5: Sarah   Sarah is twenty-seven and has an eight-year-old son. She had been in the refuge for nineteen months at the time of interview and there was still no sign of her being rehoused. She had been going out with Maurice for about three years when he arrived one day with his bags:

> 'He virtually just moved in. I mean we were going out, and one day a neighbour came and said: "Oh he wants you outside." And when I looked out of the window, he had taken all his things out of the car. He just moved in. We had been going out for about three years, but that didn't entitle him to move in automatically the way he did. But I didn't really say much. I just sort of asked him, you know, what was happening. He said he thought that was what I wanted . . . Apparently he shared a flat with another woman who had a child for him. They had apparently broken up, so I thought – you know – "What the heck?" She threw all his clothes out and then he came and said he thought it was what I wanted.'

Maurice was a self-employed decorator, while Sarah did full-time office work. Their relationship deteriorated after he had moved into her council flat.

'He started abusing me and being aggressive, you know. I mean he'd never done it before – he always said, "Oh I'll never hit a woman. I'll never hit a woman," and I always believed him. In all the three years I've known him he's never hit me before.'

They fought over 'silly things' – if she used the car (which was hers) when he wanted to, or being five minutes late to collect him, for example. This resulted in unexpected consequences:

'I went up the stairs to close the door and I just felt one punch on the back of my head. In my flat you go down as you enter the door, so I went flying down the stairs and crashed into the wall. He just started beating me and kicking and swearing – fucking this and fucking that. I couldn't understand it – that I was too out of order, that he don't know who I think I am and all this. Until I was knocked out unconscious. When I woke up I was so mad. I wanted to kill him, but because he was so big and tall I knew that if I hit him I was going to get twice the hit I gave him back. I thought I was due to die that day because Wayne [her son] was at his aunty's. It was just me and him in the flat. Wayne was gone for the weekend. I was just so mad – I started trembling, I couldn't stop myself, I couldn't control myself. I just started to shake and then he said, "Yeah, you fucking pretend you're sick, you go on and fucking pretend you're sick." And I said, "I want some water – can I have some water?" My lips just dried up and I was just trembling. He thought I was joking or something. Then he realized that I was genuinely shaking. I couldn't keep myself still. He ran to get the water and everything. And then they took me to the hospital – he took me to the hospital and everything – he lied to them and told them that I fell over and banged my head. I just told them that I didn't want him in there. He wouldn't leave because he knew that if he leaves me I would tell them.'

Assaults of this sort had longer-term effects on their relationship; not only was making up and saying sorry followed by other attacks, but the nature of their relationship changed:

'After he started being aggressive I suppose I became afraid of him. But I always pretended – I never showed him that I was afraid of him. If he said anything, I always said it back, and that – "I'm not frightened of you." "Not frightened of me? I'll give you fright," he'd say, and I'd be sitting there thinking, "Oh God, please don't let him hit me." He was always threatening before that incident . . . On the other occasion he didn't actually get to abuse me much because I jumped out of the window. I mean he would have killed me. He threatened and then slapped me in the face. I ran through the kitchen and locked the door and took the key. He ran round to come in through the front window, and I said to him you just put one foot through – he lifted his foot and I was over the balcony. I had on something skimpy, it was raining, I had nothing on my feet. Looked like a tramp. I didn't care – I just wanted to get away from him.'

Sarah explains his violence thus:

> 'I think he was insecure. He was jealous of the fact that – because I've always been independent, like now I'm a student and everything. I've been saving up money because I do people's hair at home and I charge them £50. I'd been saving up my money and I bought a car. He didn't like the fact that I always went out and got my things – whatever I wanted. He detested that you know – he always wanted me to have a baby for him. And I've always said no because I want my career first. "Fucking career" – he didn't like it. He did not like the fact, he just wanted me to be a slave to him. I don't know. He just seems really insecure.
>
> 'Things got worse as time went along. He just got over-possessive – he wanted me to be under his spell – at his beck and call sort of thing. I don't know why. I suppose because his parents – his mother always cooked for him and washed for him even though he was living with this other girl, he always went to his mother's for dinner. At Christmas everyone goes to his Mum's and she spoils them. And that's what he expected of me. Cook dinner every day and make sure it's no rubbish.'

Violence also had a negative effect on her son:

> 'He was hyperactive. I had to take him to a child psychiatrist because of all the ups and downs; it disturbed him a little bit. Maurice would shout and Wayne was frightened of him. He used to say things like – "I don't like Maurice because he hits my Mum," you know – things like that. Sometimes when he got violent Wayne would wet his bed. It was obvious that that is what it was. He was frightened for me. When we took him to the child psychiatrist, I didn't go in with him, and the things he told her – I couldn't believe it. At the time he was about five – I thought what does he know about this? He knows everything and it affects him. I cried when she told me that.'

Meanwhile, the mother of Maurice's first child had another baby for him, much to Sarah's distress, since he had denied that he was continuing to have relations with her. She explains why she put up with him for as long as she did under those circumstances thus: 'I don't know. I must have loved him.'

Case 6: Mary   Mary was interviewed at her council house in north London where she now lives with her three-year-old son. She has never stayed at a women's refuge. She is a thirty-two-year-old woman of Jamaican origin who had a strictly religious upbringing in her Pentecostal family. She entered the church and engaged in missionary work in the Caribbean, and describes herself as having had very little experience of life when she met the man she married. She did not live with him before they were married, and they settled in Hackney. Since they could not find anywhere to live, they were grateful to be offered the use of Neville's sister's council flat. At that stage the relationship was far from violent. It was:

'Great – wonderful! It really was. If he swore he used to apologize – it was always – "Oh I'm sorry!" I think it was because prior to that I had spent seven years in the church, so I was a total fool. He could see that, but I think that's the reason why he was so courteous and gentle – I think that had a lot to do with it. I jumped out of the church and into his arms!' [laughter].

After four years of highly sheltered married life, Mary found her life had ceased to have meaning for her. She left her husband and went to live in Belgium for two years while they got a divorce. When she returned from abroad, she was again homeless, all her family having returned to Jamaica some time previously. She stayed with her now ex-husband for the time being. While she had been away he had met someone else, whom he continued to see – an older woman who kept him supplied with the drugs that he had developed a dependency on.

'He wanted both of us – he didn't want to choose. So he'd be spending some of the time with her and some of the time with me.'

He went through violent mood changes and their relationship deteriorated again. On one occasion Neville took Mary's tape recorder to the other woman's house, and she angrily phoned him there. He returned and subjected her to her first serious assault:

'He came home, opened the door – I was in the kitchen and he just laid into me, left, right and centre. That was the very first time it had ever happened. I was in hospital for two days. I was traumatized and shocked. I had a lot of bruises – my eyes were out here, and I was just really lost. I was really dazed. My family had gone back to the West Indies. My mother had gone, my sister had gone – everybody had gone – I was completely alone. Well almost – I have a brother and sister here, but I couldn't really go to them – it was my younger sister and I don't think my older brother would have understood somehow. So I was alone – I did feel alone and more than that I felt ashamed, so I couldn't go to them. That was really bad. It was the shame more than anything. I couldn't understand it. I mean I had never experienced violence of that kind before. It had never happened – I've got five brothers and sisters – a large family – and I'd never known it to happen to them. I'd heard of violence, obviously, and as far as my father and mother – I'd never seen it. I'd never even met anybody who had experienced it. I think it was partly because I was in the church, and led a very sheltered life. I'd never expected it.'

After this painful experience, Mary reacted in a way not uncommon for isolated victims of domestic violence:

'When he realized where I was, where I'd gone, he turned up at 12.00 that night, but the nurse had told him to come and see me in the morning, and he came back the next day. After about three days, he was really contrite, he hadn't meant to do it and what have you. It sounds a really funny thing to say but, even though I knew what he had done, he was the only person I wanted comfort from. Do you understand what I mean? Although he'd put me in this position and what he'd done and what have you, he was the only person that I really wanted. I didn't feel to reject him. And I went back to him. And then I fell pregnant' [laugh].

It was after this that she discovered her partner to be a user of hard drugs, and their relationship continued to deteriorate.

'There were instances when we'd be in the car, and he'd just get into a rage – "Why don't they get out of the way!" – as if he wanted to kill everybody. Depending on his mood, I couldn't speak to him, without fear of being snapped at. He was on cocaine, and I think that had a lot to do with his violence towards me.'

In the end, and after further violence, even in her pregnant state, he agreed to move out. Since it had been his sister's flat however, he continued to visit and disturb her. All Mary's desperate attempts to be transferred by Hackney council failed.

Case 7: Yvonne Yvonne is twenty-five years old and has three children. Her ex-partner, Roland, is a British Rail engineer. They cohabited for a couple of years, somewhat intermittently, after he moved into her council flat with her.

'He'd say I'm stepping out of line. I'm getting too big for my boots, I must remember I'm only little and things like that . . . I never had any broken bones, but I've been swollen up and bruised, which is enough. He was just sick. I remember one time I ran away, down to his Dad's house, and he even beat up his Dad so he could come in and beat me. He phoned the police. But by the time the police came he said – "It's alright – he's calmed down now – it was a domestic affair, it's alright." '

The violent attacks to which Roland subjected Yvonne, particularly when he came out of prison after being remanded for other violent offences, were clearly life-threatening. She was rehoused twice by the local council, and spent long periods in reception centres. He found out the address of her second home before she had even moved into it, from the housing department. Yvonne has essentially been trying to escape from his violence for the last four years; this has included being attacked on the streets when he has spotted her. Their youngest son was born two days before Roland was taken into prison on remand for a different violent offence. Roland appears to have had some mental disturbance:

'About two days after Mikey was born he went into prison. When he came out he goes to me: "When did this take place? Where did this baby come from? It's not my baby." So I said to him: "During that space of time that you was in prison you forget I had a baby?" I said: "Obviously, as far as I know my two children got the same father, so if this one ain't yours, that one ain't yours." He told me that it's either his Dad's child because he's got his Dad's name, or his brother's child. And then he started to name untold amount of his friends – it could be any one of them, so I was supposed to have laid down with all of them.'

His hostile feeling towards their youngest child erupted in one of his violent attacks:

'He claims he never saw the water boiling. We were having an argument, I was in the kitchen making a bottle for Mikey. I'd just turned off the fire, and the water was still there bubbling and he come in and brought the argument from one room through into the kitchen, and picked up the water and flung it like that. I had Mikey in my arms, I had him in my hand. He didn't hold it over me – he held it over Mikey – like that [demonstrates] and the water splashed upon me, but I didn't get burned. Mikey got burned from his head right down to his chest. All they did was give him a six months' hospital order, and he kept running away, so he only served about three. After a while they said they didn't want him there no more . . . I phoned the ambulance – and I mean this is how stupid he was – he said to me I must tell them I was giving the baby a bath. Now stupid as some women are, they don't put a baby in the bath head first. When the ambulance men came they asked what had happened and that's what he told them. I never said anything in case he thump the ambulance man down and then thump me down afterwards. He wouldn't let go of the eldest one. He said I must go to the hospital with Mikey and get myself treated and Mikey treated and then come back. The ambulance man said, "It's alright love, I know what's happened," and he phoned the police on his radio thing.'

Perhaps the most alarming thing about Yvonne's case is the nature of intervention by the statutory agencies that were repeatedly involved in the case. Her experience highlights the complete lack of protection available to black women, even when their assailants have criminal convictions for violence and have been subject to psychiatric orders.

Domestic violence against women of Asian descent

Case 1: Sangita   Sangita is a twenty-two-year-old Ugandan-born woman who has a three-year-old son. Her family moved to Britain in 1971. She was married to her husband, a Kenyan-born twenty-eight-year-old, at the age of nineteen, after he had visited her family for about nine months. They lived with his mother for about a year until they were given a one-bedroom council flat. She describes her husband during the courtship:

'Before we got married he used to come around. We didn't go out, but we did sort of sit and chat. He was very shy. Very quiet. But he seemed a nice person. He never showed any signs that he'd be a violent person. Very quiet and shy.'

Three months after they had been married another side of his character emerged:

'Usually when he was drinking at pubs and all that, someone would say something to him and he'd hit – he'd blow his top. Or he didn't beat them up, he'd just get angry. With his brothers and sisters he didn't get violent – just get very angry . . . He hit my sister-in-law once because she was trying to protect me. And he hit his own Mum once, but that was because she was trying to protect me as well. He used to kick me, throw things at me. Kick me, punch me – he used to throw me about the room. He used to pull my hair to pieces . . . No broken bones, but I've had black eyes and I've got scars, loads of scars to prove, because he used to have quite long nails – he'd just grab hold of me and the skin would sort of come away . . . I always used to say if you want to hit me don't do it in front of the child because it would affect him. It has affected my son, but now he has calmed down a bit.'

Various, often trivial 'misdemeanours' sparked off violence:

'If he didn't like anything I was doing. If he didn't like the cooking – because he used to be a meat eater, if I made vegetables he'd just throw the pans everywhere – throw the food everywhere. If I didn't talk to his parents properly, his Mum properly. If I was talking to his sister – he didn't like that. If I went shopping without telling him. If I left the house. So I was just a prisoner in my own home. I wasn't allowed to go out anywhere.

'When I did refuse to have sex with him, he'd say to me – Are you sleeping with another person? You must be. He was so suspicious. He'd often say to me – You must be sleeping with other men. And he'd sort of force himself on me. Yes, it was very painful.'

Interventions by Sangita's female relatives on her behalf only exacerbated the situation.

'My sister-in-law used to tell me, you know – Go to the doctor. But I was too scared to go out of my own house, in case he caught me going anywhere. I just sort of locked myself in. But I did tell my health visitor once. At that point I was really breaking – cracking up you know.'

Sangita was then referred to a community centre that did not assist her in any way. Eventually it was her mother and sister who helped her to escape to an Asian refuge in another part of town.

Case 2: Smita Smita, now twenty-eight years old, has one daughter and is a community worker. She comes from a Pakistani Muslim family that settled in Britain in 1960. She was about to sit her O-levels when she was married:

I was about sixteen and he was about thirty years of age at the time, so I let my parents make the decision at the time. I think what they were looking for more than anything was that he had a good job – he was well settled and they thought I'd be looked after. That was all they were looking at – the material aspect of the marriage. I was very worried, but I didn't think I had a say. I think the way I was brought up was – I didn't have a choice. They were making the decision that they thought was right for me.'

She was subjected to her first assault the day after the marriage:

'Immediately after the marriage, because I'd offered my sister a drink. After the wedding she'd come to stay with me for a week. I'd offered her some orange juice and he said I didn't have the right to do that . . . It was bad from the start really. He was very oppressive, very authoritarian mannerisms. Thought he knew everything that was right for me, totally controlling. I was totally controlled and it was almost like living with one's father. I played a very menial role of cooking and cleaning and that's all. I wasn't asked anything and I didn't have any friends. I wasn't allowed friends actually. I had no contact with the outside world. Virtually a prisoner in my own home. It was a very sort of numb feeling – that one wasn't really living – a horrible existence. I was kept indoors and not allowed any opinion even – suddenly my life had changed from being a free, easygoing schoolgirl to one that was almost a prisoner. I didn't think it was my fault, all this – I hadn't done anything to deserve this.'

The violence was severe, including:

'Kicking, pushing, threats of using a knife. He pushed me against the radiator once – he would push me against hard objects. Punching and kicking. I actually ran out of the house and my nose was bleeding. Yes I did have injuries – head injuries. I stayed in hospital for about two weeks. After that I suffered depression, and had amnesia for a long time. Bouts of amnesia when I would forget things. I've been very depressed since it all. I used to get blackouts and just keep forgetting things. Frightening actually.

'When I was six months pregnant he pushed me down the stairs. And then he just wasn't around when I'd had the baby. There was no caring in him at all; there was no love, there was no care.

'When the baby was born, when she started crying too much he just put the pillow over her face. It was so awful to think that. In a way I was getting in his way. I mean the fact that he'd married me, now I was getting in the way of him having other relationships – just me being around wasn't nice for him. I don't think I can remember a time when he wasn't being abusive. We couldn't have a conversation because he didn't think I was worth having a conversation with – I was too stupid to have intelligence. He was always putting me down.

'There was another spell after that where I was beaten up on the street and he had beaten me up so violently that I again had a blackout and I was in hospital for about five or six weeks after that . . . He punched me and I fell against the concrete. I was very, very badly beaten up. No one helped me, everybody walked away. They didn't get involved. That was the first day of my breakdowns. After I had recovered from the physical injuries I just lost control and I had a nervous breakdown in hospital. I was transferred to a psychiatric ward.'

Smita was put into group therapy, which she found intimidating. Her family do not appear to have been much help. In fact her father had been violent to her own mother for years, so that domestic violence was probably a normal and accepted occurrence in their family relationships:

> 'I think they were angry because I'd ended up in the psychiatric hospital, because they had all the old myths. Suddenly I'd lost control of my life and I wasn't an able citizen any more. I wouldn't say they were supportive really.
>
> 'Although the marriage lasted for seven years we didn't really live together because he – his lifestyle meant that he stayed away mostly because he was having lots of affairs with other women and he had his own flat.'

When she went back to college after the birth of her daughter, his violence got worse. Prior to that she had courageously kept her books and tried to study for her O-levels in secret, a difficult thing to do in her mother-in-law's house. Smita then took a job to sustain herself and her daughter as well, since her wealthy husband had ceased to provide any income whatsoever. After she escaped to a women's refuge, the court awarded custody of their daughter to Smita's husband, ostensibly because he could provide a better home. She is still involved in the court battles around custody and divorce, five years later.

Case 3: Madina   Madina is twenty years old, of Bangladeshi origin, with an enthusiastic character that immediately endears her to people. She went to school and grew up in Tower Hamlets and was married five years ago when she was fifteen, to a Bangladeshi man who came to Britain from Kuwait to marry and settle here.

> 'I'm brought up here obviously, so I didn't want an arranged marriage but I had no choice. I was forced into the arranged marriage bit and well – that was that. But I thought I could cope with going along with my husband and with the idea of a housewife and whatever. I thought I could cope with it, but at the beginning . . . He sort of . . . I don't know how to explain it.
>
> 'He thought I was too Westernized. The violence started from the beginning. Every time I tried . . . I couldn't get myself to fall in love with him. Even though I pretended. I then tried to forget about that part of life and just be a complete housewife, but he . . . it just sort of . . . he used to see me in a peculiar way. He never acted to me as a husband – the way a husband should act. That's what I think anyway. Then after about two months of my marriage I just couldn't handle it any more. I wasn't happy! With the marriage, with my husband, with the way I was living. He didn't understand me, and I didn't understand him. I did understand him, but he didn't understand me. I left him and went to my Mum's after two or three months. I just left him because I couldn't cope with being depressed all the time. Four years of marriage and I was depressed every day of it. I was married for four years and that was four years of being depressed all the time.'

Madina's family persuaded her to return to her husband several times in those four years, although her mother was fairly supportive. She continued to try:

'I had Sima, my daughter, but day after day it was as if he never noticed I was there. He used to work. I was there for the cooking, the cleaning, the um – for his bedtime, to look after Sima – that was all I was there for. I didn't exist as a person. I felt so depressed sometimes . . . He used to pick on anything he saw I was doing, whether it was right, wrong, even if it was right he'd find something wrong with it. He used to just pick on it to find a way of starting an argument with me. So we were always arguing and through the arguments he used to sometimes hit me.

'I don't blame myself in any way, because – I mean I know I'm saying this – I'm defending myself, but he couldn't have asked for someone better. I did my role: I was a mother, I looked after the kid, I stayed at his house all the time. I was a complete housewife. A complete Indian housewife! Even though I've been brought up in this country, but he just couldn't accept that. I don't know why.

'He was so big-headed that he thought whatever he said and whatever he did was right, because he was my husband he had the right to hit me and abuse me and things like that . . . I was just an object for him.'

After Madina left him, her husband went to Bangladesh, making no attempt at reconciliation.

Case 4: Shireen   Shireen is the British-born daughter of a Pakistani Muslim family. She is nineteen and has a nine-month-old baby boy. She was married to a twenty-five-year-old man of similar background, just before her sixteenth birthday. She had planned to leave home at the earliest possible opportunity, having been subjected to violence and abuse at the hands of her father. Her mother had been coerced into being his second wife after an unwanted pregnancy, and had been forced out of the marital home by constant violence and abuse. Shireen's mother had to go to the police herself to try and stop her husband harassing her. So Shireen had borne the stigma of her mother's fate, and been raised by her father and his other wife. She had been promised to an older man, and when that fell through her father arranged her marriage and she was told of it a week before. Yet she looked forward to a way out of her miserable home life:

'I realized that I was going to be married and I thought, Wow! Brilliant! I'm going to break out of this vicious circle. When I got talking to my husband and had a nice relationship I thought it was fantastic. So I was really happy about it when I got married. But bit by bit their true colours started to come out.'

Shireen found her in-laws strict and begrudging towards her. There was a great deal of violence in the family, and it emerged that her husband had spent seven months in prison, out of a fourteen-month sentence for GBH. She discovered her husband to be having affairs, taking drugs, drinking and gambling. His violence started while his parents were in Pakistan:

'First it was once or twice a month. He was a part-time boxer and he's six foot six. I am not exaggerating; he's really fit to look at him – he's really handsome, proper –

what a girl would want in a man. He beat me up and he used to do weight training at home. He used to lift the whole weight up in one hand and put the punch bag in the middle of the room and box that. Then when he used to hit me, it wasn't as if he was hitting a fragile woman. Women are fragile – it's not as if it were man to man. He used to really lay into me, punch me about. He would hit like a man to a man. Punch me – really get the punch out as if he was in the boxing ring. I got beaten up so badly that he broke my nose. Blood clots and long strings of blood – the whole works.'

Shireen got no support from her own family. Rather she was further humiliated:

'My father used to stick up for my husband. He used to stand up for him and I always used to be in the wrong. The last time I saw my Dad he made me cry. He insulted me in front of the whole family, in-laws too. Then they thought, well, if she's nothing in her father's eyes, then she's got no respect, no status. Then they started, you see. If my Dad had shown a bit of respect in front of them, it wouldn't have been that bad. Fair enough a father should tell his daughter off, but it could be done between us and I wouldn't have bothered. He could have said anything – he could have beaten me up or anything, but as long as it was done in private.'

Shireen was subjected to quite extreme violence, and lost her first pregnancy. It was therefore her second pregnancy that resulted in the birth of her son:

'When my son was born, my husband turned round to me and said to me, listen – I've got what I wanted out of you and that was a son. After that that was it. There was nothing to our sex life and he had other women.'

On one occasion her husband dragged her down the stairs to throw her out of the house while she still had stitches in from a miscarriage brought on by the violence. Her father-in-law accused her of aborting herself after she lost that baby. The neighbours called the police on several occasions. Shireen was driven to desperate actions:

'My husband beat me up so bad on one occasion that I was in the kitchen and as he went out there was a glass bottle and I smashed it on the sink and started jabbing it in my arm. He got the bottle off me and took me to hospital and I had bandages. I couldn't look after my son so I left him at my mother's. She asked me what had happened to me and I said I fell over on the floor.'

One day, after a fight with her mother-in-law, followed by her husband punching her in her bed that night, Shireen took her son and escaped. She has changed her name and plans to raise her son lovingly, and to study to become a lawyer.

Case 5: Sunita   Sunita is a British-born Indian woman who grew up in a suburban home. She was married to a man of similar background, in what

turned out to be an attempt by his family to extricate him from a relationship
with an older married Indian woman.

> 'He was in love with her before we were married, and then he was okay with me for
> a month. And then he became so distant. He just completely changed. At first he
> was loving and caring and would always consider me in everything. Then he just
> became distant and he would never be at home. If I wanted to talk to him he'd never
> be there. I was always just left with the in-laws, and he'd be away with this other
> woman. They have another house, which is my husband's . . . My husband told me
> himself that he had this woman and he loved her and he could never give her up.
> He was saying that he can't leave her and he wasn't going to leave me either. I'd
> have to stay at home – you know – stay there as I was doing.'

After two and a half years, Sunita left, with the help of a social worker. She has
not had any family support throughout her sad marriage:

> 'My parents are very upset about it. They keep sending letters through my social
> workers and telling me to come home because it's their reputation at stake. All they
> keep saying is "don't change". But I gave them all that time before for them to do
> something. I told them what I was going through. They said that they can't do
> anything. And now I've made a step, all of a sudden they're caring and want me
> back. I know my Mum cares a lot about what people say. She's just worried – what
> can she say to people, and back home in India what is she going to say? It's their
> reputation – that's all they're worried about.'

Her husband for his part has received the divorce petition:

> 'He just keeps saying that I'll end up being a slag, being used by men. That I'll end
> up being a very lonely person. He tells me to come home now, while both families
> want you. Later on in life nobody will want you and you'll be very lonely . . . I've
> told him he's a free man now – he can bring her home and she can look after his
> parents and be a daughter-in-law and bring their children up. He said I was just
> acting like an English person now. He thinks that men should do that. He goes,
> "You think what I'm doing is bad. Loads of men do worse than that. People hit their
> wives. I've never hit you." He thinks what he was doing to me wasn't bad.'

Case 6: Hamza   Hamza is a Kenyan-born woman of Punjabi Sikh origin who
fell in love with and married a Kenyan-born man of Punjabi Hindu origin.
Her family were unhappy about the marriage because her husband's previous
marriage had broken down. He became extremely over-possessive and
violent immediately after they had married.

> 'Right from the first day of marriage, he became so possessive suddenly. Very, very
> possessive. He just wanted to control me completely; he didn't want me to have any
> friends, he was jealous of everyone I knew or associated with. He didn't want me to

wear this, that and the other. He completely changed. He kept saying "Now you're married, so you have to do this, now you're married you must not do that". I was shattered by all this experience, and I couldn't just go back to my parents because I was unhappy, they would just have said "We told you so!" I was completely in a daze. I just didn't know what to do . . . The first time he hit me was a week after the marriage.'

He wanted her to abandon her teaching job and stay in the house, although financially this was not a realistic option, and beat her for insisting that it was necessary that she continue working. In any case she was soon grateful that she had some life outside her unhappy marital situation. She left him several times because of the violence, but did not wish to be a burden to her own family.

'Every time there was a fight because he wanted me to leave my job. I said "No", because I knew we couldn't really survive without my income. I used to have bruises, but nothing that would really bleed – no cuts. But I would have lots of marks. Gradually as time passed he realized that if I was beaten on the face it left marks and then I had to pretend I was sick. So I couldn't go to school and that created a lot of complications because my mother would come to visit me also. When he realized this, he started hitting me on my head and back, where it wouldn't be really seen.'

In 1982 they sold up and moved to Britain, where they bought a house jointly. Hamza hoped that they would have a fresh start. Unhappily, things only got worse, and she was now completely isolated.

'When he used to hit me it wasn't because we didn't have a good sexual relationship, but he used to complain many times that I was not – that I was frigid, he would say. I guess I couldn't respond ever because of the way he used to treat me . . . He would hit me at any time. It didn't bother him that I was pregnant. In fact he hit me with a stick once, when I was eight months pregnant with my first baby. I lost that baby anyway . . . I don't know whether it had anything to do with the beating, but . . . it was born a bit early – four weeks – and didn't have a lung, so it died.'

In England, both of them were at home all day, since she never got a job in Britain, and her husband was self-employed. Hamza eventually found the strength within herself to take her children and leave her husband. She went into a refuge. She had been there for well over a year at the time of interview, with no prospect of being rehoused by her local authority, since they are awaiting the outcome of her divorce settlement.

Case 7: Georgina   Georgina is of Malaysian-Chinese mixed origin. She has a five-year-old daughter and works for a local authority, having escaped from a violent husband and gradually rebuilt her life in the ten years since their marriage. She had known her Nigerian student partner for one year, then they cohabited in a council bedsit for a year and then married and they moved into a one-bedroom Camden council flat. Ten months after they were married, he became verbally abusive and threatening, and then subjected her to serious assaults on three occasions.

'The final attack came when I was four or five months pregnant. I remember I was asleep – he was out as usual – out all day and all night. The next thing I knew someone just dragged me onto the floor and kicked and punched me, and then all this verbal abuse while he was doing it. I was so shocked. Because I was asleep at the time it was like a nightmare. I wasn't sure it was really happening. But it was – I felt the pain and everything. I remember saying, "Don't come near me, right?" I remember grabbing a badminton racket and saying, "If you come near me I will hit you." The next thing I knew was that he had overpowered me and took it from me. Then I was hit right down on my head. I had a cut on my forehead and I've a scar on my chin here. The next day I didn't go to work or anything. I was sort of at home. And then I started to bleed heavily. The doorbell rang, and when I went to the door it was his best friend. When I opened the door and he saw me, he just freaked out, and I remember him going to call an ambulance. He said, "I'm going after him, but before that I have to go with you to hospital." I went to hospital and had a miscarriage.'

Violence had other, longer-term effects on her as well as the immediate and traumatizing damage she suffered.

'My whole personality had changed from that violence. For two years I withdrew myself completely . . . I became isolated and kept away from everybody and everything. I was like a robot. I suffered from a lot of headaches.'

On being discharged from the hospital after her miscarriage, Georgina went to all the various statutory agencies for help, but was turned away unhelpfully, and was often even more upset as a result of their treatment. Her husband continued to be violent towards her until she found a particularly original way of handling the situation, with the help of her workmates and friends.[4]

Case 8: Sui Wong   Sui Wong is a thirty-seven-year-old woman of Cantonese birth who has three teenage children. She was married for eighteen years to her husband who is now sixty-one years old and worked in a takeaway restaurant while they were married. He became violent soon after the birth of their first child. Sui's husband turned out to be an alcoholic, and when drunk became verbally and sexually abusive and, like many alcoholics, incontinent. Being a traditional Chinese woman, she lived with this for years, and was very reluctant to confide the extent of the horror she was living to family members. Indeed, her attempts to find a way out of her situation were largely in vain. She speaks very little English and could not afford the fees that a

Chinese solicitor demanded from her when she enquired how to file for a divorce. She started doing piecework at home to try and establish some economic security for herself and her children.

In sober moments, her husband denied all his terrible behaviour completely; even when she left the evidence for him to see, he merely accused someone else of making the mess. She received little family support: 'They all know that he has a drinking problem, but they think the men are like that. That she ought to accept it. They find it acceptable.'

Eventually, after eighteen years of misery, during which she grew to thoroughly despise her husband, Sui heard of the Chinese Information and Advice Centre. She contacted them and was advised. She is now divorced and lives in a bed and breakfast with her children, as another homeless single-parent family. She still has no family support: 'They used to think she was wonderful to cope with it, but they look down on her now that she's divorced.'

Her husband won access rights to the children in court and visits every week. Sui says she hates him and wishes she could never see him again. [Interview conducted through translator in Cantonese.]

Case 9: Shuwei   Shuwei is a thirty-year-old medical doctor who specialized in acupuncture. She originated from Shanghai. She married a man of Malaysian-Chinese origin who was also an acupuncturist and they bought a house in his name and set up in private practice together. One month after their marriage, he became violent. All the money from their work went into her husband's account, and she was kept without money most of the time. Worse still her husband often did not bother to work.

Shuwei worked at acupuncture during the day, and in a restaurant at night to try and keep things going. She also did all the household chores, while her husband watched TV and periodically assaulted her. When she became pregnant and stopped the restaurant work, her husband insisted that she have an abortion, as he did not want any children.

She describes feeling sick every day from being hit in the head and throat. After six months of this treatment, Shuwei was hospitalized with broken ribs. All her resources, and all that she had worked for were in his control. When she got home from the hospital, her husband asked her why she had come back and not died. Shuwei left, so beginning an alienating ordeal of staying in hostels and refuges, disadvantaged by her limited use of English. It was only after months of homelessness spent in racist and unsuitable temporary accommodation that she was able to find herself another job which, fortunately in the circumstances, had tied accommodation.

Case 10: Su Chang   Su Chang comes from a middle-class Chinese family and was going out with a fellow student of the same age from Hong Kong for about six months before she agreed to marry him, in secret, and against both

of their families' wishes. As a result for the first seven months of their
marriage they did not actually live together, until Su told her parents she was
going to live with four other Chinese girls, and moved in with her husband.

'Before we got married he was extremely nice, extremely understanding, extremely
mild-tempered. The things that he didn't like about me, came out after the
marriage. Yet I was the same person before and after the marriage. Our problems
were things that he had said he didn't mind. For example I smoke and he knew that
I smoked before the marriage – he said, "Of course girls can smoke, why can't girls
smoke – it's fine." But after the marriage it was a case of – "My wife can't smoke,
but girls can smoke." He had seemed very open-minded and liberated about
everything. He never expressed anything in particular that was different from my
own opinion. He was easygoing, very generous and very humorous as well. I'd been
very honest with him about the things I had done in the past. I went out with a
number of guys, and he went out with a number of people as well. We actually
joked about the people we went out with. I didn't know at the time that he would
remember everything I said about my previous boyfriends. He became an
extremely possessive and very jealous person. I wasn't aware of that before because
he had said that he didn't mind that I'd been out with people before. He didn't
mind anything in particular. I didn't think I'd done anything wrong. Nothing out of
the ordinary for girls over here as far as I know. Then after we got married, things
started. If we were arguing about anything he would start quoting examples –
"Why did you do this in the past, why didn't you do that?" And then he would
insinuate that I was cheap to have slept with people, although I stress that I only
slept with people that I felt for. I don't sleep around, you know – for the sake of it.'

Her husband's jealousy grew worse as time went by:

'He started minding me going out with my friends. Especially ex-boyfriends. Some
of them I still know as friends. He disliked them so much that it got to the point
where I couldn't see them. If I made arrangements to see them he would make it
very difficult when I got back. He would question this and question that. He was
quite rude when he saw me with any of my friends. It got to the point where I
avoided going out with my friends, and I hated bumping into people in front of him,
because he can be very abusive as well.'

He used the fact that she had confided in, indeed married, him as well as
physical beatings to try and exercise this type of control:

'I thought of leaving him actually, quite early on in the marriage. I threatened a lot
to go for divorce. At the same time he would threaten me with going to my parents,
and telling them that I smoke – my parents didn't know that I smoke. And that I was
married to him, and the fact that I had had an abortion as well. But that was because
of him – it wasn't with someone else – it was with him. All these things that Chinese
parents just couldn't take. My Dad has always been a very tough person to get
around, and I've always been frightened of him because of his temper. I just

couldn't face the consequences of my husband telling them everything that I did in the past. It was blackmail. As a result of that I gave up my friends, I gave up going out with the people that I used to know – they were all people that he knew. They all come from overseas and – especially the blokes – they've got very male chauvinistic attitudes.

'I was smoking behind his back when he was away, thinking he wouldn't know. When he came back from Hong Kong he said: "Have you been smoking in the summer?" I said, "No." He asked: "Are you sure you haven't?" And that's when I started to think, "Oh my God – he's found out." And then he said: "You've lied to me! You have smoked." And then he slapped me. He slapped me so hard he sent me flying across to the other end of the room. He pushed me around and swore at me, said that I'm cheap, I'm a prostitute, I'm all sorts of things under the sun, you know? – How could I be with someone who doesn't even earn my trust? And for two days he made my life hell. For some reason I was extremely submissive to him. I was just so scared of him going to my parents.

'He just couldn't get it out of his system, that I'd been out with guys, that I'd slept with guys – he couldn't forgive me. Especially this guy who I had been out with who was still a friend. I don't know why, but for some reason he kept on thinking that I would be unfaithful to him. If I made a comment about someone on the TV – even how ugly they were – he would get so mad that he would start throwing the furniture around the house, breaking my china ornaments and things like that, just causing a complete mess.

'At one time, before we moved, we lived in this grotty place near Bethnal Green. It was a really awful place, really dark, very scary. I'm just scared – so scared of being on my own and he knew that so whenever we had a fight he would take the car and go off to stay with any of his friends, in the middle of the night and not come back for two days. Until I eventually phoned him, to beg him to come back. Going through the night on my own was the most frightening thing for me. I would have all the lights on in the house. Cry myself silly until I was eventually so tired I was too exhausted to do anything but fall asleep. Then the next night it would be the same thing again. Until I couldn't tolerate it. Then I'd phone him and literally beg him to come back – I'd say it was all my fault, everything was my fault, I shouldn't have done this or that. It was a vicious circle.'

Su explains why she stayed in such a destructive relationship for as long as she did, beyond the blackmail already mentioned:

'I think I did actually believe time and time again that he would change when he cried and apologized. I thought about him every time, because he seemed so lost and helpless. I just didn't have the heart to tell him "No, I'm not going to give you another chance", when he was in such a state. He even tried to commit suicide, when I really threatened to leave him once. He's driven me to several suicide attempts.'

One day, in a fit of pique, because Su was visiting her family, he marched into the house:

'He's just walked through the door and said to my Mum: "Did you know your daughter's married to me? Did you know she smoked and did you know she's sleeping around like a prostitute as well?" – you know – just one after the other, he just completely bombarded my Mum with it all. She was so shocked she burst out crying. She looked at me and said, "Will you tell me this person is lying to me?" I looked at her and I couldn't. I didn't know what to say. I wanted to die that minute.'

So ended the marriage. In the end Su was reconciled with her family and got a divorce, living with the terror of threatened underworld reprisals against her and her family on the one hand, and hardening her heart to her husband's pleas on the other. She suffered acute damage to her self-esteem as a result of her experiences:

'For a long time after my marriage I thought I would never go out with anyone again. I didn't think anyone else would want me.'

Case 11: Linda   Linda is a thirty-one-year-old Filipino woman with a two-year-old son. She met her English husband while she was working for a cosmetics company in the Middle East. They went out together for about eight months, and then he returned to England but they kept in touch by post:

'We went out together – to dinner parties. He's a very nice man. I think that's why I fell for him. He is very gentle, very kind, very romantic.'

This 'gentleman' sent for her to join him in England and they were married. Within two months of marriage things changed drastically:

'When he's drunk he gets violent, even over just a small thing. Like he says he doesn't want me to wear jeans. Or use any word of American – like "kids". I mustn't say kids I must say children. And he is very jealous, for no reason. He's older than me – he's fifty-something.

'The first time he beat me we were in America. He took a job for two years and we were staying in a hotel. We were just having a drink after working with some of his colleagues, and I was talking to one of the blokes and he didn't like that. When we got to our room he started calling me names and beating me and all. I tried to run away, but he found me in the station.

'Whenever he comes home I feel edgy, like maybe he'll start again. Every time I say something, he'll say no, that's not right. He thinks I'm stupid or dumb, I don't know anything. He's always trying to teach me. You won't believe that he even tried to teach me to operate the cooker. How to put the bed sheets on the bed and all that. I couldn't believe it.

'I don't think he trusts me. He's very insecure. Every time I go out he is with me. I can't even go out on my own – even to the butcher, or to go for my check-up. After we came to London we confirmed that I was pregnant and we were both happy. I thought things will change. I should give it a try. When I went for my check-up he came with me, right inside the surgery. After that he had a bit of drink and then start an argument, calls me names and I just ignored him. I was so depressed. I thought, "My God, is this what marriage is all about?" I wanted to run away but I don't know how. I don't know anybody here and I got no money.'

It was the beating she received in her third month of pregnancy that drove Linda to run away:

'I had the beating and then he threw me out of the house. He said he doesn't want me any more. He calls me all the names that you can think of . . . I had a few punches all over the place and he kept hitting my head against the wall, so I packed my things and left. I stood outside the door. I didn't know what to do. Hoping he would call me. He did call me back. Took my suitcase into the bedroom and apologized. He swore to me that he would never touch drink any more. He won't beat me again. So I believed him. But that was only for one day. The next day he was good. And then the next day again he started beating me. He came home drunk while I was cooking. I nearly burned my cooking. He kept calling me in the sitting room. I was very scared. I didn't answer because if I answered, whether I was right or wrong, I was still wrong. So I thought not to cause any argument I would keep quiet. But then he gets angry if I don't answer. I just kept moving away from him, that's all. And I was shaking. He punched me in my tummy. I was already three months pregnant at the time. I thought I will lose the baby. He threw me out of the house. I didn't want to move. He said, "Get out, I don't want you any more you whore." So he grabbed me by the shoulder and threw me out of the house. So I stood outside the door, and he came out and pushed me. He pushed me four times, until I reached the main road. The fourth time he pushed me I fell over and I had some bruises on my knee, and my wrists were bleeding. I was praying that one of the neighbours would come, and at least he would stop. But none of them came. I was just running on the road, shouting for help. None of the people helped – they just stare at me. He was running after me as well, but I was running faster than him because he was drunk and he was unsteady. I got to the crossing and I saw this police car coming. I stood in the middle of the road and shouted "Help! Help!" And heard the screech of the car.'

Linda got little sympathy at the police station, but so began the long process of seeking a home for herself and her future child.

Domestic violence against African women

Case 1: Mabel   Mabel is a thirty-three-year-old Ghanaian with two children; a five-year-old son and a four-year-old daughter. She ran her own small business and lived in a council flat and has lived in London since 1974. Nine years ago she met Kofi, a Ghanaian tailor, who shared her strong Christian faith, and after two years they were married. She attributes some of their problems to his family:

'They didn't seem to get on with me. They interfered a lot, and I won't take that. I don't want anybody to tell me what I have to do in my own home and things like that. Kofi was pressurized by the family: they said I was having a good time, taking the money from him or whatever. I don't know what they were thinking of, because I always worked hard. Yes, most of the time I provided everything. And I didn't really demand of him. But because of the way they see me – I love to look good, that's me. So when they see me dressing up well, they think that it's from him.'

Her husband's violence was irregular:

'One week he's alright, and then the next he's like a monster. It was on and off for about ten months.'

At other times he was:

'a very nice man. A very nice father. He is wonderful. He really cares for his children. But when the monster comes, you know . . . Then he'd cry. Whatever he did, he'd start crying and asking – "Why did I do it?" – talking to the little boy as if he was a big man and all that . . . He is a believer, a Christian, and he didn't believe in psychiatrists or whatever they call them. He always believed in – well – we do have demon spirits anyway, so that could come in. Like those were behind everything. As far as I'm concerned, because he can be as nice as anybody and can be as nasty as a monster.

'He would break down, he would kiss my feet like Jesus did and he would quote from the Bible – "The Bible says this, the Bible says that." But yet he'd do it again. I mean what can you do? "How long would that go on?" I always asked him, "How long?" '

They turned to the church and to prayer, but to no avail. Instead Kofi went on to inflict quite serious injuries to her, and she saw the effect this was having on her children:

'I had to go to hospital for head X-ray. And I was taking tablets for migraines. He left me with bruises almost everywhere, bite marks and all that.

'I didn't want my children to see us fighting all the time. It got to a time that whenever the two of us sat down to talk, my little girl, Suzie – at that stage she was only a year old – she would come and stand in front of us and sort of look at Mummy, look at Daddy . . . and the little boy, especially, when he was about four years old would start and shout – "Don't shout at Mummy, Daddy, stop talking to Mummy, go away! Don't fight Mummy, you want to kill my Mummy!" I really felt sorry for my son because I didn't want him to grow up and have that kind of thing in his mind at all – that one time my Daddy wanted to kill my Mum, or that he was beating Mum all the time. Otherwise he would probably – God forbid – grow up and behave like that. I just couldn't allow that to happen at all.'

Mabel persuaded her husband to move out, but could get no peace from him. Eventually she abandoned her flat and her business and went into a women's refuge, where she was staying when we interviewed her.

Case 2: Iyamide   Iyamide was brought over to England by her husband in 1977. He was much older than her, but she had known of him in her community for years. Since living in London she continued her career as a nurse, while he worked in a large department store. They lived in a house they rented from their local authority, once they had the children. Their relationship deteriorated from the time he brought her to England:

> 'You know African men – when they've brought you here, they think that you are a slave. Especially when they are older than you. They want to make their power over you.'

Her husband, a teetotaller himself, took exception to her drinking an occasional glass of wine. She found herself alone, without friends or relatives in this country. Her husband worked and they had no social life at all:

> 'We go to work during the day. Then he goes to bed. I have nobody to talk to. We have no social life. It was a miserable life actually. Even if he came to sit down, he'd be over there sleeping. Since I have joined him, we can't go out. He goes to work, comes and lies down and sleeps.'

On the other hand:

> 'If I introduce any friends to him, he would be after them. After I went back home to visit, one of my friends who used to come – we used to be very close – she just cut off. When I asked her what was wrong, what have I done? She said to me – "Iyamide, you are very good to me, but all the time your husband is harassing me to make love to him."
> 'I had three children for him, and the way he insults me! I can never stand it. Each time I think about it I don't want to make love to him.'

She was beaten and kicked repeatedly, on one occasion until:

> 'My eyes were bleeding. When he saw my eyes were bleeding, saw the blood, he called the ambulance. By the time the ambulance had come, he had washed everything, cleaned the whole corridor. He didn't want the people to see that. When the doctor attended me he asked if my husband did this – because of the way they saw my eye full of blood. I went back because of the children. Since 1980 I was staying because of the children. They love him so much.'

Iyamide had to go to hospital three or four times, where she had X-rays. Her vision has been permanently damaged by repeated blows to her eyes and head.

> 'When the youngest baby was born he beat me. He tried to strangle me. My voice all went. I couldn't even talk. He was on top of me, holding my neck like this

[demonstrates]. After that I just tried to hold on to something and I banged him on the head. Otherwise he would have finished me that day. From that time until today we never made love.'

Iyamide left her husband shortly after this. I heard her disturbing account of what happened to her after that in what the council call 'temporary accommodation'.

Case 3: Patience   Patience is a Nigerian store manageress who has been in a relationship with Ransome for nine years. They have a young son and got married a year and a half ago. She has left him many times because of his cruelty to her and their child.

'Last Easter he took me and stripped me in front of his friends. He was beating me, punching me and pushing me about. I had come in from the kitchen because I heard him saying some nasty things in front of his friends, trying to be funny by making fun of me. So I came out from the kitchen and I told him he would regret the things he was doing. As I was going out he started rough-handling me – shouting and pushing me. As he was doing all that my zip had come down, and my breast was coming out – I didn't even notice – I was busy trying to restrain things so as not to display anything to those people. He started slapping my breast and shouting "Cover yourself!" All in front of his friend and the wife, while they were looking on.'

Ransome has been consistently unfaithful to Patience. Probably partly because she grew up in a polygamous home herself, what disturbs her most is his degrading behaviour towards her and his taste for pornography. When she leaves, he begs and cajoles her to come back.

'He hasn't spent long in Nigeria. His Dad is here and he's spent most of his years in this country, yet he says to me "Our tradition is that women should live with their men". He is not serious!'

She has been subjected to pressure from elders in her family (all men) who are concerned that she should have all her children with the one husband. For her own part she does not feel it would be in her interests to get a divorce from her student husband because as she put it, 'I have worked hard for him.' Custody or maintenance rulings in British courts would be of no use to her when they return to Nigeria, where (in her community) taking legal action against one's husband is not an acceptable way of solving marital problems. Her own friends have tired of advising her to permanently leave Ransome. Patience has been multiply abused; not only has her husband injured her on numerous occasions, but on one occasion when neighbours called the police to intervene, they took the opportunity to arrest her and subject her to racially and sexually humiliating ridicule and then assaulted her at the police station.

Discussion

The case material presented here illustrates the enormous diversity in the manifestation of domestic violence. Culture, material circumstances such as bad housing and economic stresses, drug abuse, childhood relational experiences, sexual insecurities and jealousies, deep mistrust and suspicion, misogynistic attitudes, and lack of communication are just some of the recurring themes of the material. These factors are not specific to domestic violence between black people, since very similar themes recur in European and American literature on the subject (Dobash and Dobash 1979, Yllo and Bograd 1988, Women's Aid Federation England 1988). Orthodox clinical approaches to 'family violence' tend to treat social and economic factors as 'confounding variables' rather than as variables that should be integrated into the analysis of domestic violence (Bolton and Bolton 1987). Yet social and economic factors constantly appear in women's accounts of their partners' violence towards them as rationalizations and reasons given, as women struggle to comprehend their partners' behaviour.

Preliminary research indicated that in the present housing climate, relationship breakdown was seldom grounds for rehousing by local authorities. Where there were written policies on relationship breakdown, these were not being implemented at a time when only homeless persons were being housed in many boroughs. In any case, in terms of local authority rehousing practices and policies, domestic violence is often treated as an extreme instance of relationship breakdown.

Many women would not have been condemned to tolerate violence if there had been any possibility of one or other of the couple securing alternative housing in the earlier stages of relationship breakdown. The high incidence of black male and female homelessness resulted in many couples living together more through lack of options than through choice. Since single men have no access to public housing at all, black male homelessness can be seen in a number of cases to have been a major factor in determining the decision to cohabit in the first place. In this context the nature of relationships themselves is affected. Sometimes men had simply moved in with black women who had local authority tenancies. Many of these had previously been staying with other women or their mothers on a semi-permanent basis and had never had tenancies of their own. As such they would constitute part of the 'hidden homeless' population that has no statutory right to housing. Local authorities (in theory at least) are statutorily obliged to house people who have dependent children living with them, so that parents (who do have their children living with them) have a means of gaining entry to public sector housing that is not open to women or men whose children are not living with them.[5] When relationships deteriorated, men in these living arrangements not only became violent, but quite often also refused to leave, so forcing mothers and children out of their local authority accommodation to join the long queues awaiting housing in hostels, reception centres and refuges.

The degree to which violence against women in their homes is tolerated in Britain has long been condemned by the women's movement here, but this has largely been from a Eurocentric feminist perspective. The class, race and cultural dynamics of agency responses to domestic violence have been grossly neglected by feminists, except for the more vociferous Asian women's organizations (such as Southall Black Sisters). Regarding women of African and Caribbean origin, community groups have focused on police brutality, rather than the more sensitive issue of woman abuse. Police brutality is less of a contentious topic within the black communities because it is an oppression delivered by the 'Other' – in this case the state. Woman abuse remains a shameful and buried phenomenon, only made worse by its private nature. This privatization protects the abuser and facilitates further violence. The collusive silence around the issue has the effect of limiting the options that abused women have. Seeking help from the authorities is often regarded as an act of betrayal and several women in the sample who had been forced to seek police assistance as a result of serious violence, now live under threat of death for doing so. Black women are expected to bear their beatings (as if these too were not a betrayal of humanity), and actually to understand that they are a result of the black man's oppression. Yet, as many survivors have pointed out, being beaten by the man one has taken as a sexual and emotional partner is itself a crude and degrading form of oppression.

In October 1988 a black community meeting, entitled 'Violence within the System' (and billed as the first ever), was held on domestic violence. During this meeting participants exhibited something of a consensual understanding that black men beat black women because they themselves are brutalized by state repression. While it is commendable that such a meeting was held and that discussions took place with seriousness, this kind of analysis can feed into the collective abdication of individual responsibility for brutal and anti-social behaviours. However, many people in the black communities recognize that it is now time to seriously address the problem of violence against black women in Britain, so that more organized collective responses can be developed.

Our findings demonstrate that high levels of violence and cruelty to women by the men they are or have been in relationships with, are being tolerated, by the communities themselves, as well as by statutory organizations. They also indicate clearly that domestic violence occurs in all the cultural and religious groups we investigated. The fact that this practice may have culturally specific content is also evident in women's accounts. In the examples above we saw Muslim and Rastafarian men using religion to assert their patriarchal authority and misogyny.

Women also often referred to tradition, but in their case it was usually to describe how they had tried to conform – to become the ideal wife – only to find that nothing they said or did satisfied their spouse, or stopped the violence. While women of Caribbean origin referred less explicitly to established orthodoxies, it was clear that the men they were involved with often held quite unrealistic expectations about how 'their' women should behave and conduct themselves, and often felt they had a right to use violence to enforce these. Women (who may well have been born and brought up in Britain as Madina was) were often criticized and beaten for the 'crime' of being 'too Western', sometimes by men who had also been brought up in Britain. Some of these husbands, like Smita's, continued to have sexual relationships with English women throughout their marriage (presumably to meet their own 'Western' desires).

Others did not refer to religion or tradition, but simply held and tried to enforce expectations that the women found to be oppressive and unrealistic, for example not being allowed to have friends or go out, being expected to stay at home and cook (even when this was not economically feasible as in Hamza's case) and anger over the women's cooking (as Elsie described).

There were Asian women who had both arranged and 'love' marriages.[6] Contrary to what racist discourse would suggest, there was nothing to suggest that either form of marriage was less violent. What did emerge was that when a woman had married a partner of her own choosing, she had less access to family support if her choice contradicted her own family's wishes. Having made an individual choice, she also had to cope with the consequences of that choice on her own, so that such women sometimes found themselves in a more isolated and vulnerable position than they might otherwise have been. In other words it is not whether the marriage is arranged or not, but the woman's family's attitude to that marriage which affects how much support she will get.

For others, conforming had not meant exemption or protection from abuse, and often (as in Smita's case), respectability, and their daughter being suitably married meant more to her family than her safety or well-being. Many different cultural and relational factors can therefore prevent a woman's family from giving her any support after marriage. In Smita's case, her family's conformity and the fact that her mother had also been abused by her father meant that she got no support. In Shireen's case, the fact that she was the daughter of an abused first wife meant that she was held in contempt and beaten in her family home, so that her own family's behaviour towards her only worsened her situation after her arranged marriage to a sadistic man. In other words culture or 'tradition' comes into play through interpersonal (familial) relational dynamics, as well as through male assertions of power and urges to dominate.

Within the communities, extended families sometimes intervened posit- ively, although on some occasions, they did not feel able to intervene (for example where the woman's father was dead or absent). In other instances the woman's own relatives made the situation worse (as in Shireen's case).

In some cases (women of Asian and African origin in this study), migration had meant being isolated from family and community support, so that violence reached dangerous levels. For example in Iyamide's case, violence began when her husband brought her over to England.

In-laws were often involved in exacerbating the conflict (as in Mabel's case where they were jealous of her and wanted greater access to her husband's income), and sometimes as perpetrators of violence themselves, so that some young wives were multiply abused. In Elsie's case, her cohabitee's doting mother used to watch indifferent, so perhaps giving tacit approval, while her son assaulted 'his' woman. Several of the Asian women living with their in- laws had been married to men who had no interest in them and continued to pursue their relationships with other women. As traditional wives, these women were expected to live in the family home to serve their in-laws and husband (when he appeared). Smita's wealthy husband actually kept a flat of his own where he continued to live as a bachelor, returning to terrorize and impregnate the young wife with whom he had no real relationship. Sunita's husband continued his relationship with a woman his family did not approve of, expecting her to be satisfied with having been married at all even if there was no relationship between them. He continued to threaten her with ostracism and condemned her as having 'Western' ideas when she finally left and told him to find the courage to bring the woman he was relating to into his family.

In short, double-standards which indulge abuse and neglect of women and wives are quite explicitly upheld by families and conformist elements within the black communities. This indulgence of sons of the community has detrimental effects on the women and children, who are expected to live with them while being denied many basic human rights in the name of 'respectability'.

Professionals within the black communities also often appear to condone violence. Recalcitrant responses to domestic violence have been observed in the white community, so it is perhaps not surprising to find that black professionals, too, often adhere to patriarchal values and fail to assist abused women. There were incidents in which women were told by doctors from their own communities that 'women should not leave their husbands'. Sometimes women who did not speak English sought legal assistance from lawyers in their own communities and were not given proper legal advice, as in the case of Sui Wong who could not afford the fees of the Chinese solicitor she went to, but who was also not advised to seek legal aid.

The lack of protection for women in the privacy of their homes and families emerges starkly. This applies even where the police have been, sometimes repeatedly, involved. In Yvonne's case, for example, it is clear that her assailant was mentally disturbed and a danger to both her and her children. Even when he badly scalded the baby, he was still able to return to continue terrorizing her. Other women were being battered by men who had drug addictions or criminal records for other crimes, yet few were encouraged to prosecute, and one woman who had attempted to prosecute (Yvonne, on a different occasion from the one cited here) had had her case thrown out.

This study also found that women are often unprotected from men they have ceased having a relationship with. Ex-husbands and ex-boyfriends were not deterred from assaulting women. This upholds the notion 'that once a woman has engaged in any form of sexual relationship with a man, his social dominance over her is assumed . . . and this includes the right to physically assault her'. In some cases indeed, the man only became more violent at the point when the woman tried to end the relationship or alter the terms on which it would continue. Yvonne is only one of the examples where women had been coerced and intimidated for a long period (several years) after they had ended their relationships with assailants who kept seeking them out and returning to further terrorize them and their children.

The evidence from many of the women in this study (particularly those of Caribbean origin, but also from women of African and Asian origin) contradicts the Western feminist analysis of domestic violence which relates it to women's economic marginalization, and concomitant dependence on their spouses' income. Many had been assaulted by men who depended on them. This indicates that men continue to dominate women emotionally and physically even when they depend on those women. Indeed, the evidence is that this can be an exacerbating factor. Many women cited the fact that they were working and had some economic independence, as a source of antagonism.

At one extreme were a number of women whose men contributed nothing to the homekeeping or upkeep of children, and assumed they had rights to the woman's earnings. Recall that Sukie's partner actually resented her using the money she earned, to buy clothes and food for their children. Zoey's cohabitee never worked, but pimped and beat her, accusing her of cheating him while he sold her sex to obtain a flat, a car and other material needs for himself.

Not all these men were without incomes of their own, and some exploited the sexism of the cohabitation rule to collect and control social security payments to the family. Sarah's partner earned several hundred pounds a week, and started assaulting her after he had moved into her flat. Only then did he feel confident enough to violently express the resentment he felt towards her for having a career instead of having a baby for him, even while the mother of his other two children had a third for him. Charlotte put all her resources into a business with her man, only to be kept in a state of near starvation during her last pregnancy, while he impregnated another woman.

This material also shatters the stereotype of the 'strong' or 'castrating' black woman. Rather, these women are both providers and slaves whose labour supports men who then degrade and abuse them. It seems that when women have even a limited material advantage over the men they have relationships with, this in itself may in fact provoke those men to assert their male authority literally with a vengeance, through violence. This dynamic suggests that the frustration felt by men who are unable to conform to patriarchal standards, manifests itself in misogynistic behaviour towards the women they live off. Thus we can see that socio-economic jealousy may operate in a way that parallels sexual jealousy and often links up with it.

Notes

1. The word 'black' is used politically to embrace women of Caribbean, Asian and African origin.

2. A small number of women interviewed had been subjected to violence by other parties. If this was in addition to violence from their sexual partner, cohabitee or husband they were included in the study. Several of the Asian subjects fell into this category, having been multiply abused by in-laws as well as spouses. One older Caribbean woman was assaulted by her son when he grew up, after she had been subjected to years of violence at the hands of her husband. If however their experience of violence did not include violence from the man they were having or had been in a relationship with, they were excluded from the data analysis. There were six such cases including, for example, Lalita, a Filipino domestic worker who suffered abuse at the hands of her employer, and Sharon, a twenty-three-year-old woman of European and African parentage who was sexually abused by her stepfather and stepbrother and then violently assaulted when she matured and at the age of sixteen tried to resist having sexual intercourse with them. The others were Asian women who were assaulted by in-laws, like Neelim, the thirty-four-year-old Asian woman who had her nose smashed leaving her face permanently deformed by her sister's husband or the teenager who went into refuge with her mother, having been beaten by her father for trying to protect her mother.

3. 'Runnings' is a Jamaican term for 'what's going on' and 'how things work' within a particular subculture.

4. Georgina's workmates rallied around her by coming to stay and collectively ousting her husband.

5. Parents are not eligible if their children have been taken into local authority care (perhaps – in a cruel irony – because of homelessness or bad living conditions that threaten their health and safety), or are living primarily with the other parent, or abroad with relatives, for example.

6. 'Love marriage' was a term that women used to describe marriages to partners of their own choosing.

5

Black Women and the Police: A Place Where the Law is Not Upheld

Amina Mama

Introduction

Although violence against women in the home is a 'crime' the police are highly unlikely to arrest the man, preferring instead to advise the woman to take out an injunction against him. If the man is black, however, they are more likely to arrest him, but black women are confident that this is motivated by racism rather than out of any concern for the woman's safety. If either the woman or the man is black, the entire case may become one not of protecting the woman, but of an immigration investigation (McGuire 1988).

In recent years, substantial criticism has been directed at the response of the police forces nationally to domestic violence. Edwards (1986, 1989) has conducted the most substantive research into police response in London. Her findings reveal the widespread recalcitrance of the Metropolitan Police when it comes to upholding the law, where the crime is deemed to be 'just domestic' by police officers called to the scene. The non-criminalization of this particular form of assault (often serious enough to amount to attempted murder), appears to be widespread. Records of calls not being kept (and where incidents have been recorded, information has often been incorrect), reports not being submitted, and violent incidents not being categorized as crimes, have all emerged as common practice in the areas of London included in her study. Edwards's research indicates that the police receive approximately 60,000 calls concerning domestic violence every year in the former GLC area. Her work also indicates the wide variation in police responses, and in their implementation of the 1987 Force Order. Research like this has also precipitated the recent establishment of two 'Domestic Violence Response Units' in Tottenham and Lambeth.

These too need to be critically assessed, particularly because of their location in areas that have been subjected to particularly coercive policing, and where black women have been the victims of such policing in at least two deeply disturbing recent incidents: Cherry Groce (paralysed from the waist down after being shot in the back in a police raid) lived in Brixton and Cynthia Jarrett (who died of a heart attack during a police raid on her home) lived in Tottenham.

Prior to Edwards's work, a number of feminist criminologists had raised serious questions around gender and the law (Smart 1976; Smart and Smart 1978; Edwards 1984, 1985; Carlen 1985). These works have tended to concentrate on the analysis in terms of the patriarchal character of capitalist society, and have shown, for example, that women convicted of crimes are likely to be treated as 'mad' or 'sick' rather than 'bad'. They have also demonstrated that women are sentenced particularly harshly when their behaviour contradicts gender expectations (for example in the case of women convicted of violent crimes). In these studies much of the sexual inequality prevailing in law and law enforcement is attributed to the fact that males dominate the police forces and the criminal justice system, and that the dominant social values within these institutions, as in the wider society, are still anti-feminist and even misogynist in their ideological content. It is these values that inform police perceptions of domestic violence as being 'not real police work' and lead to it being accorded only low priority, since it is not viewed as being the kind of work that will lead to promotion. The evidence also suggests that policemen often abuse their own wives.

Little of this work has attempted to address the differential treatment meted out to different groups of women (i.e. class and racial inequalities being reproduced by the same institutions). One of the few studies to incorporate racial as well as sexual considerations into criminological study in Britain was an investigation into the imprisonment of women, commissioned by the GLC women's committee in 1986. *Breaking the Silence*[1] did not, however, look at the 'service delivery' aspects of policing or the criminal justice system, since it was a study of the processes by which women generally, and black women in particular, end up in prison, and their treatment once they are inside.

This researcher is not aware of any existing research that focuses on the issue of police responsiveness to crimes committed against black women. This, then, is the first time the subject has been addressed. In considering black women and the police, this study suggests three major areas of concern which need to be taken into account:

(i) The reluctance of black women to call in the police even when serious, if not life-threatening, violent crimes are being committed against them;

(ii) The reluctance of the same police to enforce the law in the interests of black women when they are called in to do so; and

(iii) The evidence that the police themselves perpetrate crimes against black women.

Statutory and voluntary organizations that have been set up to monitor the police in the public interest (e.g. Local Authority Police Units and organizations such as Newham Monitoring Project and Southall Monitoring Group) have uncovered widespread abuses of women by the police. Many of the cases they deal with stand in contrast to the sociological literature which frequently chooses to highlight 'man-to-man' confrontations between 'black youth' (who are invariably male) or black men and members of the police force (see for instance Pryce 1979; Cashmore and Troyna 1982). This is unfortunate in that this focus does not facilitate the development of the broader political understanding of the relations between coercive state apparatuses and the civilian population that a race, class and gender analysis highlights. The results are police ineffectiveness and a lack of accountability.

More alarmingly, police assaults are individualized and marginalized from considerations of how to develop police services in the interests of the citizenry. In the current political climate, policing is becoming increasingly coercive and intrusive, furthermore police powers were massively increased to the detriment of civil liberties by the Thatcher regime (Christian 1983). In other words developing a better police 'service' in the interests of the population has not been of as much concern as increasing police power. The wider socio-political context in which police powers have been massively increased without much effective opposition, has been explored elsewhere (e.g. Hall 1988). It is necessary to note however, that the mobilization of popular opinion in support of rather than against increased police powers, has for some years relied on racial constructions of rising crime rates (see Hall et al 1978). As Paul Gilroy (1987: 111) puts it:

> The discourse of black criminality has been articulated not just by the police, who have sought to mobilize popular support for the increase of their resources and the expansion of their powers, but by the extreme right who have organized marches and protests against the levels of black crime and sought to link these fears to the argument for repatriation.

Police–black community relations have been investigated by many studies which have been generated or inspired by police attacks on black people (Lambert 1970; Humphrey 1972; Roach Family Support Committee 1989). In recent years there have also been a number of campaigns over police brutality and deaths of black people in custody, and against increasing police powers (e.g. the Roach Family Support Committee, the Brixton Defence Campaign, the Campaign Against the Police and Criminal Evidence Bill). The success of these campaigns is hard to evaluate. The inner city disturbances up and down the country during the 1980s, and some more recent abuses of power, have also generated enquiries into policing practices, particularly with respect to the black communities (e.g. Lord Scarman's enquiry into the Brixton disorders of 1981; Lord Gifford's enquiry into the Broadwater Farm disturbances of 1985).

However, much of the existing material is androcentric and needs to be criticized.[2] None the less, despite the gender-blind nature of this work, there is sufficient evidence to show that it is not only black men who are subjected to the peculiarly coercive and aggressive forms of policing most evident in inner city areas.

The Institute of Race Relations recently published the alarming catalogue of evidence that they presented to the Metropolitan Commissioner Peter Imbert in October 1987. This documents the prevalence of police misconduct towards black people in their own homes, on the streets and in police stations. Thus, for example, when black people attempt to report crimes, they are frequently subjected to harassment, or their cases not taken seriously (see also Gordon 1983, 1986). Among the hundreds of cases included in the IRR evidence, are a number involving police brutality towards women. A few of the better-known examples are quoted below:

On 5 October 1985, Floyd Jarrett was stopped by police as he was driving through Tottenham, North London, and arrested for suspected theft of a motor vehicle. The police, who had no grounds for suspecting Mr Jarrett of stealing the vehicle, then proceeded to search his family's home for stolen goods.

The search of the house was carried out by four officers, with a District Support Unit held in reserve. The officers let themselves into the house with keys taken from Floyd Jarrett while he was at the station – but when asked how they got in they told the family that the door was open. The home was occupied by Mrs Cynthia Jarrett, Patricia Jarrett and two young children.

During the search an officer brushed past Mrs Jarrett, pushing her out of the way. She fell, breaking a small table. The police continued the search while Patricia Jarrett called for an ambulance. The officers then left the house. When they realized Mrs Jarrett was seriously ill, an officer returned to the house to give her mouth to mouth resuscitation. Mrs Jarrett was dead on arrival at hospital.

Although the police deny Patricia Jarrett's statement that at no time was a search warrant shown, the Broadwater Farm Inquiry was not convinced that the police had a search warrant, and believed it was possible that one might have been filled in only after Mrs Jarrett had died (Institute of Race Relations 1987: 25). Other accounts suggest that Patricia Jarrett asked for assistance and was ignored, which would imply that they either did not take any notice, or worse still, that they knew of Mrs Jarrett's condition and did nothing.

On September 1985 a team of armed officers went to the home of Mrs Cherry Groce in Brixton, South London to arrest her son Michael, who was wanted for armed robbery. In fact Michael Groce no longer lived there. The officers smashed down the door with a sledgehammer and then an inspector rushed in shouting 'armed police'. He put his finger to the trigger. Mrs Groce says the officer suddenly rushed at her, pointing a gun at her. She tried to run back but he shot her. She is now paralysed and confined to a wheelchair (*The Times*, 16 January 1987) (Institute of Race Relations 1987: 26).

In February 1984 Linda Williams lodged an official complaint after the police arrived at her Peckham home and demanded to see her son, Errol. Mrs Williams says that when she asked to see their search warrant she was dragged downstairs by the hair and, while on the ground, was repeatedly kicked in the back, as another policeman stood on her legs. Mrs Williams was pregnant at the time (*West Indian World* no. 649, 8 February 1984) (Institute of Race Relations 1987: 24).

In April 1983 an Instant Response Unit arrested a black youth, Emile Foulkes, who was sitting on a wall near his home in Waltham Forest, East London and accused him of taunting a group of white youths. According to Emile, the police grabbed him and called him a 'black nigger'. When his mother, Mrs Esme Baker, attempted to intervene, she was forced into the van, her dress was torn open and her breasts exposed. An officer prodded her in the breasts with his truncheon and said: 'I didn't know a nigger woman had breasts.' Both Emile and his mother were later acquitted of charges of threatening behaviour and assaulting the police. (*Searchlight* no. 89, November 1982) (Institute of Race Relations 1987: 18).

Other cases of police and immigration officers' misconduct (including denying women much needed medical care while in custody, planting heroin in homes, coercing African immigration defaulters into having anal intercourse with them) were identified by the women's imprisonment project (Mama, Mars and Stevens 1986), and need not be repeated here.

Lack of Protection in the Community

Black women subjected to violent assault in their homes may well have no alternative but to become involved with the police. Often, the police arrive at the scene as a result of being called by neighbours. A significant proportion of the women in this study were single women, many of whom lived in quite isolated conditions. For many others, their assailants were persons who lived with, were staying with, or who were visiting them. Often children tried to intervene, but clearly were unable to protect their mothers. Sometimes children were injured by their mother's assailant (accidentally or deliberately). Black women are particularly isolated if they live in white areas. While some of their white neighbours might adhere to the stereotypical view that such things constitute 'normal behaviour' for black people, others may simply lack concern when it is black women who may be being beaten to death.

In black communities black women are no more assured of protection against violence. There is evidence to suggest that many black people have internalized white stereotypes, or have come independently to believe that woman abuse is 'black' behaviour, so that black neighbours may also choose not to intervene. It may also be the case that people living in 'ghettoes' or on 'sink estates' in inner London, are forced to become accustomed to high levels of violence. In such circumstances they may also decide that domestic violence is something they will have to grow accustomed to, and therefore will not intervene or call the police.

Here, one needs to consider the history of black people's relations with the police. It has been observed, for example, that black people who have been subjected to racial attacks are sometimes subjected to further abuse and victimization by the police. More commonly, the police refuse to enforce the law, and so do not protect black people from white racial violence and abuse (Institute of Race Relations 1987: Chapter 2). As the studies referred to earlier have shown, this forms part of a broader pattern within which black people have been abused, victimized and harassed by the police both on the streets and in their homes. It may well be therefore that black neighbours who have themselves had bad experience at the hands of the police, are reluctant to have any further contact with them.

The reluctance of neighbours and friends to intervene when they hear cries and screams, while perhaps being understandable at one level, does need to be questioned and investigated further. Many of the women in this study found themselves in life-threatening situations with absolutely no other form of support available to them on a twenty-four-hour basis. Some, like Linda and Sulochana, ran out on to the streets to escape or, where they could, ran into neighbours' homes. Men often assaulted the women in this study during the night. Sometimes neighbours or other concerned parties called the police, either to complain about the noise, or because they feared for the woman's safety.

None the less there are many cases of violent assault in the home that the police are not called to (nearly half of the women in this study), or where their intervention is too late. The tragic death of twenty-four-year-old Denise Moncrieffe in October 1988 is a case in point. Her fully clothed body was found one Monday afternoon, in the ground-floor flat she shared with her cohabitee. She had suffered internal injuries after being kicked and punched repeatedly in her stomach. Police interviewed fifty neighbours, many of whom remembered hearing her screams, but did not interfere. Her common-law husband, a twenty-eight-year old mechanic, was charged with her murder and remanded in custody (*Hackney Gazette*, 7 October 1988).

Many black women in this study also described being attacked on the streets in broad daylight, without anyone responding to their cries for help.

> Yvonne for example was kicked down the stairs of a bus in Brixton after the man she had abandoned her home to get away from, spotted her and the children as he drove past. He leapt on to the bus and proceeded to attack her while onlookers observed.

Selena was followed on her way back to the refuge in which she had sought shelter, and attacked in Shepherd's Bush market in broad daylight, but nobody intervened.

This does not only happen when women are attacked by partners or ex-partners, but far more generally, since when a woman is attacked, members of the public may assume that her assailant is someone she knows, especially if they are both black. Or, again if the attacker is black, they may be particularly afraid to intervene because of the general racist paranoia about 'violent black men'.

Hindi, a twenty-three-year-old student of mixed Nigerian and European origin was harassed and assaulted, by a Caribbean man she had never seen before, on a bus on her way home from college while her (white) fellow students looked on and did nothing.[3]

Women in the study also reported instances of respected members of the community, who were asked for help, refusing to assist. Mumtaz, one of the women in this study, had an Asian GP who told her that 'women should not try to leave their husbands'. Meena, a forty-two-year-old mother of two, also sought help from her Pakistani GP who sided with her husband and kept her addicted to tranquillizers instead of helping her. Others like Shireen knew better than to confide in their family doctors. The fact that other women in this study were advised and assisted by their GPs indicates that GPs, like other members of the community, can play a more positive role. Medical practitioners who, after all have sworn oaths to protect life, have a responsibility to be supportive to women they know are being abused.

In those cases where the neighbours are concerned or disturbed enough to do something, they may well opt for calling the police, rather than attempting to intervene directly and perhaps put themselves at risk. In addition, given the fact that quite often nobody intervenes at all, many women find themselves in a situation where the police are the only agency that can be called upon to deal with the immediate problem of them being violently attacked, either in the home or on the street.

Police Involvement

The experience that Britain's black population have had of the police forces goes some way perhaps towards explaining why nearly half (47 per cent) of the women interviewed had not had any contact with the police throughout their ordeal. This is a high percentage when one bears in mind that most of the women in this study had already been forced to leave their homes. A significant proportion of the remaining 53 per cent who did have some contact with the police did so only because neighbours or friends had called them.

The fact that the majority of these women also became homeless subsequently, suggests that even where the police were involved, their response did not assist the woman sufficiently to prevent her from having to flee her home for her own (or her children's) safety. Despite the extreme violence that most of the sample had been subjected to, and despite the fact that there may have been nowhere else to turn, it is notable that very few had called the police on their own account. This suggests that many black women will be severely injured and face other dire consequences of violence rather than involve the police or make use of the law.

Quite apart from the poor opinion that women, and particularly black women, have of the police, there is some evidence to suggest that fear of reprisals combines with a sense of loyalty to discourage black women further. A few of the women had violent partners who were engaged in other criminal activities and were afraid that the latter would take it very badly if 'betrayed' by partners they already disrespected enough to abuse physically and emotionally. For example:

> At the age of fifteen, Marlene became involved with a much older man of Caribbean origin who dealt in drugs. On one occasion she had served a prison sentence for possession of drugs found in this man's flat while she was staying there. They fought a lot and his extreme violence culminated in an incident during which he threw her from the seventh floor of the tower block they lived in. She spent seven months in hospital, several of which were spent in traction, and was left permanently disabled by an incident that went down as 'attempted suicide'. In her case the fear of her partner, combined with her own experience of law enforcement agencies, prevented her from exposing her partner. After her release from hospital, Marlene was rehoused in the same area. However, the same man later broke into her flat and smashed the place up so badly that she left and went into a refuge.

Women who expect little from the police or the law, perhaps because they have been brutalized by police and prisons (and/or because they have been involved with men engaged in non-legal activities, and perhaps participated in these themselves) are likely to try and find other (legal, illegal or extra-legal) ways of dealing with their assailants.[4] However, a number of women in this study have also developed such an attitude because in the past legal avenues had failed them dismally or made their situation much worse.

A number of women were in relationships with men who they knew had already been harassed and brutalized at the hands of the police.

> Georgina Ming for example was one of the women in the sample who gave the fact that she and her Nigerian partner had been stopped and harassed by the police as a reason for not calling them sooner than she did. When she did call on them to assist when her ex-husband returned to the flat and tried to break in, they refused to come until she told them that he was 'damaging council property'.

It is sometimes suggested that black men beat black women because they are themselves brutalized by the police, unemployment, and other manifestations of racism.[5] The question of where this leaves oppressed black women remains unanswered. So too is the question about the community loyalties of black men who assault their partners (or tolerate and condone the domestic violence of other men in their communities), in the firm knowledge that a so-called 'right-on' black woman will not seek police protection, and so risk incriminating a violent black man.

When the police were called, their presence sometimes did have positive effects. For example:

> Charlotte called the police on an occasion when she felt her partner was going mad and had threatened to kill their children. When they arrived she was able to collect a few possessions and be escorted out of their home to a women's refuge in another part of London.

> Kiran's neighbours called the police when they heard her drunken husband beating her. The police came and took her to a local black women's centre. The workers found her a place in a women's refuge.

Responses of this type are immediately helpful to the woman and are a good emergency procedure. It would also be desirable, however, for the police to advise the woman that there are various possible courses of legal action if she is interested in pursuing the matter and, for example, retaining her rights to the home. This happened in some cases, but there were many where it did not. There were also instances in which the police dumped the woman in a hostel where she was not wanted or accepted. This may sometimes happen out of necessity, when local refuges are full, but it also happens when the police do not even know that refuges exist, or are reluctant to use refuges for reasons of their own. Lily Chang and Shuwei both had unpleasant experiences at hostels to which they were taken by the police who insisted that they be taken in. They did not get sympathetic or supportive treatment. Lily felt that the treatment of the wardens was racist. For Shuwei, who did not speak English, it was a particularly unpleasant experience because her arm had been broken and the hostel made all the residents stay out during the day. She was therefore forced to walk the streets endlessly.

> In another very disturbing case, the police were called to Yvonne's home on numerous occasions as a result of the repeated and severe violence she was subjected to by her partner, Roland. Roland had a long record of offences and was intermittently remanded in custody for other offences, including assaulting police officers and GBH, but either he did not get custodial sentences, or had already served enough time on remand when he went to court. Yvonne described a typical police response:
> 'They say "come on lads, it's [nickname] again" and all ten of them would come out and put on their steel caps ready to come and get him.'

The police themselves would assault Roland, but on one occasion they did get as far as the court. To quote Yvonne again:

'When the policeman was in court last time he said to the judge "Really and truly she's been in front of you before. What are you going to do? Wait until he takes her guts out and they're lying on the street, before you lock him up?" The policeman told him it was a mockery, and the judge said he'd have him for contempt of court, so he said he could have him for what he liked.'

This is clearly an instance in which the police were quite zealous in their response, but found themselves frustrated at the courts. Later, Roland was imprisoned on remand for another offence. When he returned, he appeared to have become quite paranoid, and to be hallucinating – seeing and hearing things. In a fit of jealous rage he accused Yvonne of being unfaithful to him and dashed a pan of boiling water over the baby. On that occasion the ambulance men consoled Yvonne that they did not believe him when he said she had burned the baby while bathing him. Roland was later sentenced to six months in a psychiatric facility, where, according to Yvonne, he went on hunger strike to avoid the drugs they were prescribing, and was forcibly injected. He escaped and returned to her home after only three months, still in a disturbed state. Yvonne abandoned her home once again. She had been rehoused twice, after staying in reception centres and refuges when we interviewed her, but Roland had found her addresses (once from the housing department) and she had to move on each time. She has since moved to a different part of the country with her three children.

Her case illustrates the fact that women and children can be left unprotected even from mentally disturbed men. It also illustrates the hopeless inefficacy of the responses of the police, the law courts and the mental health facility in which he was placed. It seems that he will be left until he kills someone, and then locked away in a top security hospital indefinitely.

To give one final example of police responses in cases which appear, on several occasions, to have warranted arrest of the man or at least some law enforcement action, let us consider Elsie's experience. Her assailant had broken her nose twice and split her head open so badly that she had to be hospitalized. On another occasion bystanders called the police when they saw her partner trying to force her over the balcony:

'One of the police officers took me outside the flat and sat me in the van. One asked him his side of the story and one asked me my side of the story. Then they conferred notes, and agreed that it was just a domestic argument and let's go home – "Why don't you kiss and make up?" '

Her partner found her after she had moved into a refuge, and the refuge workers called the police:

'They came with a big van, so [the police took him into the van]. I was saying good – take him away, and then these two young coppers got out of the van, and they said: "Why don't you sit down and talk? Come on you sit here and you sit there." They took us into this van, and we sat opposite each other and the two coppers stood at the doorway of the van and they kept us there talking for about an hour. "What was the problem?" the copper would say. At the end of this hour of conversation they agreed with me, and then this young copper said, "Why don't you just kiss him goodbye?" . . . They were more like marriage guidance counsellors than coppers – saying "Well actually I had a little row with my wife, but I didn't hit her." '

Elsie described their reaction to the situation as 'pathetic'. When asked if she thought they realized the extent of the problem she replied:

'Yes, I've been in there with black eyes and blood trickling down my face all over my white T-shirt. I mean Mike followed me one day into the police station and told the policeman that he'd done it. He said, "Yeah, I did it. She wouldn't cook my dinner so yeah – I licked her round the head with it." And the blood was trickling down my back.'

The police did not inform her about women's aid or take any legal action, yet they found time to take up amateur marriage guidance. Their apparent amiability should not be allowed to mask their failure to enforce the law.

Use of the Police as a Weapon by Men

'If there is one thing the police enjoy more than assaulting and locking up black people, it is finding ways to deport us instead.'

BLACK COMMUNITY WORKER

When police are called to a scene in which a black woman is being assaulted, they have to decide a course of action: they may choose to enforce the laws outlawing assault, or they may turn the whole affair into an immigration investigation (Mama, Mars and Stevens 1986; D'Orey 1984; Gordon 1981). A solicitor specializing in domestic violence whom we interviewed pointed out that in some of her cases the police have been known to arrest the woman, pending enquiring into her immigration status.

In this study it emerged that not all woman-beating men shun the police. In a number of cases, men actually threatened their wives with the police and the immigration department in the course of their disputes.

Jameela is a twenty-one-year-old Pakistani woman who was married by arrangement in Pakistan to a biochemist with British nationality. Jameela was brought into Britain as a fiancée in 1985, although they were already traditionally married. Her problems began soon after they started married life in the family home, when her brother-in-law tried to rape her. Her husband was himself sexually violent and abusive to her, and did nothing about his brother. On the one hand, he regularly threatened to have her deported back to her family in Pakistan in disgrace, while on the other told her that if she tried to leave the room, in which he kept her locked for days (with no toilet), the police would catch her. Even during her pregnancy, her husband refused to allow her to see a doctor, and kept her so malnourished that on one occasion she fainted from hunger. Her only relative in this country is a sister in a very similar predicament, who is married to a relative of Jameela's husband. They live several hours away and cannot see each other. Jameela was deeply depressed when we found and interviewed her at a women's refuge.

In a number of cases the husband was able to mislead the woman about her immigration status and terrorize her with the threat of deportation, when she did in fact have independent status, or did not know what her status was.

Arifa is a fifty-year-old Afghan woman whose Indian husband used her sheltered upbringing against her. Since she knew very little about the law or her rights in Britain, he was able to stop her from getting a British passport and so keep total control over her. They were married for over twenty years and he was violent to both Arifa and their children. He often used her economic dependency on him punitively, making them go hungry for days on end.

In view of the number of recent cases where the Home Office has actually issued women escaping violent husbands or partners with deportation orders, there is in effect a collusion going on between the patriarchal power that men wield over their families and the state power of the British authorities, against the interests, if not human rights, of many black women.

In some of these cases the man has dominated the interaction with the police, because he is male (or perhaps because he has a better command of English) and they have therefore elected to listen to him rather than to the woman he has assaulted, so that once again they turn and leave perhaps after a few words about disturbing the neighbours.

Shaheeda is a twenty-seven-year-old Asian woman who was abused by her father. At fifteen she ran away to London and ended up in a homeless persons' hostel. There she met a white English man from a middle-class family, who was himself a 'problem child'. Eventually they set up home together. Their relationship was 'rocky' from the start and once they lived together he became physically violent. Shaheeda had three children, one of whom was taken into care and later adopted. She tried to leave a number of times and the police were involved, but according to Shaheeda 'they always took his side because he is white'. Eventually, during her third pregnancy he assaulted her so badly that she did leave and go to a refuge.

Mei Ling is a thirty-two-year-old Chinese woman whose husband became violent to her after she gave birth to a daughter when her husband wanted a son. He beat her repeatedly seizing upon whatever trivial excuse he could find, and subjected her to violent rapes. On two occasions he threatened to kill her, and she called the police. They did not offer any assistance. Eventually he began torturing their baby by blowing a whistle loudly in her ears, so that Mei Ling ran away with her baby. She still lives in a bed and breakfast, and is very isolated and unsupported, but visits a local advice centre. She has not been able to get housing, and her husband still refuses to give her a divorce.

In other instances, the man has instructed the police to remove the woman. One man actually pointed at his wife and suggested that the authorities should deport her for him. The police duly arrested the woman pending enquiries about her immigration status.

The general point is that men are able to use the police and immigration to terrorize women. In many cases they are merely exploiting a situation in which racist and sexist immigration legislation and policing practices do mean that these agencies are often threatening and coercive towards black women.

Consequences of Police Non-response: When a Non-response is a Response

In a number of cases the police have arrived at the door having been called by neighbours who heard the screams and thuds that accompany domestic violence. Even this sometimes made the men seek vengeance on their victims. More often than not there was a lack of response on the part of the police, so that when they left the scene, the man felt even more confident.

If the police are called in and do not make clear the criminal nature of woman assault, this can have punitive effects on the victim. Indeed, her assailant may punish her further if the police have humiliated or unnerved him without also taking steps to prevent further violence. For example, one victim described how her husband's violence towards her was actually reinforced by the police coming, but refusing to take any action.

One Asian woman in this study described how the police responded when she called for help. They sent an Asian community policeman, who told her off severely in her own language and then told her to stop misbehaving and to try to be a 'good obedient wife'.

Non-collaboration by the Woman

When other parties have called the police, the woman sometimes did not admit that she was being assaulted prior to their arrival.

Shireen is only nineteen years old, but she has tried to kill herself twice. Her husband beat her severely throughout their married life, on two occasions so badly that she had miscarriages. Her in-laws turned round and accused her of having abortions. Her husband tried to drive her out of the house, but she did not know where to go for help. On one occasion the neighbours called the police, but Shireen refused to press charges against her husband. Her husband was later sentenced to seven months imprisonment for assaulting someone else. Shireen subsequently left him and stayed in a number of refuges.

For an economically dependent wife, pressing charges may not appear to be in her own interests. She may be afraid of being left destitute and disgraced in her own community. Others fear reprisals, or have had negative experiences of the police's response in the past. Alternatively, the manner in which the police respond may be perceived as offputting to an already frightened and traumatized woman.

Uniformed male officers may be the strongest deterrent to a violent man, but they may also frighten the woman. The police guidelines on domestic violence issued on 24 June 1987 recommended, inter alia, that more women officers should be used. However, since only 10 per cent of the force are women, this will be difficult to implement. Police responses should bear in mind the fact that many women, particularly black women, will be too terrified or suspicious to trust them.

Changes in the law, and in the practice of the courts, in the direction of coercing women to give evidence are not necessarily the best way of tackling the problem. Worse still they may serve further to deter women from reporting violence and seeking legal support.

Black women are right to be concerned about the potentially negative impact the sweeping increase in police powers introduced in the 1984 Police and Criminal Evidence Act will have on black people. We have already discussed the evidence that police often refuse to take violent crimes defined as 'domestic' seriously. Under these circumstances, if the police are repeatedly called to a woman who then denies that there is a problem, they may well use this as an excuse for not taking any action in the future. If women do deny that there is a problem when the police come, it may also worsen her situation by giving her assailant more confidence. Even worse, racist police may take the opportunity to harass her themselves.

Punitive Police Responses to the Woman

In some cases, the police respond in ways that are more actively punitive and abusive to the woman.

Patience is a Nigerian woman married to a Nigerian man brought up in Britain who subjected her to violent abuse and other forms of degradation. She often slept in the factory where she worked rather than risking further assaults at home. Her husband's violence did not stop. On one occasion, the neighbours called in the police when they were disturbed by screams and bangs. When the police arrived her husband (who had a better command of 'the Queen's English') told the police that she had been damaging property in his flat and instructed them to arrest her. The police ridiculed the pair of them. Patience quoted the police as saying 'Eenie meenie minie mo, catch a nigger by the toe' while they decided who to arrest. They opted for Patience, and dragged her off in a half-clothed state, refusing to allow her to collect her bag or proper clothing. When they arrived at the police station she was roughed-up and then kicked down the stairs into the cells, where she was locked up all night, shivering with cold. She was ridiculed and racially humiliated (remarks about her husband not wanting to 'fuck' her any more, about a dirty smell in the station etc.). A woman police officer witnessing all this laughed with amusement, telling her colleagues to 'take it easy, lads', while Patience wept and pleaded for mercy. In the morning she was driven to the edge of the borough and dropped on the street. No charges were brought against her.

Horrific experiences like this can only be understood in the context of police assaults on black people, most of which continue to go unchallenged.

Conclusion

It is clear that police responses to the women in this study were very mixed. They ranged from being helpful and supportive (for example assisting women to collect their children and belongings and leave the scene), to the worst type of intervention which was damaging and abusive. In most cases better legal advice and support could have been given. Only a minority of the women in this study who had contact with the police said they were in any way encouraged to press charges or prosecute, suggesting that the police often assume that they will not pursue the matter.

For many black women (as for white women) the police often become involved whether the woman calls them or not. It is therefore imperative that work is done to improve the ways in which the police respond. This work has already begun through, for example, the exposure of the inadequacy of police responses by Edwards (1986a). None of this work, however, has examined the race and class dynamics of police responses.

The findings of this research do suggest that police may be particularly insensitive, and on occasions brutal, towards black women. The experience of Patience is particularly disturbing, as are the experiences of women threatened with deportation, under existing law.

The most helpful police responses relied on the existence of black women's centres and refuges. Specialist facilities are far from adequate, and those that have been established are struggling to stay open in the face of cutbacks in funding. The importance of the work these do in supporting black woman must be recognized, more must be established, and the police must be encouraged to refer black women to these agencies. The experiences of women like Shuwei and Lily, who were dumped in quite unsuitable and unsympathetic hostels which did not provide any of the necessary support, demonstrate that it is important that the police refer black women to the right places.

Encouraging black women to make use of the law for their own protection
and in their interests is another role that the police should play. The police
should also refer black women to other legal agencies, whom they might find
less intimidating, regardless of the women's willingness to press charges. The
police should be equipped with lists of lawyers who specialize in this area of
law, as well as law centres and women's centres that they can advise women to
approach, perhaps after recovering from the immediate trauma and when
they feel strong enough to do so.

Generally, it is clear that the police role should centre around appropriate,
effective and efficient enforcement of the law as it relates to domestic
violence. The issue of the police not following up cases or taking appropriate
legal action to enforce injunctions and other aspects of the law, remains an
important one. The Police and Criminal Evidence Act of 1984 empowered
the police to compel women to prosecute. Similarly, the Police Force Order
of 1987 aimed to encourage police to act, and to prosecute violent men, even
if the woman does not wish to pursue the matter.

However, since the police were already empowered to arrest assailants
prior to this legislation (the main problem has always been police non-
response or under-response), it is somewhat paradoxical that it was decided
to extend their powers further. In the light of the evidence on police racism,
there is good reason to fear that this extended power will be used against black
people. Certainly, it may well serve to further deter women, particularly if
they or their partners are black, from calling the police. From the perspective
of the women whose experiences have been documented here, these recent
changes are also of concern because of the evidence that the police are often
racist and punitive towards black women. There must be some doubt that
increased and ill-defined police powers, bearing in mind the lack of accountability particularly of the Metropolitan police force, will operate in the
interests of black women. Indeed these developments may well present black
people in general, and black women in particular, with specific problems.

Notes

1. *Breaking the Silence: Women's Imprisonment* (researched and written by Mama, Mars and
Stevens in 1986) was subsequently republished by the Women's Equality Group of the London
Strategic Policy Unit and is available from the Campaign for Women in Prison.

2. Having witnessed first hand the violence meted out to black women, as well as men, during
the Brixton uprisings of 1981, this researcher has no illusions that being female counts for much
in relations between black women and the police in Britain.

3. This woman was not one of the sample for this project, and had not experienced domestic
violence, but recounted her experience to the researcher, in the course of explaining why she was
afraid to go out alone in London.

4. Generally, black women (including those who have committed very minor crimes) are left
with a deep mistrust and suspicion of both the police and the courts, often because they feel they

were unfairly treated and took extra punishment in one way or another. This is not surprising, given the treatment of black women at all levels of the criminal justice system and the racism within women's prisons (Mama, Mars and Stevens 1986).

5. This attitude was, for example, evident amongst some of the participants at a black community meeting entitled 'Domestic Violence within the System' held in Lewisham on 8 October 1988, organized by the International Women's Day Planning Committee.

6

We are a Natural Part of Many Different Struggles: Black Women Organizing

Claudette Williams

Introduction

Historians and contemporary writers on international labour migration have invariably failed to examine the contribution of women to the process of settlement, finding accommodation and employment. Such an omission, argues Gerda Lerner (1973), is indicative of the general failure to 'recognize that there is a female aspect to all history, that women were there and that their specific contribution to the building and shaping of society was different to that of men'. This assessment is equally true in the case of the migration of black women from the Caribbean to Britain. Though some of the problems women encountered were the same as those of men, there were additional, gender-specific dimensions. Women from the Caribbean in post-war Britain were instrumental in finding employment, finding accommodation, saving money to 'send home', either to repay the loans which had financed their passage, or for their children or family. Black women also had a high profile in organizing around issues outside the home: setting up community meeting places, social clubs, community newspaper and political organizations. In the late 1960s and the 1970s the late Olive Morris was prominent in spearheading the demands for better housing in the Lambeth squatting campaign. Women were in the forefront of campaigns demanding an end to bussing and segregation in state education, in setting up black supplementary education; in the campaigns against police harassment; in the fight for union recognition and support against the racist practices of trade unions and employers. Women's involvement spanned the entire spectrum of concerns affecting the black community. Within the black community women began both to challenge black men's sexism and to demand recognition for their crucial contribution to the overall struggle of the community.

On board the *Empire Windrush* when it docked in Britain in June 1948, was a woman stowaway, twenty-five-year-old Averilly Wauchope, a dressmaker from Kingston (Fryer 1984). She was to be followed three months later by a further fifteen women on the *Orbita*. In 1949 forty-five more women arrived. As the number of men arriving increased so too did the number of women and children. Direct recruitment by London Transport and British Hotels (Sivanandan 1982) brought in more Caribbean women. Hence, from the outset, black women featured in the process of migration.

What do we know about these women? Where and how did they survive in a hostile racist climate? To what extent did their experiences reflect the experiences of other migrants as well as differ qualitatively by virtue of the simple fact that they were black *women*?

Early Struggles

The struggle to find living accommodation was hard. Landlords either refused to let to black people or charged increased rents. In its report, the Committee on Housing in Greater London observed:

> landlords clearly barred coloured people [sic] and only 6 per cent (of 1,258) indicated that coloured tenants would be welcomed . . . as to rent levels . . . higher rents are asked and obtained from coloured immigrant tenants for comparable accommodation . . . Rent seemed to be far less determined by relevant objective criteria – such as the size and quality of the accommodation provided – than by fortuitous subjective ones, such as the date of the tenant's arrival at the landlord's doorstep, his or her colour. There was apparently a 'newcomer's tax' , and on top of that a 'foreigner's' levy high especially in the case of coloured people (Field and Haikin 1971).

From overcrowded, expensive rented accommodation women organized and drew on survival techniques brought from home. The 'sou sou', or 'pardner hand' helped to support families in the Caribbean as well to provide the down payment on a house in this country. Women were central in maintaining these structures and generating means of increasing incomes. In the case of the 'blues dance, house-selling party', women would be the organizers of food, drink and security, and would be responsible for hiding goods and money in case the dance was raided by the police or declared illegal. The form that this participation took 'behind the scenes' was clearly defined by gender. Men took care of the music, whilst women's involvement was confined to the more 'private' activities associated with domestic responsibilities such as food, drink and financial management. In other words, it was confined to those very activities which were essential to the success of the dance.

Within the church – another area of high visibility for women – the organization and running of the institution often rested on women's leadership. The rejection experienced by black people attempting to attend the conventional church, and the absence of 'our kind of religion' propelled women to set up and run their own prayer-meetings, and subsequently churches, to meet their social and spiritual needs. The well-researched dramatization of *Motherland*[1] by students of Vauxhall Manor School in South London powerfully depicts many of the obstacles, humiliations and joys experienced by black women during the 1950s and 1960s. The slogan 'the personal is political', which became popular in the Women's Liberation Movement (WLM) during the 1970s had as one of its bases the very brutally-lived experiences of black women. Sixty-seven-year-old Edna Parker[2] recounted thus her personal struggles with employers:

> I remember when I went for my first job. I was asked: 'You as a black person, don't you feel ashamed of coming to England and asking for a job?' I said, 'I come from India, and there are white people there. Aren't they ashamed to work in India amongst the black people?' He said 'No', so I said 'Why should I?' And he said to me 'Oh, the job is yours'. I said, 'No, I wouldn't work for you. You need to have a little more education for me to work with you. For if you, as the boss, think that, I can imagine people working under you' (*City Limits* 1983).

Even before Britain's post-war economic decline became apparent and pronounced, an upsurge of racist and fascist attacks on black and migrant workers had become commonplace. The onslaught of the teddy boys going on the rampage in Camden Town, Notting Hill and elsewhere (Sivanandan 1982), petrol bombing the homes of black families, the weeks of 'nigger hunts' by Mosleyites and the White Defence League under the watchful eye of the police, called for an organized response from the black community. The murder of Kelso Kochrane in 1959, the increasing calls for the introduction of immigration controls and racial violence in Nottingham and Notting Hill impressed on the black community the need for greater organization and militancy. In collaboration with individuals like Amy Ashwood Garvey, Claudia Jones (Johnson 1983), a Trinidadian-born communist deported from the United States for her political activities, began to mobilize the Afro-Caribbean and Asian communities in Britain. Through the pages of *The West Indian Gazette*, a forum of communication and public education, support was mobilized for those arrested while defending themselves and the community against racist attacks.

The Gazette argued consistently for a West Indies Federation free from imperialist domination. Its major efforts were designed to stimulate political and social thinking and to forge unity. In Jones's own words, its aim was to act as a 'catalyst, quickening the awareness socially and politically of the West Indian, Afro Asian and their friends'. Its editorial advocated a 'united

West Indies, political equality and respect for human dignity for West Indians and Afro Asians in Britain, for peace and friendship between a Commonwealth and world people'. The struggles for freedom from imperialist domination of our homelands; freedom from racist attacks; and an end to racism and disunity within our communities were all issues around which Claudia Jones, together with other political activists, agitated (Jones 1964). Such agitation provided the platform on which many political organizations of the 1960s and 1970s were able to build. As Paul Robeson said of Claudia Jones on her death in 1964:

> She left behind a legacy of struggle and inspiration; she continued in our day the heroic tradition of Harriet Tubman of *Sojourner Truth*, the struggle of the Negro liberation for women's rights, for human dignity and fulfilment (Johnson 1985).

Her resoluteness in mobilizing and urging women and the black community to organize has become the model for many black women organizing today. Her assiduity in forging unity between the migrant communities in Britain continues to be a major political task in our struggles against racism in Britain. The legacy of Claudia Jones contains many political lessons for those who are active and struggling on all fronts in this country.

The Rise of the Black Women's Movement

In order to locate specifically the development of the black women's movement, it is necessary to identify initially some aspects of the Black Power Movement (BPM) and the Women's Liberation Movement (MLM) of the late 1960s. The BPM in the USA gave rise in Britain to the development of several organizations. One of these was the Black Panthers, a militant political organization aimed at combating racism and developing a class-conscious perspective amongst black people in Britain. This occurred at a time when racism and state harassment were intensifying, with the police targeting activists and singling out black youths for 'special treatment'. The high level of women's participation within this movement threw up tensions between men and women activists and heightened the inadequacies of black power politics. In the movement, important political questions relating to women, childcare, sexism, sexuality, the nature of women's participation, and, crucially, the question of free, safe, legal abortion, were marginalized.

Women initially arranged meetings outside the organization, in each other's homes, arranging to share childcare and facilitate discussions, out of which grew specific women-related campaigns. From these discussions, too, it soon became clear that involvement within our original organizations increasingly placed us in politically compromising situations. The need to establish an alternative space within which to clarify and further develop issues specific to us as women, was becoming more and more apparent. The issues and campaigns considered were not in any way marginal to the 'wider struggle' but were rather an integral part of the same struggle against racism and for human liberation. Sexism, racism and economic exploitation interlocked to oppress us as black women. All these strands needed to be recognized and challenged simultaneously. There was to be no hierarchy of oppression. However having come to this conclusion, and even with the inspiration of women like Claudia Jones, we were not confident about articulating our views within the wider black movement. This lack of confidence, together with the hostility with which gender issues were greeted in mixed black organizations, was to act as further impetus for the formation of black women's groups. One of the first such groups was the Brixton Black Women's Group which was set up in 1973.

In the WLM, too, which had as its fundamental principle the liberation of women, black women experienced a similar process of marginalization. At issue was the inability of the WLM to acknowledge that racism shapes and is a fundamental part of the experiences of black women in Britain.

The ideology, goals and strategies of both these movements have greatly affected and changed our lives. Nevertheless, our experiences and consequent disillusionment with the movements have encouraged the development of a politics which was both anti-racist (unlike those of white women) and anti-sexist (unlike those of black men).

The lessons gained from being in the BPM and the WLM provided the re-affirmation of our ability to organize, identify and determine how we engage in a struggle and what those areas of struggles were to be. What we learned was that our experience as black women was a fundamentally legitimate area around which to organize because of the way it unified the various dimensions of oppression and exploitation. Consequently, there could be no ordering of those dimensions into primary and secondary since to do so would be to deny the specificity of our experiences, and to deny the struggle for human liberation a dimension which was sorely needed. As Barbara Smith (1983) aptly concludes:

> we examined our lives and found that everything out there was kicking our behinds, race, class, sex and homophobia; we saw no reason to rank oppression, or as many forces in the black community would have us do, to pretend that sexism among all other 'isms' was not happening to us.

The antagonistic response to black women organizing autonomously has been and still continues to be problematic for many within the black community (Brixton Black Women's Group 1983). To organize autonomously is to create a favourable climate for understanding and evaluating the intricacies involved in the goal of self-liberation as well as to expand the whole political struggle. Throughout history black people have formed autonomous organizations in the belief that it is only those who are oppressed who are best equipped to liberate themselves. No one else can do it. This is a lesson which we as black women have had to re-learn.

Another area of hostility has been the constant criticism that women articulating and challenging sexism within the black community have been divisive and detracted time and energy from the black struggle as a whole. Such argument is puerile to say the least. More fundamental and serious, however, is the implicit suggestion behind this argument that relations based on gender are somehow 'natural'. By definition this means that they are not social relations and should therefore be removed from the realm of political struggle. This is somewhat ironic given that many critics are themselves engaged in an ideological struggle to unmask the social nature of another set of relations which are also said to be 'natural'. Sexism can no longer be relegated to the sidelines; and the political agenda should address both the rampant sexist oppression perpetuated by black men subscribing to the belief that the best position for black women should be 'prone' (Cleaver 1968), and the more 'liberal' approach which regards the question of black women's struggle as 'cool' but nothing to do with them.

In practice this means women can no longer be expected to contribute to the movement only in ways determined by black men if we are to take our specific (as black women) and collective (as black people) struggle forward. Organizationally our roles can no longer be confined to those of coffee makers, cooks, typists, fund-raisers and willing sexual partners, while the men conduct the 'important' business of the struggle. Sexism intersects with class and racial oppression. Regardless of their differing class position, black and white men participate in the perpetuation of sexual oppression.

Of course black men are victimized and exploited by the institution of racism, as are black women, but acts of gender and sexual abuse and exploitation are also perpetuated by black men. They oscillate between the positions of oppressed and oppressor. This oscillation, however, could offer a potential site for political struggle for black men. To underplay the social position of oppressor is to develop an inadequate analysis of black people's situation. For progressive men to deny this position is to fail to understand that although sexism crosses class barriers, it only acts in the interest of our common oppressors. Similarly such a denial devalues black women's efforts to create a better life for ourselves from which all black people would benefit. The addition of the gender dimension to the black struggle clearly has common benefits for us as a people. As a social construction based on sex, gender is necessarily prescriptive for both men and women. As such its transformation has the potential of freeing us all from the strait-jacket of 'masculinity' and 'femininity'. For black people gendered categories cannot be separated from racial stereotypes. As a result, any attempt to deny the need to negate gendered relations would represent an automatic denial of a real anti-racist struggle.[3]

Why OWAAD?

In 1978 African women active in the African Students Union (UK) launched the Organization of Women of African Descent (OWAD). The major concern then was to engender support for liberation struggles in Africa. African women came together with other black women living in Britain to plan a conference in 1977 in Coventry. Differences in priority emerged from that conference: support for liberation struggles at home, and the development of strategies to survive here in Britain. The conference also felt that there was a need to connect with African and Asian women living permanently in Britain. The organization thus became known as the Organization of Women of Asian and African Descent (OWAAD). Its aims were:

- to campaign and struggle on all issues which affect black women in Britain;
- to oppose and struggle against all forms of sexism and discrimination against women and all forms of racism and discrimination against black people;
- to support those struggles of the working class which further the interest of working people;
- to support all anti-imperialist struggles and national and neo-colonial domination;
- to support the right of nations to self-determination;
- to encourage the formation of and build links with black women's groups;
- to develop a better understanding of our economic, sexual and racial exploitation and oppression through working, struggling and discussing together (Brixton Black Women's Group 1984).

OWAAD was to be a forum in which black women came together to plan, discuss and organize support for liberation struggles in our countries of origin, as well as to organize to survive here in Britain.

A major element of our organization and struggle had to be finding ways of surmounting the historical antagonism between Asian and Afro-Caribbean peoples. As women we recognized that our shared historical experiences as victims of colonialism and our experiences as second-class citizens in a racist society formed the base on which to build resistance and thereby unity. Racism, sexism, economic oppression manifest themselves in different forms, and pit us against each other for 'capital's favour'. There is however little distinction between the kind of racial and sexual abuse and insults to which we are subjected as black women. While cultural and ethnic differences could not be ignored, it was recognized that these differences could be built on rather than be treated as sources of division. While OWAAD remained numerically dominated by Afro-Caribbean women, the recognition that Asian women were a significant part of the organization confirmed the correctness of our analysis.

At the first OWAAD conference in 1978, over two hundred and fifty women attended from all parts of Britain to discuss our position in this society. On the agenda were health issues, education, law and immigration. 'Women who came were greatly inspired and went away to form black women's groups in their own communities' (Brixton Black Women's Group 1984). This conference marked the birth of the black women's movement in Britain. Though many black women left the WLM because of its inability to recognize how racism functions to shape our lives and must therefore be a critical element of our analysis and strategies for resistance, it must be stated that OWAAD was not conceived as an alternative to WLM. The success of black women's groups identified a comprehensive understanding of the forces of racism, sexism and economic exploitation. The recognition of the fusion between these three elements was crucial to the development and advancement of strategies of resistance. Armed with such an analysis we were able to make political alliances with those organizations which recognized our form of struggle as legitimate, and a vital part of the fight against class, race and gender oppression.

By OWAAD's second conference in 1980, a structure had been developed to sustain the work of the organization: a media committee collected and disseminated information in *Forward*; a Calendar and Diary committee put out a black woman calendar. Women could join any of these committees. Planning committees were drawn from women in women's groups and individuals affiliated to OWAAD to plan the next conference. No elected leaders were appointed. It was deemed that an important feature of the structure was that leadership would be exercised according to the situation. Of course there were difficulties. OWAAD never explored satisfactorily the implications that Afro-Caribbean Unity posed for practice, and the question of sexuality which had been bubbling beneath the surface from the second conference, was to be forcefully placed on the agenda of the third conference.

What had become clear was that we – the BWM – had succumbed to homophobia, and had reduced sexual orientation to heterosexuality, i.e. as the interplay between women whatever their class or race background. In challenging our traditional cultures and cultural imperialism we had correctly placed on the political agenda a black feminist discussion of gender which examined the oppression of women and the structures and processes which reproduced the conditions of oppression. However, in this analysis we did not go as far as to discuss the social and psychological forces which lead individuals to choose sexual partners from the same sex. 'We became the unwitting victims of our own and our communities' "homophobia"' (*Feminist Review* 1984). The time had come to throw off accusations and step outside the yoke. We were not all 'frustrated lesbians', we were frustrated at having to keep within the boundaries of male-defined politics. It was time to affirm that sexual orientation was part of the personal, and we had all agreed that the 'personal was political'. Lesbianism, homosexuality and heterosexuality were personal and political, and as black women organizing we could not allow ourselves to be undermined by the threat of being all labelled lesbians. Sexual orientation, sexuality, and sexual oppression are part of our political struggle, and important aspects of black women's feminism. Like Afro-Asian unity, sexual orientation and sexuality will continue to be worked through, developed and integrated as part and parcel of our political struggles.

The uprisings of 1981 had an enormous effect on women organizing. Women were arrested, beaten up. Homes were invaded by the police and children, lovers and husbands dragged through the courts and imprisoned. Despite the input of women – mobilizing support, fund-raising, gathering information for evidence, and working on defence campaigns – we again allowed ourselves to become marginalized. Our experience of organizing did not erase our uncertainties and lack of confidence, about how we struggled and prioritized issues specific to us as women without having them eclipsed by the 'larger struggle'.

The uprisings took many women from their women's groups. Such were the women who felt that the needs of black people would be better served in mixed organizations or who felt uncertainty about the validity of women-only groups. OWAAD's fourth conference in 1981 with black feminism as the focus appeared insignificant to many of the new women who attended. (This too had a history since there was always a back-log of discussion from one year to the next.) Hence the focus of discussion for 1981 appeared to many inappropriate. Criticisms ranged from saying that women organizing were out of touch with women 'on the street', to saying that women who articulate and mobilize were middle-class and thus misguided. These criticisms as well as internal weaknesses within their own women's groups hastened further the break-up of OWAAD. However many lessons have been learned, the major one being the networking and organizational skills which workers in OWAAD have developed. To some extent we have learned to appreciate our different cultures, understand our experiences and distinguish between these differences and objective political differences. The questions of gender relations and sexual orientation have been placed legitimately on the political agenda. OWAAD succeeded in firmly establishing black feminism as a vital and valid area of black people's struggle, one which must remain central to our understanding and advancement of our complete liberation as black women and as black people.

Rethinking Feminism

There existed many points of divergence within the Black Women's Movement. One such point is the rejection of feminism by some black women as a European/Western idea that has nothing to do with the lives of black women. Part of this distancing comes from the continued failure of the women's liberation movement to acknowledge racism as a central plank of analyses of self and community. Hence events such as 'reclaim the night' marches which mobilize women to march through predominantly black communities calling for 'better policing', to 'make the streets safe for women', fail to acknowledge the racist nature of such demonstrations. Implicit in these actions are notions that it is only black communities which are unsafe for white women. Furthermore, these marches refuse to take account of our struggles against police harassment and community intimidation by the heavy policing of our neighbourhoods. The streets were never safe for black people; and the presence of more police will only guarantee that black people will experience more harassment. Black women have rightly felt unable to support such actions and consequently are at odds with such groups.

The black male activist who continues to perceive women organizing autonomously as a threat, as 'dividing the struggle and fragmenting the cause', tends to relegate feminism to the domain of 'white girls' things'. A hostile climate is thus generated which forces black feminists to reaffirm constantly that feminism is not an exclusive theory for white women but a theory which underpins the struggles of women against systematic oppression based on gender. Our status as black women places us at the intersection of all forms of subjugation in society. This means that we are a natural part of many different struggles both as black people and as black women.

Among black women who have rejected or are about to reject feminism, there has occurred a shift towards the appropriation of Alice Walker's 'womanist' definition, on the grounds that 'womanist' comes from a black 'rootsy' tradition. In *In Search of Our Mothers' Gardens*, Alice Walker writes:

> Womanist 1. . . . From the black folk expression of mothers to female children, 'You acting womanish,' . . . 2. *Also*: A woman who loves other women, sexually and/or nonsexually. Appreciates and prefers women's culture, women's emotional flexibility . . . and women's strength. Sometimes loves individual men sexually and/or nonsexually. Committed to survival and wholeness of entire people, male *and* female. Not a separatist, except periodically, for health. Traditionally universalist . . . 4. Womanist is to feminist as purple to lavender.

Such a definition of 'womanist' should not be posed as an alternative 'feminist' although it is located within a black culturist frame of reference. Rather 'womanist' should be an intrinsic part of any understanding of self. As such it is crucial to our continued development as black feminists. However to substitute 'womanist' for 'feminist' is to limit our understanding of the nature of our total oppression and hence the inherent complexity of our struggle. In their newsletter, Camden & Islington Black Sisters Group wrote:

> Black womynism: is it goodbye to black feminism? Many of us never even said 'hello' . . . we can develop our own philosophy and ideology to suit ourselves and to guide our practice, black womynism is about living in dignity. It is about equal responsibility and our right and ability to determine our destiny. Black womynism has to be about the daily lives of ordinary black women as opposed to the static nature of feminism which does not seem to be going anywhere constructively.

The systematic oppression of women on grounds of gender affects our lives. But systematic racial, economic, sexual, political and psychological oppression affects us in specific ways; and this is what we as black women seek to identify and to struggle against. Black feminism necessitates an understanding of these forces and how they come to bear on us as black women and are played out in our communities.

To understand our situation is to understand the roots of women's oppression both historically and cross-culturally. We need to examine and analyse the inter-relations and connections between the various factors which form the basis of women's subjugation. Such factors have to be examined not in isolation but in relation to the whole oppressive capitalist system. The struggle for women's liberation has to be part of the concrete struggle against class oppression. As women, we cannot consider our oppression and exploitation separately from either the international oppression and exploitation perpetrated by international capital in our countries of origin or from our experiences here in Britain. Womynism does not embrace the totality of our struggle. Instead of rejecting feminism, we need to continue to identify, reflect and reject those elements which compose and construct our feminism specific to us as black women. If womynism allows for this rethink, it is progressive; but, as in the case of feminism, we must evolve and mould our experiences into useful knowledge to advance our understanding and sharpen our analysis to forward our struggle.

Notes

1. *Motherland* by Vauxhall Manor Girls, 1983, directed by Elyse Dodgson, based upon the lives and experiences of twenty-three women who migrated from the Caribbean to Britain during the 1950s and 1960s.

2. Edna Parker migrated in the 1950s from India where she was born to a Caribbean father and an Indian mother.

3. A particularly eloquent vision of the effects of transcending the constraints of gender is given in Alice Walker's *The Color Purple*.

7

Indo-Caribbean Experience in Britain: Overlooked, Miscategorized, Misunderstood

Steven Vertovec

Introduction

Just as the Indian experience in the Caribbean has been relatively unacknow-ledged in both public awareness and academic inquiry, so, too, in Britain has been the presence of Caribbean-derived persons of Asian descent. As Dabydeen (1987: 10) suggests, the former oversight has led to a flawed conception of the Caribbean region as being of wholly African heritage; by extension, the latter oversight has brought about a similarly flawed conception of the Caribbean diaspora.

Having settled in the region since the mid-nineteenth century, Indians (or, as they are sometimes called there, 'East Indians') are found throughout the numerous territories of the Caribbean and account for about half the population in both Trinidad and Guyana. They also formed part of the large-scale migration of West Indians to Britain in the 1950s and 1960s. While in the Caribbean Indians represent an historically significant economic and political force, in this country they have been overlooked (since many British are ignorant of the Indian presence in Britain), miscategorized (on paper they appear as 'West Indian' due to country of birth, while physically they appear 'Asian'), and misunderstood (in various ways by whites, Asians and Afro-Caribbeans alike). The following essay points to certain salient features of the Indo-Caribbean presence in Britain, how various misapprehensions among others have arisen, and what the consequences of such misapprehensions have been for Indo-Caribbeans themselves and for the general understanding of the Caribbean diaspora.

Indians in the Caribbean

Following the abolition of slavery in British colonies between 1834 and 1838, colonial sugar planters desperately sought new sources of labour. The newly freed Africans did not flee from plantations, as historians once rather thought; most were willing to continue working as wage labourers (Hall 1978). But by calling for a cheap, controllable workforce from outside their colonies (even in times of low actual labour need), planters could ensure locally depressed agricultural wages and also mitigate the possibility of the African ex-slaves becoming a proletarian class which might threaten production and profits by making demands and withholding their labour. Beginning in 1834, planters in Mauritius were fairly successful in importing contract labourers from India; their model soon spread to sugar colonies around the world. The pervasive framework of British colonial administration provided the substantial organization that was needed, in India and overseas, to create what was deemed in its own time, 'a new system of slavery' (see Tinker 1974). Even given the cost of recruitment and transport (often underwritten by local colonial administrations which were dominated by sugar planters), Indian migration was quickly accepted as the most beneficial (that is, owner-profitable) solution to the post-Abolition situation.

British Guiana (today's Guyana) received the first Indian immigrants in 1838, Trinidad in 1845, Jamaica in 1854, and other West Indian territories in subsequent years (see Table 7.1). In many of the smaller islands, Indian migration halted after a few decades mainly because their economies could not support the cost of recruitment and transport (Erickson 1934). In the largest receiving territories, namely British Guiana, Trinidad and Dutch Guiana (Surinam), Indian migration continued until 1917, when the system was halted throughout the British Empire. Between 1838 and 1917 over 2.5 million Indians ventured abroad under this system to such far-flung places as Fiji, South Africa and the Caribbean – the latter of which alone received over half a million Indians.

Indian migration to all of these places was governed by a system of indenture contracts. Though the details of contracts varied over the years in each colony, the most common features of indentureship included: recruitment by indigenous agents throughout vast areas of northeast and southeast India; inducement to enter into contracts to labour for at least five years on a foreign plantation; transport to and maintenance in the port of embarkation (Calcutta or Madras) and abroad; receipt of a basic pay, often on a task basis, while supported with rudimentary housing, rations, and medical attention during the course of the contract; and partly or fully paid return passage to India following the expiration of the contract (and, often to be eligible for fully paid passage, a further five years' labour in the colony). While providing a

Table 7.1 Indentured Indian migration to the Caribbean and population by country, 1980

Colony/Country	Period	Indian Immigrants	Estimated Indian Population	Indians as % of Total Population
British Guiana/Guyana	1838–1917	238,909	424,400	50.8
Trinidad	1845–1917	143,939	421,000	40.7
Guadeloupe	1854–85	42,326	23,165	1.0
Jamaica	1854–85	36,420	50,300	1.7
Dutch Guiana/Surinam	1873–1916	34,000	124,900	31.0
Martinique	1854–89	25,509	16,450	1.9
St. Lucia	1858–95	4,350	3,700	3.0
Grenada	1865–85	3,200	3,900	4.2
St. Vincent	1861–80	2,472	5,000	5.5

Sources: Roberts and Byrne 1966; Tinker 1974; Dingaravelou 1990; Barrett 1982

kind of migratory outlet for Indians in the economically devastated and famine-struck India of the late nineteenth and early twentieth centuries, indenture on plantations in the Caribbean proved harsh through the system's own ways of creating poverty, disease, malnutrition and social oppression (see Mangru 1987; Vertovec 1992a).

Notwithstanding dire conditions on the plantations, around four out of five Indian immigrants in the three largest colonies opted to stay in the Caribbean following the expiration of their indenture contracts. They did so largely because opportunities for land acquisition and social mobility were deemed potentially better in these places than back in India. Yet the patterns of post-indenture settlement varied significantly in each colony – patterns which subsequently had much to do with the local nature of emergent Indian ethnicity and race relations in the Caribbean (and which, in accordance, had much to do with conditioning features of later migration to Britain and elsewhere).

Ehrlich (1971) provides a useful comparison of Indian settlement patterns in Jamaica, Trinidad, and British Guiana. His central argument is that:

> communities organized around modified cultural patterns failed to develop in Jamaica as they did in some other areas because of historical and ecological factors during the post-emancipation period in the British Caribbean (Ehrlich 1971: 166–7).

Due to various financial problems surrounding a declining sugar industry, Jamaica received far fewer indentured immigrants than either Trinidad or British Guiana. However, it was not the paucity of numbers that disfavoured the creation of a sense of community among Indians in Jamaica; rather, lack of geographical concentration after indenture contributed most to the weakening of communal sentiments and the adoption of non-Indian social and cultural habits. 'A large ethnic population spread over a wide geographic area,' Ehrlich (1971: 169) suggests, 'would not in all likelihood maintain ethnic ties as well as a smaller population highly concentrated.' St. Mary, Kingston and Westmoreland were the areas identified most with Indian settlement in Jamaica, but in these places no exclusively Indian villages developed. Instead, Indians came to reside in villages and agricultural settlements alongside the numerically dominant Africans. Shepherd (1988) describes how, for decades, Indian–African relations in Jamaica were quite good until the period 1930–45, when economic competition in a time of scarcity led to a deterioration of such relations, sometimes to the point of violence. Although few aspects of Indian culture and society remain in Jamaica, Ehrlich (1976) observes, social differentiation and self-perceptions persist by way of racial segmentation.

Similarly, in the smaller islands of the British West Indies, Indians settled in a dispersed way such that collective activity and shared, pre-migration cultural phenomena eventually gave way to traits wholly indicative of the colonial Caribbean. One telling example of this is the case of Grenada, where in 1960 only eight Hindus and six Muslims were recorded in a population of 3,768 Indians (within a total population of 88,677): the balance was comprised of Christians of many denominations (Steele 1976).

In British Guiana and Trinidad, however, things were different. At different times in these colonies, various schemes were created such that Indians could acquire plots of land following the expiration of their indenture contracts (see Nath 1950; Wood 1968). In British Guiana, the topography of the colony limited agricultural settlement to a narrow coastal strip. Consequently, the proximity of Indian lands and homes was physically circumscribed. Although this coastal strip, which is only fifteen to twenty miles wide, also served to concentrate the other ethnic groups, Despres (1967: 58) points out that immigration policies and labour laws – along with ethnic groups' different strategies for resource exploitation – acted to confine the groups to spatially separate areas. Indians came to be located primarily in rural districts of East and West Coast Demerara and Berbice, while Africans became identified with the urban vicinity of Georgetown.

In Trinidad, ex-indentured Indians were offered plots in the vicinity of existing sugar plantations. In this way, the Indians could develop new arable lands while providing a seasonal workforce for the estates. Numerous homogeneously Indian villages sprang up throughout the island's central 'sugar belt' – a large area of the country which is still pervasively Indian today. Such demographic concentration in both British Guiana and Trinidad played a large part in providing for the reproduction, from generation to generation, of Indian social, cultural, and religious practices – all of which fostered strong ethnic sentiments.

Such strong sentiments in each colony (and eventually, in each independent country) were also hardened by sometimes tense relations with the numerically comparable Africans. In many respects, such tenseness can be traced to attitudes formed soon after the arrival of Indians in the region (Brereton 1979). The white planters were glad to foment antagonism between Indians and Africans, as they hoped that in the case one group rebelled, the other would come to the side of the whites. In the earliest days, Indians generally viewed the Africans as crude, lazy and licentious, while the Africans saw the Indians as a heathen, stingy, scab workforce. Further, some scholars have suggested that, at least initially, Indian distancing or outright prejudice against Africans was drawn from caste-based notions of ritual pollution: since in north India the lowest castes were often associated with dark skin, it is suggested that the Africans encountered for the first time in the Caribbean must have therefore been regarded by the immigrant Indians as a highly polluted people (Moore 1977).

Yet it is a subsequent history of resource competition and structural inequality, rather than initial prejudice, which has overwhelmingly conditioned race relations in Guyana and Trinidad (see Cross 1978). Arguably a large factor in this has been the continued predominance of Indian residence in rural areas, where poverty and unemployment were always most rife. Yet further, in each country throughout the 1950s and 1960s (when migration to Britain was most common), Indians were shown to be under-represented in the civil services, to have the lowest incomes of any ethnic group, and to be blatantly discriminated against in many economic sectors (Harewood 1971; Cross 1973; Hintzen 1985). And although Indians also long exhibited the highest number of unskilled workers and the lowest number of professionals, they have demonstrated an increasing desire for education, social mobility and high-status occupations (Cross and Schwartzbaum 1969; Graham and Gordon 1977; Nevadomsky 1983; Hintzen 1989).

The situation of Indians in Guyana and Trinidad was worsened by the emergence of a notorious state of racial party politics (see Ryan 1972; Premdas 1972–3). In Guyana, the Indian (mainly Hindu)-dominated People's Progressive Party (PPP) enjoyed two brief periods of power (1953, 1957–64) over the African-dominated (and often Indian Muslim-backed) People's National Congress (PNC) before being ousted each time with the collaboration of the British and American governments. Following race riots in 1963 and 1964 in which 150 people were killed, the PNC came to power (with a weak coalition partner, after British manoeuvres to instal proportional representation to prevent the communist-prone PPP from gaining power). The PNC governed the country through independence in 1966, and have ever since consolidated their power through internationally observed intimidation and vote rigging. In Trinidad, the Indian-dominated People's Democratic Party (PDP, eventually to call itself the Democratic Labour Party or DLP) was virtually indistinguishable from the country's Sanatan Dharma Maha Sabha, or national Hindu organization. The PDP/DLP never experienced government except by way of opposition, however, and the African-backed People's National Movement (PNM) maintained total control of the nation from the mid-1950s, through independence in 1962, until 1986 (and have, recently, been re-elected once more). In each country, the governing African party was seen to favour its own racial constituency (Hintzen 1989); hence, the weight of perceived political oppression added to Indians' poor socio-economic plight. Africans, on the other hand, saw the Indian parties as striving to establish their own, communally patronistic regime (pointing to the rhetoric and makeup of the DLP in Trinidad in the 1950s and 1960s, and the favouritism which the PPP allegedly showed Indians during their term of government in the early 1960s).

In racially mixed neighbourhoods, towns and villages throughout the Caribbean, day-to-day relations between Indians and Africans are usually not bad – indeed, great inter-racial friendships, mutual cooperation, and inter-community events are often hallmarks of such local scenes. As with any racialized context, however, when it comes to making generalizations about history and society with reference to 'the other' (not so-and-so nearby who one knows well, but 'Indians' or 'Negroes' generically), negative stereotypes and characterizations of race relations arise among both Afro- and Indo-Caribbeans in every Caribbean country.

It is this background which must first be understood in order to appreciate the experience of Indo-Caribbeans in Britain.

Indo-Caribbean Immigration and Settlement in Britain

As mentioned previously, the movement of Indo-Caribbean migrants to Britain occurred mainly as part of the larger immigration of Caribbean peoples during the 1950s and early 1960s. This larger migration was not so much due to population pressures in the Caribbean as to opportunities offered in this country (Peach 1968). By far the greatest influx of West Indians took place initially prior to implementation of the 1962 Commonwealth Immigration Act, when thousands migrated for fear of having the door permanently shut.

Although Indo-Caribbean immigration occurred within the general Caribbean influx, the nature of their move differed in important ways. Indo-Caribbean immigrants in Britain tended to exhibit higher pre-migration educational backgrounds than the bulk of Afro-Caribbean immigrants, and sometimes higher occupational levels as well. (Yet this may be said generally of all Trinidadians and Guyanese, since these countries have been noted for their substantial 'brain drain': Andrews 1975; Boodhoo and Baksh 1981.) As explained by informants and noted in questionnaires, highly motivated

Indians chose to come to Britain basically to work and study on levels higher than they deemed possible (through lack of facilities or through racial or religious discrimination) in Guyana and Trinidad. Most informants claim they originally intended to return to the Caribbean at some point after gaining credentials or amassing considerable capital. It has also been suggested that well-to-do Guyanese of all races emigrated from Guyana in the early 1960s due to the PPP's Marxist policies (Milne 1981: 25), while racial fears during the riots in that country prompted further flights (particularly by Indians, who suffered the brunt of the violence; cf. Enloe 1982).

In terms of overall numbers, West Indian immigration to Britain declined through the 1960s and 1970s, yet immigration from Guyana and Trinidad remained substantial. The 1961 Census of Great Britain shows a total Trinidad-born population of 9,273 and a Guyana-born one of 10,889; by 1981 the Trinidad-born population registered 16,334 (an increase of 7,061) and the Guyana-born population, 21,686 (having increased by 10,797). The intervening period was one marked by heightened political and socio-economic fears among Indians under the ever more powerful PNC and PNM regimes during a time when both economies were plunging. Thus Indian emigration from Guyana and Trinidad grew considerably at this time. Boodhoo and Baksh (1981) indicate that between 1969 and 1976, Indo-Guyanese increasingly comprised between 31 and 47 per cent of total Guyanese emigrants. There is little reason to assume the ratio would be drastically different in Trinidad (although as the 1970s progressed, Indo-Trinidadians fared better through oil boom spinoffs and sugar price hikes (Vertovec 1990).

Due to the lack of a 'race' question in British censuses which could be correlated to country of birth, we can only guess at the current number of Indo-Caribbeans in Britain. If we count as Indo-Caribbean a conservative proportion of between 30 and 40 per cent of all Trinidad-born (16,334) and Guyana-born (21,686) persons in Britain in 1981, we arrive at figures of a possible 4,900–6,500 Indo-Trinidadian immigrants and 6,500–8,700 Indo-Guyanese. If we then multiply these figures by two, roughly to indicate offspring born in Britain (following the pattern shown by the Labour Force Survey 1986, in which the total West Indian population of Britain is twice that of West Indians by place of birth), we obtain figures of 9,800–13,000 and 13,000–17,400 respectively, or an Indo-Trinidadian/Indo-Guyanese population of some 22,8000 to 30,400.[1] In addition to being a rough deduction, furthermore, this is, of course, an underestimate of the total Indo-Caribbean population in Britain, especially since it does not take into consideration illegal migration, nor does it include the unknown numbers of Indians from Jamaica, Grenada, St. Vincent and elsewhere in the Caribbean.

The great majority of British Indo-Caribbeans reside in London. Using the same reasoning as above, based on Trinidad- and Guyana-born persons in Greater London and the outer metropolitan area, we arrive at an estimated number of between 17,534–23,378 Indo-Caribbeans in the region, or 77 per cent of the presumed total Indo-Caribbean population of Britain. They are spread widely across the London area, with a modest concentration in Balham and Tooting, Brixton and Catford. Almost all the persons who were interviewed or who responded to questionnaires indicate that they have moved many times since immigrating (from the early 1960s through the early 1980s), yet practically all have done so merely from one vicinity in London to another.

The bulk of British Indo-Caribbeans migrated to work and study, most had not established families back in the Caribbean which they planned on supporting with remissions. As individuals who 'came to go back' – set on gaining credentials, experience, and capital – most married (usually back home) only after some time in Britain, only subsequently establishing families in this country. Thus most have children wholly raised in Britain.

Initially, a few individual 'pioneers' came to Britain, usually having lived in the urban environs of Georgetown or Port-of-Spain (where they had gained a higher level and quality of secondary or advanced education than most of their rural compatriots, and where they had perhaps more readily been able to accumulate funds for the journey). According to one of these early Indo-Caribbean migrants (who arrived in 1954), initial accommodation was far more difficult to gain than a job. Racism in the housing market was blatant and rife at a time when 'No Coloureds' signs frequented the windows in London lodging houses. Many of the first migrants lived around Notting Hill Gate, Earls Court, and Hammersmith, where some bed-and-breakfast hotels were more liberal (or were owned by members of other immigrant groups). Then, such 'pioneers' had to face the fact that, as an informant attested, due to racism 'you couldn't get a civil servant's job, or any job, in fact, that's commensurate with your education'. Dishwashing, assembly line work, streetsweeping, and other manual labouring jobs were taken by individuals trained to be teachers, accountants, and administrators. Nursing was the main occupation into which women went; although this provided housing (in largely West Indian-occupied nurses' homes), training and a skilled profession, wages were poor, chances for promotion were minimal, and the duties given to the immigrants were the most undesirable.

The first 'pioneers', further, served as contacts for subsequent migrants – and therefore, as anchors or central nodes in growing immigrant networks. Persons back in Guyana, Trinidad, or elsewhere in the Caribbean would simply have one of their names (knowing it was someone from their neighbourhood, a relative, or friend of a friend), and that was as good as an invitation. The then-settled 'pioneer' migrant would receive a letter stating that so-and-so would arrive on a certain date, and in a most unselfish manner, he or she would dutifully meet the new immigrant at the boat train, put them up for a few nights, and give them tips on making their way in a new and sometimes hostile society.

Many of the first Indo-Caribbean migrants were quite isolated socially. One recalls that he practically 'lived in a shell', going to work, school, and studying while knowing only a few kindred souls. Some began to frequent the West India Student Centre in Earls Court, where they had meals and basically 'limed' (hung around and chatted). There, however, they often encountered ignorance and exclusion by small islanders – especially the many from Barbados who never had encountered Indo-Caribbeans before (since during colonial times that island did not receive indentured Indians).

Just as the majority of Indo-Caribbeans in Britain attest to having moved, since originally immigrating, several times within the London area, so, too, do most indicate a succession of occupational changes. This is particularly – and not surprisingly – the case among those who came in the late 1950s and early 1960s: often they had originally undertaken unskilled or semi-skilled occupations while studying for British credentials (in law, medicine, accounting or engineering) deemed more meaningful to employers here than those credentials they had gained in the Caribbean. Eventually, most Indo-Caribbeans in Britain embarked on a course of upward occupational mobility. Later arrivals, who often came with degrees from the University of Guyana or the University of the West Indies – and who were often pursuing advanced degrees from one of the London universities – usually did not have to undertake the same, initially low entry into the British job market as did their forerunners. Usually having working-class origins in the Caribbean, British Indo-Caribbeans may now be characterized as being broadly middle-class, engaged in a range of professional, administrative and white-collar occupations (though one should not, of course, pigeon-hole an entire community so as to overlook the numbers of working-class and unemployed Indo-Caribbean women and men).

Although British Indo-Caribbeans are not, then, geographically or occupationally clustered, they do remain quite distinct socially, culturally, religiously, and through shared experiences of racial and ethnic exclusion by whites, Asians and Afro-Caribbeans. The following section points to such features and experiences, suggesting certain implications these have had for the formation of British Indo-Caribbean collective identity and community organizations.

Dimensions of Distinction

Over the course of 150 years in the Caribbean, a variety of Indian social, cultural and religious institutions were transformed in significant ways. This is not especially remarkable, for it is in the nature of society, culture and religion to transform constantly in discourse with its changing demographic, political and material surroundings; indeed, many key features of society, culture and religion in India itself have changed significantly over the past 150 years. Among Indians in Guyana and Trinidad, important changes have included: (a) the attenuation of the caste system, such that only a few caste identities remain, while a complex system of caste relations is wholly absent (see Schwartz 1967; Vertovec 1992a); (b) the creation of an Indian *lingua franca* by means of sifting, modifying and combining aspects of different Indian languages into one (see Durbin 1973; Gambhir 1988); and (c) the formulation and institutionalization of an 'orthodox' Hinduism based on certain general, north Indian traditions (see van der Meer and Vertovec 1991; Vertovec 1992a, n.d.).

Many other characteristics set Indians apart in Guyana and Trinidad, including aesthetic preferences and traditional manners of dress, musical styles, cuisine, and patterns of sexual or familial relationships. Still, a great variety of wholly Caribbean traits have come to characterize Indians there, especially the use of the local creole dialect of English, certain mannerisms, forms of joking, other aspects of cuisine, games and an avid participation in cricket (though in this sphere, tensions often arise: while Indians often complain they are discriminated against in selection procedures for the West Indian side, they do often play prominent roles on national teams; and although Indians are keen supporters of the West Indies in international tests, that support always switches to India when the two sides compete – hence, sometimes uncomfortably, racializing India–West Indies test matches in Port-of-Spain and Georgetown). In Trinidad, carnival and calypso/soca are often eschewed by rural or other tradition-steeped Indians (though often even the most chauvinistic Indo-Trinidadian can recite and take delight in lines from certain calypsos) – hence, much debate has arisen over the place of Indians in the 'national culture'.

When these developments are viewed in light of the history of racial stereotypes and racial politics, one can begin to understand Indians' self-perceptions of distinction – in some spheres, tinged with feelings of similarity – vis-à-vis Africans and others in the Caribbean. In Britain, these self-perceptions are compounded by a host of factors.

It is not possible (or desirable) to make any single generalization regarding relations between Indo-Caribbeans and Afro-Caribbeans in Britain. Just as in the Caribbean itself, personal relations are often quite good and friendships, sincere; yet broad statements about 'the other' frequently are stereotyped and coloured by reference to politics. In the early days of their mutual presence in Britain, Indo- and Afro-Caribbean immigrants (that is, primarily those from Guyana and Trinidad) regularly socialized together in boarding houses, clubs and associations. Over the years, however, these patterns of consociation have given way to more communal ones as settlement became dispersed and family-based, and as exclusively Indo- or Afro-Caribbean recreational space, organizations and activities emerged. Currently few formal arenas exist where the two are mutually active, save for foreign branches of certain political parties (namely the Working Peoples' Alliance, or WPA, for Guyanese and, at least until recent years, the National Alliance for Reconstruction, or NAR, among Trinidadians). Although some Indo-Caribbeans notably involved themselves together with Afro-Caribbeans in aspects of the (politically designated) 'black' struggle in Britain as it developed essentially since the 1970s, on the whole most first-generation British Indo-Caribbeans maintained their own course of community development – always bearing in mind their perceptions of Indian socio-economic and political plight at the hands of Africans in the Caribbean.

Although 'Asian' in appearance, many Indo-Caribbeans report to have been rather disdained by members of various Asian communities in Britain. This is due largely to the different social, cultural and religious forms which Indians created in the Caribbean. Indians from the subcontinent do not wholly understand the Trinidad and Guyanese Bhojpuri (dialect of Hindi) sometimes – if at all – spoken by Indo-Caribbeans; they find strange certain features of Hindu practice as they have evolved in the Caribbean; they are puzzled that Indo-Caribbeans often do not know exactly where in India their ancestors came from, or what were their caste and clan origins; and they (wrongly) believe that the original indentured migrants to the Caribbean were predominantly from low or untouchable castes – or worse, in their eyes, believe (again, wrongly) that Indo-Caribbeans have miscegenated with Africans over generations. Hence, British Indo-Caribbeans have said of their subcontinental counterparts, 'They don't see me as one of them,' 'As an Indian from the Caribbean, they look at you as an oddity, as an ignorant cousin,' and 'We are not regarded as true Indian.'

British Indo-Caribbeans – who are, in other words, Asian West Indians – have a rather anomalous position since they harbour no close identification with either self-defined groups of 'Asians' or (Afro-)'West Indians'. Many British Indo-Caribbeans feel excluded from both categories, an experience noted by the Indo-Trinidadian novelist Sam Selvon:

> As for the Caribbean man of East Indian descent, he was something else. He wasn't accepted by those from India, and he wasn't wanted by the others because he wasn't a black man and so he couldn't understand what was going on. If he could play cricket, he could join the team, but leave the politics out (Selvon 1987: 18).

Further, by way of statistics, and in terms of formal British ethnic categories, they are indeed 'West Indian' due to their countries of birth; and, perhaps more importantly, in the eyes of British whites, they are 'Asian' – or, unfortunately more commonly expressed, 'Paki' (since racism acknowledges no distinction of heritage). These obfuscations and indignities have, over the years, increasingly stimulated British Indo-Caribbeans to go their own way in a number of fields.

The density of social networks among Indo-Caribbeans has facilitated the establishment of formal associations of different kinds. Initially, the process of immigration and settlement was itself largely a product of social networks, as friends, relatives, co-villagers and others facilitated the travel and arrival, housing and even employment of one another. Continuous communication with those back in the Caribbean, and frequent return visits there, have served to maintain such connections. In this way, news of people and events 'back home' (a term still often used by people settled here for thirty years or more) quickly gets around; similarly, through such grapevines Indo-Caribbean activities (social, cultural or religious) organized here are easily publicized.

The most prominent sets of activities first institutionalized were religious. In the mid-1950s, a half dozen or so Hindu immigrants from the Caribbean organized, by means of their overlapping social networks, religious rites on a regular basis. These soon grew in size – especially since, at that time, participants included many Hindu migrants from India. By 1957 they formed the Hindu Dharma Sabha, originally meeting in someone or other's flat but soon renting larger venues such as the Royal Overseas League, Railton Road Community Centre, and Lambeth Town Hall. By the early 1960s, as the subcontinental Hindus gradually founded their own organizations, the Sabha changed its name to the Caribbean Hindu Society in order to cater more specifically for Indo-Caribbeans. The society bought premises in Brixton in 1972, where a sizeable temple remains today and where rites and gatherings are undertaken reflecting a unique heritage and strong sense of identity (see Vertovec 1992b).

A similar process occurred among Muslim Indians from the Caribbean. Drawing upon the social networks of Trinidadian and Guyanese Indian immigrants, small domestic gatherings in the 1950s evolved into the North London Islamic Association and the North London Jamaat during the 1960s. Today these have been succeeded by the United Islamic Association, based in Haringey, a *jamaat* or congregation still comprised predominantly of Indo-Caribbeans (see *Asian Times* 19 February 1988).

Secular organizations have arisen in latter years. Of particular note is the UK branch of the People's Progressive Party (PPP), which not only engages in political activity and lobbying, but organizes fund-raising activities and dances serving the Indo-Caribbean population (see *Asian Times* 18 December 1987). In 1988 – a year marking the 150th anniversary of the Indian presence in the Caribbean – the Indo-Caribbean Cultural Association (ICCA) was established. Among its stated objects are: 'To promote educational, social and leisure facilities for Indo-Caribbean peoples and their descendants' and 'To promote knowledge of Indo-Caribbean history and culture, and thereby to work for the betterment of the welfare of all Caribbean peoples.' Among its activities, the ICCA organized a series of annual 'cultural extravaganzas' bringing to Britain Indian singers, dancers, musicians and authors from the Caribbean to demonstrate their arts and, thereby, to emphasize and to celebrate Indo-Caribbean identity.

Social networks turning to formal organizations is not a process confined to Indo-Caribbean experience in Britain only. Throughout the period from the 1960s to the 1980s there has been an exodus of Indians from Guyana and Trinidad. This has emerged through worsening – indeed, in the case of Guyana, often abhorrent – economic conditions and increasing fears of political indifference or prejudice against Indians. Hence British Indo-Caribbeans now have kin, friends, and other social ties throughout America (mainly New York City) and Canada (mainly Toronto). Such ties have been institutionalized internationally by way of new organizations linking Indo-Caribbeans worldwide through conferences, fund-raising activities, political lobbying and printed media (see *Asian Times*, 20 January 1989).

Thus Indo-Caribbean collective sentiments have been increasingly mobilized and institutionalized on a variety of levels since first arriving in Britain – both as a kind of 'resistance' to felt exclusions on behalf of British whites, Afro-Caribbeans and Asians, and as a manifestation of felt 'difference' or distinction on their own behalf (and sometimes, as the result of inherent racism on the part of certain Indo-Caribbeans, especially in relation to Afro-Caribbeans). Yet British Indo-Caribbeans have not necessarily achieved unity in all their undertakings: strong attachments to Guyana, Trinidad, Jamaica or elsewhere in the Caribbean still hold sway. Such attachments are bolstered through particular social networks tying British Indo-Caribbeans to others 'back home' (especially those based on kinship and villages or neighbourhoods in each Caribbean country), dialect differences, and national or regional social and cultural habits sometimes joked about or stereotyped. Such localized identities or community sub-divisions are characteristic of all Caribbean peoples in Britain, however, especially small islanders (cf. Philpott 1977; Peach 1984).

Whether such evolving patterns of mobilization and institutionalization, or such maintained patterns of national or regional ties, will remain among Indo-Caribbeans born and raised in this country is yet to be seen. So far, subsequent generations of British Indo-Caribbeans for the most part appear to harbour few of the sentiments regarding Guyanese and Trinidadian politics or attitudes towards British Asians and Afro-Caribbeans (although their experience of white racism has been much the same). Some young Indo-Caribbeans took up a wholly 'West Indian' identity and its Rastafarian manifestation during the 1970s, while today many have adopted a kind of pan-British Asian 'youth culture' while seeking to explore their roots in subcontinental culture (for example, through learning Hindi or Indian music

and dance). Overall, most young British Indo-Caribbeans seem much readier
to adopt a general 'black' political identity than their parents, and in practice,
they have emerged as a truly 'multicultural' generation.

Conclusion

Just as the Caribbean should not be characterized as a region wholly
populated by people of African descent (nor of one African-derived culture),
so, too, should not the Caribbean diaspora in Britain. Failure to recognize the
presence of Indians and others in both parts of the globe contributes to a
broader failure to understand the historical movements of peoples, the
legacies of imperial rule, processes of cultural change, dynamics of political
struggles, ramifications of emergent race relations, and the institutionalization of ethnic identities. Indo-Caribbean peoples in Britain have been
overlooked by observers of all kinds – academics, the media, and the general
public alike; they have been miscategorized in official statistics and in social
perception; and they have been misunderstood by almost all they have come
into contact with in this country. Such a variety of obfuscations by others –
contrasting with their own self-knowledge of a long history, vibrant culture,
and firm identity (both before and after settling here) – has been foremost in
the experience of Indo-Caribbeans in Britain.

Note

1. I wish to express my thanks to Ceri Peach for his helpful discussions regarding possible
numbers of Indo-Caribbeans in Britain.

8

Psychiatric Racism and Social Police: Black People and the Psychiatric Services

Errol Francis

Introduction

Nowadays black people are almost synonymous with the idea of madness, but there used to be a time when black people, Africans in particular, were considered almost too primitive to experience 'complex mental illness'. In the romantic notion of the 'noble savage', to be mad was more or less a possibility of the civilized mind. The savage occupied an existential space somewhere between childhood and adolescence. Madness was, and still is, defined as irrationality and unreason; so how could the essentially 'irrational' mind of the 'savage' experience madness?

The savage was the very incarnation of irrationality and unreason – the Other of civilization. As late as 1937, psychiatrists like Laubscher (1937) would say:

> Insane ideas having particular reference to personal experience are so much in harmony with the generic ideas, that differentiation between the particular irrational and the general irrational (witchcraft) are indeed a difficult task for the normal pagan native because so much of his beliefs belong to the universe of irrationality.

Concepts of insanity thus become a means by which racial difference can be articulated. The figure of madness is a crucial element in the historical construction of race, racism and racial difference. Psychiatrists were foremost in the articulation of race along biological and cultural lines. The rise of psychiatry, and especially comparative psychiatry, occurs parallel with European colonial expansion abroad and industrialization at home. As a prerequisite for such expansion there is an imperative to understand 'Man' on a domestic and global scale. The realization of colonial domination owed as

179

much to a knowledge of Man as it did to a knowledge of geo-political territories. Thus the practices of the human sciences are of paramount importance to any consideration of classical or contemporary racism. Take, for example, somatometry – the measurement of the human body.

Anthropologists towards the end of the nineteenth century were obsessed by somatometry. The object of measurement was mainly the body of the 'savage', criminals, and the 'lower classes'. The object was to try to ascertain if social (class) or racial differences could be identified and measured in physical attributes. (In the 1920s the proto-Nazi eugenics movement in the United States would turn their callipers on the bodies of black Americans to record their dimensions and 'defects' in the wishful belief that the 'Negro' was on the verge of extinction because of innate genetic inferiority!) But for the early somatometrists, their principal interest was in the physique – especially the head – which would be measured to see if, for example, there was a particular facial angle or profile applicable to criminals or deviants. When it came to black people the interest in the physique was more general, involving the dimensions of the whole body. Haller (1970) points out that:

> From an initial emphasis upon the enumeration of races, the nineteenth-century science of man moved into somatometry through ingenious efforts to determine racial peculiarities. The hallmark of anthropology in the nineteenth century was somatometry.

In the late 1890s, at a British penal colony on the Andaman Islands in the Bay of Bengal, a typical exercise in somatometry was undertaken. The aboriginal population were infected with pneumonia, syphilis, measles and influenza, and by the turn of the century the native islanders had been all but wiped out by a colonial presence which considered them expendable. 'It was not the policy of government to raise revenue from the aboriginal population' because 'financial interests were confined to the penal settlement' (Portman 1895).

As a means of rendering the Andamanese more knowable, and 'recording them for posterity', the assistant chief superintendent of the penal regime, M.V. Portman, went about the task of calibrating the primitive with uncommon zeal. He perfectly combined the role of colonist/ethnologist, beginning his project with photographic portraits of his aboriginal subjects and with scenes depicting their cultural habits. Then there were studies in which the Andamanese were photographed in front of metrical grids so that their physical dimensions could be instantly read off. Portman recorded their height, average number of heart beats, temperature, weight and personal characteristics. The detail went as far as the folds of skin 'at the inner angle of the eye'; the shape of the face and the profile of the nose; and the size and condition of the genitals. And to complete the totality of the project, Portman produced a treatise on the Andamanese languages so that communication between the colonial regime and the islanders would be enhanced (*The Imperial Gazetteer*, 1908).

Other studies would ask: how heavy is the primitive brain? Is the weight of the human brain proportional to intelligence? Or is intelligence expressed in the size of the cranium, the cell content of the pre-frontal cortex, or the volumetric capacity of the skull? (Vint 1932; Haller 1970). All these physical attributes were measured in relation to theories and hypotheses about racial difference, genetic inferiority and comparative intelligence.

Although these theories and experiments may now seem outlandish compared with contemporary theories of racial difference, there is more of a continuity with the present than orthodox histories of science would have us believe. What these early scientific attempts at identifying and quantifying racial difference represent is an imperialist desire to find a universal norm by which all human attributes can be judged. The modern practice of IQ (Intelligence Quotient) is just one example from the domain of psychometrics whose procedures and aims – the arithmetical gradation of human mental aptitude – can be traced back to the early science of comparative psychology and psychopathology. Race will become crucial, and psychiatry all the more instrumental, in the assembling of a global concept of madness, not only by the imposition of a Western version of rationality with which to judge the normal and the pathological in any race; but everything that falls outside of this Western rationalist domain will be made a negative reference point for concepts of madness and rationality within. As Jung (1970) would put it:

> The inferior man exercises a tremendous pull upon civilized beings who are forced to live with him, because he fascinates the inferior layer of our psyche . . . [1]

What Jung means is that the image of madness, as defined in the West, is personified and incarnated in the 'normal' culture of the primitive. The chaos of the unconscious – that 'inferior layer' of the white man's psyche – is the other, the primitive underbelly of consciousness and rationality. It is the image of savage nature which the white man strives to overcome, and it is also the psychological figure of the inferior opposite which is the normal cultural mentality of savages. Culture thus becomes important to psychiatric diagnosis as part of the rubric of what is normal and what is pathological. The psychiatrist, often doubling as anthropologist, will then occupy a position of power by being able to delineate the boundaries that define and separate acceptable behaviours from madness.[2]

The Social and Police

The emergence of psychiatry in Europe in the latter part of the eighteenth century owes as much to a politico-economic need for an effective means of policing the social as it does to a psychological-cultural regime of norms. Here, psychiatry is concerned with individuals as elemental, molecular formations within the domain of the social. But 'police' should not be understood in the militaristic sense of prohibition and negation. Police, in its original sense, refers to those governmental concerns, practices and discourses whose aim is the maintenance of the social order – the population. Pasquino (1978) gives the definition as:

> Isolated persons, individuals. This is what constitutes a population, that abstract concept which is none other than the object of administration of police.

Consequently health, welfare services, social services and education are all forms of police in that these spheres reflect the policy of the state with regard to the preservation of the social order. Social police, and policy, is the threshold of where the state becomes the estate of the social. The emergence of psychiatry occurs in response to a need for better social police following the consequences of industrialization. There came to be a realization by the middle of the eighteenth century that governments, to be successful, had to pay more attention to the regulation of the social domain. Psychiatry was one response among many to the problem of pauperism, indigence, vagrancy, prostitution and delinquency – in short the multifarious iniquities that followed the restructuring of society to satisfy the needs of capital. We find, therefore, that at the time of psychiatry's emergence as a discipline centred upon the asylum as the place where insanity is detained, the whole spectrum of anti-social delinquency is represented in the population of the asylum. As Scull (1980) reminds us:

> At the outset of this period [between the mid-eighteenth and mid-nineteenth centuries] . . . mad people for the most part were not treated as a separate category of deviants. Rather they were assimilated into the larger, more amorphous class of the morally disreputable, the poor, and the impotent, a group which also included minor criminals, and the physically handicapped.

The function of early psychiatry with regard to this variegated population of the asylum was to separate and classify different forms of delinquency as pathological, anti-social, indigent, defective and so on. Psychiatry became a scientific ally of medicine in the classification and treatment of mental disorders as individual instances of disease cut off from any social origin: this is 'the medical model'. But the problem with the medical/psychiatric strategy is that whereas medicine, the father figure of psychiatry, would be able to devise techniques of intervention into diseases by by-passing their social origin, psychiatry remains comparatively ineffective as a 'curing' agent.

Psychiatry's advances have been in the sophistication of means of containment and in the management and discipline of insanity – and in its role as a
regulatory force vis-à-vis individual aptitude and the social order.

Race Relations and Psychiatry

This essay is an attempt to outline the importance of psychiatry and psychological knowledge to the configuration of contemporary racism in Britain. It is
also an attempt to identify certain historical continuities and discontinuities
which still have a presence. Contemporary race relations theory and practice
is centred on a set of themes remarkably consistent with the old biological/
taxonomic imperatives of classical racism – only that the biological has been
replaced by the cultural. There is a tendency of race relations discourse
towards a metropolitan anthropology of the social, using conceptual models
first devised for deployment at the colonial periphery, but renovated as a
means of governing an explicitly racialized social police at the centre. This
social police, specifically charged with race relations as an instrument of
government, and whose aim is variously concerned with racial integration,
pluralism or multi-culturalism, has an oblique relationship with psychiatry.
One concern of this essay is the way that the anthropological tendency in race
relations occasions the interests of psychiatry and psychology.

Race relations discourse, and the political set-up typified by the Commission for Racial Equality, emerged after the exclusionist era of British racism.
The advent in the late 1950s of race relations as a political objective aimed at
'integration' represents a shift from earlier positions of governments in
relation to the presence of black people as a permanent feature within the
British social formation.

Whereas governments around the time of the first substantial settlements
of black people in the late 1940s had considered the black presence as
temporary, or at least insignificant, requiring no attention in terms of
citizenship or other rights, later governments, facing a growing political
challenge from black militancy, had to be seen to take the race question on
board. As Sivanandan (1982) has written: 'To stop black militancy infecting
the body politic, the government embarked on a programme of integration.'
The problem was how to define and conceptualize racism, as an official
reason behind the acknowledgement of such a programme. It is the redefinition of racism as a problem of culture and identity (rather than power) which
allows the human sciences to be deployed. An anthropologically-inclined
sociology, linked with psychology, will redefine the black presence in the
British social body as a problem of integrating 'alien cultures' within the
'British way of life'. Attention is turned to the culture of 'immigrants', their

lifestyles, family structures, diet, reproductive patterns, religion – all being identified as obstacles to integration, and recorded with the same obsessional detail that Portman put into recording his primitives.

Racism will be seen to be caused almost by immigrants themselves for failing to be intelligible, in cultural terms. And it is as a direct consequence of this cultural reductionist interpolation of racism by the human sciences that social police will be deployed as a means of control rather than integration. The redefinition of racism as a culturalist problem of social police may be done under the guise of 'integration' or positive measures to combat 'disadvantage' but it merely authorizes several state agencies to act in concert, as a circuit of control, using as their rationale the idea that black people are a serious threat to the social order, as a malignant pathology, for which special social police controls are needed. The point of entry is the cultural and the pathological.

The Psychological Complex – Schooling

With regard to race, the school is the object of contradictory yet complementary forces. One the one hand there are the 'anti-racist' positions which target the school as a place of cultural domination (Garrison 1977); and on the other there are the bureaucratic-administrative interests of race relations which propose an understanding of race that is located in the cultural and the personal. Both positions end up complementing one another and set the stage for the total psychologization of black children in the British school system. And it is this 'psycho-cultural' targeting of black individuals that will set the stage for the intervention of other agencies, besides the school, bringing the black child properly within the circuit of control described here as social police. Consider this early assessment of racism in education.

In 1971 Bernard Coard, a Grenadan school teacher working in London, published a fifty-page book under the title: *How the West Indian Child is Made Educationally Sub-normal in the British School System.* The book received considerable attention at the time because of its attempt at an authoritative explanation of why black children were being kept at the lowest level of educational opportunity. Coard would focus on the category of educational sub-normality (ESN) and the practice of IQ testing as the principal instrument with which education authorities separated normal from sub-normal. Coard presented Inner London Education Authority (ILEA) statistics showing a massive over-representation of Afro-Caribbean children within ESN units. He focused on techniques of IQ testing by the Schools' Psychological Service because they appeared pre-set for black children to fail. Coard also showed that once placed in an ESN unit, black children had a poor prognosis with regard to returning to a normal school. But the way that he conceptualized the reasons for the entrapment of black children in the ESN category is problematic. Referring to the IQ test as 'the single most important indicator to the Educational Psychologist' that a child is ESN, Coard identifies three 'biases' which he held to be responsible for the over-diagnosis of educational subnormality in black children. First of all is culture (Coard 1971). There are:

> Linguistic differences between West Indian English and 'standard classroom' English. The West Indian child's choice of words, usage and meaning of words, pronunciation and intonation sometimes present tremendous difficulties with the teacher and vice versa.

Then there is the 'middle-class bias':

> in a middle-class institution . . . viewing the child through middle-class tinted glasses, the child being working-class in most cases . . . feeling that he is somehow inferior, and bound to fail (Ibid.).

Finally, the 'emotional disturbance' bias:

> Many of the problem children . . . are suffering a temporary emotional disturbance due to severe culture and family shock, resulting from their sudden removal from the West Indies to a half-forgotten family, and an unknown and generally hostile environment (Ibid.).

While one would not deny that such phenomena exist, and that they are a factor in the practice and experience of racism, they cannot be held to be the principal objects of concern in an analysis of institutional racism in the education system in Britain. Yet Coard goes on to build his entire critique of both the content and manner of administering the IQ tests on the basis of these three biases. He constructs a picture of racial domination primarily in terms of culture (although class is at times mentioned) and he identifies 'attitudes' of the teachers and 'anxieties' of the children as the principal terms of his analysis. The solution, by way of an institutional response, will merely be 'culture-free' tests and a demand for more black professional workers to administer the tests. His analysis of emotional disturbance reads like a psychiatric diagnosis: a picture of psychological alienation, personality disorder and identity crisis – and the now familiar stereotype of the black family whose structure has been completely shattered by the experience of immigration and whose offspring – 'caught between two cultures' (Kapo 1982) – are debilitated by 'culture shock' and an inability to cope with the way of life in the metropolis. Coard's critique therefore falls short of being an effective analysis and a whole series of less well-intentioned versions of this sort of analysis would follow from a burgeoning cadre of race experts (Garrison 1983).

Ten years after the publication of Coard's essay, the Rampton Committee, which was commissioned by the Department of Education and Science (DES), published its report *West Indian Children in Our Schools* (DES 1981), and in it we find a choice of themes remarkably consistent with Coard's. To begin with, racism is defined as a 'set of attitudes and behaviour' (DES 1981) – which is the first indication that a cultural-reductionist analysis is to follow. We see the black family picked out and blamed as a site of nascent pathology and incipient language defect because:

> West Indian parents may not fully appreciate the need to spend time talking and listening to their children to develop their language skills (DES 1981:12).

On the all-important subject of behaviour the Rampton Committee will report that:

> Head teachers who commented on discipline consistently identified West Indian pupils as the immigrant group with which the most discipline problems arose (Ibid.).

And for the ultimate test that the Committee would make on how well a school had tackled racism, it would be:

> The extent to which these [ethnic minority] groups are positively represented in displays around the school building (Ibid.).

So all that is meant by 'racism' is that grey psychological area of inter-personal relations at the boundary of black and white. Nothing more. Psychiatry is never very far away when there is talk of positive representation (displays = positive images = identity), for the solution is always to be found in altering individuals and not institutional practice.

With these two parallel and complementary strands of discourse represented by Coard and Rampton have come practical initiatives and remedial interventions into the school system, and a whole new body of professional expertise: race relations and multi-cultural experts who have usurped black dissatisfaction with the education system and turned the issue into one of cultural identity. Black positions on culture, which were once radical, have thus been weakened and transformed into reactionary positions on 'accultu-ration' and personality disorder. This has irresistibly drawn psychiatrists to black people as psychologically maladjusted.

After more than a decade of multi-cultural practices in schools the entrapment of black children in the category of sub-normal continues, not only in ESN units but in Support Centres, Intermediate Treatment and Educational Guidance Centres – all those agencies that offer specialist remedial facilities for children deemed to have behavioural, psychological or 'special' educational needs. It is in these units that black children tend to remain, as Coard observed with ESN. It is these same agencies that offer most opportunity for the collaboration of other agencies: like social services, psychiatric and psychological services, the courts, probation and even the police. There is now a whole range of on- or off-site facilities for 'problem' children. ILEA statistics (ILEA 1985a) indicate that:

> In different types of special schools Afro-Caribbeans are over-represented in special schools for the language impaired, schools for autistic children, and schools for children with emotional and behavioural difficulties.

In 1981 28 per cent of the children in Support Centres (disruptive units) were 'West Indian or African' (ILEA 1981). The largest over-representation was in units for children with language impairment where 43.6 per cent of children were Afro-Caribbean (ILEA 1985b). The figures also show that there is a low success rate in terms of correcting or improving academic performance of most children referred to special units. Where they do show an improvement is in the area of discipline.

There has now been a rearguard action by the state to deflect attention away from psychological techniques like IQ testing as being instruments of racism. The Swann Report (which was the second tome of the DES inquiry which began life as Rampton's *West Indian Children in Our Schools*) has this to say about IQ testing:

> There is no evidence that IQ tests are more biased against working-class children . . . or against black children, than are conventional exams or measures of performance (DES 1985).

Throwing away the cultural-reductionist crutches which once supported Coard and Rampton, the Swann Report is, in fact, a backlash against the cultural biases identified by Rampton. Swann dismisses these out of hand, the subtitle of the report, 'Education for All', emphasizing a contemporary Tory impatience with any suggestion that schools deny black children educational success. Rather it is now the pupil's family alone that is seen as the problem. Tucked away in an annex to the main report, an academic paper which the Committee commissioned from two social scientists quietly tries to lay the IQ scandal to rest. They say that criticizing IQ tests for reflecting class difference is rather like 'blaming the weighing machine when it shows an under-nourished child to be below weight' (DES 1985: 127). Quoting another sociologist, they say:

> If a child has been deprived of intellectual stimulation or educational opportunity, it is small wonder that his intellectual performance will reflect this fact (Ibid.).

From this position of blaming, by suggestion, the cultural and family back-ground of Afro-Caribbeans as being the source and cause of academic failure, the sociologists move on to a well-tried ethnic comparison, with Asians:

> [If] the suggestion that the Asian community in this country suffers less racial discrimination than the West Indian seems hard to defend [then how is it that] children of Asian origin by and large do better than those of West Indian? (1985: 139).

The punch line is provided by yet another education sociologist, Sally Tomlinson:

> West Indians are more boisterous and less keen than Asians. This is well known . . . (Tomlinson 1981 – quoted in DES 1985).

So nothing is to be blamed on the institutional set-up of the education system, or the content of curricula. Black people, or black behaviour, are the problem, and everyone is making too much of IQ tests. In a patrician tone Swann concludes: IQ has long been a sensitive and emotive issue. We hope that it can now cease to be so (DES 1985).

But the very arguments put forward in race relations discourses like the Swann Report, that educational failure arises from dysfunctions within black families and from personality and culture, is the very analysis that will authorize further medicalization of black people by psychology, psychiatry, social work – that is from agencies of social police. The IQ test and categorization as ESN is therefore effective in more ways than the placement of children in special units. ESN categorization triggers responses from other agencies. Intermediate Treatment (IT) is a case in point.

Black children are over-represented in IT Centres as in other remedial facilities for children deemed to have special educational or emotional difficulties.[3] IT was introduced by the Department of Health and Social Security (DHSS) in 1972 as a multi-disciplinary practice (involving teachers, psychologists, social workers and probation officers) aimed at children classed as either under-achievers, with behavioural or personality difficulties or as criminally delinquent. During their first year of operation the DHSS described (quoted in Simpson 1980) the object of the centres as:

> [To bring] the child into contact with a different environment and give . . . the opportunity of forming new personal relationships and developing new interests.

The intention at the time was a benign psycho-social approach aimed at reforming personalities in a manner that was ostensibly non-penalizing but nevertheless aimed at correction in medical rather than expressly legal terms. But after the famous 'short, sharp shock' speech by William Whitelaw in 1979, IT centres became an explicit instrument of law and order in the drive against juvenile delinquency. The way was then opened for the further use of psychological expertise for controlling and disciplining children. The centres would gradually fill up with black children deemed disruptive, disturbed or criminal. The formal brief of IT centres is to cater for those who cannot be assimilated into normal schools; but the effect is rather a form of containment – to separate, differentiate and pathologize so that the established momentum of the school can go on uninterrupted by those who do not conform to normal expectations. The over-representation of black children in the category of ESN and in all the special schools is thus a consequence of the predominant definition of black children as being in special need of intervention from psychological expertise and those concerned with behavioural disorder and social hygiene. The analysis of this situation in terms of culture is therefore wholly inadequate and demands, instead, a more rigorous interrogation of institutional practices and the theoretical discourses governing them.

The Psychological Complex – Asylum

There is much about racist medicalization in schools which allows a direct comparison with the mental asylum. Michel Foucault (1980) has argued that both institutions have a normative and regulative function vis-à-vis the social: a way of pathologizing and diagnosing as defective those personalities which violate dominant norms. More specifically Foucault identifies both the school and the asylum as places of disciplinary power and correction. They produce 'docile bodies' and 'obedient individuals'. The asylum and the school, with their infinite rules of institutional conduct, can exercise the same degree of disciplinary power to modify individual behaviour as, say, the prison or the military. The asylum, then, as much as the school, is about the transposition of social and political realities into the realm of individual pathology and normative aptitude.

The failure of psychiatry to achieve a uniform and 'objective' frame of reference means that its asylums are still the depository of the 'anti-social'. Patients tend to be a group of people trapped in the equilibrium of illness or else mobile, at times categorized as insane, at others as criminal, and sometimes as delinquent or socially maladjusted. With this fluid, undefined, definition of pathology (or at least a conceptualization that is all-inclusive), psychiatry and the asylum become prime sites for the medicalization of racism, just as ESN categorization medicalizes racism in schools. If schools can operate 'multi-cultural imperatives' which claim to remedy racism by turning its victims into personalities lacking identity, then we must especially interrogate the procedures of the asylum, which have as their basis a concept of insanity charged with racial signification anyway.

Black people are massively over-diagnosed as mentally ill. In particular, the major psychotic illnesses are diagnosed at up to five times the rate for the rest of the British population, with particular emphasis on schizophrenia (Cochrane 1977). The legal sanctions under the 1983 Mental Health Act, whereby individuals can be compelled to have treatment, are also exercised more often in relation to black people (Runnymede Trust 1983). Then once they are compelled or otherwise admitted to a mental asylum, the medical treatment accorded to black people is often an open form of harassment bordering at times on torture, with rampant over-use of medication and numerous instances of physical abuse (Mercer et al 1984). But a thorough-going analysis of these issues from the point of view of black experience has been obscured by the ground that has been taken by the professional liberal conscience of psychiatry – the so-called 'transculturalists'.

The act of diagnosis (and thereby the doctor–patient relationship) has been singled out by the transculturalists as the problem that needs to be solved so that psychiatric racism can be interpolated as a problem of culture and anthropological knowledge. However, culture and anthropology are part and parcel of the medical tradition of diagnosis anyway, so in this respect the transculturalists are proposing nothing new. What is new is the tactic of bringing culture and anthropology to the fore as a means of explaining away racism itself and absolving the psychiatrist of any role in the institutional and political mechanisms which are entrapping black people in psychiatry. What they are now saying is that it is in the act of diagnosis that certain 'errors' are made in the interpretation of black behaviour (Littlewood and Lipsedge 1981). In a subtle version of the old 'blame the victim' ploy, it is the alien who is the root of the problem, who gets haplessly mistaken for mad when, in fact, he is acting quite normally in the norms of 'his' culture. The deceit in the transcultural position is exposed in the comparison with stalwart old classical racists like the South African Laubscher complaining that he cannot tell the difference between irrationality and the culture of the savage. In the nicest possible way, the modern transculturalist will announce:

> We continually found ourselves looking upon a particular type of behaviour as abnormal, but later as 'only a cultural phenomenon' . . . Often it seemed impossible to distinguish the normal from the pathological (Ibid.).

Culture and anthropology are now being highlighted by psychiatry with the proposition that the over-representation of black people in psychiatric asylums is the result of 'cultural misunderstanding'. It has been said that the 'normal' modes of black cultural expression can be easily misunderstood for pathological symptoms (Tewfik and Okasha 1965). But what these explanations ignore is the already unstable scientific theoretical premisses of psychiatric nosology and the inherent difficulties in their application to any racial group. What is also ignored is the complex links between psychiatry and other welfare/social control and correctional agencies which often act as filters or 'decanters' for those persons who fail to meet their specifications or are considered too dangerous to be assisted. One needs therefore to concentrate much more on processes and modes of admission to hospital rather than the reductionist spectre of cultural difference as it is played out upon the site of the asylum.

Procedures of Admission

The lack of a coherent medico-scientific definition of mental illness, and the importance of psychiatric intervention as a means of discipline, occasions an enormous reliance upon the law, as a partial definition of pathology and as a framework for the referral of patients. Black people are noticeably over-represented in all categories of compulsory admission under the 1983 Mental Health Act (as was the case with the previous 1959 legislation). I shall now look in particular at sections (abbreviated 's') 2, 3, 4 and 136 of the present legislation (Basaglia 1980). The various legal procedures under the Act allowing for compulsory detention of individuals in mental asylums are variously concerned with admission in emergencies (s2 – 72 hours), assessment (s3 – 28 days) and for long-term treatment (s4 – 6 months). These sections can be brought into force with or without the consent of the patient's nearest relative, because doctors and approved social workers are authorized by themselves to sign section papers. Section 136 of the Act empowers the police to apprehend individuals found in a public place and considered to be 'a danger to themselves or others' and to take them to hospital. Section 136 is, for obvious reasons, the most notorious section of the Mental Health Act, because of the ample opportunity it gives to police both to criminalize and to medicalize.

We can begin to make sense of the excessive use of psychiatric compulsion by considering the concept of dangerousness as specified in the Mental Health Act and how it functions in relation to black people. The Act says that compulsion is necessary in cases where the individual thought to be mentally ill has become a danger to themselves or others. And this is justified in practice by the assumption that severe forms of mental breakdown, particularly those diagnosed as 'psychotic', involve a loss of the individual's ability to think and act in his or her own best interests, or in the interests of 'the public'. Thus the state will assume control of the lives of those defined as mentally ill. As Franco Basaglia (1980) reminds us, in his discussion of dangerousness:

> That which psychiatry defines as sick is, in fact, that which the social set-up defines as dangerousness for its equilibrium, according to its changing requirements.

Thus the traditional social control equation by which psychiatry operates (sickness = danger) is made potent by the addition of race (black sickness = danger x 2), therefore the necessity for compulsion is increased. In any case mental sickness has always had an oblique relationship with race: the construction of 'irrationality' is almost equivalent to 'uncivilized', so black madness, or even the suggestion of black madness, is enough to alert the local state to act often as a pre-emptive and precautionary strike. The killing of Winston Rose in 1981 is a typical over-reaction of psychiatry and social police to a supposed threat of black danger. It is necessary to quote at length from the description of events leading up to the death of Winston Rose given by the solicitor who acted for his family at the inquest.

> In the case of Winston Rose, it appeared, in his wife's view, that he needed more help than she could give him, and she very properly went to his family doctor to ask for help. Now after that, a situation arose in which all the authorities who dealt with him were in some way or other reprehensible. His general practitioner appears not to have given sufficient thought to the method – if he had to be involuntarily detained in a mental hospital – the method by which he ought to be detained. One also had brought into it the social services, the psychiatrists and the police who were called in to actually effect his apprehension.
>
> Now he was a gentle man who had never displayed any violence towards his family or anybody else. He was, at the time that they were seeking to take him to a mental hospital, sitting in his shed at the bottom of his garden reading his Bible. He was jumped on by police who held him round the throat in an illegal neck hold and literally choked him to death. He was put on the floor of the police van and they claim that they did not realize until the van was on its way that he was dead.
>
> Now this was a man that wasn't a criminal, wasn't a danger to anybody or to himself . . . [he] was in a period of crisis and needed . . . help towards treatment. Instead of which he had police unleashed on him who said that they had no direction at all as to what they were meant to be doing. One of them said at the inquest: 'All I knew was that he was big and coloured.' And it was that crude, racist approach that led to his dying. Why couldn't an ambulance have been called and his wife, who deeply cared for him, have been asked to sit in the ambulance with him and proper trained medical people be with him? It was a most disgusting, disgraceful situation and the inquest jury came up with the verdict of unlawful killing which means, that this is the way that they were directed [by the coroner] that the negligence of those concerned was so extreme that it could not be 'lack of care' – it became unlawful killing. But to the best of my knowledge nothing has ever happened to discipline those people who were involved in his death. One would include here the doctors and the local authority.[4]

Within the frank racism of the policeman's outburst ('all I knew was that he was big and coloured') lies an assumption that will extend right up to the consultant psychiatrist: a black person experiencing mental distress is ipso facto a danger. For the policeman, ignorant of the nuances of psychiatric language, the traditional-commonsense image of the insane-as-violent is fused with the racial stereotype of black crime, muggers, rapists and so on. For the diagnosing psychiatrist, it will be more subtly put as 'psychosis and the aggression with which black patients present symptoms'. This complex interplay with, on the one hand, legal concepts of social danger, and on the other, medical concepts of mental pathology – added to racism – are the proper objects of blame for the increased rate at which schizophrenia is diagnosed in black people, and in the use of compulsory sections. To cite 'culture', as the transculturalists do, is merely to divert attention from the real objects of concern. Culture, in fact, is a problem of racism rather than the means of its analysis.

It is culture that will be given as the excuse for psychiatry to invent entirely new pathological labels tailor-made for black people when traditional categories do not fit or have come under fire from black criticism. 'Ganja psychosis', for example, will be formulated as an 'illness' following the use of marijuana to be explicitly applied to the lifestyles of Rastafarians and young blacks in general.[5] 'Atypical psychotic reaction' – a special sub-category of schizophrenia – was invented in the late 1970s as a way of continuing to diagnose schizophrenia under a different name when black people began to ask questions about why psychiatrists were diagnosing so much psychosis in the black community.[6]

Inside the mental asylum, the black patient labelled as chronically and psychotically ill faces two problems. First, the British mental health services today are basically the sordid aftermath of the nineteenth-century madhouses. In the old days patients were imprisoned in asylums where doctors could experiment with bizarre treatments like trephining and hot and cold baths in the search for cures for madness. Today's cures are thought to be more humane than the old remedies because the major form of modern psychiatric treatment, medication, is thought to leave the patient's physical dignity intact.

The first 'tranquillizer' was, in fact, a chair into which patients could be strapped and immobilized but the new high-tech neuroleptic drugs provide an even greater degree of physical and mental quiescence without the need for medical staff to physically control the patient – except of course in the often forcible administration of the injection. Every patient, black or white, faces the squalor and degradation of a system that has outgrown itself. But the antiquated nature of the British mental health services is more than an old system needing modernization.

Chronic under-funding by the NHS and poor management and a bias in resource allocation towards medical services rather than social services like housing and benefits have also played their part in ensuring that the social needs underlying psychiatric breakdown are not met. A television documentary (Multiple Image Reproductions 1986) paints a picture of asylums and doctors as obsessionally attached to medical treatment to suppress symptoms of mental breakdown without trying to listen to the patient's problem. Nurses and other staff are shown to be more concerned with the discipline of the hospital than helping people over a crisis; and social services are shown to be lacking in their vital supportive role. A young mother who complains to her general practitioner that she would like somewhere to rest away from the pressure of the family house is instead sectioned to a psychiatric hospital.

Furthermore, the already highly coercive and disciplinary set-up of the asylum regime – consisting of cancelling out psychological disturbance with drugs or incarceration – is applied with a different emphasis in the case of black patients. For a start, black patients are thought to require, and are consistently given, higher doses of medication on account of racialized assumptions of an excess of black aggression resulting from physical prowess and innate psychological alienation. Similarly, there is a tendency to contain black patients in locked and secure facilities in mental asylums (locked wards and interim secure units) for less reason and for longer periods than is the case with white patients. One also finds that of the various treatment options available to psychiatrists (drugs, electro-convulsive therapy – ECT, counselling or behaviour modification) the most often selected for black patients are drugs and ECT, the most destructive of the available treatments in terms of the style of administration and the serious side-effects for patients. There can be no doubt that this reliance on physical therapies at the expense of treatments relying on verbal communication with the patient is also a reflection of the view of black madness as all aggression, all psychosis, all bodily expressed, rather than the more 'reasoned' characterization of mental breakdown suggested by the label 'neurosis' which is rarely applied to black patients. Thus, in deciding on which treatment option to deploy, psychiatrists fuse their traditional supposition that psychotics do not generally benefit from psychotherapy with a racist notion that the invariably psychotic/schizophrenic black patient is too inarticulate, even when sane, to benefit from psycho-therapy or psychoanalysis. Such options are reserved for the archetypal neurotic-articulate white.

The classic picture of black asylum inmates is one of young people, male, with a schizophrenic diagnosis, on a compulsory section, contained in locked facilities, drugged to the point of unconsciousness, and facing the prospect of repeated admissions with an ever worsening prognosis. This cruel cycle must not be underestimated in terms of the damage that it can do to individuals, families, and communities. It can end in death, as in the case of Winston Rose. But we should not be led to believe that the Winston Rose episode is an isolated one or in any way excusable because of the ignorance of the police of the proper means of handling the mentally ill. The catalogue of black people dying at the hands of the psychiatric system is lengthening with a recent addition to the list being Michael Martin, whose death at Broadmoor

Special Hospital in 1984 brings out many of the problems outlined in this essay. It is worth dwelling on his experience for a moment.

Michael Martin was typical of the group of young black males suffering under psychiatric racism. A young man of twenty-two, he was diagnosed as schizophrenic and was a long-stay patient at Bexley Hospital, a large mental asylum which serves southeast London. He underwent at Bexley the usual endless trials on major tranquillizers, which instead of improving or abating his illness, seemed, in his family's view, to steadily deteriorate his mental aptitude, adding nothing to its stability. Michael was also remarkably tolerant of the conditions of boredom and incarceration.

In 1984 the Martin family was informed by the consultant psychiatrist at Bexley that Michael would be transferred to Broadmoor Special Hospital to 'stabilize' him because, in the jargon of the psychiatric professions, he had become a 'management problem' at Bexley. That is to say he could no longer be controlled by Bexley and care staff had given up attempting to have a therapeutic relationship with him. Therefore he was decanted from Bexley to Britain's best-known hospital for the criminally insane, whose inmates include Ronnie Kray (Francis 1985; Ritchie 1985; Hansard 21 March 1986 – adjournment debate on death of Michael Martin called by Labour MP Gerald Bermingham).

Michael Martin languished at Broadmoor. Attempts by his family to have him released were consistently refused by the authorities. There is evidence of physical violence towards Michael by staff over the years that he was under their care. His family noticed a definite downward trend in Michael's mental condition brought on, they feel, by his realization that he might never be released from Broadmoor. He was right. The end came suddenly in June 1984 following an altercation between Michael and another patient who had been taunting him with racist abuse. According to evidence given by a patient at the inquest, Michael tried to complain to a nurse on several occasions. Finally, exasperated, he attempted to strike the nurse but missed – but within minutes nurses arrived from all over the hospital to restrain Michael who was by now pinned down on the floor by up to a dozen nurses. He was soon overwhelmed.

Michael was carried to a side room where he was stripped, then frog-marched, naked, down several flights of stairs to a seclusion room where he was injected with the maximum 500mg dose of one tranquillizer (Sodium Amytal) and 200mg of another (Sparine). He was then left, unobserved, for a period of time until it was discovered that he was dead. The post mortem revealed that death occurred as the result of various factors: asphyxiation due to strangulation (following the neck holds by the nurses' violent restraint after the quarrel) and the almost paralysing effects of the massive doses of sedatives that had been administered to Michael on a full stomach, causing him to choke on his own vomit. As often happens when a black person dies in suspicious circumstances, the jury did not return a verdict of unlawful killing, they brought one of 'accidental death aggravated by lack of care'. The 'lack of care' rider did not lead to anyone at Broadmoor being disciplined, or to any thorough-going reforms.

Five issues arise from the death of Michael Martin which are relevant to the situation that black patients face in general.

Dangerousness

When one considers the criteria used for the transfer of Michael Martin from Bexley hospital to Broadmoor, one comes up against the problem, alluded to earlier, of the assessment of dangerousness. Michael Martin was sent to an asylum for the criminally insane because he was seen, in the eyes of the Director of Broadmoor, as a 'highly dangerous and unpredictable individual' but the facts that ought to accompany such a description are nowhere to be found in the case history of Michael Martin's detention in psychiatric asylums. All the evidence points to a young man in the grips of psychological disorder, yet able to relate affectionately to his family and to fellow patients. His 'danger and unpredictability' were reserved for the quasi-gaolers, the so-called nurses who could only detain him but offer no comfort to his mental distress.

The therapeutic regime

The routine that psychiatric patients must undergo is demoralizing and oppressive in the extreme. Even the judge who presided over the enquiry into Michael Martin's death had to admit that the regime at Broadmoor was one that inspired nothing but apathy among both patients and staff, and outbursts of violence were thus not altogether surprising (Ritchie 1985). Patients sit around all day long like prisoners, with the occasional exercise, but no programmes of physical or mental recreation. Therapy and counselling are virtually non-existent since, as one psychiatrist declared at a recent meeting of the Royal College of Psychiatrists: everyone in special hospitals has diagnoses of psychopathy therefore therapy is ruled out of order.

The only therapy is the submissive tranquillity which the syringe forcibly injects into patients. Drugs in psychiatry are the panacea that produce docility and obedience. Drugs, rather than other therapeutic treatments or material benefits to patients, ensure a greater turnover of patients in hospitals; a sort of efficiency where the asylums can be seen to behave something like medicine – or factories. Patients can be doped up on long-acting tranquillizers and discharged back into the community, leaving beds free in the asylum for other patients. Every illness ends up being treated by a succession of phenothiazines until, sometimes bordering on toxic overdose, the cycle of drugs is repeated over and over with doctors reporting a worsening prognosis, that the patient will be dependent on drugs for the rest of his or her life.

Compulsion

The legalized nature of psychiatric detention fixes patients in the role of infidels who have transgressed social norms. Dangerousness (to one's self or others) is a code word that authorizes the use of compulsion. To quote Basaglia (1980) again:

> In the case of psychiatry, the necessity of keeping the patient in custody, defined by the law as the condition and form of treatment is, in fact, identified with the treatment itself and has frozen the contradiction between the individual body and the social fabric and made them irreconcilable opponents.

Not that being an opponent of the British social order is all that bad. It is just that in the case of black people and mental health, we are experiencing the paranoia of a state that is obsessed by the 'enemy within', where the necessity of making precautionary strikes against its opponents, who need not be political, but social, becomes habitual. One continually comes across these pre-emptive and aggressive acts by social police. The Afro-Caribbean Mental Health Association in London, a black community mental health project, related a case where a woman, whose unborn child the local social services wanted to take into care, was herself sectioned to a mental hospital specifically as a means of containing her until her child was born. The mother was incarcerated in a locked ward until her child was born, and then promptly released as soon as social services had taken control of her child.

Racism

The way in which racism is mediated through psychiatry is complex and paradoxical. Michael Martin's experience of racism was of the brute force kind, in which he is crudely depicted as a dangerous snarling animal against whom confinement in Broadmoor is a minimum precaution. On the other hand there is the more subtle tactic of cultural reductionism where a pseudo-concern is expressed for black patients by a liberal wish to 'empathize' with racism (Basaglia 1980) and where transculturalism is brought in. Here racism is interpolated in terms of psychological (rather than physical) danger and the psychiatrist absolves himself of over-diagnosing illness with the assumption that there is a prevalence of psychological trauma among black people as an effect of a racism construed in terms of psychological and cultural prejudice. The black patient thus gets caught up in a double bind where he must be mad because racism is conceptualized as a thing of the mind.

Mental asylums as closed institutions

The callous indifference with which Michael Martin's family were treated when they tried to enquire after his well-being illustrates how mental asylums operate as a law unto themselves, answerable, at best, to government, but having no obligation to account for their conduct to patients. In Michael Martin's case, the psychiatrist refused to discuss any aspect of treatment with his family. Broadmoor as a whole is protected by its status of 'Special Hospital' for the criminally insane and will do everything in the name of security because every one of its patients is supposed to be highly dangerous. Yet there are an increasing number of black people sent to Broadmoor for trivial offences that have been given a psychiatric interpretation. And once in Broadmoor, the prospect of release is bleak.

The psychological complex – legal psychiatry

There is a traditional and specific role that psychiatry plays in relation to the legal system which rests on the axis of dangerousness in much the same way that agencies of social police are concerned with psychological danger. It is not merely that there is a medicalization of crime – which we would in any case expect from the coincidence of both psychiatry and criminal justice having similar imperatives to control individual conduct. With legal psychiatry the definition of danger is perfectly congruent with the legal conception of criminal danger. Psychiatry thus has two major objectives in relation to its involvement in legal proceedings. First, as a means of assessing whether individuals brought before courts are 'rational and sane' at the time of an alleged offence. And secondly, as a consequence of the first assessment, psychiatry must advise the courts of the appropriate means of disposal of convicted criminals – whether an individual should be imprisoned or hospitalized, or in cases where the court makes a non-custodial sentence, psychiatric treatment should be attached to a probation order. The overriding aim of psychiatry is to advise courts of the level of danger posed by offenders in terms of the severity of their mental disorder.

The object here is to attempt to articulate how racism is implicated in this legal/psychiatric process, and in particular how the concept of dangerousness is formulated and acted upon in relation to black people. But first of all, a few words need to be said about the traditional role that psychiatrists have occupied in forensic psychiatry.

Michel Foucault (1978) argues that the involvement of psychiatrists in court came about as the result of a shift in the understanding of criminal responsibility. Up until the end of the eighteenth century, the criminal justice system sought to punish offences corporally or capitally simply according to their seriousness, but by the beginning of the nineteenth century prosecutors and jurists would be also concerned with the motivation of crimes and the personality of criminals. According to Foucault, this shift came about because it was no longer possible to explain certain bizarre crimes such as parricide and fratricide that seemed to have been committed without 'reason' or 'rational motivation'. Psychiatrists thus offered themselves up to the legal process as experts in assessing motivation. They were able to deploy an already socialized 'notion of psychological symptomatology of danger to the notion of legal imputability of a crime' (Ibid.). In other words, according to a new rationale which demanded logical explanations for crimes (even if the criminal himself could not give any) any offence which was apparently unmotivated was not a mere crime but more or less an act of mania.

Psychiatry must tell the courts how likely it is that criminals will re-offend or relapse. It must say what likelihood there is of recovery; and what sort of treatment is required in what sort of conditions, for how long and on what sort of legal basis. Above all psychiatry must say how dangerous is the individual if left to liberty. But we should not believe that such assessments are made only in the case of serious offences. Foucault (1978) also points out that:

> The psychiatric question is no longer confined to some great crimes; even if it must receive a negative answer, it must be posed across the whole range of infractions.

That 'whole range of infractions' is anything from shoplifting to murder. The psychiatric 'expert opinion' is not an occasional appearance, as a specialist asked by the court (the defence or the prosecution) to support a particular point of view on the motivation of an enigmatic crime. Rather, psychiatric expertise, in terms of its 'scientific opinion' and its institutional facilities, is an integral part of the judicial apparatus – both as a means of rendering criminality and the personality of criminals more knowable to the state, but also as an option in sentencing.

Prins (1980) conducted a survey of magistrates asking for 'the types of offences on which they would ask for a psychiatric opinion'. In descending order they cited 'sexual offences, drugs, damage to property, shoplifting, violence, obvious police haters [sic], taking and driving away, infanticide and cruelty to children' as offences on which they would seek a psychiatric opinion. And when asked 'which factors other than the nature of the offence' would lead the magistrate to ask for a psychiatric opinion, they answered that these would include:

Appearance and demeanour in court;
Previous offences of the same type;
Offences out of character with previous conduct;
Previous medical/mental history.

It is with these criteria that the opinion of psychiatry (as objective science and social police) is called upon to render objective the reactions of magistrates and judges to the criminals who appear before them. In terms of racism, a legal notion of criminal risk, already targeted on a supposed excess of black crime, will be conflated with the extra psychological danger of black madness.

The psychological assessment of offenders and the plea of diminished responsibility is now commonplace and not only made in relation to murder. Although not referred to as diminished responsibility, a person convicted of an imprisonable offence can now be 'sentenced' to a mental hospital, and one must ask whether the widespread psychiatric involvement in the sentencing of criminals actually offers mitigation or rather punishment by medical means. Two further questions must also be asked of the psychiatric involvement in this process. First, having persuaded the court that a particular offence has been committed under diminished responsibility, it follows that the criminal act and the person of the offender have become the concern of medical competence. And if, by proving diminished responsibility, psychiatry has managed to identify abnormal conduct which only it can deal with, one needs to know how the psychiatric strategy of dealing with offenders differs from legal punishment. In other words one needs to know how penalization differs from psychiatric confinement; and how psychiatric diagnostics differs from legal diagnostics.

For serious offences found to have been committed under diminished responsibility, hospital is a common solution, ordered by the courts. But hospitalization as a result of legal proceedings can end up being more long-term and constitute a more total suspension of individual liberty than imprisonment. So how can diminished responsibility offer mitigation?

As far as black people are concerned, the difference between being criminalized by the police, courts and prisons, or medicalized by psychiatry is merely a choice between two different forms of oppression. In a context when black people are criminalized and over-represented in the criminal justice system, we are being decanted from the penal justice system to psychiatry in disproportionately high numbers compared with other groups. One will find high concentrations of black people in special hospitals, secure units and as patients sent to asylums on hospitals orders from courts.

Courts can remand offenders to hospitals pending trial, and for the purpose of obtaining psychiatric reports under section 35 of the Mental Health Act, or for treatment under section 36. A crown court can make a hospital order (s33) for an indefinite period for any convicted criminal found guilty of an imprisonable offence. Or the court may apply a restriction order (s41) which, along with the application of section 37, can hospitalize offenders for an indefinite period, and can only be terminated with the approval of the home secretary.

For offenders sent to prison in the normal manner, there are means whereby they can be transferred to an ordinary hospital or a special hospital if they are found to be mentally ill and 'a danger to themselves or others' while serving a prison sentence. The period of time spent in hospital, it must be stressed, is not related to the original prison sentence since the further application of section 49 brings into force a restriction order which, like section 41, can only be terminated by the home secretary.

There is increasing evidence that black people are being caught up in this legal/psychiatric referrals system in a casual and punitive manner (SNHDC 1985). It appears that an increasing and disproportionately high number of black people brought before the courts are being remanded for psychiatric reports, and that the high incidence of custodial sentencing is leading to more black people being sent to hospital under the orders of courts (Ibid.). Guided by a medico-legal conception of black danger, and reinforced by scientific and commonsense racist stereotypes, the psychiatric expertise deployed by courts is as powerful as any other legal procedure at the disposal of the criminal justice system. Take, for example, the social enquiry report.

Social enquiry reports are of routine but paramount importance to the psychiatric/legal process, and they are the site of a discourse where social services or probation provide the background to the character of individuals brought before courts so that sentences can exactly fit the social position of the offender – in order to assess what sort of person he is, from what sort of background and posing what sort of danger. This discourse will always proceed under the guise of 'what is best for the individual offender' in terms of what the court may decide by way of a custodial or other sentence. But in this context all the fears in relation to the social, criminal and psychological risks posed by black people can be brought into play at once. In the following extract from a psychiatric report on a Jamaican man accused of indecent assault and abduction, the psychiatrist begins:

He is a powerfully built, physically fit negro. His hair is dressed in 'dreadlocks' although he maintains that he is not a rastafarian . . .

The patient exhibits gross delusions of persecution, by means of systematic intimidation . . . [and] has experienced auditory hallucinations consistent with the diagnosis of schizophrenia . . .

> His large stature, his lack of insight, the intensity of his paranoid and grandiose
> beliefs and his clear preparedness to use violence . . . suggest that were he at large
> he would be a grave danger to the public. His later after care would be greatly
> facilitated by the imposition of a restriction order.[7]

In prisons psychiatry has also become an instrument of punishment. The
option for prison discipline staff to use psychiatry as a means of punishing
prisoners has become too tempting for them to ignore. And psychiatrists
themselves often treat and diagnose prisoners on the judgement of discipline
staff. Psychiatrists as a matter of routine will participate in punishment by
giving medical clearance that a prisoner is fit to be punished by solitary
confinement or, if he is fit, for adjudication. Community groups have
recorded numerous cases of prisoners being punitively drugged with tranquillizers and sedatives for control purposes. The report of Her Majesty's
Chief Inspector of Prisons 1984 denies this with the assertion that 'there is no
evidence that psychotropic drugs were being used indiscriminately' (HMSO
1985). But the latest report on the prison medical services by the House of
Commons Social Services Committee (1985–86) now euphemistically
admits that:

> In all probability prison doctors are on occasions pressured by the Prison Depart-
> ment to tranquillize a difficult patient less for his sake than for the sake of a
> peaceful prison.

It has taken a long time for the state to admit this much. Black people have
been protesting for years about what prison discipline staff will do 'for the
sake of a peaceful prison'. In 1979 Steve Thompson was transferred from
Gartree Prison to a mental hospital for refusing to have his locks shaven off
(Mercer/BHWPG 1984). In 1984 Cirus Noor was an activist in the Hackney
and Stoke Newington Defence Campaign which was formed to protest at the
mysterious death of Colin Roach in the foyer of Stoke Newington police
station. Noor was jailed for attempted arson – a fake attack on a police station
to draw attention to his campaign – and soon after his arrival at Wandsworth
Prison he was diagnosed as psychotic and transferred to a special hospital. In
fact he had been protesting about the conditions of black prisoners at
Wandsworth. Both men were released following pressure on the Home
Office by the black community. It is not therefore surprising that MIND (the
National Association for Mental Health) estimates that black prisoners are
twice as likely as whites to be transferred from prison to hospital.

Conclusion

This essay is an attempt to open up the field of psychiatry as an area of
political priority for black people. In this brief commentary space has not

allowed a fuller examination of a problem which seemed to grow in complexity as work on this article progressed. But despite its brevity, one hopes that it has been possible to set out the scope of what a black politics of psychiatry ought to include. At one level, the problem seems unjustifiably academic and historical but it seems to me that without some idea of the part that psychiatry has played, along with other branches of medicine and the human sciences, in the construction of scientific racism it is less easy to pick out the continuity of classical racism in contemporary theory and practice. The cultural reductionism that one can see at work in race relations sociology (for example in explanations of 'racial disadvantage' which explain away racism by appealing to 'culture') is firmly rooted in the colonial tradition of anthropologically enlightened racism where the natives deserve domination through their own backwardness. The difference with the new cultural reductionism is that the inferiority complex is bolstered by subtler theories emanating mainly from the psychological disciplines, sociology and elements of anthropology. The political effect is clear, as Sivanandan (1982) reminds us, that techniques of colonialism have been revived for use in the metropolis.

Similarly the dreary academic-bureaucratic discourse of race relations seems to have little to do with psychiatry. Yet when one examines the discourse around levels of black academic achievement in schools one finds another version of cultural reductionism, this time containing elements of both classical biological racism (as for instance in the eugenic theories of the psychologist Eysenck) as well as an idea of culture straight from the notebooks of colonial anthropology (as in prying into black families' culture in vain efforts to find out why black children are not properly served by the education system). Here psychiatric racism is effected by means of psychology, as a major sub-discipline of education science; and the whole issue of educational subnormality and black children's behaviour is the zone in which psychology blurs into psychiatry because of the obvious pathological implications of educational backwardness and behavioural disorder.

For mainstream psychiatry centred upon the asylum, everything comes to a head in the stereotype of an epidemic of black madness. As mental health becomes recognized as an area of concern for black people, the proper objects of blame are being passed over in favour of a blame-the-victim approach. Psychiatry itself forms the basis for an explanation which extends common-sense racist assumptions about black aggression and culture and combines these with a part sociological, part medical explanation that black people must be going mad in great numbers, simply as a reaction to racism! It is what two black American psychiatrists have called 'the mark of oppression', a concept in which black people's personality is defined by white psychiatry 'in terms of the stigmata' of their social condition in America. It is a thesis in which:

The stress of racist discrimination has produced not merely an inerasable mark but
a deformity in the black man's psyche (Thomas and Sillen 1979).

And this comment is quite consistent with the British experience where, in
their hurry to erect a cultural-reductionist excuse for psychiatric racism, most
accounts of black people's contact with psychiatry will ignore the objective
facts that have a bearing on psychiatric admissions, like housing, employment,
social services. And in the medical management of pathology racism affects
psychiatric practice in the conceptualization of treatment and in the therapies
accorded to patients. Here psychiatric racism takes the form of an explicit
social control, in its refusal to acknowledge social and economic determinants
to mental ill-health.

But nowhere is psychiatry more exposed as a form of control than in
forensic psychiatry. Nowhere is the penalizing nature of the practice of
detaining madness by force in custodial institutions more apparent than in the
deployment of psychiatry in the criminal justice system. In the psychiatry
practised in courts and prisons the bankruptcy of the medical model, and its
failure to provide genuine help to victims of mental disorder, is revealed by
the perfect congruence of criminal and legal diagnostics and in the similarity
of hospitals to prisons. Psychiatry is an elusive power, able to occupy and
reinforce different institutional contexts by applying itself to the differing
needs of social police – as a tactic of government in the management of the
social, and as a theory for the interpretation of social conflict. It is not a
monolithic power but a 'discreet' form of domination with its semi-autonomous
parts linked together as a 'circuit of control' – to borrow Franco Basaglia's
phrase. The elements that make up this circuit of control have been seriously
under-estimated as forms of domination because they appear 'soft' when
compared with the power of the police force for example. But the description of
psychiatry as a form of social police is an attempt to recognize psychiatry as a
power to be reckoned with, and to describe the ultimate nature of its power as
it affects individuals at the psychological level. The word police has been revived
in its original sense of management, regulation and administrative control of
populations – as an addition to the contemporary sense of police as prohibition.

It needs to be said, however, that the problem of psychiatry, even for black
people, is not exclusively about race. Psychiatry is a class problem because it
has always transposed social, economic and political reality as disease and
illness. Psychiatry has always had problems with diagnosis as a consequence
of the failure of the medical model when applied to psychological phenomena.
And psychiatry has always revealed itself as a form of control. It has been
instrumental in the oppression of women, as well as being a leader in the
articulation of scientific racism. For there to be an effective politics of
psychiatry, gender, race and class would therefore need to be acted upon
together.

Notes

1. See also Jung (1928: 137) in which he warns that the white man 'must defend himself against the Negro by observing the strictest social forms' otherwise he 'risks going black'.

2. See for example, Carothers (1954). The psychiatrist is here explicitly aligned with the colonial regime and offers his slur on the Kikuyu people so that 'some knowledge of psychology and psychiatry may throw some light on the Mau Mau movement in this colony and might point the way to some solutions to this problem'.

3. See ILEA statistics quoted above.

4. Interview with Gareth Pierce (solicitor), 9 June 1986, quoted in Brackx (1989).

5. For the 'ganja psychosis' theory, see Carney and Bacelle (1984).

6. On the special sub-category of schizophrenia see Littlewood and Lipsedge (1981).

7. Anonymous medical case notes passed on to the author.

9

Carnival, the State and the Black Masses in the United Kingdom

Cecil Gutzmore

Introduction

To a major extent, violence and open confrontation between what I call the black masses in the United Kingdom and the British state tend now, and in the recent past, to involve what might be called the *cultures* of the black masses.[1] That might be surprising. The explanation might be that we are not confronted by the British state, or involved with the British state significantly in a physical confrontation, or violence-producing context, in our other areas of existence, i.e. at work, precisely because there are already pre-existing forms of control there. The forms of control at work are obviously the organization of the work pattern: the role of supervision, the use of the notion of 'skill', and the trade unions. These are at least some of the significant *control mechanisms* at work. And they function more or less satisfactorily as control mechanisms for black workers except when the latter rise up against the direct effect of racism in the place of work, which has happened in a substantial number of cases, where you get specifically *black industrial action* (cf. Gutzmore and Cambridge 1974–75).

These confrontations, and this violence, around the culture of the black masses, are worth looking at. They have taken place in relation to a number of aspects of black culture. First of all, in relation to *cultural events*. One thinks of the Brockwell incident – riot, affray if you like – as men were certainly charged with affray arising from that incident some years ago in Brixton. It was basically a Bank Holiday crowd, mainly black people. The police came along and tried to do certain things that people objected to and before long stones and bricks and bottles were flying across the park and hundreds of policemen were coming and trying to 'do their thing' in relation to black youths and getting repulsed.

There are other incidents like that. For example, two years earlier, there was the Leeds Bonfire Night incident which led again to an affray charge, and to the trial of several young black people, all of whom, incidentally, got off because the police used illegal violence against them once they got into the police station, and extracted confessions from them which didn't then stand up in court. The Notting Hill Carnival is perhaps the most spectacular of those cultural events that actually led to violent confrontation between the black communities and the state.

In addition to cultural events, *cultural venues* have also attracted violence, or been the scene of this sort of confrontation. I will name a few, and some of you might know them, and some of you might not. But the Carib Club incident, of late 1974, which, again, led to a massive trial – thirteen people charged, twelve with affray; none of them incidentally went down, because, here also, the police, having gone into this place, 'arrested' forty-odd people and randomly selected twelve and then stuck charges on them in the most arbitrary way, couldn't actually defend that case when it came to the reality of the courtroom and evidential proof, when it came to standing up against the quite serious and truthful allegations concerning the level of brutality the police used on the night in question. And similar things have happened in relation to clubs like the Burning Spear, which was in Harlesden, north-west London; like the Four Aces club, which is in north London; like the Mangrove restaurant in Notting Hill. Several bookshops, also in their way cultural venues, have been targets for violence – Bogle L'Ouverture, Unity and so on – although the perpetrators of violence *there* have not been the police, but other elements of the British sub-state violence mechanism.

Then *cultural forms* within the black communities have also been arenas of violence. These have included *dances*, quite ordinary dances; policemen come, and they explode. Blues dances, which are different from dances in the sense that they are heavier, the music tends to reggae, and the people tend to be 'rougher', and when there is an incident the police tend to get knifed – they are just 'rough' and 'tough'. But those things produce violence, as do ordinary *house parties*, like wedding parties. After a wedding – black people tend to have fairly lively weddings which go on late – people drink; the police arrive on the scene, and before long they are in the house bashing people over the head. People resist. These cultural forms, which you wouldn't think lead to violence, have in fact done so between the black communities and the police, over the thirty or forty years of the mass Caribbean emigration to this country.

Finally, *cultural practices*, so called, have produced violence between us and the state, though these practices have been of the most innocuous variety. For example, black youths choosing to walk on the street *jauntily* are subjected to violence from the police. Young blacks walking *in groups* on the street too have been subjected to violence by the police. Blacks choosing to *walk on the street at all* – and I'm not sure that's a cultural practice – have actually experienced violence because police officers come up and say, 'I want to search you.' They're supposed to have reasonable grounds but they can never specify these to the satisfaction of anyone except the participants in their machinery of self-investigation. What constitutes *reasonable* grounds for them is manifestly *unreasonable*; it's the fact that you have dread-locks, or the afro, or whatever, or are just in a black skin. And that's sufficient cause for searching blacks. The fact that young blacks choose to walk on the streets well-dressed needs to be explained – so the police think. Since they 'know' that substantial numbers of youths are unemployed, and assume that none of them ought to be able to afford to dress well, and when they do, obviously they must be stealing from somewhere, the 'flash' clothes must have been shop-lifted. The police *do* come up and say, 'Nicely dressed . . . ' and, before long, there are three Black Marias and ten police cars, and there's a really heavy scene.

Now, all of those forms and appearances of black culture in this society have attracted at different times and in different degrees at different levels quite brutal responses from the police, who are the *key civil repressive agency of the British state*. But they also attract violence from organizations like the *National Front* which can be regarded as *the main manipulator of anti-black non-state political violence within the UK*.

The Perspective on Carnival

Now, if one takes what has been said so far as a starting point in relation to the Carnival – and you will note that Carnival was mentioned as one of the cultural events that have actually produced violence – then what one is saying, in effect, is that this perspective is to be regarded as a political-theoretical standpoint for the analysis of the Notting Hill Carnival *in general*, and also, *specifically*, for the analysis of the violence in the Carnival in the years 1976 and 1977. What I am proposing to make quite explicit is this: *that there is state repression of what is perceived to be dangerous, or potentially dangerous, or disruptive, or undisciplined culture on the part of the black masses*.

If one takes that as the perspective it would produce a number of tasks, that I shall not take up. The first would be this: to establish, or at least to suggest persuasively, that *cultural repression*, or the physical repression of cultural forms of the masses by the state is, or tends to be, a general feature of the way in which bourgeois states, which might also be racist states, relate to the culture of the masses within the nation state in question.

In other words, it is useful to demonstrate or at least to suggest as persuasively as one can, that it is generally the case that within bourgeois states, which might also be racist states – which indeed tend, in the real world, to be racist states – there is cultural repression of sections of the masses, be those sections black or otherwise objectionable or potentially *threatening*. That's the first thing that would have to be, I repeat, proven, or suggested.

It seems to be that this can be done in relation to the United Kingdom, certainly, since that is the state within which we're actually functioning. Anybody who knows even a little of United Kingdom history will know that, within the urban working class – white in the main – in early capitalist England a whole series of cultural events and practices have in fact been systematically suppressed. (There were blacks here but they were never part of the urban working class, because nobody let them work – Phillips 1975–76). I'm not particularly cultured, in European terms, but I know that if you look at Hogarth's prints, you will see that he has some quite intriguing drawings to do with events like Southwark Fair which no longer exist. If you check out what they were, you will find that they *were occasions of jollity, mass jollity*, on the part of the eighteenth-century urban working class. And you will find, if you ask what happened to those functions and fairs, that they no longer exist because they were systematically suppressed by the British state at different times. The last one to be suppressed by the British state was called the Blaydon Races, which was a northern urban working-class jollification around Newcastle-upon-Tyne. On the last occasion when there was violence, it was suppressed: they simply prevented it happening the next year, after bringing in the 'dragoons' to put down the rioters. There are several other examples of this. Indeed, it is possible, although it is no business of mine here, to analyse in similar terms the battle between so-called 'football hooligans' and the police. Remarkably, what happens to the so-called 'football hooligans' tends not to get noticed at all by the press, or to be glorified as correct. A group of white youngsters set off; when it became rumoured that they were going to fight another group of white youngsters, the police then assembled at the railway station leading in to the particular town and confiscated the boots, shoe laces, braces and such like things that people actually need to function with – you know, when you're in public – from these youths. And the popular press glorified it. If I were a white working-class person I would really be concerned about this, and it'd actually make me angry. But since I'm not a white working person, it's no concern of mine here, OK?

I just mention it here in passing as an example. So there has been and there still is cultural repression at home by the British state.

There has also been cultural oppression or repression abroad by that state under *colonialism*. A good example actually relates to our present topic. The Trinidad carnival, which is part of the history of the Notting Hill Carnival, started off as a mode of cultural expression by, initially, white people, and then by black people, in Trinidad. Extraordinary efforts went into trying to suppress the carnival in Trinidad in the last and present century. Who was trying to repress it? Precisely the local white representatives of the British colonial state. The elements that were involved included the church – they objected to people being jolly, in particular to black people being jolly, on Sunday. And so the first thing they did in trying to restrict carnival, historically, was to prevent it happening on Sunday. From the 1830s in fact, they brought in legislation cutting out carnival jollification on the Sunday when it was supposed to take place. This is, incidentally, very well documented in a book by a man called Errol Hill, entitled *The Trinidad Carnival* (Texas University Press, 1972). Now, Hill points out, among other things, that various administrators, governors – colonial functionaries (all white men) – tried, in the 1850s, to suppress the carnival, and came up against physical opposition. There were also riots around the defence of carnival in Trinidad in the 1880s and in the 1890s – physical violence on the street, people actually dying, the *local defence forces* actually being called out. And, I repeat, that's cultural repression by the colonial power – Britain.

Now, they also tried to suppress the drum – would you believe it? – as one of the features of musical cultural expression inside of the carnival event. Indeed, they didn't just try to suppress our (African) drums, but when the Indians came to Trinidad, they tried to suppress their drums as well. And several Asians in Trinidad died in defence of the humble drum. Would you believe it? But it actually happened, in that part of the world. Because *men who are oppressors take very seriously the possibility that culture can be used as a vehicle for the organization of protest or rebellion or, dammit, revolution which is the most worrying thing of all for them.* And there is a history of all of that, and of how it happened, and of why it happened. I'm not sure that Hill has got a definitive account, but it's there and should be checked out. The fact is that in the context of Trinidad, as possibly here, I will suggest later, carnival came, for the black masses in that country, to be regarded as a period of freedom during which the maximum cultural expression would be claimed as a 'right'. It was a period, therefore, in which anybody who tried to stand in the way of that was an enemy and *deserved* to be physically cut down; and sometimes literally was. I suspect that that feeling of identification with the carnival as a period of freedom for the black masses represents, although it's not the whole basis, a political defence of the carnival within the United Kingdom. I simply mention that certainly in Trinidad that is how the carnival came to be regarded, and that in the United Kingdom an element of that either carried over from Trinidad or was built up in this context independently of any Trinidad association. So that, I hope I've managed to suggest at least to some extent persuasively, the state represses culturally and seeks systematically to do so on historic occasion after historic occasion, which either can be or is documented.

Carnival in Context: 1958–76

The second task that arises from the perspective that I'm seeking to use is this: *that it would be necessary to show that the experience of the Notting Hill*

Carnival is precisely such a case of state cultural repression. And I believe that this can be shown; but it can only be shown within a historical context in this country, and I'll try to establish that context first, before attempting to look at it in some detail.

The starting point for establishing that there has been cultural repression in relation to the Notting Hill Carnival would have to be the Notting Hill race riots of 1958. Why do I say that? Because it seems to me that between 1958 and 1976, the year of the first 'Carnival riot', there were *no major attempts* in Notting Hill by the white community or state to confront or to suppress the black masses as a whole, or indeed systematically to suppress any major cultural activity of the black masses. Unfortunately, that is not to be taken as a plus for the state, as I will show in a moment. The reason is this: in 1958 the black masses responded with strikingly well-organized counter-violence to the manipulators of violence by white sub-state agencies – in that case it was Mosleyite fascists, and people like that. This 'strikingly well-organized counter-violence' has never been properly investigated. What actually happened in Notting Hill, and maybe even Nottingham in 1958, was this: the state defined that *riot* as a 'race riot'. And 'race riot' should mean two groups of people coming out in some sort of equal way and attacking each other. But no 'race riot' ever means that. Usually, it means black people rioting on their own, or well-armed white people attacking black people. And if you check the history of so-called 'race riots' in the United States you will see that's what they always are – either one of those things, never equal groups of people confronting each other. In the Notting Hill situation, what happened was that groups of white thugs, basically, with the approval – tacit and sometimes active approval – of the Metropolitan Police Force, attacked black people in brutal and destructive ways: attacked their homes, put shit through their letter boxes, put petrol through their letter boxes, chopped them up on the street, and so on. This is what happened on British streets in 1958. Black people left their homes to get to work, and never got to work; left their work to get home, and never got home, because they had been chopped up by armed groups of bicycle-chain-wielding or knife-wielding white people. After that had gone on for a little while and a number of isolated black people had got chopped up, it was decided, quite correctly, by blacks in Notting Hill and elsewhere, that they were not going to stand for this. And certainly blacks in the West Indies (and most of the blacks in 1958 were West Indians) have never stood for that sort of violence from anybody. So they organized themselves. And they organized themselves to the extent that they gathered in one house on one occasion with petrol and bottles, and started to prepare petrol bombs with a view to defending themselves. Importantly also, they got into cars and went as far afield as Southampton to sort out white people who had been physically doing up black people. Once that happened and it became clear to the British state that they weren't dealing with people who would sit down under physical brutality from anyone, the state then decided that it had to do two things.

It had, it decided, generally to *reassure* its new labour force – because that, as far as the state was concerned, is what we were. That's the first thing it had to do. And it got into the business of so doing by grabbing hold of some of the whites who had been manipulating the violence and passing exemplary sentences. Some very fine speeches were made in court concerning what it was not right to do to black people, who were here to work, and were decent citizens, and should be left alone, etc. That's what the verdicts in court against those white youths who were using violence against black people were about. They were reassurances to us generally because they needed our labour in this country to work for them, as a substitute for investment, in exactly the way I have argued elsewhere (Gutzmore 1975–76).

The second thing that the state decided was that it needed specifically to *reassure* that same labour force that we needn't organize for counter-violence against anyone because there wasn't going to be any violence to organize a counter to; they were going to stamp it out. They were extremely concerned that we should not organize for counter-violence, and never see any necessity to do so. That was the second activity involved in state reassurance, in and following 1958. A lot of white so-called liberals entered the field as race relations experts. Some of them left unfinished theses in places like Oxford . . . to engage in this business of reassurance to black people about not needing to organize for counter-violence. Institutions such as the church also took on the task of reassurance – a Methodist mission to Notting Hill was launched. At least one institution, the Notting Hill Social Council, was specially created. That's what British state and non-state propaganda was principally about during that period. Side by side with this there emerged a clear decision on the part of the state to curtail the growth in the UK of this dangerous group – the blacks from the Caribbean. The Commonwealth Immigration Act 1962 was the legislative outcome. It came into operation in mid-1962 and since then there have been further severe restrictions on entry into the country.

What 1958 showed the white manipulators of violence – and I mean the Mosley people and the fringe Mosley people and the white working class generally – is that if they *fucked* with black people from the West Indies, to use that sort of language, they were going to have some trouble coming. And it's quite important to use that sort of language, because that is precisely the way in which the thing was projected by the blacks who were on the ground, and it was precisely the way in which it was understood by the whites who needed to understand it. Basically, what happened in '58 was that we sorted out, as a community, the manipulators of violence against us on a large and organized scale. Since then, there has been no mass-organized non-state violence against black (Afro-Caribbean) people in this country, because they know what will happen if they come against us in an organized and public way. That's important, because since 1958 we have faced no challenge by white manipulators of political violence, and our community has faced – to return to something I was saying earlier – no real attempts, no major attempts, to suppress it on the streets of Notting Hill, and probably nowhere else in the United Kingdom. The challenge of '58 is, however, once more in the air.

I have said that this wasn't a big plus for the state, and for this reason: that our culture was expressed in extremely private ways, primarily, between '58 and '75 in this society. Our culture was expressed in the ways, largely, that I have already enumerated. In particular the black masses – the men and women who work for their living, or hustle for their living – in churches, in clubs, in shebeens, in 'roots'/basement restaurants, in private gambling dens, in their homes, and so on. White people, other than the police, other than the state itself therefore, left us completely alone.

It was only in 1975 that we went onto the streets in large and challenging numbers (an exception was the large political demonstration against the British invasion of the Caribbean island of Anguilla), in a way that made us look threatening to the state. And it was within that context that they called out, or so I'm wanting to argue, those large numbers of police against the 1976 Notting Hill Carnival. We are at the moment trying to document what happened: there is a commission into police brutality which is being run by some black people there, including myself – we're trying to gather evidence relating to this issue. What is known to us are these things. I've already mentioned what the police did in '58; but throughout the '60s, and early '70s blacks were systematically brutalized in shebeens and house parties and so on; the Mangrove restaurant was constantly harassed up until the period of the demonstration which led to those arrests and the trial that is now famous as the Mangrove Nine trial; the Metro youth club was also harassed, and it's still symbolically harassed – the Mangrove is again the object of regular and increasingly blatant harassment. So that, although I say there were no major confrontations, or at least no major moves by the state at suppressing major elements of culture, there were moves against all the small manifestations of *black culture*, the culture of the black masses. And that, as I say, is largely because the culture of the black masses was expressed indoors, and if it didn't particularly impinge on the white working class, and even if it had impinged on them, they had learnt the lesson in '58 that you leave it to the police, because black people will back really heavily. It should be noted that the British state also attacked and destabilized the political organizations of the black masses in this period.

The Cultural Challenge of Carnival

The Notting Hill Carnival started within the framework of culture – it was a cultural event. What it emphatically did not start as was *potentially challenging culture*. It never looked, until recent years, as a piece of expression by the black masses that could challenge in significant ways the state or its police force. And so, for the first several years of its life, the Notting Hill Carnival was left alone. Why was that so? A number of reasons. The police participated, incidentally, in the Notting Hill Carnival for all of those years, and they got enormous propaganda out of it: reassurance to the black community that they were nice people, although we knew differently; reassurance to the great white public that they were nice people relating enjoyably to black people – and we knew differently again. Specifically, the question has got to be asked, why was it that the Carnival didn't look threatening for its first eight years? Let's say it started in 1966. The reason is this, that it was organized in the early days by white people. A woman called Raune Laslett was one of the whites who was central to the early organization of the Notting Hill Carnival. Later white organizations like the North Kensington Amenity Trust, which is a control agency for the local borough council, then run by a white liberal, called Anthony Perry. I say he's a white liberal because I've seen him operating as a white liberal in Notting Hill; because he made a white liberal film about the 'Mau Mau' situation in Kenya which said precisely nothing, which misrepresented the revolutionary potential of the struggle of the Land Freedom Army. So we know about him, and I call him a white liberal on the basis of some evidence.

Though organized right through, in dominant ways, by whites there were a few blacks involved, but these were largely subservient, though not necessarily being people who were subservient in themselves. The early black organizers were men and women who were black culturalists, not into confrontation with the state, who weren't necessarily into the culture of the black masses in this society. I cite one person, a Trinidadian gentleman called Junior Telfer, who was a member of the Carnival committee until he left the United Kingdom in 1977. He tells a story of being involved in the early days, of being one of the early organizers. He was fond of saying that the Carnival started in a club called the Ambiance located in Queensway which he ran in the 1960s. I have to believe him – it may be incorrect. But the key thing about him, whatever his level of involvement, however great or small, was that he, and several of the others, were culturalists, non-conflict-oriented black people who were not interested in the sort of black culture that automatically produces conflict with the white state.

There were early battles within the Carnival for control by black people, to take the thing out of the hands of white people. Later, there was competition between blacks for control of the Carnival. It's possible, for example, to name names. The man who was the most important organizer of the Carnival to date, a man called Leslie Palmer, joined in the teeth of opposition from the man who organized, or who was the director of one of the present committees, Selwyn Baptiste, and in the teeth of organized opposition from the man who organized, or who was the secretary of the Carnival and Arts Committee of 1977, Granville Pryce. They (Pryce and Baptiste) were friends at the time (I believe they remained friends) and not on opposite sides of those days – this was 1972–73. They fought and lost their battle with Leslie Palmer because he got the backing of one of the white organizations I've mentioned previously, the North Kensington Amenity Trust. That is how Palmer, who had enormous talents and skills, and not a little insight – I'm not saying he's a revolutionary, or even a radical – he's just a brilliant publicist if not so much a brilliant organizer, although he can organize. His 'successful' Carnivals of '74 and '75 were not technically well-organized Carnivals in the sense that they didn't flow, that everything wasn't got together on time, and so on. I mean, if you were looking at it in purely technical terms, you wouldn't say they were well-organized, although they were successful in terms of numbers – I'm coming back to that. Palmer's victory over Pryce and Selwyn Baptiste was the transforming agency in the Carnival situation. That's what transformed the Carnival from what it was in the earlier period to what it later became: from being something out of which the police could get reassuring publicity for white people and black people, into something that the whole state perceived as *threatening*.

Palmer's tools were publicity and organization. But crucially, extremely crucially, he recognized that there was another, broader, possible cultural base for the Carnival. I'll come back to that also.

What had been the cultural content of Carnival earlier? I've talked about who organized it in those days, but what had been its cultural content? Carnival was about two things, really: first, African bands, like Ginger Johnson, played an important part, and, secondly, steel and costume bands from the Eastern Caribbean, in particular Trinidad, manned by men from that part of the world. That's what it was into, culturally. That was the musical space it occupied, so to speak. The African polyrhythms of Ginger Johnson like the mellifluous sounds of the steel band are totally *unthreatening* to them. And as long as the Carnival continued to be culturally about those two modes of music, everything was 'cool', 'wonderful', 'beautiful' and allowed for 'close vibes'. A few people were disturbed, there were a few fights; Granville Pryce had to tear down some fences one year because an attempt was made to stop the Carnival having use of a piece of ground that it wanted. There were the occasional battles with the police about how big an area should be covered, which streets shouldn't be part of the route, and so on. But nothing of any real significance – no conflict. And then Palmer decided that he would do something to *appeal* to a *different element* – I don't know whether he consciously or otherwise decided on this; I haven't interviewed him, but it is certainly what happened. In any event Palmer took action which raised the cultural appeal of Carnival, because it included a new cultural content. And that cultural content concerned the vast majority of the culturally Jamaica-influenced Caribbean or West Indian migrants in this country. That is to say, Palmer introduced *reggae music*, the music that moves the vast majority of the young people – and, if you check the 'blues parties', the old as well – from the Caribbean in this country. The *Sound System* is the medium of the *reggae* message. And in addition to using *sound* in great enveloping sheets dominated by drum and bass rhythm, they soup up the music in all sorts of ways. Of special importance is a cultural mechanism called *toasting*.[2] So that in addition to the record being on, there is an extra microphone into which the DJ will make additional, *toasting* sounds, so as to enhance the total impact of the record. And the sound can be either *nonsense sound* – depends on what you do with nonsense. It's not always sounds in English, or even creole, although the sound always, as I understand it, has significance of some sort: it might be rebel language, it might even be revolutionary language. The sound system for all these reasons is an extremely powerful medium inside the black communities. Such is the way in which they have grown that, if you say, this sound is on here tonight, and put up some posters, many hundreds of people will come. And if they're playing in the open for free many thousands of people will come. The top, the 'baddest', the best sound in London today is *Sir Coxone*. They have that sort of pulling power and impact. Now that's what Leslie Palmer introduced into the Carnival when he came in. In addition to that, he used the media massively. Palmer used Capital Radio and Radio London. But particularly Capital Radio was used on the scene of the 1975 Carnival, inviting young people to the Carnival. He had great banks of sound systems all the way up along the Westway motorway – I don't know if you know the geography of Notting Hill – but he had great banks of sounds all the way up along there. And he had massive publicity beforehand. Naturally five hundred thousand people, or thereabout, attended the Carnival. Once that happened, five hundred thousand people – they weren't all blacks – even a quarter million black people – in those streets, the police were terrified out of their tiny little minds: they really were.

Once that had happened, the Carnival entered the domain of *threatening culture*, because it was then mass culture, active mass culture, and it had therefore, to be suppressed, or controlled. But, the difficulty about suppression is that you can't suppress anything in this society unless it's illegal or violent. It's very difficult to do so, because people will object, I mean, they'll actually ask you why, and you'll have difficulty controlling it as well. If you're talking about five hundred thousand people, or even two hundred thousand people, on the streets of Notting Hill, there is enormous difficulty controlling that crowd. If they riot, you're in difficulty – as agents of control. And even if they don't riot, you're in difficulty, because you're worried about the possibility that they might riot. You then have to have two alternatives. You either have to move the Carnival into a space in which you can control those numbers – and there is no space of that sort in England, apart, possibly, from open parks, which incidentally, represent the same sort of danger. The largest ground in the country, I think, is the Glasgow Rangers ground, Ibrox Park; and it only holds a hundred and fifty thousand people. There are no indoor spaces that can hold those sorts of numbers. So, when you say, move the Carnival to an indoor space, you're actually talking about drastically reducing numbers. You're talking about the fact that the police have enormous experience with controlling indoor spaces, and that they have great experience with controlling even vast numbers in indoor spaces.

So once that had happened, once those five hundred thousand people – let's say, three-fifths of them black – turned up on the streets of Notting Hill in 1975, the state took the view that the cultural gauntlet had been thrown down, and that that gauntlet had to be picked up! That's what the remainder of the history of the Notting Hill Carnival is about.

Now, all my talk about non-state manipulators of violence comes into play here. You would have thought, as is usually the case in Britain, that when you want to suppress something you organize civil (sub-state) opposition to it. Such civil opposition might have a physical element to it, but it will certainly rely heavily on a propaganda element. Now, there was no physical element to call upon in Notting Hill because we, the black community, had, a decade or more before, sorted them out 'good and proper'. But there were some people, bodies, to mobilize. They were mobilized, and I've got their letters in my file. But who were they? They were old women and men, in a road called Cambridge Gardens, who said, probably quite correctly, that they'd been disturbed by aspects of Leslie Palmer's Carnival in 1975. No doubt they were. Those sound systems do make a hell of a noise. And when you have a great bank of them up along the road, not only can't you hear your mellifluous steel bands but, unless you like the music, you're pretty likely to feel affected in some way. Further, the local authority hadn't anticipated the numbers – nobody had, really – and so they made no extra provision at all for sanitary arrangements, even of the most basic kinds. There weren't any extra loos on the street, and some of the public loos were shut. And people's gardens got pissed in, people's porches got pissed in: and they objected, I mean, quite rightly. The council should have done something about it. They did in following years – in '76, although by then we had moved away from *public cleansing* problems *to public order* problems. Once those numbers arrived, although the propaganda battle could only be articulated in terms – civilly – of public cleansing and *public disturbance*, and possibly *public control* a little bit, when you got the nitty-gritty of what the state, through the police and the council were saying, they were talking about *threats to public order*.

But there was a long battle following the 1975 Carnival, for the preservation of Carnival itself, and for the retention of it on the street. That battle involved some very weak leadership on the part of the Carnival Committee, while on the other side were some groups that were already discredited as racist. For example, there's a group in Notting Hill called the Golborne 100, which is supposed to be a local 'community control' association. It has got publicity as such. (The man who was in charge of it at the time is called George Clarke, who's another excellent publicist, and a known racist locally, but who has a national reputation in the 'community control' movement.) It mainly used the tougher Irish element who, although they had a physical presence, and would defend themselves against anybody, were living in a sort of uneasy truce with the black community. I mean, blacks rarely fought them, and they rarely fought us because they knew that somebody would die. And it's roughly still like that, although that area, the Golborne, has been gutted: the people have largely been moved out, and it's being rebuilt. So that the physical personnel-base that George Clarke once had isn't there, for the moment. That was one of his weaknesses as a mobilizing agency against the Carnival. He did, however, get into it at the propaganda level. He offered a sort of carrot and stick. He said, the Carnival has now become a sort of 'national event': therefore move it to Hyde Park and integrate it in the Jubilee. 'What a splendid gift to the West Indian community,' he said, 'this would be.' That was the carrot. The stick was to do with him saying that 'pimps', 'spivs', 'crooks', 'wide boys' and 'hucksters', had taken over the Carnival and that it was really no longer at all a wholesome thing, and that, what is more, people were pissing on people's doorsteps, and that was naughty. You can read this thrust in his community magazine called *The Golborne*: the September issue is the crucial one.

Additionally, there were the old women, and the relatively old men, who had been genuinely disturbed, and who, some of us were concerned, should not be disturbed, certainly not in those ways – it was unnecessary for them to be disturbed so heavily. These people lived on Cambridge Gardens and they tried to mobilize. They tried to mobilize white tenants' associations, and things like that, but it never got very far. They were rather old, slightly ineffectual people; some of them were too middle-class for the people they were trying to mobilize. One or two of them were very racist Irish women. They just had no conception at all of what was happening to them in Notting Hill. We rang rings round them. One of the things one of these women – with whom I appeared on a radio programme in April '76 – said was, 'You've already got one carnival in Trinidad, what do you want another one for?' It was sometimes at that level – just basically pathetic. They were really completely outmanoeuvred. And so it was necessary for the local state and for the state proper to be called into play. The local state – local council or local authority – has muscle. Unfortunately, since there had been no threat to public order, no disturbance proper, in 1975, the council had no basis for seeking a ban on the Carnival. Although the women I've mentioned, and the men, from Cambridge Gardens, actually thought about getting an injunction, they hadn't a clue about how to get it, nor had they the money to spend on the expensive business of getting an injunction. So much of the opposition to Carnival was either simply ineffectual, or ineffectual because discredited as racist, or ineffectual because they had not the legal basis upon which to proceed.

The state proper as represented by the police was a different matter altogether. They also had the major disadvantage that the local council had, namely that they had no legal basis on which to seek a ban by the home secretary. So all they were able to do was to try, by brute force, threats and restrictions, to force the black community off the streets for Carnival in 1976. But they also offered the 'carrot' before they came with the 'stick'. Their carrot was that money could be made out of the Carnival. The council agreed. The way to make money out of the Carnival was to privatize it – set up a private trust. Movements were made towards that – they called it the Carnival Development Committee within the West Indian Steel Band and Cultural Association. Both were private associations with no legitimacy in the local black community. Certainly, I didn't know of their existence – and I should have done – until they came publicly into being. So that sort of privatization was going on. Like the council, the police argued that if you privatize the thing, and then move it into some indoor place, you'll be able to have gala performances – the works. We will be satisfied, they said, because you can still have your little march on the street, and then you can march the whole thing off, off our nice streets, into some park. They offered the White City, but that happened to be occupied with dog races on the relevant day. So they offered instead the Chelsea football ground – note the football crowd association. And the council was instrumental in trying to get the Carnival use of the football ground. Obviously, those of us who were in community politics in the area opposed all of that, and we're on record as so doing. But interestingly enough, they found, in those people who privatized the Carnival, support and a base for trying to move, restrict and ultimately destroy it. And we found, my organization did, as also did several people 'on the street' and community organizations with whom we work in Notting Hill, that the Carnival Committee, which by then was the Carnival Development Committee, part of the West Indian Steel Band and Cultural Association, was no longer listening to us, because they were now relating to much more important people. They were relating to the police, who were powerful, you had better believe it. And they were going to be able, because the council had money and because the police had power, to buy all the bands off the street and take them to Chelsea, whatever we said.

They proceeded to organize on that basis, until the council showed them the economics of the operation, which we had been telling them all along anyway. We said that you are going to be moving the Carnival into a space that belonged to the 'man'; that the 'man' was going to have control of the food preparation; that basically all you were going to have was control on the gates; that he was going to put his people on the gates, and that he was going to give what he wanted out of the gate receipts. And you were going to get nothing. We were telling them that. But it wasn't until the council sent them a letter which said that clearly, that they backed off the idea of going with the Carnival to Chelsea football ground in 1976. This is documented.

Now, after the Carnival Development Committee had backed off going to Chelsea, because it was no longer going to be profitable, the police brought out the big stick. The Carnival Committee had meetings with the council and the police jointly and meetings with the police on their own. The police said that they were going to enforce 'law and order'! That they were going to uphold the letter of the law. And in the context of the Carnival, that means, basically, no jollification. It represents a major challenge to every cultural space that Carnival is. And it was obvious that the black communities weren't going to like it, and I wrote a letter threatening that the black communities wouldn't stand for it. The police ignored us. We wrote, hoping . . . you know. I understand the British political system, so I wrote to the commissioner of police and I copied the letter to *The Times* – major opinion organ, you see – and to *The Guardian* – major wielder of liberal opinion; to the local community relations officer (CRO) in Westminster, the state's man on the ground; to the home office; and to Jennifer Jenkins – the home secretary's wife, who was also chair of the local North Kensington Amenity Trust. Nothing happened. The police continued to mobilize their operation. They said, no illegal sale of drinks, no smoking ganja on the streets: basically, no jollity. They also said, no sound systems on the street; and they got support for that from the 'Trinidadians' on the Carnival Committee, because they had been offended, regrettably – understandably though – by being 'swamped' by reggae music, and by all those 'Jamaicans' who really, they said, 'don't understand Carnival at all', coming to the Carnival and just swamping their music – nobody was able to hear the steel bands. And they really did, and still do, resent it very deeply. The Carnival Committee was always dominated by Trinidadians – I think Mr. Chase and Mr. Bukari, respectively past and present chairmen of the Carnival and Arts Committee, are the first non-Trinidadians to chair any of the committees organizing Carnival. There are never very many people from anywhere else on it, if you check down any of the lists of members. The state, then, announced all these prohibitions. There was to be no 'illegal' selling of drinks; but the Carnival wasn't to have a drinks licence. There was to be no illegal selling of drinks; but publicans and off-licences/off-sales people were to be encouraged not to sell. So it was going to be a dry Carnival, a spliffless

Carnival, a completely joyless Carnival. And what is more, it was going to be an incredibly heavily policed Carnival. Because all of those prohibitions were going to be enforced. Indeed, the Carnival itself was going to be controlled. They were going to organize the routes. They did, in exactly the same way that they organize football crowds. And so they sectored the routes, the whole area, into six parts. They said that bands should flow inside of each sector, but there would be no movement between sectors. They said that the most difficult area of control within the location was going to be the Acklam Road/ Portobello Road area – the geography of the area's quite important – and only one band passed, presumably by accident, through the space during Carnival '76.

Given that those prohibitions and controls were going to be enforced, the police needed massive numbers on the grounds. They said to the Carnival Development Committee that they were going to have a *serial* round each band. But its members never understood what a serial was – it just happens to be twenty policemen. And there jolly well were twenty policemen round most of those bands in Carnival '76. I kid you not – we have photographs of them. And in addition to the policemen who were not functioning in serials, that is, not in surrounding bands, including kids' bands, there were policemen in fours or eights with one or two sergeants on every street corner and on most parts of most streets, throughout the two days. And towards the end of Sunday, the numbers increased massively. Their business was enforcement of all the prohibitions that I've mentioned. It was initially a total humiliation. I kept hoping, as did anybody else with any spunk at all, over those two days, that, from somewhere within the community, resistance would come.

The police enforced their thing, ruthlessly. Our organization has an office at 301 Portobello Road – and that road was not open to public traffic at all. They had a vast ambulance unit from Weybridge, belonging to the London Ambulance Service, there. They had several other ambulances there, as well as a police command post and several police vans. What had been part of the heart of Carnival in previous years was occupied in that way in that year. The officer in charge was a man called Paterson. He was actually second in command on that day, but he planned the operation, with the full backing of Scotland Yard. And they were filmed doing it by the BBC who have lots of films which would be very revealing if they were not discarded. But even the stuff they have screened is still very revealing. Paterson came to the door of our organization when we'd put up a stall where we sell records outside on Saturdays and on occasions when there are likely to be people there to buy. And my colleague said, 'Who's giving this order? What legitimates that?' And the man said, 'The Carnival Committee.' The response was, 'Go and bring your chief steward, and I'll get my cutlass and one of you touch my sound and see who gets what today.' And Paterson went mumbling to the TV crew filming the encounter that the stall would only make a 'normal' noise. But another sound system that was further down the road was moved on. And the Carnival chief steward came – a very muscular man – and watched them move it, and encouraged the moving of that sound system. There were very few sound systems present in Carnival 1975.

Resistance

Now, how did the violence arise? I have said that the police enforced prohibitions throughout. There was a raid on the Mangrove restaurant on the Sunday morning. There were raids on several other black centres in the locality. The whole area was full of green and blue buses packed with policemen being held in reserve. There were people who had in previous years sold beer who were just picked up and carted off. And even when one man said to the police, 'Look, take the beer, take it all, just leave me alone, I'll accept the loss, don't arrest me', he was still carted off and put into a van. Fortunately he had the gumption to give them a wrong name. They were probably too busy on that day to check. Usually, if you give them a name and address, they go and check it now, before they let you out, because lots of people have told them wrong names. But in the early part of Carnival, that man got away. Several black people were arrested in that way. And several people lost hundreds of pounds, because the police seized their goods and when you're seized selling illegal booze, you don't get it back.

The police said that pickpocketing was going on. Possibly. But because they had so much force on the ground, they didn't feel any need to arrest with any gentility. So they didn't. Several black youths went past our post, on the Portobello Road, bleeding, in the hands of policemen. And, finally, you will have heard that the flashpoint of the violence was on the corner of Acklam Road and Blagrove Road, near the Acklam Hall. It is said that was the flashpoint because pickpocketing was occurring there. Again, there might have been pickpocketing, but the flashpoint didn't happen because of pickpocketing. Rather, it was because of the massive and indiscriminate violence which the police used against black youths they thought were pickpocketing. The girl who was secretary to the Carnival Committee until shortly before the 1977 Carnival was in that corner at the crucial time on Carnival Monday '76. She had difficulty sleeping for months afterwards because of the way in which she saw policemen use batons on the heads of black young men and women in that corner on that afternoon. Fortunately, there were enough black youths around there, and enough missiles in that space, for a resistance to be put up and supported. That resistance was not pre-organized, and it spread so fast, that nobody was able to control it. I oughtn't to say this, but as the move by the youths, throwing stones at policemen, and bloody policemen being brought out

from down in that corner by their colleagues, developed, there were stalls on
the Westway side of Acklam Road, one of which belonged to the Black
Liberation Front. Perhaps they would have preferred to continue selling what
they were selling on that stall, which was books and posters, and things like
that. One person operating the stall tried to get the black youths to stop.
Indeed, one of them looked round and said, 'Stop doing that', as the half
bricks were coming over. They packed up their stall and a few hours later they
had a militant leaflet out against the police action on the afternoon, and
supporting the youths. But at least one of them tried, temporarily, to intervene
to stop the resistance happening. Just temporarily, but it was too big.

The reason why the resistance was so dramatic is that the terrain was full of
weapons. Adjoining that space was, until recently, an extended building site.
Indeed, on the corner of Acklam Road and Blagrove Road there is still a GLC
building site. That is what I mentioned earlier when I said that the Golborne
Ward area is being taken down and rebuilt, and George Clarke's Irish base is
temporarily not there any more. That's where it started from, and there were
bricks there, half bricks, and whole bricks, and there were also bottles in
abundance, beer cans full and empty, and soft drinks cans full and empty.
And the police were almost unarmed. They just had their sticks and their
numbers. But numbers were absolutely no use, in effect, against those
weapons. They were roundly beaten. Hundreds of them were injured.
Absolutely justifiably – because what they were attempting to do seemed to us
in the community to be totally unnecessary. We had warned them about what
would happen. They might just have got away with it if they had attempted to
do it with a little bit less brashness and a little bit less brutality. But, in fact,
they did it both brashly and brutally, and they were confronted and defeated
on that terrain, in the second most important single battle fought by the black
masses in the UK – the first being, of course, the black resistance in 1958.

The Survival of Carnival

Now, after Carnival 1976, the question was: was Carnival to be banned or
not? It wasn't banned. Was it to be off the streets or not? It wasn't taken off the
street. The main reasons why neither of those things happened was this: that
the police had been caught entirely on the hop. Not only had they been
defeated physically, but in propaganda terms they had also been routed.
Because it was patently clear that they had over-policed; it was patently clear
that they'd used too much brutality; it was patently clear that they had ignored
the warnings from inside the community about what was likely to happen if
they acted in those ways. Given that that was so, the state could not say,
although there had been a disturbance of public order, that the black

communities had been the cause of that disturbance, because the police clearly were the cause. And so the Carnival was not banned. But what then had to happen was that, in some way or another, the Carnival had to be moved out of that geographical terrain; it had to be put into the hands of people that the state liked; and it had, as far as possible, to return to its traditional Trinidad Eastern Caribbean cultural base. The prevention of these developments has been the battle that the community has faced in relation to Carnival since 31 August 1976.

How did that go? Darcus Howe said that 'the state will determine'. Has the state determined? And what did it determine in the year between Carnival '76 and Carnival '77? A number of things happened – and I'll try to be extremely brief about this, some of it is very recent history. What happened, I say, was this: that the council – the local state – and the state proper decided that the weak link, the manipulable element, inside of the black community where Carnival was concerned, was around the man called Selwyn Baptiste, whom they had almost outmanoeuvred in the previous year. He was the man in charge who had almost taken the event to Chelsea, and to the White City stadium; he had been the man who had not understood what police serials were, and who had not issued any warning to the community about over-policing, and so on. Now that was the man that the state chose, and he got help from the local state, although they would deny it; did deny it subsequently. There were disagreements: the state is not, for internal purposes, homogeneous. Certain people inside the local state knew how weak Baptiste was, knew he 'couldn't organize', and thought that they should deal with 'better' organizers. Some of them also knew the truth, about how he operated in the period immediately after Carnival '76.

The process of privatization that he'd started earlier, by setting up those two associations I mentioned, was later carried to ludicrous extents. He moved away from the Carnival office in the Acklam Road into his private flat, somewhere else in Notting Hill. He told the Post Office to disconnect the phone. He tried to arrange for the Users Collective controlling the buildings in which the Carnival office was located to repossess it. There were repeated vandalizations of the Carnival office in Acklam Road. In the meantime, he set about trying to constitute a Carnival committee round himself. The first attempt he made was that it would be multi-racial. I don't have any objection in principle to that, but the people he chose were very effete and reactionary indeed. After they failed, he chose black bourgeois people from largely outside Notting Hill who had contact with the state through the work of the CRC and so on. That initiative too failed, because we destroyed it. And then, finally, he imported, or accepted the forced importation of Darcus Howe of *Race Today*, and a reconstituted Carnival Development Committee following Carnival '76.

In the meantime he tried to present Carnival once again as a 'Trinidad'-based, mellifluous, pretty spectacle. There were jamborees in the Common-wealth Institute, and I don't have to tell you who owns that and what it functions as. There were jamborees in the Architectural Association – I don't know anything at all about the Architectural Association and will make, therefore, no accusations! Baptiste tried further to suggest that his Carnival Development Committee was the same committee, in terms of personnel, as the one which had organized Carnival '76, which it wasn't. In fact, he was one of only two people from the Carnival Development Committee '76 who went over into Carnival Development Committee '77. So it wasn't the same people at all. All the old people remained, and battled with him, along with us – the community organizations and individuals who tried to get Selwyn Baptiste to come back to the community at least to explain what had happened. We knew, of course, what had happened; but there really ought to be some grace exhibited in terms of offering an explanation and an apology when you screw up like that. He never came. He decided, as he had done prior to Carnival '76, that we were not important enough to bother with; that, provided he got a show on the road with sufficient momentum, all would be well. We waited until January 1977, five months after Carnival '76, before we started really mobilizing. After that, we, the community groups in the area (the black community as organized in that area, unorthodox organizations, possibly, but they're there and they function politically, and they can stand up against enemies inside the community and outside when necessary), organized, and re-created the Carnival committee, under a different name – now the Notting Hill Carnival and Arts Committee – because the 1976 name had been hijacked by Baptiste. But in membership it was the old committee, largely, most of the personnel from the previous year were still there, except in the instance of the resignation of Mrs. Pansy Jeffries, who was the treasurer; or had gone off somewhere else, as was to happen eventually with Junior Telfer, who I've mentioned previously. The battle then raged between a committee constituted by election in the community and a committee constituted on three different occasions with three different memberships, by some persons largely unknown. And yet the 'liberal' press, and yet the 'liberal' state, and yet the 'liberal' state institutions, supported the Carnival Development Commit-tee rather than the committee constituted by the community.

Why did they do that? Because they were afraid of a physical community base for the Carnival; because they wanted to move it back to its old, non-threatening, modes of culture; because they wanted black youths to be out of it, for it was they who had wielded the weapons in '76. The state almost succeeded. The way they did it was that they propagandized black individuals and community organizations. They accused me and my organizations of being crooks and other things like that. They said we were 'mysterious'; they said we'd got £50,000 'public money' and hadn't accounted for it – not true: we had accounted for it to those who for their own reasons were giving us the funds to carry out work. They called upon every medium of opinion, including the *West Indian World*, which (because of the Trinidad connection and despite an earlier political attack by *Race Today*) came out in favour of the Carnival Development Committee under Darcus Howe. The West Indian Standing Conference, a band of desiccated black conservatives, came out in favour of them; so too did the Caribbean High Commissions and the personnel of the CRE (CRC) and so on despite the obvious legitimacy of the alternative committee.

It was decided also, that since the Carnival was going to be on the road, that it should not have any money. That way it couldn't pay for discos, sound systems and bands and would thus not attract people. That way, too, the 'threatening masses' would be removed. The local state spent a long time clearing the ground of weapons – the weapons that had been used, the missiles, in 1976. They told people to board up their shops. The police prepared for battle plan, which they disguised behind a so-called 'low profile'. They closed off streets and alleys and people, including myself, got arrested, allegedly for trying to take down barriers and to re-open alleyways so that there could be the normal flow of people, both in the context of the Carnival and also within the community, because those alleyways are places that we traverse normally.

What surprised me, and what I have to condemn formally, was the role of *Race Today* – as a black political organization, an organization that's explicitly political and purportedly revolutionary – in supporting the Carnival Development Committee against the community-based elected committee. I want to mention a statement of theirs, in order to show the perfidy and opportunism of their political position in relation to this matter. *Race Today* wrote an open letter to the Carnival Development Committee on 8 September 1976, in which they roundly condemned Selwyn Baptiste, and called upon him to come back to the community and explain. Selwyn never did. But Darcus Howe went and joined him. (Incidentally, before Carnival '76, *Race Today* played quite a progressive role in terms of organizing opinion inside the black communities in the UK, and maybe even internationally, in favour of a Carnival.)

The *Race Today* collective talked about a 'power base' for Carnival. What is the base that they enunciated? Mass-bandsmen, steel-bandsmen, stall-holders, and local West Indian businessmen. Then they accused the Carnival and Arts Committee of being hustlers. Now, with the best will in the world, some of those groups itemized above as the 'base' function on the basis of hustle. Much more importantly, they tend to be culturalists, they also tend to be apolitical. Thus their response, the response of the steel-bandsmen and the mass-band people to the 'riot', to the resistance of black youth, in Carnival '76, was 'Is all dem Jamaican youths who don't understand Carnival who

cause all dis trouble'. Importantly, the so-called 'Jamaican' youth turn out to
be not all Jamaican in origin. They were simply black youth in resistance.
That's what they said. What is more, since most of them were not involved in
the resistance, and didn't even know about it until they saw the TV, they were
quite sure that it was all the Jamaican youths who didn't understand Carnival
who caused the violence, because they themselves were involved in bands,
away from Acklam Road and Portobello Road, and the area of the Metro, and
the area of Ladbroke Grove; and saw no 'violence'. They just heard about it,
or saw it later on television. So that those men are not a political base, in fact
they are a systematically apolitical, even anti-political, base. Darcus Howe
said that what he had against the community-based committee was that it was
'populist'. And by populist, he seemed to mean that any- and everybody could
participate. But that was not the case. We controlled the mode of election
quite tightly. And the only reason the quality of the committee wasn't better
than it was, was that we're short of good personnel on the ground. This is
always the case in ghetto situations. Darcus, therefore, and the *Race Today*
collective, as I understand it, acted out of pure political opportunism in
joining with the Carnival Development Committee. They made no contribution at all to the fight, to the articulation of the fight against the state and the
various sub-state agencies in the disposition of police forces in the area. They
said nothing at all about the fact that the local Amenity Trust moved away its
stalls – mounted them out of the community – so that they wouldn't be
available for stall-holders during the Carnival. The *Race Today* people said
nothing about these things.

In the meantime, the Carnival Development Committee was busy at the
Commonwealth Institute. When there was trouble on Carnival Sunday
afternoon – the first day of Carnival '77 – they said, 'That's nothing to do with
us.' When there was again trouble on Monday, that really had to be dealt
with in some way, because the whole basis of our mobilization against the
police was that we, the black community as such, could gather on the street
without being perceived as a threat to public order in this country, that to so
perceive us was racism; and that we were going to fight them on those
grounds. That was the basis, of course, on which my and several of the other
community groups and the political people in the area mobilized.

We mobilized, I say. But we didn't exactly win the battle. There were more
policemen there in 1977 than, conceivably, there were the year before. They
had an open terrain; it had been cleared of weapons. When they moved in
finally, having first been attacked by the youths, they swept all before them.
That's significant and should be talked about. The police didn't attack the
youths in the first instance in 1977. Rather the youths launched a direct
frontal attack on them, and that has got to be looked at and analysed. Did the
youths know that they were fighting on a weaponless terrain? Did it matter
to them if they knew that they were fighting on a weaponless terrain?

Had they worked out means of escape afterwards? What was the meaning of the tactics that they employed? – tactics that seemed, on the second day of the Carnival, to be used doubly, for theft, and then, later, for politics. Is theft also politics, in this context? All of these questions have got to be asked. Finally, the stewarding. Having provided no stewards, Darcus Howe said that the stewards were thugs – he had a lovely Indian word, which I suspect he borrowed from Farrukh Dhondy, who's the man inside the collective who knows the Indian sub-continent – he used a lovely Indian word, which I've forgotten. It means gangsters, thugs – Goondas! So they said that the stewards were thugs. Now, the stewards were undoubtedly heavy! But what actually happened over those two days? And I was one of the stewards, although I used no violence against anybody. What actually happened was this. There had to be some 'policing' of that crowd by the black community. And when black people started ripping off inside something that we had said was ours, and was important to us politically, we had to try to defend against it! That's what the stewards were at. When they tried to do this, they were faced with ruthless young black men, who have got to be understood. The youths pulled knives, and used those knives against stewards. It was only after those knives had been pulled and used against stewards, whose names I have – they're people I know – that the stewards went in with those sticks that they have been photographed wielding, plastered over the *Daily Telegraph* and the *Evening Standard* and the TV screen, and so on. Now those stewards were ordinary black people who were trying in those conditions, probably wrongly, and certainly they took it too far, to do what they felt was necessary to protect a cultural event that we had said had some value to us, and that a set of youths were saying had no value, or had only a value as a venue for robbing with violence. I repeat, theft may be political, so the argument is in a difficulty there. Certainly, theft by black youths in this society cannot be apolitical, because it's produced by the operations of the capitalist economy (from which they are massively excluded) and its acquisitive, individualist culture. Nevertheless, that is what happened. And those are some of my views on the Notting Hill Carnival, and that is why I insisted on saying that I was going to talk about Carnival, the state and the black masses in the United Kingdom.

Notes

1. This is the text of a talk given by Cecil Gutzmore on 20 November 1978 at the Polytechnic of Central London. The forum was the course on Black Culture. Gutzmore was invited as a worker for the Black People's Information Centre in Ladbroke Grove, Notting Hill. Though not on any Carnival committee, this 'grassroots' black organization was substantially involved with Carnival.

2. *Toasting*, in the better quality of reggae music, is improvised 'oratory' about the social structure, political and cultural class practices or sexuality. Comments on these aspects – which the toaster introduces spontaneously – usually generate certain 'phases', 'terms', and 'nonsense' sounds which can trigger off responses ranging from being 'cool' to being 'rebellious'.

These 'terms', 'phases' and 'nonsense' sounds are normally taken into everyday 'street language' of the black masses and function there as reference points against racism, cultural subordination or economic exploitation. In this way, the 'roots language' of the *toaster* is evoked in the voices of young blacks. Similarly, a toaster may affect the 'speech' patterns of *the* youth.

The greatest toasting innovators are *U-Roy, Big Youth* and *Prince Far I*. After them it became normal practice for every *sound system* DJ to *toast*.

10

Migration, Racism and Identity Formation: The Caribbean Experience in Britain

Winston James

It is the white man who creates the Negro. But it is the Negro who creates négritude.

FRANTZ FANON

A waan free up de system
cause it a meck me feel
dat we cyaan get no satisfaction
until we chop off we right han

so me waan fi drape it
inna it shut
till it bus up

fi meck dem know
dat a jus fed-up
dat when dem a chat dem fart
bout fi add more nought
we just chip een
an meck dem know
dat a fi-we time now
fi tell dem two plate claat
an meck dem understan
we rass claat predicament
dat dem got we a live inna

So meck we free up de system
fi meck we dance
to a new rhythm
an just mash dem ism

MICHAEL SMITH

231

Introduction

Although much has been written on the forces behind Caribbean migration to Britain, and on the social and economic conditions in which black people in this country live, precious little work has been done on the nature of the national and ethnic identity of Caribbeans and their descendants here. The following remarks are therefore primarily concerned with an exploration of the issue of black identity in Britain with particular reference to people of African Caribbean descent. There is, however, another, albeit somewhat secondary, ambition behind this project, one of more general import – it is that of a case study of identity formation and change.

It is now generally acknowledged that ethnicity and ethnic identity, however defined, are not static and eternal in their constitution but are profoundly dynamic, always in the process of being made, unmade and re-made. Moreover, it is evident, that the phenomenon of migration and the encountering of new challenges in a new environment quite often accelerate the process of such changes.[1] But although the issue of identity, including that of 'black identity', has become a veritable intellectual cottage industry of late, there is still a virtual absence of *concrete* analyses of identity formation and change.[2] What is therefore attempted in this essay is a concrete case study – an analysis, vis-à-vis this issue, of the experience of African Caribbeans in Britain in the post-war period. It explores the relationship between the phenomena of migration and racism, on the one hand, and the formation of ethnic identity, on the other. Thus it attempts to lay bare the dialectics of Afro-Caribbean ethnic identity formation and discusses some of the political implications of the new identities being forged by black people in Britain. And as I shall endeavour to show, the exploration of aspects of black identity is by no means an academic exercise in the pejorative sense of the term: the way in which black people identify themselves within British society has a direct bearing upon their political capacities and practices. Consciousness and action are inextricably intertwined.

For our purposes it is appropriate to look at the differential nature of identity formation between the first generation of migrants and their descendants. It should, however, be emphasized at the outset that this mode of procedure does not in any way imply – contrary to the popular British stereotype (reinforced, incidentally, by much pernicious writing, especially in recent years, going under the banner of 'social science') of Afro-Caribbean people – that there is a Chinese Wall between the first and subsequent generations. It is merely deployed to assist in the necessary periodization of the analysis as well as to help indicate some of the genuine differences, forged by fundamentally dissimilar life histories and cultural experiences between the first and subsequent generations of people of Afro-Caribbean descent in

Britain. It will also be shown that, although many white Britons do not apparently know this, black people, old as well as young, *do* learn, *do* adapt to their environment and *do* devise new strategies (individual and collective) to confront the problems that they face.[3] Again, contrary to the stereotype of increasing generational conflicts between the first and second generations of people of Afro-Caribbean descent in Britain, it is noticeable that since the early 1970s in particular, there has been a remarkably sharp convergence in the diagnosis of the 'British problem' by older Caribbean people and their offspring in Britain.

The First Generation and the Caribbean Historical Backdrop

As is to be expected, the harsh and perennial winter of British racism has, in a number of respects, helped to create an identity – which perhaps under different circumstances would not have developed – among Afro-Caribbeans living in Britain which is more commensurate with their concrete situation and historical experience. Inter alia, the crude binary (black/white) allocation of ethnic groups within Britain has contributed to the severe and unrelenting undermining of the at once nauseating and pathetic hierarchy of shades which has vitiated the Caribbean psyche. To bring this and other points into full relief it is necessary to make an historical detour.

As elsewhere, colonization in the Caribbean did not only entail the economic, political and military domination of the indigenous and colonized population, it also involved a sometimes overt, but often surreptitious process of cultural oppression. One of the major facets of this cultural domination was the more or less open undermining of any positive self-image which the colonized might have had. Frantz Fanon, with his exceptionally sharp gift of perception, was acutely aware of this and grasped its implications:

> Colonialism is not simply content to impose its rule upon the present and the future of a dominated country. Colonialism is not satisfied merely with holding a people in its grip and emptying the native's brain of all form and content. By a kind of perverted logic, it turns to the past of the oppressed people, and distorts, disfigures and destroys it (Fanon 1967: 169).

The days of slavery

In the Americas, arguably as a direct consequence of the trade in Africans and the enslavement of millions more, the image of Africa and Africans was continuously and systematically maligned.[4] In the eyes of the slave owners, humanity in Caribbean slave society was not only conceived to be congenitally hierarchical (with the European in the superordinate position) but the African barely reached the lowest rung of the human species.

Not surprisingly, a complex hierarchy of human shades, what one prominent Caribbeanist (Lewis 1969: 80; 1983: 9) has aptly called a 'multilayered pigmentocracy', commensurate with this *Weltanschauung*, evolved wherein those who approximated most closely to the European type (in terms of hair texture, skin colour, facial characteristics, etc.) were accorded high status (which almost invariably corresponded with their location within the class structure of the society), and those deemed to have been without, or with few such characteristics, were likewise relegated to the bottom of the social hierarchy. Thus the 'coloureds' (the so-called 'mulattoes') – offspring of the union of Europeans (almost invariably men) and African (almost invariably women)[5] – were regarded as congenitally superior to 'pure Africans' and moreover, *were treated as such.*[6]

The coloureds were quite often manumitted and, moreover, were bequeathed substantial property by their slave-owning fathers. Of such significance was this practice of granting property to 'mulatto' offspring that in Jamaica, for instance, in 1761, after an enquiry of the House of Assembly of the island had discovered that property already bequeathed to 'freedmen' (people who were born into slavery but later manumitted, the vast majority of whom were 'coloured'),[7] was valued at between £200,000 and £300,000, legislation was promptly put into place that made it unlawful for whites to leave real or personal property worth more than £1,200 (sterling) to any coloured or black person. 'The whites,' concluded one historian, 'had decided that it was more important to keep the land in European hands than to follow parental instincts' (Heuman 1981: 6). This Jamaican Act, like similar attempts elsewhere in the Americas did not, however, in any way undermine the material privilege of the coloureds over the Africans in the Caribbean pigmentocracy. Indeed, even when they were kept as slaves, the coloureds were given preferential treatment and occupied 'superior' positions in the slave hierarchy: they were given a greater opportunity to learn skills to become artisans and many worked as house or domestic slaves – positions much sought after by the slaves, male as well as female, who had to work more arduously under a harsher regimen in the fields.[8] It is also instructive to note that in the early years of the slave system, in correspondence with its colour hierarchy, many of the enslaved Africans who were put to work as house slaves, in Jamaica at least, were the ostensibly 'light-skinned' 'Madagass' slaves – so called because they were imported from the island of Madagascar (Henriques 1968: 33).

The point being made is important and deserves emphasis: not only did the pigmentocracy operate at the level of ideology per se, it also performed as a *material force* joining tightly together colour with class position and privilege, neatly overlapping, over-laying and imbricating them, thus generating and upholding the *forced coincidence* of colour and class in Caribbean societies which has lasted to the present day.

Slave societies in the Americas were profoundly race/colour-conscious. A whole plethora of social types based upon 'race' were designated and hierarchically structured in such a thoroughly and consciously organized manner that by comparison, the obnoxious triad (white, coloured, black) of contemporary apartheid seems singularly crude. In the British colonies, for instance, the following categories obtained (Braithwaite 1971: 67; Hall 1972: 196; and Higman 1976: 139):[9]

Negro: child of negro and negro
Sambo: child of mulatto and negro
Mulatto: child of white man and negress
Quadroon: child of mulatto woman and white man
Mustee: child of quadroon (or pure amerindian) and white man
Mustiphini: child of mustee and white man
Quintroon: child of mustiphini and white man
Octoroon: child of quintroon and white man

The Spanish and Dutch colonies had even more multitudinous categories. The former, for instance, in their *castas* had *saltatras* (mulatto/quadroon), *givero* (sambo Indian/sambo mulatto) and the almost incredible *tente en el aire* (translated literally as 'suspended') which designated the offspring of the union of quadroon and mustee. Indeed, in Spanish America, no fewer than 128 gradations were possible (Brathwaite 1971: 167; cf. Mörner 1967; Rout 1976; and Knight 1970) and in Brazil, Marvin Harris counted 492 different categories (Harris 1970; cf. Bastide 1974). According to Mörner these hierarchies were, inter alia, illustrative of 'the almost pathological interest in genealogy' that was characteristic of the age (Mörner 1967: 59).

In the British Caribbean (with the sole exception of Barbados), one was designated legally white after the category of mustee and became automatically free.[10] One way, therefore, of becoming legally free in Caribbean slave society was to literally breed out the 'African blood' from one's system over a series of generations. Thus we have the underlining of the concatenation of blackness and servitude (and the absence of human attributes) and whiteness and freedom (and the epitome or attainment of human status).

But even after such a perverse and viciously self-immolating journey had been undertaken, the aspiring traveller to whiteness even after passing through the stations marked 'Quadroon', 'Mustee', 'Mustiphini' and so on, never quite reached, never *really arrived*, at the great 'City of Whiteness'. Gad Heuman cites the case of a white patroness of a ball in the eastern Caribbean who 'strongly criticized a British captain for having danced with a "costie"', a term describing a person who was *one-sixteenth coloured*. The woman sponsoring the event then provided the captain with a list of the various castes between mulattoes and 'costies' and 'presumably', conjectured Heuman, 'the rules of behaviour for an English officer'. This remarkable incident, an exhibition of the astonishingly sharp social and racial demarcation which existed, occurred as late as the middle of the nineteenth century, two clear decades *after* the abolition of the enslavement of African people in the British Caribbean (Heuman 1981: 76). It was difficult to become 'white' and humiliating to have been 'un-white' – including being 'coloured', not just being 'black'. It was far *easier*, and needless to say, much more noble, to have raised a rebellion of the masses.

While the coloureds were being demeaned and humiliated by the whites, even after death,[11] they, in turn, bloated with what the eighteenth-century planter-historian Edward Long aptly called 'the pride of amended blood', had few qualms in pouring scorn upon Africans, including upon those who were legally free like themselves. According to Long, they:

> despise the Blacks, and aspire to mend their complexion still more by intermixture with the Whites. The children of White and Quateron are called English, and consider themselves as free from all taint of the Negroe race. To call them by a degree inferior to what they really are, would be the highest affront. This pride of amended blood is universal, and becomes the more confirmed, if they have received any smattering of education; for then they look down with the more supercilious contempt upon those who have had none (Lon 1774, vol. II: 332).[12]

Excluded by the whites, the coloureds held their spectacular balls from which Africans, but not whites, were excluded. The coloureds also expressed their social insecurity by ruthlessly oppressing the African slaves in their possession. They were notorious, even among the white plantocracy, for exceptional cruelty against slaves.[13] A common Jamaican saying among the African slaves reflected this state of affairs: 'If me fe have massa or misses, give me a Buckra one – no give me mulatto, dem no use neega well.'[14] According to Mrs Carmichael, who spent most of her time in the Caribbean in Trinidad, 'To be sold to a coloured owner is considered by a Negro to be an extreme misfortune' (cited in Campbell 1976: 57).

After his examination of the equivalent dynamic between whites, mulattoes and Africans in pre-revolutionary Haiti, C.L.R. James declared in resigned exasperation: 'It all reads like a cross between a nightmare and a bad joke' (James 1963: 43). His remarks apply with equal poignancy and sorrow to the conditions which obtained in the rest of the Caribbean and to those of the Americas as a whole.

Understandably, the African slaves and their descendants were – depending upon the historical specificities of the particular social formation – to a lesser or greater degree affected by the values attributed to different human 'types'. Indeed, so much so that even in Jamaica, an island renowned for its relatively high retention of African culture in the Americas, contemporary eighteenth-century accounts testify to the contempt with which the newly-arrived African slaves were often met by other – 'creole' (or local-born) – slaves. Newly-arrived Africans, traumatized successively by capture, the march to the coast, the horrendous middle passage across the Atlantic, the humiliation of 'inspection' by prospective buyers, the branding of their bodies as if they were cattle, were derogatorily referred to by some creole slaves as 'salt-water negroes' and 'Guiney birds'. This is the observation of one early-nineteenth-century commentator:

> The one class, forced into slavery, humbled and degraded had lost everything and found no solace but the miserable one of retrospection. The other, born in slavery, never had freedom to lose; yet did the Creole proudly assume a superiority over the African . . . (Patterson 1967: 146–7, 152).[15]

Such were some of the ironies of Caribbean slave society; that cross between a nightmare and a bad joke that James talked about.

The legacies of the long night

The post-slavery period was marked more by continuity than by change in the colour–class complex which was firmly laid in place over a period of more than three centuries of African chattel slavery in the Americas. A somewhat subconscious element of self-doubt if not self-contempt afflicted the African section of the population during and after slavery. It could hardly have been otherwise, for, as Marx recognized: 'The tradition of the dead generations weighs like a nightmare on the minds of the living' (Marx 1973: 146). Various symptoms reflected this state of affairs: the straightening of the hair which was described to a Jamaican sociologist by one hairdresser as, significantly, the 'cultivating' of the hair,[16] the bleaching of the skin and the obsession with skin colour are some of the most well-known expressions of the colonial legacy in the Americas.[17]

In an otherwise solid analysis, Errol Lawrence (1982) has grossly under-estimated some of the negative legacies of colonialism in the Caribbean and is far too defensive about their manifestations. Criticizing aspects of Nancy Foner's work, he writes:

> The fact that hair straightening is one among a range of ways that Afro-Caribbean women have of dressing their hair and the fact that lotions for whitening the skin are not the only items in their cosmetic repertoire, appears to be lost on Foner (Lawrence 1982: 101).[18]

The issues, to my mind, are wrongly posed by the author. What ought to be explained is: first, *why should* hair straightening, which is not only damaging to the hair but can be deleterious to the overall health[19] of the individual who indulges in such an activity, be a means of dressing the hair *at all*?; and second, the question should not have been whether the use of lotions for whitening the skin is or is not the only element in the so-called 'cosmetic repertoire', the question ought to have been, *why should* lotions for whitening the skin (the application of which has been known for decades to be damaging not only to the epidermis but also to the general health of the individual due to the characteristics of their chemical components) be applied *at all*? Being 'tempted', if only in a footnote, to 'speculate as to whether the practice among white women of curling their hair, and the practice among white people generally of going to extraordinary lengths to get a "suntan", should also be seen as evidence of a "negative self-image" among the white population'[20] is not only completely unproductive, it is also tantamount to the trivialization of an extremely important human and sociological problem.

It should be noted that the idea of black 'negative self-image' was not occasioned by white reactionaries but by black nationalists and revolutionaries (such as Marcus Garvey, Claude McKay, the Rastafarians, Aimé Césaire and the *négritude* movement, Frantz Fanon, Malcolm X and Walter Rodney) who were desperately worried about the economic *as well* as about the psychic state of their people. Consider the following passage:

> West Indians of every colour still aspire to European standards of dress and beauty. The language which is used by black people in describing ourselves shows how *we despise our African appearance*. 'Good hair' means European hair, 'good nose' means a straight nose, 'good complexion' means a light complexion. Everybody recognizes how incongruous and ridiculous such terms are, but we continue to use them and express our support of the assumption that white Europeans have a monopoly of beauty, and that black is the incarnation of ugliness. This is why Black Power advocates find it necessary to assert that BLACK IS BEAUTIFUL.

This is clearly not written by some white reactionary bent on demeaning black people, yet it alludes to the recurring motif of 'negative black self-image', 'we despise our African appearance', etc., which Lawrence finds so objectionable. In fact the sentiments quoted above were expressed by one of the most courageous and exemplary children of the African diaspora, Walter Rodney, in a speech which he made in Jamaica in 1968 (Rodney 1975: 32–3, first emphasis added).

The fact of the matter is that colonialism has, not surprisingly, done us tremendous harm in a whole variety of ways. Our task is to understand the nature of the harm done, how it occurred, how it persists and how we ought to combat it. The process of reflecting upon some of them, especially on paper, is painful and sometimes even embarrassing to some. But the alternative of silence and misinformation is far more detrimental to the cause of our people.

The internalization of the pigmentocracy, however, did not take place to the same depth and range by Afro-Caribbean people regardless of class. The evidence suggests that those most affected by what the Caribbean sociologist Fernando Henriques has termed the 'white bias' in Caribbean society are the coloured and black middle classes.[21] It would however, be a mistake to assume that the 'white bias' is merely an expression of Caribbean petty-bourgeois *angst*.[22] The coloured and black middle class are most affected by it, but the working class and even segments of the peasantry do not go unscathed.

The British Experience

It is from such a cultural milieu – albeit one persistently punctuated by African resistance[23] to the European value system foisted upon them during the colonial era – that the post-war Caribbean migrants to Britain emerged.[24] In the 'Mother Country' no regard was paid to the complex hierarchy of shades by the 'host' society: the pattern of racism which the Caribbean migrants experienced here did not correspond to the pigmentocracy which they left behind in the Caribbean. They were regarded monolithically as 'coloureds', 'West Indians', 'blacks', 'immigrants', and even 'wogs' with no reference to differential shades. As an Indo-Trinidadian writing about his experiences in Britain in the early 1960s accurately observed:

> Leaving the West Indies and coming to Britain is like entering a land where the natives suffer from a curious kind of colour blindness in the contemplation of human groups. This special form of blindness manifests itself in an insensitivity to racial discriminations and variant shades *within* the category 'black'. It registers two crude categories, black and white.
>
> The West Indian consciousness is outraged by the crudity of the categorization. In the rarefied atmosphere of the mother country the delicate instrument ceases to function. All West Indians are black (Ramchand 1965: 28; emphasis added).

A prominent compatriot of the author of the above passage, a man of Portuguese-Madeiran extraction, was certainly outraged by the shade blind-ness of the British. 'I was accepted as a white person in Trinidad. For all practical purposes,' he complained, 'I am coloured in England' (Gomes 1973: 53; cf. Madoo 1965). Over the years, this dichotomy of black/white in British 'race relations' has helped to undermine, if not totally destroy, this hierarchy of shades of black to which the Caribbean working class had itself, by and large, adhered. The erosion of this hierarchy of shades, if not the means by which it has been achieved in Britain, is, without doubt, a positive political development. In a remarkably moving and courageous autobiographical essay by a 'light-skinned' (her expression) Trinidadian woman studying in Britain during the early 1960s, the following conclusion was reached:

> The whole experience of living in England, though at first almost traumatic, is of extreme value for the West Indian student, particularly the light coloured student. I have no knowledge of what the experience does for the African or the Indian, but I cannot help feeling that the consequences for the light coloured West Indian student are more wide ranging. He [sic] had removed an incipient white-type colour prejudice; he has his position as a member of one of the coloured races clearly outlined for the first time; he has a whole series of class prejudices overturned; he has the colonial myth of his almost British personality completely destroyed. In the end realization of this makes it impossible to be bitter about his stay in England. The English have at last rendered him a service (Madoo 1965: 61–2; cf. Hinds 1966: 5).

The second discernible way in which the experience of migrating to Britain has brought in its wake political demystification for Caribbean migrants is to be found in the undermining of 'island chauvinism' and antipathies which are extant in the Caribbean. Divided by the expanse of the sea – the distance between Port of Spain (Trinidad) and Kingston (Jamaica) is the equivalent of that from London to Moscow – and mutual suspicion in the Caribbean, the passage to Britain has brought Jamaicans, Barbadians, Grenadians, Kittitians, Guyanese, Trinidadians, etc., in close proximity to one another for the first time. Although island loyalties still remain, the people of the Caribbean have been brought together by London Transport, the National Health Service and, most of all, by the centripetal forces of British racism to recognize their common class position and common Caribbean identity. It was hard work for some Caribbeans, at least in the early days of migration, to overcome their insular prejudices, but even they recognized the good sense of public solidarity with other Caribbeans in a hostile environment. 'I talk plain. I not fighting Bajans [Barbadians],' said a fictional Jamaican character in Brixton. 'Out there in the street, on the bus, we are one. I ready to stand by them in anything. But – and that is a big but – when it come amongst us I touch them with a long stick' (Hinds 1972a: 94). No doubt the remnants of island chauvinism still linger on in the metropolis (Pearson 1977, 1981; Hinds 1966), but it is equally true that this phenomenon has waned over time.[25]

The somewhat innocent journey to Britain has also served as an unparalleled eye-opening experience to the 'West Indian pioneers'. In the Caribbean few have ever seen the European in the class location of the working class;[26] in general, they had never seen Europeans in positions of subordination and poverty. A Guyanese female migrant related the paradigmatic experience:

> I learnt very early to associate being white with being wealthy. A man who left my village long before I was born returned when I was about ten. He brought back a red-skinned woman with him. Probably she was no more than a whore he picked

up in Georgetown [Guyana's capital], but she was very fair with long hair down her back. She must have been a half-caste, or something. But this man, I think his name was Adam, could not afford to give her a car and servants. You know, every day I expected the police to come and arrest Adam for making this white or near white woman walk around the village barefoot, carrying tin cans of water on her head? Yet all the time we were walking barefoot. That was the point, black was something you associate with poverty. Now and again I would be taken to Georgetown and I would see the girls in offices working away at typewriters. I wanted to be able to be a typist too, but never dared to tell anyone, for working in an office meant a pale skin. I had an aunt who used to work for some white people in New Amsterdam. I went there once and saw the little fair-haired children skipping about the place. My aunty warned me that if they spoke to me, I should be very polite and should never forget to call them 'master' and 'miss'. My aunty would never work for a black man even if he was made of gold. She would never call a little black boy master, or a little black girl miss. It was all so very confusing (Hinds 1966: 11–12).

An Indo-Trinidadian man confessed: 'I had not the slightest idea of the existence of a working class in Britain' (Hinds 1966: 15; cf. Patterson 1965; 15). One Guyanese migrant who arrived in 1958 was so 'flabbergasted' by seeing *white* porters at Victoria station that 'I went up to a bobby and asked him whether I was in London!' (Morrison 1987: 25). The shock of discovering the existence of a *white* working class in Britain was by no means confined to those who lacked a formal education. As George Lamming, the distinguished Caribbean novelist, informs us, the petty-bourgeoisie also experience a sense of bewilderment at discovering that Britain has *white* workers. To him the shock of this discovery had not so much to do with a lack of knowledge about England per se, but more with the strength and persistence of what he calls 'the *idea* of England'. Lamming's illustration is worth quoting at length:

> As an example of this, I would recall an episode on a ship which had brought a number of West Indians to Britain. I was talking to a Trinidadian civil servant who had come to take some kind of course in the ways of bureaucracy. A man about forty to forty-five, intelligent enough to be in the senior grade of the Trinidadian Civil Service which is by no means backward, a man of substance among his own class of people. We were talking in a general way about life among the emigrants. The ship was now steady; the tugs were coming alongside. Suddenly there was consternation in the Trinidadian's expression.
> 'But . . . but,' he said, 'look down there.'
> I looked, and since I had lived six years in England, I failed to see anything of particular significance. I asked him what he had seen; and then I realized what was happening.
> '*They* do that kind of work, *too?*' he asked.
> He meant the white hands and faces on the tug. In spite of films, in spite of reading Dickens – for he would have had to at the school which trained him for the

civil service – in spite of all this received information, this man had never really felt, as a possibility and a fact, the existence of the English worker. This sudden bewilderment had sprung from his *idea* of England; and one element in that *idea* was that he was not used to seeing an Englishman working with his hands in the streets of Port-of-Spain (Lamming 1984: 25–6; emphasis in original).

Like white people in the Caribbean, the white Britons *as a whole* were conceived to have been above manual labour. On arriving in Britain the scales fell abruptly from the Caribbean migrants' eyes.

As Mrs Stewart put it: 'In Jamaica we used to take white people as gods. We always look up to them; they put on such a way you can't understand. People I know work for whites and would make their bath and bring them coffee, like slaves. The whites put themselves on such a pedestal, you really thought they were something.' Thinking back to her previous attitude, she gave a bitter laugh. For in England whiteness is no longer synonymous with high status occupations, large incomes, and authority; many whites are members of the working class performing menial tasks and living in relative poverty. 'What makes things strange,' one man told me, 'is that when I came over here, I was surprised to see the state of a lot of the English, I expected something else, not a lot of drunks, some even begging. That's what I don't rightly understand. A lot of white folks see us as worse than them. Some of the time it's not even true' (Foner 1979: 51; cf. Sherwood 1980: 318–19; and Schweitzer 1984: 30).

Many Caribbean people were appalled at what they regarded as a lack of personal hygiene on the part of the British. To them the British (especially, but not only the working class), apparently had an aversion to water – the allegation was that they seldom saw the need for a bath and acted accordingly. They could not understand why bread had to be sold unwrapped and why fish and chips had to be sold in dirty newspapers. For a people to whom the saying 'Cleanliness is next to Godliness' is taken very seriously, the British were a rather dirty and ungodly lot. And one of the things many Caribbean people had resented most about racist Britain was the way in which their own standards of hygiene were compromised by the overcrowded conditions in which they were forced to live by the racially segmented housing market. For whatever reason, the low opinion which they held of British standards of hygiene is hardly ever mentioned in the sociological literature and yet it is something that has frequently recurred in my conversations with older Caribbeans over the years. Sam Selvon has alluded to this phenomenon in his fiction. Donald Hinds, however, a black migrant himself, reported a conversation which took place in a youth club in the summer of 1964 in London; the participants are a young man who had recently arrived from the Caribbean and several young white women. Part of the conversation went as follows:

First girl: '[T]he fact still remains we are different. Brought up differently. We have different standards of hygiene, and everything.'

West Indian: 'Please don't think that the white race has a monopoly on cleanliness. I know a white woman who has one bowl in which she washes herself, prepares the vegetables, washes the children's clothes and mixes pastry. On a national scale a recent television programme has proved that the standard of hygiene at the abattoirs is the worst known anywhere. I for one strongly disapprove of the way the British display unwrapped bread in shops. In the West Indies, bread must be displayed in a glass case. The presence of one fly would cause the whole lot to be destroyed. Do you seriously believe that it is hygienic to wrap fish and chips in an old newspaper?'

Second girl: 'What would you do if someone called you Nigger?'

(Hinds 1966: 115–16)

There are two particularly noteworthy consequences of such experiences. First, they help destroy the erroneous association of white people *qua* whites with superordination: the mystique of whiteness dissolves in the air of a class-stratified English society. And second, coupled with the Caribbean migrants' encounter with racism in Britain, they generate a corresponding valorization of blackness on the part of Caribbean people. As Fanon, a Caribbean himself, recognized long ago: 'It is the white man who creates the Negro. But it is the negro who creates négritude.'[27] Indeed, the whole experience of living in a white racist society has helped to forge a black identity where in many cases such an identity did not exist previously or was not consciously thought about. 'The colour of your skin matters here. In Jamaica it is class not colour,' stated, somewhat too categorically, one of Foner's respondents. Gordon Lewis captures well the subtleties and specificities of race in the contemporary Caribbean, and in the process offers a good corrective to this common error:

[I]f there exists a West Indian myth about English society there exists, correspondingly, an English myth about West Indian society. It is applauded, by West Indian nationalists and English liberals alike, as a successful multi-racial society. In relative terms, beyond doubt, that is true; the West Indian Negro, unlike the American, has little of the ghetto mentality because he has known little of the ghetto experience. In absolute terms, however, it is different; and West Indian life is in fact that of a multi-layered pigmentocracy suffering from its own private disease of subtle 'shade' prejudice. What takes place, thus, is not that the migrant comes from a harmonious 'race relations' system to a system of incipient racialism but that, rather, he moves to a classificatory system that has taken over the American black–white dichotomy so much more brutal and insulting. Like the Puerto Rican in New York, he suffers deep shock as he moves from a system comparatively benign to a system designed to strip him of all self-respect (Lewis 1969: 80).

It is the *brutal* nature of the racism encountered in Britain which helps Foner's respondent to forget that race and colour also figure negatively in Caribbean society. No one on the spot in Jamaica would seriously concur with the claim that she makes. But *compared* to life as a black person in Britain or

America in the 1950s and 1960s, the Caribbean one had left behind *would* seem like a paradise of racial harmony. 'I think most of my friends *feel* Jamaican. The English helped us to do it,' concluded another migrant.[28] Needless to say, the English also helped Afro-Caribbean people in Britain to '*feel* West Indian' and '*feel* black'. We also find, in the early period of settlement, the fumbling – what Roland Barthes called 'stammering' – and somewhat inchoate emergence of a new vocabulary of self-definition commensurate with a new identity in the making brought about by a new and challenging social configuration. We hear the stammering utterances of a new language being born: 'Respondents generally use the term "black", "coloured", "West Indian", and "Jamaican" interchangeably (many times in the same sentence) when speaking, both informally and in answer to direct questions, about their position in English society. This was so even though the interview questions always used the category Jamaican' (Foner 1979: 144).[29]

The growth in racial consciousness and the implications of black people's position in the wider world came quickly after the discovery of blackness. We hear the discernible sentiments of a maturing pan-Africanist consciousness: 'I think people lose respect for us when we let them think we want to be black Englishmen. We are going to be reckoned with the blackheads of this world, when they are being counted. We must see ourselves in this context.' This was the new wisdom of a St. Lucian migrant imparted in an interview in the 1960s (Hinds 1966: 16–17; cf. Schweitzer 1984: 32). What we have then is the development of the phenomenon that McKay and Lewins called 'ethnic consciousness' where ethnic traits assume 'considerable importance' and where 'ethnically conscious individuals manifest strong sentiments about their uniqueness' (McKay and Lewins 1978: 416).

The over-determining salience of race in Britain led many migrants to close ranks regardless of class. Thus in one study as many as 70 per cent of the interviewees felt that all Jamaicans were in the same social class (Foner 1979: 134–5). Stunned by the class-blind racism in Britain, the Afro-Caribbeans themselves have become, understandably, somewhat blinded to the class differentiation and class formation taking place among people of their own colour and cultural background. The *Labour Force Survey*, the most authoritative source of its kind, has consistently shown that, although Caribbean people in Britain are overwhelmingly concentrated within the ranks of the working class, they are nevertheless by no means all located within this category.[30] But for most black people the pain of racism was more intense and unrelenting than all others.

Despite the horrors of their exile in Britain, it would be a mistake to believe that the first generation of Afro-Caribbeans regard their experience of living in Britain as an unmitigated disaster. They have experienced the suffocating consequences of racism in their everyday life and they occupy in their vast proportion the lowest rung of the social hierarchy in Britain. Nevertheless, in material terms, the majority enjoy a standard of living in Britain which many could only have dreamt of back in the Caribbean.[31] It is therefore not unexpected that their conception of Britain is an ambivalent one. As one migrant explains:

> These have been the hardest years of my life. I think about them, and I ask myself, Sonny, tell the truth, coming here, was it a good decision or not? Think before you answer, like your dead mother used to say. So I think. And I answer, 'Yes,' it was good that we came and that we stayed. I found work, my wife is happy, happy enough. My children are happy and healthy. I thank the good Lord for all of that. I thank Him everyday, just as my dead mother told me I should. I pray to Him and I ask Him. I wish too. I wish this could be like this and that could be like that. I wish I were with my family, my father, my brother, my cousins. I wish I lived in a newer home, and made more money, I wish I could have come here and be treated like I was equal by all these people. But I came as someone they thought was a dope smuggler, and that's about the way they treat me (Cottle 1978: 16).

Another captured this painful ambivalence thus: 'It's all right here, basically, but we are kind of treated inferior' (Foner 1975: 198). In recent years however, many, having been made economically obsolete by a Thatcherite Britain, have become distinctly hostile and bitter about their rapidly deteriorating social condition. Many more than hitherto are returning home.[32] But even more feel 'trapped' within Britain because they are incapable of mobilizing the financial wherewithal to resettle in the Caribbean: 'The majority of us are trapped' (cited in Selbourne 1983b: 258). In his study of 'race relations' in Nottingham, Lawrence (1974: 28) found that 78 per cent of his West Indian respondents were intent on returning home (cf. Foner 1979: 210, 1977: 137; AFFOR 1981: 33). 'Trapped' in Britain during their lives, a considerable number make detailed plans and get relatives to promise that their bodies will be returned to their native land to be buried as soon as possible after their death.

Others in the evening of their lives or chronically ill return home for one reason only: to die. One thirty-seven-year-old Jamaican woman, who was known to the writer, realizing that she was about to die from the cancer she had suffered from for years, flew to Jamaica and died within twenty-four hours of her arrival. She wanted to be in Jamaica when she died and she wanted to be buried in her home town. Going home to die and arranging for their bodies to be sent home to be buried does not only reflect the love and attachment of Caribbeans to their native land. For Caribbean people it also serves as an index of the extent to which they have been made to feel unwelcome and unattached to British society – regardless of the length of time spent here.[33] Even those who consciously decided to live in Britain permanently, plan for their remains to be taken to the Caribbean. To be buried in Britain is almost always a second choice foisted upon the relatives of the dead largely because of financial constraints.[34] When George Adamson, a working-class Barbadian (who in 1983 had been living in Britain for twenty-eight years) told David Selbourne that, 'There's not one in a million [Caribbean people] who wants his bones to be buried in this country', there is, I am afraid, no good reason to doubt his words (Selbourne 1983b: 258). One Caribbean shipping agent, who in 1989 was handling in an average week the cargo of five families returning to the Caribbean, was of the opinion that for Caribbeans in Britain 'The greatest fear is possibly dying here and not returning before you've passed away' (Thames TV 1989). Folarin Shyllon, the Nigerian scholar, is right to remind us that since the sixteenth century the bones of black people may be found in 'cemeteries all over England', and that that should count for something for the rights of the living (Shyllon 1981: 111). But the fact remains that if black people have their way very few of their corpses will be interred in British graves.[35] It is also worth noting that a considerable number have returned home to the Caribbean and discovered, to their great cost and chagrin, that the meagre financial resources which they have scrimped and saved over the years in Britain were not enough to facilitate resettlement – in the land they have loved and romanticized during their painful sojourn in Britain – in circumstances of high unemployment and rampant inflation in the Caribbean.[36] These, woefully dejected, have had to return to the Britain they had fought and worked hard to escape from, savings depleted, to virtually start all over again to remake their lives in a hostile environment a long way from home. There are also others who have returned home and realized that they had stayed 'too long' in Britain and could not re-adapt to a relatively parochial Caribbean life-style.[37] These too have trekked back to Britain or have moved on to North America. One man has informed the writer that on his return 'home' to Jamaica for a visit he discovered that he was regarded as a 'foreigner in my own country'.[38] Resentful of his being dubbed, albeit jovially, 'the Englishman', and with the growing realization that all his friends and relatives were either in Britain or North America, he decided to remain in Britain – a decision which radically overturned his twenty-seven-year dream of the return – where his immediate family and closest friends reside.[39]

But the experience of return and disillusion has been registered as early as the mid-1960s. Indeed, the phenomenon had existed from the 1940s when ex-servicemen returned to the Caribbean. A former member of the Royal Air Force explained:

> I think we were responsible for triggering off migration. Many of the boys went home after the war only to discover that they did not fit in. Just think of it. Some recruits left school and went straight into the service. After four years or so when they returned to the West Indies, they were like migrants searching around for a foothold. The romance of the schooldays, followed by the adventure of war and the glamour of uniform were no help in the rough and tumble of a society like the West Indies. After the freedom of jumping on a train and ending up in Edinburgh or

Portsmouth where there was always something happening, to be cooped up on a tiny island of perhaps less than two hundred square miles, where everything happens in its own sweet time, all that was unbearable. If there had been any sign of the polemics of a people trying to strike out on their own there might have been something to fight for. Again most of them were broke in a short while and did not want to go back to the land. That was the time that the ss *Empire Windrush* became a household word in the West Indies as ex-servicemen and their close relatives trekked north. After a while people started writing to us, asking us to meet their relations and see that they received some sort of accommodation (Hinds 1966: 56–7).

Also in Donald Hinds's remarkable book of Caribbean testimonies we encounter Frank. Frank had left Jamaica when he was eight. After ten years in Britain, 'I returned home,' he declared. 'I had thought of Jamaica only as paradise. Nothing was important but the sun and the beach which were the things my parents talked about.' But the Jamaican reality rushed in on him from the time he landed in Kingston:

> The dream of returning was not so romantic when I reached the airport. It is a fact that the place is very elegant. But returning migrants are considered tourists. The taxi drivers are out to squeeze everybody they can get hold of. You have to stick out or they would 'thief' your eyes out of their sockets. Jamaica is not a poor man's country! Wages are still low and jobs are very hard to come by. There are no labour exchanges in the country, so what do you do? You get hold of a paper and look down the 'situations vacant' column. You might find something which would keep body and soul together, but no one seems to care very much . . . (Hinds 1966: 191).

Frank witnessed the callousness of the police: 'I cannot tell the horror of seeing a police officer beating up a boy'; he saw an old woman knocked down by a truck which did not stop; the ambulance took half an hour to arrive. 'Things like these made me shudder and I tend to forget the beauty of the beaches and the glorious sun which we do not have in Britain.' Frank's nightmarish experience did not end with these incidents:

> The behaviour of people too is shocking. I went to a bank in Kingston and had to wait for a long time in a very slow-moving queue. A white man walked in and went straight to the head of the queue where the clerk was just about to stop attending to a black man and to serve the white man. I was bristling. Suddenly a little man jumped out of the queue and with the aid of a few choice four-letter words told the clerk that if the white man got served before the rest of the people he would drag him across the counter and beat the life out of him. The white man turned on his heels. And the clerk quite shaken returned to attending to the man at the head of the queue. As it turned out the man who kicked up the fuss had been to England and had learnt to respect the queue! My return to Jamaica was the greatest illusion of my life. I have not ruled out the possibility of returning to Jamaica, but brother, I would know what to expect. That is something that many people do not understand . . . (Ibid. 192).

This was recorded as early as 1966.

Needless to say thousands of migrants have returned from Britain to the Caribbean and have successfully re-adjusted to Caribbean life (Taylor 1976; Rubenstein 1982; Thomas-Hope 1985). Although having more than a little contemporary resonance, Frank's experience was undoubtedly an atypical one. The dream of the return is still a powerful and recurring one. The importance and value of home is never more appreciated than when one is in exile. And in a hostile land the dream of return becomes a burning desire. And yet strictly speaking, it is never ever possible to return. Just as it is impossible to stand in the same place more than once in a flowing river, so it is impossible to re-enter a society at the point of departure. It is impossible to return for two reasons.

Firstly, no action can be separated from time and space. Action takes place *in* space and is temporally defined and bound. The notion of return implies the impossible – the separation of space from time. One did not simply *leave* Tobago in the process of migration; one left Tobago at a particular point *in time* – there is no other way to have left. And so, not to put too fine a point on it, one left Tobago on a particular day, in a particular month, in a particular year. Thus Mr. Johnson left Tobago on 8 February 1954. And as a consequence of the temporally defined nature of this leaving one can never return, as one cannot turn back the hand of time. What many 'returnees' forget is that when they 'return', they inevitably return at a different point in time from when they had left and as a consequence, have 'returned' to a different place – because place is always bound by time.

The second reason why it is impossible to return is also connected with time. The individual exists within time. And even if it were possible for a particular place to be exempt from the temporal, there would also be the relentless and inevitable impact of time upon the individual. It is not simply the case that Tobago has 'changed' since Mr. Johnson left in 1954, as not only has Tobago changed, Mr. Johnson has also changed. He left Tobago at the age of twenty-three in 1954 and after having lived in Moss Side, Manchester from 1954 to 1962, Handsworth in Birmingham from 1962 to 1974, and Stoke Newington, London from 1974 to 1982, he 'returned' to Tobago after having been made redundant at the age of fifty-one. Mr. Johnson was twenty-eight years older when he went to Tobago in 1982. Mr. Johnson was a different person – time and experience had made that inevitable.

Thus, both Mr. Johnson (the migrant) and his 'home' (Tobago) had changed. When Mr. Johnson went home in Tobago in 1982, he was a different man in a 'foreign' land. The migrant's 'return' is inevitably a new beginning, a new encounter between the migrant and what he or she likes to refer to as 'home'. Of course, the rapidity and intensity of change varies but change inevitably occurs as time marches on: everything is in motion.

The tragedy of the exile's return is that he/she forgets this and is reminded of it the hard and painful way. It is not that the returning Jamaican is 'a foreigner in my own country' (Jamaica), it is that he has no country at all and is a foreigner everywhere – in Britain as well as in Jamaica. He is indeed 'an eccentric at home and exile abroad'. Time and change have robbed him of his 'country' – he is a citizen without a nation. He can only 'return' to his homeland by coming to terms with the fact that he is indeed a foreigner: he and his country have both changed and they will both have to re-learn and learn about each other. This is the new relationship that each returning migrant has had to embark upon more or less consciously, more or less successfully. Sometimes the new relationship succeeds, sometimes it ends in failure.

Of course, there are those in exile who have been courageous enough to critically survey the wreckage of their dreams, like a pile of rubble at their feet, with the searing pain of unfulfilled desire cutting through their disarmingly honest testimonies. Few have reconciled themselves more stoically to the condition of exile, to the knowledge of irreversible change and the absence of any road back home than the nameless Jamaican who bared his soul to Donald Hinds. His remarks, reminiscent of some of the best passages of one of the better novels of exile, are worth citing at length:

If I dream tonight, you can bet your life it will be about Jamaica. I think so often about going back that the idea of returning has become as inevitable as death. Soon it will be ten years since I came to Bristol. I was eighteen when I left Jamaica and I remember boasting to some of my friends that I would be back before I reached twenty-five. My plan was to get a job and study electrical engineering by correspondence course and evening school. I was unemployed six months. When I eventually got a job as a porter all ambition was knocked out of me. Instead of correspondence course I did my football coupon. All I wanted was to get a better job. So far I have had nine jobs and none is ever better than the first. I don't mind much about that promise of returning in six or seven years because all the chaps to whom I made that promise are all over here. Some doing well at that. When I think of Jamaica, I sometimes feel as if I never had been young. The years in England are missing years. I cannot give an account of them. When I meet a man from back home who has just come up, we talk and I discover that Jamaica too has changed. My mother died since I was over here and the house in which I was born has been pulled down and the graves of my family have been trampled flat. Yet I still want to go back home. I know that I will not be going back, but we never admit it to each other. We have four children and we have a couple of rooms in a friend's house. Seven years ago we had planned to buy our own house, then the babies started coming. My wife has not been able to work since. Yet the last thing we would admit is that we will not be going home. Of course, it is not impossible. I have not given up doing the pools. Who knows? Next week might be my week for the treble chance. In reality if we are to work and save to take the family home it will take twenty years, and that would not leave us much to spend. To me the importance of Jamaica is that it is there. I asked a man the other day, who are the men who play dominoes in the village shop on Saturday night, and he said Rainford's twins. Then I remember that they were about ten when I left. Migration had settled over the country like a blight. It is a war, for none of the older men are there. I think of these things and I cannot help being angry. I have no solution to offer. I do not have any political ambition but I do not rule out the possibility of going to prison if I was to wake up one morning and find out that I was in Jamaica. Perhaps we were wrong not to have stayed to fight. We might not have got anything out of it, but we would have shown the world that Jamaica was worth fighting for. The English people don't believe all this. Sometimes I don't think I believe it either . . . (Hinds 1966: 190–1).

> Where then is the nigger's
> home?
>
> In Paris Brixton Kingston
> Rome?
>
> Here?
> Or in Heaven?
>
> What crime
> his dark
>
> dividing
> skin is hiding?
>
> What guilt
> now drives him
>
> on?
> Will exile never
>
> end?
> Will these spent
>
> tears,
> poor pauper's pence,
>
> earn him a little
> solace here
>
> bought if not given?
> When the release
>
> from fear, bent
> back
>
> unhealing history?
>
> What final peace
> consumes his
>
> ancient fury?
> So dreams
>
> so embers,
> ashes, smoke. . . . .
>
> EDWARD BRATHWAITE

The Second Generation and After

> I think the only difference between the people on the *Windrush* and our
> children is this: we came asking for our rights, they are going to demand
> them.   SAM KING, 1968

Most second-generation Caribbeans in Britain have either lived in this
country since early childhood or were actually born and brought up in Britain.
In other words, they have either spent the greater proportion of their lives in
the 'Mother Country' or for all their lives have resided here. This important
characteristic of the 'second generation' has profound implications for their
view of themselves and the world in which they live.

Unlike their parents, they compare their position and life-chance within
British society not with the condition of pre-independent Caribbean society
but with their white British counterparts. Consequently, their experience of
racism in Britain is more immediate and their perception of the phenomenon
is more uncluttered. It is therefore no surprise that their opposition to British
racism is more instantaneous and more forthright. Not for them the consola-
tion: 'It's all right here, basically, *but* we are kind of treated inferior.' For
them: 'It is *not* all right here, *because* we are treated as if we are inferior.' The
'consoling' effect of a poverty-stricken colonial Caribbean backdrop is absent.
Like the chief protagonist in Horace Ove's fine film *Pressure*, his/her yardstick
is the performance of his/her white schoolmates on the job market. In the
case of the young man in *Pressure*, he was far more qualified than his white
former classmates, yet they were offered jobs but he, who had searched far
more diligently, could not find one.

Their consciousness of themselves as a black enclave within British society
is therefore even greater than that of their parents. Certainly, as one
commentator has written (Troyna 1979), their commitment to a sense of
blackness is by no means even. Nevertheless, as an aggregate, it is no doubt
true that the vast majority consider themselves to be black and belonging to an
oppressed minority within British society.

The power of island chauvinism has waned among the first generation but,
for the second and indeed third generations of Afro-Caribbeans in Britain,
we can declare with almost complete certitude that this politically debilitating
condition has hardly infected them. Even in the cases where these prejudices
have been transmitted by parents to the young child, the centripetal forces of
racism in the school and elsewhere ensure that it never takes root. As one of
the members of this generation eloquently declared: 'As you grow older you
just see them [small islanders] as black. When you're in school you all get
harassed together, and see yourself as one – *all a we is one*.'[40]

Separated from any immediate and far-reaching experience of the society
of their parents, surrounded by what significant numbers perceive to be a sea

of white hostility, many (but by no means all), not surprisingly, have been attracted to the ideas of the Rastafarian 'Movement' in an attempt to make sense of and survive their travail in Babylon. In essence, a plebeian form of *négritude*, the signal contribution of the Rastafarian Movement is the affirmation of pride of race and the celebration of the African provenance. Despite its well-recognized, but poorly-understood, genuine weaknesses and silences, the 'ideology'[41] of Rastafarianism has made a tremendous contribution to the black counter-culture against the spell of white supremacy.

Unlike their parents, who have less attachment to Britain, the second generation of 'Caribbeans' are black Britons – whether they choose to be or not. They might speak a form of the Jamaican language and sport Rastafarian locks but in Kingston many would not be easily understood and many more would not be able to fully understand the language of their Jamaican counterparts, especially those in the rural areas. The second generation are therefore, by default, creating new cultural forms based largely – but by no means exclusively – upon the legacy of their parents and fore-parents. They are also forging new forms of resistance, like their North American counterparts, aimed at the specific problems which they face within British society.

An explanatory note is in order here. This section is necessarily much briefer than the previous one because very little – despite the chatter about 'black youths' – of genuine value has been written about youths of Afro-Caribbean descent. There are some good analyses of the situation of children of Afro-Caribbean descent in British schools, relations with the police, and black youth and the labour market. But when it comes to the study of the culture, ideology and lifestyles of youths of Afro-Caribbean descent, platitudes, ignorant romanticism and more often, negative stereotypes abound. There have been some sound critiques of some of the palpably pernicious writings on 'black youth'.[42] But ground-clearing and building, though closely related and often combined, are nevertheless discrete activities. The building still needs to be carried out: at present, despite (and because of?) the amount of ink that has been spilt on the subject of Afro-Caribbean youth, we know relatively little about the culture and ideology of youths of Afro-Caribbean descent in Britain. We know what many sociologists think of black youths, and we know what we think of many sociologists, but as far as the subject which has been much discussed is concerned, the sociologists have generated a lot of heat and virtually no light.

A Note on the Generations

As the above analysis indicates, there are noteworthy differences in the experiences of the first and second generations of people of Afro-Caribbean descent in Britain. It would be a mistake, however, to assume – as some commentators do – that the two generations have little or nothing in common. The fact of the matter is that, over time, both generations have converged in their perspectives. This is a convergence which largely arises from the simultaneity of their experiences in Britain. Many apparently do not know this, but parents, as well as their children, grow and learn from new experiences. Contrary to the stereotype of the passive first generation and a wild second generation, the evidence of the black experience in Britain clearly suggests that, despite the psychological constraints placed upon political activity by the desire to return home within a limited time frame (usually five years), the first generation of Afro-Caribbean people in Britain have – very much in keeping with the rich tradition of popular resistance in the Caribbean itself – put up some tremendous and astonishingly courageous struggles in defence of their dignity and their personal well-being in this hostile land. It took great audacity to pull Oswald Mosley, the fascist leader, off his podium in Notting Hill in the 1950s, yet a Jamaican man did just that and single-handedly. When the racists attacked in Nottingham and Notting Hill in 1958, black people organized and effectively repulsed their challenges.[43] Day-to-day resistance at the work-place was also an important element of black people's lives in Britain during the early years. Poor documentation of such resistance does not mean that it did not take place.[44] Even that *bête noire* of Caribbean literature, Vidia Naipaul, had to admire the fortitude of the early Caribbean migrants in Britain. Here he is, eavesdropping – as is his wont – on black people, this time on a group of Caribbeans travelling on the 'boat train' from King's Cross to Southampton to catch the ship to the Caribbean. The year is 1960:

The man with the baby was talking to the man opposite him of the hardships of life in London.

'Is like that Stork on television,' he said. 'Three out of five can't tell the difference from butter. Three out of five don't care for you.' . . .

'Eh! I tell you about the foreman?' He spoke easily; the train was not England. 'One day he say, "Blackie, come here a minute." I watch at him, and I say, "Good. I coming." I went up and hit him *baps*! Clean through the glass window.' He didn't gesticulate. He was dandling the baby on his knee . . . '*Baps!* Clean through the glass window.' . . .

'Tank God I didn't have the monkey-wrench in my hand. I wouldn't be sitting down in this train holding this baby on my lap today.' . . .

' "So you want rent?" the baby-feeder was saying. "I tell you I ain't paying any more than what I was paying before." He say, "Blackie, I coming up to get my rent or to get you out of my room." I watch at him and I say, "Good. Come up, *bakra*." He come up. I give him one kick *bam*! He roll down the steps *bup-bup-bup*.

'I pass round there last week. He have up a big sign in green paint. Please No Coloured. In green paint. I tell you, man, is like Stork' (Naipaul 1969: 9–11).

Needless to say, youths of Afro-Caribbean descent in Britain are by no means homogeneous in their political perspectives and activity: some are far more militant than others, and others are downright conservative. This latter category, it is fair to say, are in a minority, thanks to the radicalizing effect of British racism. The black youths have been learning from their parents and the parents have been learning from their children. Some years ago some parents would not believe the barbarities that occurred in British schools against their children. One black woman whose English teacher in Britain persistently referred to her in class as 'the savage' did not even tell her parents because she knew that they would not have believed her. The Caribbean background had not accustomed her parents to teachers behaving in such a manner. In the 1970s, due to the overwhelming evidence of racism in British schools and the emergence of extremely vocal black pressure groups, parents on the whole became aware that schools in, say, Brixton were quite different from those in rural Barbados.[45] Some years ago many parents found incredible the stories told to them by their children about police harassment; many now have a healthy suspicion of the police.

Many black youths have now realized that some of the 'authoritarian' forms of behaviour exhibited by their parents – and I would be lying if I were to deny that some Caribbean households, as other households in Britain, are characterized by 'authoritarianism' – were not merely the remnants of a puritanical Caribbean background but were largely generated by love and a profound desire to protect their children – vulnerable *black* children – in an extremely hostile environment.[46] There is now a growing sense of appreciation and indeed celebration of the tremendous odds against which their parents had to fight, particularly in the early years of settlement, in Britain.[47]

In short, there has been a high degree of convergence in the experience and political perspectives of black parents and their descendants in Britain which many commentators, blinded by the stereotype of the 'generational conflict' among Afro-Caribbean people, have hardly recognized.

Cultural Implications: the Dialectics of Pan-Caribbeanization and De-Creolization

This chapter has so far attempted to analyse and illustrate the process of ethnic identity formation and transformation. It has shown that in the case of Afro-Caribbean migrants, in the process of moving from one social formation in which race has a *comparatively* low salience to one in which social relations are deeply permeated by the idea of race and the phenomenon of racism, relatively rapid transformations have taken place in the self-perception of these migrants. Race consciousness has been awakened in these black migrants thanks to the racism of the society into which they have entered. A new identity has been forged in the crucible of racist Britain. Moreover, through the racial division of labour, especially in the 1950s and 1960s, black people from different parts of the Caribbean have been brought into meaningful and sustained contact with one another for the first time. And through the experience of working in a hostile environment they have forged bonds of solidarity against racism and for black liberation. At the level of community, the acts of de facto ethnic and racial segregation especially in the 1950s have also strengthened fellowship among Caribbeans. Furthermore, these bonds, precisely because of the anti-black racism which they oppose, have helped to create this new black identity.

This is not to suggest, however, that racism has been the sole determinant of this new identity. Clearly, migrants in a strange land, even in an unhostile or relatively hospitable one, will quite often seek out fellow migrants with whom they have a culture in common for relaxation and communion – if only to share memories of life back home and to replicate as best they can communal structures that they have left behind in their native land. Such practices are common to all migrants – regardless of race. But what is different about a maligned, racialized and oppressed group of migrants is that such practices take on a greater momentum of intensity and urgency due largely to the over-determining role of racism. They thus take on the character of defence mechanisms.

These processes generate cultural change in two crucial ways. First, they create and facilitate cultural exchange and inter-penetration between peoples from the different parts of the Caribbean. Thus paradoxically, Caribbeans in Britain and North America have a better sense of and empathy for the cultures of the Caribbean *as a whole* than the majority of their counterparts who reside in the Caribbean itself. There has thus been a *pan-Caribbeanization* of the cultures of those from the individual territories of the region. Languages, idioms, cuisines, music and so on, have scaled their individual territorial boundaries and have become far more generalized, shared and amalgamated within the Caribbean diaspora than they are within the Caribbean itself. To this extent – that is, at the level of critical exposure to the spectrum of the cultures of the Caribbean – the most pan-Caribbean of Caribbean peoples are to be found in the Caribbean diaspora – not in the Caribbean itself. As the following passage testifies, George Lamming, for one, was fully cognisant of this phenomenon. This new discovery of pan-Caribbeanness began to take shape among the Caribbean migrants on the ships across the Atlantic and on the trains taking the new migrants into London:

It is here that one sees a discovery actually taking shape. No Barbadian, no Trinidadian, no St. Lucian, no islander from the West Indies sees himself as a West Indian until he encounters another islander in foreign territory. It was only when the Barbadian childhood corresponded with the Grenadian or the Guianese childhood in important details of folk-lore, that the wider identification was arrived at. In this sense, *most West Indians of my generation were born in England*. The category West Indian, formerly understood as a geographical term, now assumes cultural significance. All this became much clearer to me when, years later, I would hear West Indians arguing about being *West Indians*. The argument would usually grow from the charge that X was not a good West Indian. To be a bad West Indian means to give priority of interest and ambition to the particular island where you were born. It is bad because your development has taught you that the water which separates us can make no difference to the basic fact that we are West Indians; that we have a similar history behind us. I know Barbadians, Trinidadians and Jamaicans who go to great trouble in order to establish that they are first of all a West Indian. This category undergoes interesting changes. Today, ten years after that March morning [when he first left the Caribbean for Britain], and five years since America, I find that I refrain from saying that I am from the West Indies, for it implies a British colonial limitation. I say rather, I am from the Caribbean, hoping the picture of French and Spanish West Indies will be taken for granted. So the discovery had taken place, partly due to the folk-lore, and partly to the singing, and especially to the kind of banter which goes on between islander and islander (Lamming 1980: 214 –15; first emphasis added).[48]

The explanation for this new pan-Caribbean consciousness is not hard to find. The Caribbean is a relatively large area (the distance from Kingston, Jamaica to Port-of-Spain, Trinidad is over a thousand miles), comprising hundreds of widely dispersed islands, it is more sea than land – a seascape, Edward Brathwaite called it, as opposed to a landscape. And although there have been improvements since Lamming wrote those words in 1960, transportation is still poor and expensive, and the majority of the region's population lacks the wherewithal to travel. It is only within the smaller and more contiguous territories of the eastern Caribbean that there is anything remotely approaching meaningful intercourse between different islanders. It is therefore in the diaspora – in North America, Europe and in an earlier period Central America, especially Panama – that ordinary Caribbeans from the different territories of the region get a chance to meet, know and strike up meaningful relations – including marriage – with each other. Sam Selvon, the distinguished Caribbean novelist, who had migrated to London on the same ship that brought George Lamming in 1950, pondered upon this remarkable phenomenon. Speaking at a conference in his native Trinidad in 1978, he reflected:

It is strange to think I had to cross the Atlantic and be thousands of miles away, in a different culture and environment, for it to come about that for the first time in my life, I was living among Barbadians and Jamaicans and others from my part of the world. If I had remained in Trinidad I might never have had the opportunity to be at such close quarters to observe and try to understand the differences and prejudices that exist from islander to islander (Selvon 1986: 9).

The essence of this sentiment is echoed a million times over in the Caribbean diaspora around the world.

There are, however, different levels of pan-Caribbeanization. New York City, despite its undeniable ethnic segmentation, has by far the highest level of such exchanges through the sheer variety and number of Caribbean peoples in that city. Miami, Toronto and Montreal would be next, followed by London, Amsterdam, The Hague and Paris in that order. It might therefore be paradoxical, but nevertheless true, that the most pan-Caribbean person in the world is perhaps a Caribbean student at the City University of New York who has ample opportunity to strike up relations with other Caribbeans from every conceivable territory of the Caribbean – from Barbados in the east to Belize in the west, from the Bahamas in the north to Cayenne in the south. Constance Sutton captures well the specificity of New York for the Caribbean diaspora:

> New York City has become the Caribbean cross-roads of the world. It contains the largest concentration and most diverse commingling of its people. With a Caribbean population of two million (this figure includes Puerto Ricans), New York forms the largest Caribbean city in the world, ahead of Kingston, Jamaica, San Juan, Puerto Rico, and Port-of-Spain, Trinidad, combined. It is in New York that the different islanders 'cross roads', learning about one another in their various encounters at work, in the streets, in schools and communities, at public affairs, and through the media. It is here that they have begun to build social bridges and alliances as they confront similar problems in their neighborhoods, the schools their children attend, their places of work, and the city at large. And it is in New York City that particular island identities become fused into broader ethnic identities: West Indian, pan-Caribbean, Third World, Hispanic and Afro-American. The wider identities point to a growing consciousness of unifying perspectives and goals, and mark a sense of new possibilities in a struggle for cultural and political empowerment (Sutton 1987: 19).

Like the international distribution of pan-Caribbeanization, the cultural exchanges and cultural inter-penetration between members of the Caribbean diaspora *within* a given country of the metropole is also uneven. In Britain, for instance, it is evident that Jamaican culture, compared to other national cultures of the Caribbean, is hegemonic – in the Gramscian sense of leadership and influence – among Caribbeans as a whole. This is due to three basic factors. First, people of Jamaican descent constitute the majority of Caribbeans in Britain. Indeed, in 1966 – by which point in time primary immigration from the Caribbean had virtually come to an end – an estimated 60 per cent of the Caribbean population in Britain had come from Jamaica alone, and thus, far exceeded the *combined* population of the remaining Caribbeans (Rose et al. 1969: 43–5). The dissemination of Jamaican cultural forms has therefore been partly facilitated through sheer weight of numbers.

Second, the appeal of Jamaican music to other migrants from the Caribbean from the 1950s to the present day has enhanced the Jamaican influence amongst fellow Caribbeans. From mento to ska to reggae, Jamaican music has ruled the roost and was hardly challenged by its nearest rival, Trinidad's calypso.

Third, as was pointed out earlier, Rastafarianism, for fairly well-known reasons, has been enormously successful in attracting young black adherents in Britain. And Rastafarianism, with its deep roots in Jamaican popular culture, carries within it modes of speech, musical forms and content that are profoundly Jamaican. Reggae music has not only been a vehicle of Rastafarianism; it has also, by default, been a conduit for the dissemination of Jamaican culture.

These, then, have been the key mechanisms through which Jamaican cultural idioms have been adopted by many Caribbean migrants and their descendants in Britain who otherwise have no direct connection to the island of Jamaica. The clear parallel here is the great influence of African American culture (most notably, but not only, music), upon the wider African diaspora as well as upon others.

There is, however, another arena of cultural change beyond that which I have called pan-Caribbeanization, the domain of intra-Caribbean culturation. This is the sphere of cultural interaction between Caribbeans and the wider British society.

Culture, defined here broadly as a way of life, is inherently dynamic. The rate of cultural change may be dramatic or it may be almost imperceptible, nevertheless everywhere culture changes. But he or she who says migration, also says, and most emphatically, cultural change. Migration, through the process of separation from the base culture or the culture of origin, accelerates the process of cultural change. This change is intensified by the entry into a new cultural environment (no two cultures are identical) which inevitably involves adaptation to a greater or lesser degree.

The extent and intensity of such cultural change, however, are dependent upon a number of factors. First, if the new environment, physical as well as social, is markedly different from that in which the migrants have their provenance, the process of cultural change, ceteris paribus, will be relatively fast. Secondly, and most crucially, the degree of power (both over nature and people) that the migrant has in the new environment profoundly conditions the rate of cultural change. Thus the more power a group has over the new environment the greater the possibility of maintaining a high level of cultural continuity. This important nexus between culture and power essentially explains the remarkable degree of long-term cultural continuity that the European diaspora has been able to maintain in even its most far-flung colonial outposts. Colonial power and post-colonial hegemony has facilitated the perpetuation of their European cultural forms. Being good colonialists, they have endeavoured, and not without some success, to change the societies into which they have entered – essentially through the mechanisms of conquest – while resisting any change on their own part. But even *they* have not been immune to the acceleration of cultural change brought on by migration. Unlike weaker migrants, however, they have had conspicuous success in the retardation of the pace of change. So much so in fact, that quite often elements of their culture become ossified anachronisms of those of their metropolitan bases.

The ratio of interaction *within* one cultural group on the one hand, and that *between* one group and another, on the other (what we may call the in-group/ out-group ratio), also affects the rate of cultural change. Clearly, the greater the degree of in-group interaction (i.e. interaction within a given cultural group), the more the cultural integrity of such a group is likely to be maintained. Whilst the denser the level of interaction with an out-group (i.e. a group different from that to which the individual belongs), the greater the probability of cultural erosion, which effectively amounts to the adoption of certain cultural attributes of the out-group. This becomes especially pro-nounced where the out-group wields more power, particularly economic and political power, than the other group.

The intensity of interaction with the home culture of the migrant group also influences the level of cultural continuity. The deeper and more frequent such contact is, the greater the likelihood of cultural continuity. The opposite obtains when the level of contact is superficial and sporadic.

And last but not least, the reception with which the culture of the migrant group is met in the new environment has direct relevance, in fairly obvious ways, to the perpetuation of the original culture. Thus the more intense the hostility to the migrants' culture, the greater the chance of cultural change and indeed, cultural erosion. Included within the process of erosion are defensive acts of the besieged group such as the erection of more effective cultural barriers and the development of what we may call cultural fundamentalism. Such developments in and of themselves constitute erosive cultural change.

With such theoretical guidelines we may explore the dynamic of cultural interaction between Caribbeans and the wider society in Britain.

The culture of Caribbeans in Britain has undergone rapid changes over the years. And by all the general considerations outlined above, the prospects are by no means good. The British environment has in general been hostile to Caribbean culture. Caribbeans as a group have the most skewed distribution of its members within the socio-economic hierarchy of the nation – fewer professionals and self-employed than all the other ethnic groups for which statistics are available.[49] We are more than any other ethnic group in Britain a nation of skilled and unskilled manual workers with the accompanying disadvantages – including relatively low pay, insecurity of employment and poor conditions of work – which these positions have borne and bear under the uniquely decrepit species of late capitalism that exists in Britain (see the essays by Harris and Lewis in this volume). This condition of economic weakness and dependence coupled with political impotence within the society increases our vulnerability and thus, that of our cultural forms.

The majority of Afro-Caribbeans in Britain possess formal citizenship, but nevertheless suffer discrimination at the hands of employers, landlords, public officials and the police. The frustration and anger this generates are just as intense as – indeed perhaps more than – that experienced by Europe's other black or non-white minorities who often find citizenship difficult to acquire. In ways suggested above, the Afro-Caribbean community is culturally vulnerable, its members accustomed to being treated without even a minimum of respect. Society has taught our children not only that they are 'black', but also, at a remarkably tender age, that they are the 'wrong' colour. However, the community does possess cultural resources which enable it to resist, despite the unequal terms of the contest for survival. The Afro-Caribbean churches help in their own way to promote cohesion and self-esteem – their following is counted in hundreds of thousands. The Rastafarians assert an Afro-Caribbean identity which has resonance far beyond their own ranks. Poets such as Linton Kwesi Johnson articulate a secular sense of resistance. The community does possess significant popular media, such as the *Caribbean Times*, *The Voice*, and a variety of magazines and journals. Adding to our music, the 1980s witnessed the precocious and remarkable emergence of an audio-visual culture of international standing, exemplified most powerfully by the work of Black Audio Film Collective, Ceddo, and Sankofa – *Handsworth Songs*, *Looking for Langston*, and *Young Soul Rebels* come most readily to mind. A few Afro-Caribbeans are prominent in the trade unions (most notably Bill Morris, general secretary of the Transport and General Workers Union) and as MPs – such as Diane Abbott and Bernie Grant. But the community's political influence is considerably less than that enjoyed by Afro-Americans in the US. While all due note should be taken of factors favourable to the cultural and political reproduction and advancement of Afro-Caribbeans, we have to contend with formidable forces of disintegration and derogation.

After the Notting Hill and Nottingham riots of 1958, there emerged on the part of both the national and local states a concerted policy of black geographic dispersal. This policy which was put into effect in the 1960s and early 1970s undermined the fragile and embryonic communal organizations which were then taking shape. This was, especially after the black explosions in the urban centres of America, articulated and justified by both the central and local state in terms of de-ghettoization as they saw it, and for 'integration'. Apart from blaming the victim the logic of the argument was based upon a classic racist non sequitur: the concentration of black people in a particular area was the cause of urban blight and racist behaviour on the part of white people. The illogicality of such an argument is easily exposed and dispatched:

> Underlying the debate over concentration and dispersal is the assumption that concentration represents the outcome of a choice that produces poverty and ghetto-like conditions. Forced dispersal then becomes a reasonable solution since it is seen as preventing the build-up of these conditions. However, if migrants are not the *bearers* of inner city malaise but its *victims*, then dispersal simply replaces one group of victims with another. If problems of racial stereotyping or discrimination and conflicts with the state are the result of assumptions deeply imbedded within the state itself, then pandering to those assumptions will never confound them . . . The concentration of powerless people in relative poverty is a real problem but it is not a problem of concentration (Cross 1983: 21; emphasis in original).

Apart from indicating what he calls the 'obvious error' of such assumptions, David Smith also registered something that the policymakers chose to ignore: 'many Asians and West Indians are limited by a multitude of factors to poor jobs, low incomes and sub-standard housing, and that, by living within cohesive communities of people sharing a common culture and recognizing a system of mutual dependence, they are making the best of a bad situation and managing to sustain a tolerable existence against the odds' (Smith 1977: 292–3). Our white liberal 'friends' of the time knew of course what was best for us; they knew that it was in our best interest to be dispersed; that our aggregation was synonymous with ghettoization; that as black people we will obviously be flattered to be placed among white people rather than having to live in communities in which the majority of people are black. They knew our needs better than we ourselves did. Our 'friends' and enemies were at one in ignoring alternative views. And so there was no room for the opinion of someone like the elderly Caribbean woman in Leicester who said quite frankly:

> I would like to get near to my people, my own colour. I wouldn't like to be in a district where there's all white there and I'm on my own . . . you will feel a bit depressed to live all amongst white people on your own, no family, no friends around (Cooper 1979: 36).

But policies are not made on the basis of logic nor with the interests of their potential victims in mind – especially if these happen to be black; there are far more powerful and over-riding considerations involved. Thus Birmingham City Council – imbibing Enoch Powell's 'rivers of blood' speech which was delivered in that city in 1968, and being intimidated by a rent strike threatened by white tenants who had concluded that their block of maisonettes were being turned into a 'ghetto' by the arrival of two black families – embarked upon a policy of black dispersal. Ignoring the specified preferences of black people to remain in the central area of the city in which the latter's friends and communal institutions were located, through so-called 'slum clearance' and the enormous powers which they wielded over people on the housing waiting list, Birmingham came up with what Colonel Oliver North would have termed a 'neat idea'. This was a set ratio dispersal policy: 'In any block of flats or in any street of houses, no more than one property in six could be allocated to black tenants' (Flett 1981: 11–12). Dispersal was synonymous with integration (Ibid.: 10). As the chief housing officer at the time explained later to a researcher: 'The average block of maisonettes has got twelve families in it, which meant out of twelve families on two landings you didn't have more than two coloured families' (Ibid.: 12). Thus between 1969 and 1975 when the practice was brought to a stop by the belated intervention of the Race Relations Board, thousands of black people in Birmingham were shunted out of the area in which they had previously lived, despatched to the white hinterland to be 'integrated'.[50] Through her remarkable investigation of the workings of this policy of racist shenanigans in Birmingham Hazel Flett found that:

> The proportion of suburban allocations to black applicants rose from 22 per cent in 1971 to 57 per cent in 1974 – and plummeted again to 32 per cent in 1976 when the policy was abandoned. The suburban 'peak' occurred not from chance but from less favourable treatment. Only one in five of black applicants in 1974 (compared to one in three whites) was housed on an estate he had requested, whilst one in three was housed in an area, almost invariably suburban, not even approximating to preferences. That is, it was possible to disperse only by over-riding black people's choices (Flett 1981: 35).[51]

Similar policies were pursued by other municipal authorities such as the Greater London Council and Manchester City Council in the early 1970s (cf. Smith 1989: 99–101); Birmingham was simply the most publicized and well-documented case.

For the black victims of these policies, such actions were deliberate and insulting acts of state vandalization and destruction of black communities in the making.[52] In any event, such developments had the effect of undermining Caribbean communal interaction and thus weakened the Caribbean cultural matrix.

Thanks mainly to a battery of viciously racist immigration bills enacted in the 1960s (1962, 1965, 1968), primary immigration from the Caribbean effectively came to an end in the late 1960s. Dependants, mainly children, were reluctantly allowed in afterwards. But the relatively large waves of the 1950s were things of the past. In fact, for the period 1973–1982 net migration from the Caribbean to the UK amounted to only 1,800 – a negligible number compared to the figures of the 1950s and to the estimated Caribbean population in Britain of 520,000 in 1982 (OPCS 1984: Table 2.3).[53] One impact of this was the closing off of further cultural reinforcement and fresh injection by newcomers from the Caribbean.

Once again the comparison with the situation in the United States is instructive.

The McCarran-Walter Act of 1952 severely restricted Caribbean migration to the USA. Many of those who had hoped to migrate to the US in the 1950s turned to Britain. In the 1960s the reverse dynamic unfolded. As the British were erecting greater barriers against *black* immigration the US were lowering theirs. The 1965 Hart-Cellar Immigration Reform Act facilitated Caribbean migration to a much greater extent than at any other time since 1924. Thus from a figure of 27,424 between 1960 and 1965, anglophone Caribbean migration to the US increased to 114,921 during the five years from 1966 to 1970. And while, as we have seen, net Caribbean migration to Britain between 1973 and 1982 – effectively a decade – numbered 1,800, in half the time (between 1976 and 1980) migration to the US from the anglophone Caribbean alone amounted to over *100 times* the level for Britain, viz, 194,606. Indeed, from 1960 to 1984 no fewer than 781,213 people legally migrated from the non-Hispanic Caribbean (including 141,109 from Haiti) to the US (Kasinitz 1992: 28, Table 2). The majority of these migrants settled in New York City. The trend, as the most up-to-date statistics indicate, continued unabated in the 1980s. Today 25 per cent of the black population (excluding 'black' Hispanics) in New York City are foreign-born. Between 1982 and 1989 Caribbeans ranked the highest in numbers of migrants to New York City. Of the total figure of 684,819 for the period, the Dominican Republic ranked first with 16.9 per cent, Jamaica second with 10.6 per cent, China third, 10.5 per cent, followed by Guyana and Haiti with 7.8 per cent and 6.0 per cent respectively. Almost 29 per cent of Brooklyn's population is now foreign-born while the figure for Queens is more than 36 per cent (*New York Times*, 1 July 1992, pp. B1–B2).

On top of the sheer numbers involved, there has historically been a much more frequent and deeper level of contact between those in the Caribbean and migrants from the region in the US. One study of Vincentians in New York found that, 'Some Vincentians moved between St. Vincent and New York so often that they themselves could not always determine which location was home' (Toney 1989: 43–4). And it was discovered that the Vincentian diaspora in New York was so important and literally well-connected to the island that 'There was more than an ounce of truth to the assertion among the islanders that, "if you want to know what is happening in St. Vincent, call Brooklyn"' (Ibid.: 48). Indeed, the depth and frequency of contact between New York and the Caribbean is so great that people have talked of an 'air bridge' linking the region with the city (*New York Times*, 4 August 1992, pp. B1, B4). And Orlando Patterson has talked perceptively of a West Atlantic

System, in which the borders of nation states of the region have become more permeable and indistinct (Patterson 1987).

Thus in relative terms the Caribbean population in Britain is rather marooned. Lower income, higher air fares in comparison to their counter-parts in the US and the absence of a flow from the Caribbean all conspire to diminish the cultural enrichment that the closer links with the Caribbean afford Caribbean New Yorkers. Of course there are the electronic media which facilitate an interpenetration of popular cultural forms. But this, in and of itself, does not, contrary to what some commentators seem to think, turn London into New York or Brixton into Brooklyn: there are limits to the capability of modern technology. And while people may call Brooklyn no one calls Brixton to find out what's happening in Jamaica.

The educational system, despite recent cosmetic changes, has been indicted and found guilty time and time again of racism and the undermining of self-confidence of black children and the maligning of the culture of their parents. Yet it persists essentially unchanged. And the recently introduced National Curriculum, manufactured by Tory ideologues, is bound to worsen this situation and exacerbate the marginalization of the non-European world as an object of study. The educational system, then, has had inevitably, given the context, a major and on the whole detrimental impact on Caribbean culture in Britain.

The Policy Studies Institute in its comprehensive study *Black and White Britain*, published in 1984, found that 15 per cent of Caribbean heads of households were in 'mixed' marriages or 'mixed' cohabiting relationships. The equivalent figure for people of Asian descent was 4 per cent. Moreover, in areas where the black population is relatively small (census enumeration districts with 4 per cent or fewer black people), the figure jumps to 26 per cent for Caribbean people and to 11 per cent for Asians (Brown 1984: 21–2, and Table 11). Given the already besieged condition of Caribbean culture in Britain, such cross-cultural[54] relationships are more likely than not to enhance the prospects of a diminution of Caribbean cultural continuity, almost regardless of the intentions of the individuals involved in such relationships. Both parties are subject to the hegemony of British culture and insofar as there may be some transmission of Caribbean culture from one partner to the other, this in and of itself can never 'make up' for the erosion of Caribbean culture already taking place within the wider society, especially when one partner is at best a relative newcomer to the culture – not someone born and brought up in that culture, even in its diasporan form.

At the wider societal level, non-Caribbeans have had some exposure to Caribbean culture. But this has, in general, been quite superficial and where it has taken place, it has largely been confined to a relatively small percentage of the white urban population (and in some areas a proportion of Asian youths), who have had some direct contact with Caribbeans. Through their dissemination of Caribbean popular music (in practice little beyond reggae), the electronic media (primarily radio and television) have, at least during the 1970s, helped to expose some small *aspects* of Caribbean culture to the wider British public. But this too has been rather superficial and also ephemeral. The whole thing was at base a commercial fad and at best a passing fashion for the mainstream British media. Such an experience most certainly, even given UB40, does not warrant us talking of a 'two-tone Britain' in which ostensibly there is some deep cultural exchange and transformation under way among both black and white youths. Though some may, I see no deep meaning, nor cause for cultural optimism in the fact that some white cockney kid in Hackney can 'cuss raas' in poor imitation of his Jamaican-descended peers.

On balance, what exists in Britain at present is a profound asymmetry in the cultural interaction between the Caribbean population and the wider society. This of course is partly explained by the fact that the Caribbean population constitutes, by the most generous of the current estimates, less than 2 per cent of the population of Britain as a whole. Thus, while there has undoubtedly been a process of pan-Caribbeanization, there has also been – especially over the past decade – and simultaneously, one of creolization-in-reverse,[55] in which the Caribbean population through the hostile forces of attrition (which are both objective and subjective) at work against its culture is undergoing a discernible *de-creolization*, in effect a process of de-Caribbeanization. This phenomenon, as I have argued earlier, *has* some positive qualities – the decline of 'colourism' or 'shadism', the undermining of island chauvinism, the demystification of whiteness and the corresponding valorization of black-ness – which most Caribbean people in Britain have grown to accept and value.

But there are negative, countervailing forces too, at work within this process of de-creolization. Most significantly, there has been the disturbing of cultural bearings which has led to a certain degree of disorientation – a most dangerous state of affairs at the best of times – on the part of the Caribbean population, in a strange and on the whole hostile environment. And this can only increase our vulnerability. We still have not fully recovered from our traumatic arrival and reception in Britain – *including* those among us who were *born* here. We are still existing in the wake of the SS *Empire Windrush*.[56] Granted, two generations is not a long time in the life of a people, but the unsuspected intensity of the hostility of the society that we came to is at the root of our deep and continued trauma. *Trauma* is *the* cardinal and ever-recurring motif one finds in the many testimonies of the early arrivants.

Now, if the current trends continue – and I am afraid I can see no reason for their not persisting – we will in the end be black and de facto British. But

British of a particular sort – *black British*, sui generis. Meaningful elements of Caribbean culture will undoubtedly exist but these will be constituents of a new amalgam transformed and in many ways overwhelmed by its British crucible. And there will also be the persistence of what Gans has called 'symbolic ethnicity', a phenomenon characterized by a 'nostalgic allegiance to the culture of the immigrant generation, or that of the old country; a love for and pride in a tradition that can be felt without having to be incorporated in everyday behaviour' (Gans 1979: 9).[57]

Some will mourn these developments, others will celebrate. I for one will not be joining the 'hybridity' revellers in the streets who are blithely complacent about the forced asymmetry of the processes at work.

The Boundaries of the Imagined Black Community

> Friends, I'd like you to know the truth and speak it.
> Not like tired, evasive Caesars: 'Tomorrow grain will come.'
> But like Lenin: By tomorrow
> We'll be done for, unless . . .
> As the jingle has it:
> 'Brothers, my first obligation
> Is to tell you outright:
> We're in a tough situation
> With no hope in sight.'
> Friends, a wholehearted admission
> And a wholehearted UNLESS!
>
> BERTOLT BRECHT

Before concluding, a significant phenomenon ought to be registered. Like all nations, nationalities and ethnic groups, Afro-Caribbean people in Britain have erected boundaries in relation to those with whom they identify. As has been argued, thanks not least to the powerful centripetal forces of British racism, a *new* sense of fellowship, akin to what Benedict Anderson has described as an 'imagined community', has been triumphally brought into being. Although the concept of 'imagined community' was developed by Anderson specifically to tackle some of the hitherto intractable problems in the analysis of nationalism, its utility extends beyond that phenomenon. As Anderson explains, the nation is inevitably an *imagined* community 'because the members of even the smallest nation will never know most of their fellow-members, meet them, or even hear of them, yet *in the minds of each lives the image of their communion*' (Anderson 1983: 15; emphasis added). Anderson's work constitutes a major advance in our understanding of nationalism.[58] And not surprisingly, it has been fulsomely invoked ever since its publication almost a decade ago. But what the epigones have by and large ignored is that the act of communion contains within itself, its antonym – exclusion, the erection of boundaries and closure. Anderson to his credit clearly recognizes and registers the dialectics of the process when he describes the nation as being '*inherently* limited' (Anderson 1983: 15; emphasis added; cf. Debray 1983). Thus the modalities of exclusion, boundary setting and closure should draw our attention as much as, if not more than, those of inclusion and the building of communion. Having so far dealt with the processes involved in the building and incorporation of the imagined black community, it is to these exclusionary processes that we must now turn in relation to the Caribbean experience in Britain.

The most remarkable aspect of this phenomenon in our case, is that boundaries have been established which exclude those whom many would regard as 'natural allies' of the Afro-Caribbean people in Britain. Although the situation is quite dynamic, it is fair to say that at present Afro-Caribbeans do not on the whole identify – in the sense of facilitating inclusion within their imagined community – with people of Asian descent in Britain.[59] Nor, it should be said, do Asian people identify with Afro-Caribbean people in Britain. This state of affairs is of course a major obstacle to the maximization of concerted action against British racism. There is a tendency among black radicals of both Asian and African descent to sweep this problem under the carpet. But to make a subject taboo, to repress it, is one thing; to make it disappear is quite another. In fact, this mode of behaviour is extremely detrimental to the struggle of black people in Britain. Indeed, I would contend that the premature demise of a number of black organizations in recent years is very much related to the silence on, and absence of an adequate handling of this important problem.

Space does not permit a detailed discussion of this issue here. What can be said here is this: anyone who has moved among Afro-Caribbean and Asian people in Britain with eyes to see or ears to hear would readily recognize that there does exist some antagonism and, more typically perhaps, a tacit agreement of a peaceful but cold co-existence between the two groups. A number of commentators have registered this phenomenon (Lowenthal 1978: 89; Lewis, 1978: 33–7; Ratcliffe, 1981: 294, 303; Sherwood 1980: 222–3, 327–8), but Daniel Lawrence is the only one, to my knowledge, to have attempted to gather data on the problem. In his study of 'race relations' in Nottingham he found that:

As many as 83 per cent of the West Indians and 43 per cent of the Indians and Pakistanis said they had most in common with the English. However, a further 31 per cent of the Indian and Pakistanis said that as far as they were concerned they had nothing in common with either. No more than 8 per cent of West Indian and 20 per cent of the Indians and Pakistanis felt that they had more in common with each other than with the English.

Lawrence also found that as many as 42 per cent of West Indian respondents commented upon the extent to which the Asians were 'different and kept themselves to themselves': 'They're clannish. Their way of thinking and behaving is entirely different from ours. I have known a few but it's hard to get through to them.' Twenty-two per cent of Afro-Caribbeans expressed explicitly critical remarks about Asians: 'A people who grab money!' 'Well you see most of the Indians, they, for some reason or another, they don't call themselves coloured – you know they think they are better than we are.' Only 11 per cent made 'friendly or not unfavourable' comments about Asians: 'They're very genuine people – they are nice' (Lawrence 1974: 156).

For their part, Indians and Pakistanis expressed more 'critical than friendly' remarks about Caribbean people. Lawrence discovered that, 'By far the most common complaint was that West Indians were rough, aggressive and generally uncultivated.'

> Well they're not like us – take crime for instance – there isn't a day when one of them isn't in the paper for doing something. They are a bit more aggressive and crude – but that's just because they are ignorant. From the day we are born we are taught that you must respect your elders – even if they are not any relation to you – and I think even among English people you don't find this sort of thing. But the West Indians don't seem to know how to behave – they are rude and rowdy you know not like Indians or the English.

And: 'Seventy-five per cent of Jamaicans do not work – all they do is go to the races and go out with prostitutes. They are tarnishing the name of the whole immigrant community. They do not use their brains – perhaps God willed it that way – I do not know. But they spoil things for all of us' (Lawrence 1974: 155–6).

Lawrence found that 30 per cent of Asians who gave their opinion about Afro-Caribbeans made favourable 'or at least not unfavourable' comments. But from the three examples that he gave, two expressed a far from disinterested admiration of Caribbean people: 'West Indians are good for *us*. If any Englishman fights *us* West Indians help *us*. Our own people run away.' 'West Indians are good. If *they* were not here *we* would not have been able to live here.' And 'West Indians are OK – they are friendly when they speak to me' (Ibid.: 156; emphasis added).

Although Lawrence, surprisingly, does not indicate specifically when his fieldwork was carried out, from the internal evidence and date of publication of the book (1974), it is almost certain that it was conducted in the early 1970s (perhaps in the late 1960s but obviously not later than 1974), that is approximately two decades ago. Since that time, there have been a number of positive developments in Afro-Caribbean/Asian relationships. The 'Bradford 12' defence campaign was to receive significant and active support from Afro-Caribbeans as well as Asian people in defence of twelve Asian youths in

Bradford who were charged with 'making an explosive substance with intent to endanger life and property' and 'conspiring to make explosive substances' during the uprisings of 1981. And more recently in East London, Asians and Afro-Caribbeans united in defence of the 'Newham 7', a group of Asian youths who were charged with affray in the aftermath of an attempted defence of their community from fascist attacks. These are just two of the better-known cases of Afro–Asian unity in action. The list could be extended. But to assume that the contradictions between Afro-Caribbeans and Asians is a thing of the past is to commit a gross error. They still remain (cf. Harrison 1983: 381). One of the most disturbing and unremarked findings of the Macdonald Inquiry into racism and racial violence in Manchester schools is the significant level of antagonism between Afro-Caribbean and Asian students. And indeed the frequent complicity and participation of Afro-Caribbean students in attacks on their Asian counterparts (Macdonald et al. 1989: see especially Chapter 25). Nevertheless, on balance it is fair to say that a relative state of indifference if not antagonism prevails over the more positive developments, between Afro-Caribbeans and Asians.

So what are the bases of this problem?

First, as the comments cited above indicate, there do exist major cultural differences between people of Asian descent and those of Afro-Caribbean origin.[60] The mutual ignorance of, if not downright disrespect for, each other's culture and the internalization by each of the British stereotype of the other help to explain this state of affairs.[61]

Second, aspects of Afro-Caribbean antipathy towards Asians are rooted in the Caribbean background. To augment labour supply and to increase their control over the labour force, the plantocracy, throughout the Caribbean, as well as others elsewhere, turned to the Indian subcontinent after the enslavement of Africans had come to an end.[62] The system, known as Indian indentureship, lasted from the 1830s to 1917, at which time, thanks largely to Indian nationalist opposition in the subcontinent, this barbaric practice, very much akin to slavery, came to an abrupt close. The motives behind, organization, practices and consequences of induced Indian immigration to the Americas are well documented.[63] The important point here is this: the process was specifically and expressly geared to breaking the increased power of the formerly enslaved Africans within the newly-created labour market. Elaborate strategies were conscientiously devised by the plantocratic bourgeoisie and its state to create maximum division between Africans and the newly-arrived and cruelly-deceived Asians in the Caribbean. These unfortunately were extremely effective: the Africans and Indians, exploited and oppressed, were thoroughly divided.[64] Mutual strike-breaking, for instance, was commonplace in late-nineteenth-century Guyana. The animosities between the groups, though less intense than hitherto, exist to the present day. The tragic state of contemporary Guyana is very much a product of this bitter legacy of intra-working-class division.[65] It therefore would have taken a miracle for some of these oppositional attitudes towards Asians not to have been brought among the cultural inventory of Afro-Caribbean people migrating to Britain in the post-war period. And the Britain to which Afro-Caribbeans came provided fertile ground for their perpetuation.

Third, the differences in the distribution, spatial as well as industrial, and location of Asians and Afro-Caribbeans in Britain – *significant* differences[66] which do exist and are often overlooked – also militate against the cohesion of these two groups in their fight against racism.

Fourth, racism in its concrete operation does not affect both groups in an identical manner. The specificities of the rhythm of Asian migration to Britain, for instance, have meant that people from the Indian subcontinent, not those from the Caribbean, have felt the brunt of racist immigration controls in Britain. Afro-Caribbeans, for their part, undergo an exceptionally high degree of state harassment on a day-to-day level. The perceived differences in the problems which each group come up against vis-à-vis the state have hampered united action based upon common priorities.[67]

Finally, clearly identifiable and *perceived* differences in the *distribution* of Asians and Afro-Caribbeans within the class structure of Britain and the lack of coincidence, and unevenness of the respective dynamic of their class formation work against the development of a unity of perspective on British racism and, even more, against combined political action. For the period 1985–87 the *Labour Force Survey* has determined that only 2 per cent of Caribbean men were in the 'professional' occupational category compared to 14 per cent of Indian and 5 per cent of Pakistani/Bangladeshi men. Indeed, the percentage of Indian men in the professions was twice that of white men, at 14 per cent and 7 per cent respectively. A similar pattern emerges when we look at the 'employers and managers' category: 5 per cent Caribbean, 15 per cent Indian, 14 per cent Pakistani/Bangladeshi and 19 per cent of white men fall within this occupational group.

The figures for women are not as comprehensive as those for men, but where they are available a similar pattern obtains: 1 per cent of Caribbean compared to 4 per cent of Indian women are in professional occupations, while 3 per cent of Caribbean in contrast to 6 per cent of Indian women fall within the category of employers and managers. The same pattern of distribution emerges amongst the 'self-employed'. For men we find that 6 per cent of Caribbean, 22 per cent of Indian and 16 per cent of Pakistani/ Bangladeshi men are self-employed. And a similar situation obtains for women: 2 per cent of Caribbean compared to 10 per cent of Indian women were self-employed over the same period (OPCS 1989: Tables 5.33 and 5.35).

There are no good reasons to doubt the general accuracy of these figures. Certainly, in relation to the 'self-employed' we may very well ask questions as to what that particular status denotes. What is clear, is that it does not automatically mean 'loadsamoney', or even a comfortable state of material well-being. Studies have repeatedly shown that, especially in the early period of such ventures, the status of self-employment often entails a high level of 'self-exploitation' and 'exploitation' of family labour (women and children especially), simply in order to stay afloat. Indeed, there is evidence to suggest that some self-employed people quite frequently earn less than they other-wise would were they working for someone else. The other side of the equation, however, should not be forgotten. There is relative autonomy in being one's own boss, there is the dual escape from the racism of white employers as well as from the 'cracker' racism of the shopfloor as it were, and many in this category do earn a very large income while a minority enjoy lucrative lifestyles, marked by an excess of conspicuous consumption.

Evidently, the categories used in the *Labour Force Survey*, such as 'pro-fessional', 'employers and managers', could bear disaggregation and would prove more useful analytically if there were. But the absence of this clearly does not render them useless or meaningless. Moreover, these *patterns* of distribution have been identified from the 1950s and not only by the *Survey*. And the *global distribution* which this information imparts is valuable and meaningful analytically. Empiricists would also say that the figures do not do violence to everyday commonsensical observations of the contemporary ethnic landscape of Britain, but rather confirm them.

In any case, these differences in the *distribution* of Caribbeans and Asians within the *class* structure of Britain – and my extrapolation from largely *occupational* categories to social *class* is based not only on the *Survey* – have, especially since 1979, some fairly disturbing political implications. What we find is that a growing *segment* of the Asian population – somewhat reflective of these trends of class formation – have, in larger proportions than ever before, been voting Tory. And rich Asian businessmen have gone so far as to deck out Conservative Central Office in the early 1980s with the best computer system that money could buy at the time (Fitzgerald 1984: 71). Clearly class, not ethnicity, is the crucial factor here. 'I'm a professional *businessman*, not a professional Pakistani!' asserts one of Hanif Kureishi's characters in *My Beautiful Launderette*, as he commands his *white* working-class hand to throw out from an upstairs window the mattress of his *black* Rastafarian tenant.

An estimated 23 per cent of Asians, compared to 6 per cent of Afro-Caribbeans, opted for the Tories in the 1987 election. And 86 per cent of Afro-Caribbeans as against 67 per cent of Asians went for Labour (Harris Research Centre 1987; *Caribbean Times*, 5 June 1987). But perhaps most disturbing of all, is the fact that there is some evidence to suggest that even when one allows for social class, there still remains a marked difference between the two groups (Layton-Henry 1984: Table 11.2). Such divergence in perspectives and trajectories clearly strains and places constraints upon political alliances and united action on the part of Afro-Caribbeans and Asians.

In short, there is a whole series of factors that inhibit and maintain the boundaries of the Afro-Caribbean imagined community vis-à-vis people of Asian descent in Britain and vice versa. And these have been far more multitudinous and persistent than the pigmentocracy and particularisms of the Caribbean background that have been battered down by the levelling effect of British racism. These forces of division need to be recognized urgently and seriously addressed if the struggle against racism, being carried out – almost by default – on a daily basis by each group, is to be more effectively waged. There are no easy nor instant solutions to this problem and in any case space does not permit serious elaboration on the possible means of overcoming this obstacle to unity. Nevertheless a few brief remarks are not only in order but are indeed necessary.

Gordon Lewis, the late distinguished Caribbeanist, in an insightful essay (Lewis 1978: 299–341), quite properly noted that:

> The mutual antipathy between black [sic] and Indian is a well-known phenomenon that if truth be told, pre-dates European colonialism. But colonialism, even so, has used the antipathy in the classic colonial condition as a 'divide-and-rule' mechanism, both in East Africa and the Caribbean . . . There now exists a real danger that with the new influx of Kenyan and Ugandan Asians the British will replicate an East African colonial situation in which Asians are utilized as a favoured buffer group between black and white, thus introducing a secondary divisive element frustrating the growth of a black–brown coalition (Ibid.: 337).

Thankfully, the 'dangers' which Lewis, writing in 1977, feared have not materialized, at least not on the East African scale that he thought was possible – and at least, not yet. He overestimated the homogeneity of the Asian population in Britain and understated the organizational capacities of Afro-Caribbean people living here. In short the 'race relations' situation in Britain is radically different from that which existed in East Africa and in reality there was very little chance of a direct replication of such a pattern within the imperial heartland. But just as the East African 'model' has not materialized in Britain, so also has what Lewis called the 'black–brown coalition' *not* come to full fruition. What is of particular interest on this score, however, is the strategy proffered by Lewis to combat these divisions and the potential colonial sandwich of 'white, brown and black'. His is a two-pronged approach based on cognition. Both minority groups, he argued, should:

> (a) develop a mutual and sympathetic *understanding* of the contribution that each has made, in their pre-European Asian and African communal societies, to world civilization as a whole, and (b) *recognize* the brutal truth that, living now in their Egyptian exile, they both suffer from the same oppression, they both are tarred by the same brush (Ibid.; emphasis added).

Although somewhat platitudinous – not to mention Lewis's unfortunate metaphor – these strategies are very important if we are to advance our common struggle against racism. 'Sympathetic understanding' of each other's history is clearly needed not only in the light of the negative stereotypes both groups quite often entertain about each other, but also because in our respective everyday life we far too often occupy and move within the ambit of discrete social worlds. Indeed, one of the noteworthy and most disturbing findings of Daniel Lawrence was the inability of a substantial proportion of his Afro-Caribbean and Asian respondents to offer 'any relevant comments' about each other. Thirty-three per cent of Afro-Caribbeans and 37 per cent of Indians and Pakistanis were unable to do so because, according to the author, 'they had no contact with members of the other group' (Lawrence 1974: 155). Clearly then, serious ideological work has a role to play.

While acknowledging the *general* validity of Lewis's second point, it would nevertheless be more appropriate to make a distinction between the *roots of,* or perhaps more accurately, the *prime mover* behind, the oppression of Asian and Afro-Caribbean people in Britain and the *patterns* of the forms of oppression they encounter. *Both* groups experience oppression (which latter ought not to be confused with exploitation) as a result of the operation of the *same* fundamental force, namely, racism. But the ways in which both groups experience racism are not always identical. The evidence indicates quite clearly that, for instance, at least in the last decade or so, people of Asian descent in Britain are more frequently subjected to fascist terror on an everyday level (brutal physical assaults and arson attacks, often executed with murderous intent and with fatal results, most readily come to mind) than people of Afro-Caribbean descent. On the other hand, the latter group, especially the youths, experience a greater degree of state harassment, and indeed some brutality at the hands of the police, than people of Asian descent.[68] As was stated above, Asians in recent years have felt the brunt of racist immigration rules, while young men of African descent (continental or Caribbean) felt the full weight of the 'Sus Laws' more than any other single group of people in Britain.

These undoubtedly different experiences have, not surprisingly, generated different responses and assessments of British racism and have spawned different priorities among the two major black nationalities. This is what all the evidence points to.[69]

The following conclusions flow inexorably from the above remarks:

(i) we need to recognize that in many instances Afro-Caribbean and Asians in Britain have different priorities in the fight against racism;

(ii) the different issues that occupy privilege status on the list of priorities by each group have to be mutually supported by both groups if we are to appreciably erode the racist structures and practices extant in Britain;

(iii) in the light of the distrust, if not downright antipathy, between both groups, it follows that, when black umbrella organizations are brought into being, this factor has got to be taken into account in the setting up and operation of structures. An organization, for instance, that is aimed at mobilizing Asians and Afro-Caribbeans and whose rank-and-file membership is equally divided ethnically should seriously consider the electing of executive members on the basis of 50 per cent Afro-Caribbean and 50 per cent Asian. In short a system of proportional representation should at least be seriously considered to facilitate the execution of such political work. A substantial part of the success of the Working People's Alliance in Guyana has been its sensitivity to intra-black divisions – between Indo-Guyanese and Afro-Guyanese – and the reflecting of these concerns in the organization and structure of the party.[70] Rupert Roopnaraine and Walter Rodney, Indo- and Afro-Guyanese respectively, were consciously paired by the WPA on speaking tours to both African and Indian communities in Guyana. There is a great deal to be learnt from the practices of the WPA – that is if people want to learn.

If these basic, indeed *elementary*, rules are not followed, we most probably will continue to 'riot' separately, fight separately, organize separately but suffer together, albeit in somewhat different ways, in this Babylon. There is nothing intrinsically wrong with cultural diversity and genuine pluralism. And unity-in-diversity is a worthy goal. But as Asian, Afro-Caribbean and white youths in some areas have shown over the years, and as black caucuses (comprising both Asians and Afro-Caribbeans) in a number of trade unions are currently demonstrating, unity-in-adversity is also an eminently sensible idea.

On Indo-Caribbeans in Britain

There is, however, a category of Caribbeans, often ignored and in many ways invisible, whom we ought to at least register in this discussion. These are those Caribbeans of Indian descent, Indo-Caribbeans, who migrated to Britain in the general wave from the Caribbean in the 1950s and 1960s.

Very little sociological work has been carried out on this group. Nevertheless, partly from personal knowledge we can and should say something, if only tentatively, about their location within the over-all analysis attempted here. There is no accurate statistical information about this group of Caribbeans (they are not disaggregated from the overall Caribbean population), but we do know that they constituted a significant proportion of the migrants who came from Guyana and Trinidad (societies in which approximately 50 per cent of the population are of Asian descent). There are, in addition, a small proportion of such migrants from other areas of the eastern Caribbean and also some from Jamaica. Steven Vertovec, the only scholar to my knowledge who has carried out research on this group, estimates that there are between 22,800 and 30,400 people of Indo-Caribbean descent in Britain having their roots in Guyana and Trinidad. But as he recognizes, this figure 'would still doubtless represent an underestimation of the total number of Indo-Caribbeans in Britain – especially since it does not take into consideration illegal immigration, nor the unknown numbers of Indians from Jamaica, Grenada, St. Vincent and elsewhere in the Caribbean' (Vertovec forthcoming).[71] Drawing upon the 1981 census figures, he further estimates that 77 per cent of Indo-Caribbeans in Britain reside in the Greater London area.

Indo-Caribbeans have over the years played an important role in anti-racist politics in Britain, constituting an integral part of what we may call the black movement in this society. Most notable amongst these have been two men from Guyana: Roy Sawh, a distinguished veteran of the struggles of the 1960s, including of the Black Power movement in Britain,[72] and Rudi Narayan, the eminent barrister. Arif Ali, who also hails from Guyana, as head of Hansib Publications, and editor-in-chief of *Caribbean Times*, has over the years developed that publication into an important anti-racist campaigning organ. Indo-Caribbeans have also been prominent and active in Caribbean solidarity movements in Britain: in Caribbean Labour Solidarity, an organization based in London, and especially in the People's Progressive Party (UK – a support group for the parent organization based in Guyana and led by Dr. Cheddi Jagan), as well as in the London-based Working People's Alliance Support Group which supports the WPA in Guyana. Indo-Caribbeans in Britain have made a contribution to the fight against racism in this country and against imperialism and authoritarian rule in the Caribbean far in excess of their actual number.

Indo-Caribbeans have also made their contribution to the artistic life of the Caribbean diaspora in Britain.[73] Most notable amongst these have been Sam Selvon, the novelist from Trinidad, author of the landmark text *The Lonely Londoners*. Some would also include the Naipaul brothers, Vidia and the late Shiva, on the list. Their relationship to the Caribbean, however, especially that of V.S. Naipaul, is to say the least highly problematic. I am not even certain that Vidia Naipaul would describe himself as a Caribbean writer. But having been born and brought up in Trinidad – the world of most of his novels – he is at least a writer from the Caribbean.[74]

So how do they fit into the wider ethnic matrix in Britain? How are they perceived by white Britons? And how do they identify themselves vis-à-vis

Afro-Caribbeans and people of Asian descent from the Indian subcontinent and elsewhere? Sadly, these are questions that have hardly been raised, never mind addressed, by those writing on race in Britain.

'To the English,' reported Selvon to an audience in Trinidad, 'as long as you were not white you were black, and it did not matter if you came from Calcutta or Port-of-Spain' (Selvon 1986: 9). Thus we have echoed the sentiments of other Indo-Caribbeans who had migrated to Britain in the 1950s and 1960s. The derogatory term 'Paki' was to come later and never really had wide currency until the early 1970s as more people from Pakistan and Bangladesh migrated to Britain, especially after the war in 1971 between East and West Pakistan out of which emerged the state of Bangladesh. Prior to this, the binary and its nomenclature, black/white, held sway in the popular mind in Britain. And it was into the black category that the Indo- as well as Afro-Caribbeans were placed. Indo-Caribbeans in Britain therefore also had their journey to Damascus.

It was made very clear to Roy Sawh who had migrated to Britain in 1958 that he was 'black'. In only his second week of working as a bus conductor for London Transport, an elderly white woman, unprovoked, spat in his face and called him a 'black bastard'. 'He pushed her and had practically the whole bus at his neck.' 'That was the end of my association with London Transport,' said Sawh, 'I left in disgust' (Morrison 1987: 26). Arif Ali, Sawh's Indo-Guyanese compatriot, had an almost identical experience when he worked as a bus driver. He vividly recalled the incident many years later in an interesting exchange with an interviewer on a radio programme:

> *Arif Ali*: One day somebody punched me on my mouth and I had to go to hospital. And he didn't call me a brown bastard because of my Asiatic background. He didn't call me anything else but a black bastard. And I never forgot that. My conductor was standing there. He said, 'But, Rif, you are not black,' and that idea then came up to me that what people describe you as, the time has come for you to accept that, and since that time, ten years before I decided to launch my publications, I have been thinking and using that sort of idea.
>
> *Juliet Alexander*: Are you saying that it took coming to this country to realize that you were black?
>
> *Arif Ali*: Yes. In Guyana, oh no, you couldn't call me black in Guyana. What's the matter, are you mad or something? In Guyana I am an Indian or a coolie (Griffiths 1984: 11–12).[75]

Ali understandably asked the interviewer if she is 'mad or something' as in Guyana no one in his or her right mind would have described him as 'black', never mind calling him a 'black bastard'. It simply would not have happened: in Guyana he was an Indian, a category sharply distinguished by all Guyanese from the African or the 'black' person. Thus it is not, strictly speaking, a case of his realizing he was black on having come to Britain; rather it would be more accurate to say that he *became* black through his experience in a racist Britain – the wider society defined him as black and he felt, as he explained, that it was sensible for him to embrace this new definition of himself, his new identity.[76]

Thus the centripetal power of British racism which helped to break down the petty antagonisms between Afro-Caribbeans from different regions of the Caribbean also assisted in bringing Afro-Caribbeans and Indo-Caribbeans closer together. Though fraught with difficulties of its own this *rapprochement* between Afro- and Indo-Caribbeans was, interestingly enough, easier to achieve than one between Indo-Caribbeans and Asians from the Indian subcontinent and East Africa. V. S. Naipaul relates an encounter which he had in an airport lounge:

> There was another Indian in the lounge . . .
> 'You are coming from . . . ?'
> I had met enough Indians from India to know that this was less a serious inquiry than a greeting, in a distant land, from one Indian to another.
> 'Trinidad,' I said. 'In the West Indies. And you?'
> He ignored my question. 'But you look Indian.'
> 'I am.'
> 'Red Indian?' He suppressed a nervous little giggle.
> 'East Indian. From the West Indies.'
> He looked offended and wandered off to the bookstall. From this distance he eyed me assessingly (Naipaul 1972: 30).

According to Vertovec this is 'typical of the experiences of most Indo-Caribbeans in Britain' in their encounters with people from the subcontinent. Vertovec's Indo-Caribbean respondents reported a range of reactions from 'Indians from India', from the positive to very negative. But by and large, these reactions have been characterized by 'amazement', 'confusion', 'surprise', and so on; in other words, very similar to Naipaul's airport encounter. Indeed, during this visit to the subcontinent in the early 1960s Naipaul was so exasperated by the innocent incomprehension of his Indian interlocutors of the idea that he was an Indian from Trinidad that he resorted to describing himself as a Mexican:

> 'Where do you come from?' It is the Indian question, and to people who think in terms of the village, the district, the province, the community, the caste, my answer that I am a Trinidadian is only puzzling.
> 'But you look Indian.'
> 'Well, I am Indian. But we have been living for several generations in Trinidad.'
> 'But you look Indian.'
> Three or four times a day the dialogue occurs, and now I often abandon explanation. 'I am a Mexican, really.'

'Ah.' Great satisfaction. Pause. 'What do you do?' (Naipaul 1972: 43).

'To be an Indian or East Indian from the West Indies is to be a perpetual surprise to people outside the region,' concluded Naipaul (1972: 33). Afro-Caribbeans being familiar with – this anomalous, 'unlikely and exotic' (Naipaul 1972: 35) creature to outsiders – Indo-Caribbeans from the region, have therefore been typically those with whom the latter, at least in the early years of migrant life in Britain, had established the closest contact – insofar as such contacts were made at all.

It should not be assumed, however, that such positive relations between Afro-Caribbeans and Indo-Caribbeans are typical of the relations between these two groups. The majority of both Indo-Caribbeans and Afro-Caribbeans do not identify with each other. And Indo-Caribbeans are not keen to be identified as 'West Indians' in Britain (Vertovec forthcoming). They in general, and understandably, perceive themselves as constituting a group sui generis:

> Indo-Caribbeans are racially 'excluded' as 'Asians' by most whites, while *also* being socially or culturally 'excluded' (or at best, held as a little-regarded, even low-status, adjunct group) by most 'Asians' themselves. Understandably, Indo-Caribbeans have mixed feelings about their identification with 'Asians' in Britain . Yet though they originate mainly from Trinidad and Guyana, Indo-Caribbeans generally do not wish to be identified as 'West Indian', this is because the term has Afro-Caribbean connotations, and in the Caribbean there is a long heritage of Indian antipathy for Africans (Vertovec forthcoming).

But some have made strenuous efforts to revitalize their Indian roots. The Brixton-based Caribbean Hindu Society (established in 1958 when it was then called Hindu Dharma Sabha), apart from engaging in religious activities also teaches Hindi, Indian music and dance (Vertovec 1992: 260–1; Vertovec forthcoming). One Gujarati woman patronizingly described Indo-Caribbeans as '*trishanku*' – a colloquialism for 'dangling' or 'floating in the air'. 'Other Gujaratis,' she said, 'did not look upon them as Hindus, while the Indo-Caribbeans themselves "realized they were not part of us".' But she admired their quest for roots and cultural affirmation. According to her, Indo-Caribbeans 'take more energetic steps' toward their ethnicity: 'they ended up learning Hindi . . . our children haven't bothered' (cited in Vertovec forthcoming).

In relation to the questions posed at the outset, we may summarize the position of Indo-Caribbeans in Britain in the following terms. For the first generation, three groups and tendencies are discernible. First, a significant minority has whole-heartedly embraced a new black identity and has also participated fully in the struggles that black people have waged in Britain. The classic example of this has been Roy Sawh, a major figure and largely unsung hero of the struggles of the 1960s and 1970s. But Sawh is not in a category of one. Secondly, there are those who are virulently anti-black, embittered by their experiences in the Caribbean. This is especially true of some Indo-Caribbeans from Guyana – and their complaints are by no means unfounded: Burnham and his lackeys *have* got a lot to answer for. As have those many Afro-Guyanese who supported him over the years. Sometimes this vicious bitterness expresses itself even in the most public of domains. I heard an Indo-Guyanese man launch a venomous tirade in the most disgusting terms against 'black' people (meaning here people of African descent) during the question time at a meeting in London at which Cheddi Jagan spoke in the mid-1980s. Most people at the meeting seemed to have regarded him as a bit of a crank but the views which he expressed are by no means exclusively held by him. Thirdly, there are those who have quietly got on with their lives and have maintained cordial if not close relations with Afro-Caribbeans. This is especially true of those Indo-Caribbeans from Grenada, St. Lucia, St. Vincent and Jamaica where the relations between Afro- and Indo-Caribbeans have not been as troubled as they have been in Guyana and Trinidad, territories with the largest Indo-Caribbean populations. As in the Caribbean, rare though they have been, there have been cases of marital unions between Afro-Caribbeans and Indo-Caribbeans in Britain.

Like second-generation Afro-Caribbeans, Indo-Caribbeans in Britain have also been radicalized by their experiences in Britain and unburdened by the painful and bitter experiences of their parents in the Caribbean close political alliances and social interaction have existed between them and their Afro-Caribbean counterparts. Particularly exemplary co-operation and alliance may be found in the Working People's Alliance Support Group in Britain where Indo-Caribbeans and Afro-Caribbeans join hands in the most selfless and moving way to forward the struggle for democracy in Guyana.

And among the young, my own observations over the years coincide with Vertovec's:

> current trends indicate lack of identification with either the Caribbean or India, whereas, instead, many seem to be adopting a generalized British Asian youth culture (symbolized by *bhangra* music) which cuts across the cultural divides of their parents. Further, at much variance with their West Indian-born parents, many Indo-Caribbean young people are equally comfortable in fields of British Afro-Caribbean culture as well – thus importantly comprising a new generation practising new ways of actually 'being multicultural' (Vertovec forthcoming).

And there are also those occurrences which Arif Ali has encountered:

> When England is playing West Indies, I'm sitting in one corner of the room backing Clive and Viv and the guys, and my sons are shouting 'Botham!' and have Botham

jumpers on, so it's one of those situations you get from time to time (Griffiths
1984: 18).

Indeed, from time to time, but not very often. British society has not had the
decency nor good sense to create enough space for such behaviour. Thus, for
the foreseeable future Norman Tebbitt shall remain a disappointed man as
the vast majority of Caribbeans, British-born or not, will continue to *wilfully*
fail his 'cricket test', the rare burst of *black* British patriotism in Arif's living
room notwithstanding.

By Way of Conclusion

Our experiences in Britain have sharpened our perspectives of our place
within the world: we have been forced, where some us were hitherto
reluctant, to recognize and validate our blackness; the 'shade'-blind and
'island'-innocent racism within British society have helped us to shed some of
the most absurd and deluding idiocies of Caribbean life. 'The English have at
last,' as Patricia Madoo rejoiced, 'rendered [us] a service.' The centripetal
effects of British racism, thus far at least, however, have not been sufficiently
uniform and strong to breach the partially antagonistic ethnic boundaries
established between people of Asian and African descent in Britain. Our
culture, for good or ill, has been dramatically changed – as was to be expected.
But in partial 'compensation', the struggle of living within the metropolis has
entailed the unintended 'privilege' of us seeing the world from the perspective
of the persecuted 'outsider'. Our vision of the world has been broadened and,
as a consequence, we are in a better position to identify with the oppressed
within and outside of Britain. It is therefore no accident that, while the white
working class engages in its periodic flirtation with Toryism, Caribbean
people in Britain in their vast majority entertain no illusions about the
Conservative Party, as their persistently high *anti*-Tory (not to be confused
with *pro*-Labour) vote in successive elections testifies.

As the dream of 'the return' of the first generation becomes more
pulverized with every passing day, and as the second generation becomes
more aware of the need to transform the Britain in which they live into a
home, the slogan 'Here to Stay, Here to Fight' rings more true than ever. But
because of the pervasive non-class-specific and non-gender-bound racism of
British society, we have and will continue to have, alas for some time yet,
relatively few allies, although those we do have are valued highly. It is a hard
road to travel. Fortunately, however, black people in Britain have long
recognized this fact – as they have recognized that the necessary precondition
for the solution of any problem is the prior acknowledgement of its existence.

Notes

Acknowledgement: I would like to thank Robin Blackburn, Barbara Fields, Cecil Gutzmore, Clive Harris and Linden Lewis for their valuable comments on an earlier draft of this essay.

1. For a valuable discussion of the conceptual confusion around ethnicity see McKay and Lewins (1978). Eugeen E. Roosens (1989) has written a particularly illuminating and wide-ranging study of the dynamics of ethnicity. Also see the fine work of Mervyn Alleyne (1988).
2. For respresentative sample, see Institute of Contemporary Arts (1987, 1988), Samuel (1989a, 1989b, 1989c), Hall (1989), Rutherford (1990), Lisa Kennedy et al. (1991), Ilene Philipson et al. (1991), Bauman (1991), Giddens (1991). I had also attempted some earlier formulations (James 1984, 1986 and 1989), upon which this essay draws and builds.
3. Karl Mannheim's pathbreaking essay on 'The Problem of Generations' (Mannheim 1952) still repays close reading.
4. Frank Snowden (1970) has shown that in previous epochs of European history the image of Africa had been quite different. Cf. James (1954), Diop (1974) and Bernal (1987).
5. For some rare and qualified exceptions see Brathwaite (1984: 13); cf. idem. (1971: 188–91). The historical records of Barbados have so far yielded one such marriage (between a *coloured* man and a white woman) during the entire period of slavery. This marriage took place in 1685. (Handler 1974: 201).
6. Heuman's (1981) is undoubtedly one of the finest case studies of this social category within the New World. For a good overview of the position within the Americas as a whole, see Cohen and Greene (1972); and also Campbell (1976) on Jamaica, and Handler (1974) for Barbados.
7. It has been estimated that in eighteenth-century Jamaica 80% of 'freedmen' (manumitted slaves, men as well as women) were coloured, whilst the remaining 20% were black (Heuman 1981: 4) – at the time over 90% of the island's population were black.
8. This is not to say that domestic slaves did not experience atrocious violations of their humanity. See Brathwaite (1971: 156–7) for some particularly gratuitous as well as gruesome examples of violence against domestic slaves. In spite of the cruelty which they quite often experienced from their so-called masters and mistresses, domestic slaves were nevertheless 'regarded by most slaves and the master as being in a more "honourable" position than the field slaves' (Brathwaite, 1971: 155; cf. Patterson 1967: 57–9).
9. According to Handler (1974: 6) this hierarchy did not obtain in Barbados. Here one was 'coloured', 'black' or 'white'. The permutations did not take the form of the ramified social categories which existed, say, in Jamaica.
10. 'In Barbados . . . no one of *known* negroid ancestry, no matter how remote, could be considered *white* with respect to social or legal status' (Handler 1974: 6, emphasis in original).
11. 'The separation of browns and whites continued after death. Each group had its own burial ground, and church bells rang longer for whites than for people of color' (Heuman 1981: 12).
12. This does not mean that political alliances did not occur between freed Africans and coloureds – they did. These, however, were in general extremely fragile, uneasy and, on the whole, ephemeral. Heuman (1981) documents this very well in the case of Jamaica. With perhaps the qualified exception of Cuba, Brazil and Puerto Rico, this state of affairs was typical of the Americas as a whole.
13. Fanon's observation of the behaviour of West Indians who joined the French Army and served in Africa before 1939 serves as an appropriate parallel here: 'The West Indian, not satisfied to be superior to the African, despised him and while the white man could allow himself certain liberties with the native, the West Indian absolutely could not. This was because, between whites and Africans, there was no need of a reminder; the difference stared one in the face. But what a catastrophe if the West Indian should suddenly be taken for an African!' – Fanon, 'West Indians and Africans', in Fanon (1970: 30). It should be noted that not an insubstantial number of Africans were owned as slaves by mulattoes. In Jamaica in 1826 they were claimed to have owned 50,000 slaves out of a total population of 310,368 (Campbell 1976: 62). In proportionate terms this amounted to more than 16% of the slave population. In Saint Domingue in 1789, on the eve of the Haitian revolution, their counterparts, the *affranchis*, owned no less than 25% of the overall slave population estimated at 500,000 (Fick 1990: 19).

14. Cited in Heuman (1981: 14). Translated: 'If I *must* have a master or mistress, give me a white one – don't give me a mulatto, they don't treat black people well.' [Translation mine, WJ.] 'Buckra' or 'backra' is derived from the Efik *mbakara* meaning 'he who surrounds or governs'. In the Caribbean it soon became synonymous with white people (cf. Cassidy 1971: 155–6; Cassidy and LePage 1980). Long, incidentally, had also suggested that 'The middle class [the coloureds] are not much liked by the Negroes, because the latter abhor the idea of being slaves to the descendants of slaves' (Long 1774, vol. II: 332).

It should perhaps be stated here that many of the damaging psychological consequences of slavery in the Americas for the enslaved Africans were not simply due to the unspeakable horrors of slavery per se, but more perhaps to the fact that *black* people (Africans) were enslaved by *white* people (Europeans). This fact of black enslavement by white enslavers in the Americas is so obvious that it is seldom remarked upon. Yet this phenomenon, I believe, has had a profound impact upon the psyche of both the enslaved and the enslavers not least because of the *symbolism* of the phenotypical characteristics of the two groups involved. In other words, from the evidence, it is quite plausible that the damage would have been quite different, ceteris paribus, were it the case that Africans were enslaved by Africans and Europeans by Europeans.

15. The citation is quoted in Patterson (1967: 152). But see Bush (1990: 105), who gives some evidence of the existence also of a more positive and warm reception of newly-arrived Africans.

16. It should be noted that in contemporary Britain hair-straightening among black people has developed, to a certain extent, into an autonomous form of black aesthetics. A form, in other words, that has to a significant degree broken with – or perhaps more accurately, has *forgotten* – its provenance in the class–colour complex of slave society in the Caribbean. The colonial legacy, however, has not by any means been completely eradicated. Cf. Caribbean Teachers' Association 1984: 38–9, and 'Are We Proud to be Black?', *Black Voice*, vol. 15, no. 3. For interesting overviews of the situation in the USA today, see 'Is Skin Color Still a Problem in Black America?', *Ebony*, vol. XL, no. 2 (December 1984), pp. 66–70; and two relatively recent brief, but exceptionally courageous, well-made and frank films on the subject: Warrington Hudlin's *Color* (1982) and Ayoka Chinzira's *Hairpiece* (1983), which have stimulated much discussion among African Americans.

17. The fact that black women are far more involved in these practices than black men is no accident: the phenomenon is directly related to the oppression of women by men and the general historical preference on the part of black men for women with phenotypical characteristics which approximate most closely to those of Europeans. With the exception of the extant Maroon enclaves (communities established by escaped slaves in the Americas in the sixteenth to eighteenth centuries, most notably in Jamaica and Surinam) it is one of the New World as a whole. Cf. Herskovits (1958: 125–6); Henriques (1968: 57); and especially Ann Cook (1970). In recent decades these practices – in tandem with the ever-widening and corrosive reach of European and Euro-American cultural imperialism – have become almost commonplace among the black petit-bourgeoisie of Africa itself: 'Whitening the skin has become a "Black" disease in Black African society,' declared Awa Thiam in her instructive book (Thiam 1986: 105).

18. The work under attack is Foner (1979).

19. Henriques found that many of his female respondents were well aware of the health risks of hair straightening. See Henriques 1968: 56–7.

20. Ibid., note 17, p. 136. Incidentally, an illuminating discussion of the genealogy and semiology of the European suntan may be found in Turner and Ash's fine and little-known study (1975: 78–82).

21. Henriques (1968: 171 et passim); Foner (1973: 27); Fanon (1970); Williams (1969: 66–7); Alleyne (1988). And perhaps most forcefully, Kruijer (1969: 22–3). For a hard-hitting and just critique of the Caribbean middle classes, C. L. R. James's 1962 essay (James 1980) is still unsurpassed in its clarity of vision and understanding. For the situation in the USA see Frazier (1957).

22. And *angst* there certainly was *and is*. Eric Williams, writing in 1942 on the middle classes, reported that 'Prospective brides *looked* for light-skinned men. They *pray* for "light" children, who might marry white. Expectant mothers *abstain* from coffee and chocolate. As the saying goes in Martinique, one who has reached the dining room should not go back to the kitchen' (Williams 1969: 66, emphasis added). Two centuries after Long wrote, his observation still rang true: 'No . . . Mulatto ever wished to relapse into the Negro.' It should be added, however, that

endeavours at lightening and whitening were by no means confined to black women, as Williams somewhat unfairly implied – black men were equally assiduous in their efforts to achieve such ends.

23. It can hardly be over-emphasized the extent to which resistance was mounted by Africans in the Americas against their enslavement. Eugene Genovese (1979) has a detailed bibliographical essay in his extremely useful (but nonetheless problematic) analysis. But special mention ought to be made of the following texts: James (1963); Price (1979); Bastide (1971, 1978); Fouchard (1981); Craton (1982); Beckles (1984); Hart (1985); Heuman (1986); Blackburn (1988); Campbell (1988); Fick (1990); and on a hitherto scandalously neglected subject, which only recently has been afforded some attention, women and slave resistance, Mathurin (1975); Brathwaite (1977); Beckles (1989); Bush (1982, 1990); Morrissey (1989).

24. The distribution of migrants from the various territories during the early years of migration to Britain has been estimated to have been as follows: Jamaica, 1953–61: 148,369; and for the years 1955–61: Barbados: 18,741; Trinidad & Tobago: 9,610; British Guiana: 7,141; Antigua: 4,687; Montserrat: 3,835; St. Kitts-Nevis-Anguilla: 7,503; Dominica: 7,915; Grenada: 7,663; St Lucia: 7,291; St Vincent: 4,285. See Peach (1968: 106–7).

25. It is not without significance that it was a woman in Montserrat – and not one in London – who, having never clapped eyes upon a Jamaican, advised against her daughter marrying a Jamaican and having anything to do with Jamaicans as they are 'the wickedest people on earth'; cited in Philpott (1977: 110). There are some first-generation Caribbeans who still hold frankly idiotic ideas about people from islands apart from their own: a Jamaican in Leicester got on perfectly well with his Kittitian neighbour but completely ostracized the latter once he discovered he was a 'small islander'. But the prize for 'island chauvinism' must go to the Guyanese (Guyana of course is a continental enclave, not an island strictly speaking) man in Brixton who said in the early 1970s: 'We Guyanese are like the English, the Jamaicans are terrible people, just peasants really, they are not good stock . . . There are too many Jamaicans in Brixton, that's why the area is full of thieves and boys who don't work – you see their island is next to Cuba' (cited in Benson 1981: 98). Although published in 1981, the fieldwork upon which Benson's study is based was carried out in Brixton between February 1970 and September 1971. It is my contention that the point in time that such sentiments are expressed is of some significance: the closer we move to the present, the more unlikely it becomes that we will hear such blatant expressions of island chauvinism.

26. For the qualified exceptions of Barbados and Grenada, see F. Henriques and J. Manyoni (1977).

27. Fanon (1965: 47) and, as the originator of the concept, Aimé Césaire, has explained, the adoption of the term *négritude* was a conscious act of defiance, not a name haparzardly or fortuitously chosen. As for its root-word, *nègre*, Césaire tells us: 'Since there was shame about the word *nègre*, we chose the word *nègre*.' See Césaire's interview with René Depestre in Césaire (1972: 73–4). Césaire's prime work of African celebration of awareness is, of course, *Cahier d'un retour au pays natal* (Césaire 1969). Cf. Jean-Paul Sartre, 'Orphée noir' (Sartre 1976): an exceptionally insightful analysis of *négritude* and an authentic expression of Sartre's anti-imperialism and solidarity with the oppressed. This essay was to have a profound influence on the young Frantz Fanon.

28. Foner 1979: 117, 143 (emphasis in original).

29. Foner's interviews were conducted between 1971 and 1972.

30. See, for example, Office of Population Census and Surveys (OPCS 1982, Table 4.25, p. 22). Cf. Brown (1984) 185 – Table 79; 197–98 – Tables 91 and 92; 201 – Table 95; 233–4 – Tables 120 and 121.

31. It must be said that this state of affairs is less of a positive credit to Britain than a major indictment of the nation states of the Commonwealth Caribbean – many of which are singly unviable as economic entities, although their leaders blindly resist talk of political union – which Britain has plundered and disfigured over the centuries, and their mimetic indigenous ruling classes who, though nominally presiding over independent states, have kept intact and have ferociously protected the fundamental pillars of the social structure erected under colonialism.

32. For a good index of this new mood among the older generation of Afro-Caribbeans in Britain, see the views expressed *in their own words* in the otherwise astonishingly insensitive and

downright mocking articles by David Selbourne (1983a and 1983b). See also Tony Kellman (1984: 9) and Thames Television, Thames Reports, 'Going Home,' 19 June 1989, where the number of pensions sent to the Caribbean by the Department of Health and Social Security was cited as being 8,903 in 1982 and 16,539 in 1988. It should be noted that the return migration of Caribbeans to the islands is by no means a new phenomenon (Rose et al. 1969: 433). On the experience of the early returnees see Hinds (1966: 191–2) Davidson (1968) and Patterson (1968).

33. The alienation expressed by a returning Barbadian man is shared by the majority of Caribbeans in Britain: 'I have been in this country twenty years and have never felt a part of this society' (Kellman 1984: 9).

34. In 1985 it cost approximately £900 for a corpse to be flown to the Caribbean and approximately £60 for ashes to be taken. In June 1992 the figures were £750 and £100 respectively. (Information from British Airways and Air Canada which books cargo for British West Indies Airways, June 1985; and British Airways June 1992.)

35. Unfortunately there is no readily available precise information on the quantity of 'human remains', to use the trade jargon, transported from Britain to the Caribbean over the years. In 1985 British Airways gave a rough estimate of approximately two corpses per week on average for the early 1980s. No doubt this figure has increased since then as more members of the 'first generation' die.

36. From personal observation there seems to be a prima facie correspondence between the frequency of visits to the Caribbean and the conceptions of the Caribbean as home: those who visit their country of origin more frequently are those who have drifted most from the utopian view of the Caribbean as home, whilst those who have not visited the Caribbean at all or visit it less frequently – precisely because their ideas of home have not been interrupted by the concrete spectacle of their native land – keep intact more successfully the romantic ideas of home which, it should be remembered, do help to sustain them in the harsh social environment of Britain. For analyses of some of the economic and political problems in recent times in the country from which the vast majority of Caribbean migrants derive, Jamaica, see W. James (1983a; 1983b).

37. Edward Kamau Brathwaite, himself an Afro-Caribbean poet and historian of distinction, has not inaccurately summarized the position of the Caribbean writer as being that of an 'eccentric at home and an exile abroad'. But this sense of homelessness and alienation is by no means exclusive to the intellectuals of the Caribbean. It can be found in equal measure among working-class Caribbean people returning 'home'. (Brathwaite's remarks are cited in Rohlehr 1981: 6.)

38. This type of experience causes tremendous pain to Caribbean migrants, especially the elderly who have never been made to feel a part of British society and are regarded as outsiders when they return to the Caribbean. A few years ago when Michael Manley, Jamaica's prime minister, and his entourage from Jamaica held a public meeting at Central Hall, Westminster, the loudest cheer of the entire evening's proceedings went not to Manley, the featured speaker, but to an elderly man who spoke. I remember his remarks well. He said: 'Missa Manley, I want yu to tell dem people in Jamaica not fe call wi "foreigner" when wi come home. Wi is Jamaicans.' His remarks clearly resonated with the overwhelmingly middle-aged and elderly audience as they immediately burst into loud applause and shouts of 'Yes!' and 'Just tell dem!' Manley smiled and clapped with the audience and promised to deliver the expatriate Jamaican's message. (From the author's notes taken at the meeting, 'His Audience and Manley', Central Hall, Westminster, 16 June 1989.)

39. Cf. Schweitzer (1984: 30). British migration statistics are notoriously inadequate in terms of precise magnitudes. But the fact that a *net outflow* of 2,800 to the Caribbean was recorded for 1982, the highest single figure for over a decade, is not insignificant and implausible. It seems equally plausible that a reversal in the trend had occurred in 1983 when a net figure of 3,000 Caribbean migrants entering Britain was recorded. The first figure seems to reflect the exceptionally strong mood for returning which existed among Caribbean migrants in the early 1980s as the economic crisis in Britain deepened and the second seems to reflect the crisis in the economies of the Caribbean when many who could return to Britain took the opportunity to do so. As a Jamaican community worker informed the writer, 'All those who can come back are doing so.' For figures see OPCS (1984: Table 2.3. p. 6 and OPCS Monitor (1984: Table 3). For a

discussion of some of the shortcomings of the statistics see Runnymede Trust and the Radical Statistics Race Group (1980: 120–9); Peach (1981a), and the ensuing debate between Peach and Jones (Jones 1981; Peach 1981b).

40. Caribbean Teachers' Association (1984: 42, emphasis in original). 'All a wi is one' is a population Caribbean saying.

41. The inverted commas are used advisedly here as the Rastafarians are so ramified in their views that it is a gross mistake to speak of *a* Rastafarian ideology in the singular. Indeed, the self-professed Rastafarians are so dissimilar in their theological and cultural outlook that it is hard to find a common denominator specific to the adherents of the faith. It is therefore very risky indeed to speak of *a* or *the* Rastafarian movement. By far the best analysis of the early Rastafarians is Post (1970), which is also developed at much greater length in his majestic trilogy on Jamaica (Post 1978 and 1981). [For appreciations of these texts see Cohen (1982) and James (1983).] Post has amplified and revised some of his earlier ideas in his paper (Post 1984). The fine, but unfortunately little-known, essay by Robert Hill (1983) is also essential reading for an understanding of the genesis of Rastafarianism. The seminal work of M. G. Smith et al. (1960) and Nettleford (1970) are indispensable. Joseph Owen's (1976), though somewhat overly romantic, is by far the best analysis of the Rastafarians in contemporary Jamaica. See also the special issue of *Caribbean Quarterly*, vol. 26, no. 4 (December 1980) which is entirely devoted to the subject. None of the numerous other studies of the 'movement' can be recommended without major reservations.

42. See in particular Gutzmore (1983a). A considerably abbreviated version is to be found in (Gutzmore 1983b); and Centre for Contemporary Cultural Studies (1982).

43. See *From You were Black You were Out*, a film documentary directed by Colin Prescod and *Riots and Rumours of Riots*, a film documentary directed by Imruh Caesar. Also see Gutzmore (in this volume), Sivanandan (1982) and Pilkington (1988).

44. Although I do not share his overly romantic reading of the period, Sivanandan's essay 'From Resistance to Rebellion', (in Sivanandan 1982: 3–54) still constitutes the best inventory and analysis of these early struggles. Cf. Bryan, Dadzie, Scafe (1985); Moore (1975); Carter (1986); Ramdin (1987).

45. For more on the struggles around education see Carter (1986: 83–103) and Bryan, Dadzie, Scafe (1985: Chapter 2).

46. For a very sensitive and moving analysis of the relationship between parental 'authoritarianism', love and sacrifice, albeit within a different context, see Sennett and Cobb (1977).

47. The video *Motherland* (1983), based upon the experiences of twenty-three women who migrated from the Caribbean to Britain in the 1950s and 1960s and dramatized by their teenage daughters, is a striking expression of this growing awareness and celebration by young black people of their parents' struggles. (The play was directed by Elyse Dodgson, and the text may be found in Dodgson 1984: 72–97).

48. Lamming develops these ideas in fictional form in his 1954 novel *The Emigrants*, (Lamming 1980).

49. See citations in note 30 above.

50. Apart from the evidence of their explicitly preferred location, the dissatisfaction of black people with being located in the 'outer ring' of Birmingham was indicated by their requests for transfers to the central area of the city where they had previously resided (Flett 1979: 46, 58–9).

51. For a variety of reasons Asians in Birmingham were hardly affected in their spatial location by these policies (Flett 1979: 48–9).

52. For some moving testimonies on the impact of such policies on the Ladbroke Grove area of London see Colin Prescod's documentary *From You were Black You were Out*, transmitted by Channel 4 in 1985 in the series 'Struggles for Black Community'; the video is available from the Institute of Race Relations, London.

53. The comparative figure for Asians from the Indian subcontinent (including those from Sri Lanka but excluding those from East Africa and elsewhere) was 196,000 (OPCS: 1984, Tables 2.3 and 2.4). Underlining the different rhythms of migration from the Caribbean and the Indian subcontinent, the Asian population in Britain in 1982 was estimated at just over a million.

54. The concepts of 'race', 'colour' and 'culture' are clearly different; but in *this* particular case there are close correspondence and imbrication of the three.

55. The term 'creole' is derived from the Spanish – the first European colonizers of the Americas – word *criollo* which refers to a person, animal or thing, born or created in the New World. Hence a creole slave (one born in the Americas) as opposed to an African slave (one born in Africa). The term creole culture refers to the culture which has emerged in the Americas out of the intermixing of different cultural groups, e.g. African, European, Native American etc.

56. The ship that in 1948 brought what was to be the first wave of post-war Caribbean migrants to Britain.

57. Gans developed the concept in relation to 'white ethnics' in America – Jews, Irish, Poles, etc., in which he sees the well nigh inexorable demise of the secular culture of their forebears in the United States. For Caribbeans in Britain, however, because of the phenomenon of racism, symbolic ethnicity, 'ethnicity of the last resort', as Gans puts it, will persist as counter-culture defences as long as racism exists. Thus for black people in Britain it should prove more enduring over the generations than for Gans's 'white ethnics' in the United States.

58. For more expansive remarks on Anderson see my review of the book, W. James (1983d).

59. Some years ago, similar but less intense contradictions existed between African and Afro-Caribbeans in Britain. For examples see Benson (1981: 40, 97–9). But a number of factors militated against this contradiction: the coincidence of the phenotypical characteristics of continental Africans and Afro-Caribbeans and hence the largely identical nature of the racism which they faced in their everyday lives; the disproportionately large role which continental Africans played in the Black Power movement in Britain in the late 1960s (cf. Egbuna 1971) and the spectacular rise of pan-Africanist ideas popularized via Ras Tafari – which itself stood on the shoulders of earlier traditions such as Garveyism – in the mid-1970s in Britain all helped to severely undermine if not totally destroy this contradiction. In any case, at least since the Second World War the continental African population in Britain has always been minuscule and more transient (many are students) in comparison to that of the Afro-Caribbean and Asian – notwithstanding the fact that there have emerged over the last two decades more settled communities of Africans in Britain, especially in London.

60. This is not to suggest that the category 'Asian' is homogeneous. Obviously many differences exist, especially with regard to religious allegiance. Nevertheless, these 'internal' divisions amongst Asians are not perceived to be as great as those between Asians as a group and Caribbeans. The most detailed discussion of the different groups of Asians in Britain is to be found in Vaughan Robinson (1986).

61. In the Caribbean, new migrants, Indian and others, quickly imbibed and adopted the stereotype established by the dominant European culture of the African. The Africans in their turn saw the Indians largely through the spectacles of the hegemonic European stereotype (Lowenthal 1972: 156ff; Braithwaite, 1975: 44ff).

62. In the case of the British colonies in the Caribbean this epoch of chattel slavery finally ended between 1834 and 1838.

63. Tinker (1974), Laurence (1971); J. La Guerre (1974); Brereton (1979) and Rodney (1981). The number of Indian indentured labourers brought into the Caribbean were as follows: British Guiana: 238,909; Trinidad: 143,939; Jamaica: 86,412; Martinique: 25,519; Guadeloupe: 45,000; Surinam: 34,304; Windward Islands: 10,026 (Source: Laurence 1971: 57). Few areas of the Caribbean were left untouched by indentured labourers – these were Barbados, the Dominican Republic, Haiti, Montserrat and apparently Antigua. Cuba did not manage to secure Indian indentured labourers but imported over 150,000 Chinese indentures in the nineteenth century.

64. By far the most thorough case study of these strategies of divide and rule in relation to Africans and Asians is to be found in Rodney's posthumously published study (Rodney 1981: 174ff).

65. For a sound recent analysis of Guyana, see Latin America Bureau (1984).

66. These have been amply documented by the *Labour Force Survey* over the years.

67. For some indication of the differences in priorities of these two groups see the survey results cited in Fitzgerald (1984: 57); Brown (1984) brings out a number of these differences on a whole range of issues, see especially Tables 116, 117, 118, 119, 136, 137, 138. Also see Harris Research Centre (1987), a survey which was sponsored by Hansib Publications, some of the results of which were published prior to the elections of 1987 in the latter's *Caribbean Times*, 5 June 1987, pp. 1, 23.

68. The relative prominence of Asians amongst those experiencing racist attacks by fascist groups and the relative salience of Afro-Caribbeans amongst those experiencing police harassment and brutality on the streets is not, incidentally, unrelated to the racist stereotypes of both groups: Afro-Caribbeans are seen as more aggressive than Asians, and thus almost by default, the latter are seen by the fascists to be fair game. Of course the second generation of Asian youths, as has been demonstrated over the years in Southall, Bradford and Newham, are making the fascists think again. The stereotypical view of 'black youths' (read young *men* of Afro-Caribbean descent) is that of a group perceived to be almost congenitally criminal and 'anti-authority' as Sir Kenneth Newman, a former commissioner of the Metropolitan Police, let slip.

69. See references in note 67 above.

70. W. James and F. Ambursley, interview with Andaiye, member of the central committee of the WPA (London, 1983). I have also had less formal discussions over the years with Andaiye, Rupert Roopnaraine and Clive Thomas, all leading members of the WPA, as well as with members of the WPA support group in Britain on these issues.

71. I am grateful to Steven Vertovec for having generously given me access to his findings prior to their publication.

72. For an informative and tender portrait of Sawh see Lionel Morrison, 'Roy Sawh, A Profile', in Roy Sawh (1987: 18–56).

73. Cf. Anne Walmsley, 1986.

74. See Lamming's warm tribute to Selvon and his comparison of the latter with V. S. Naipaul, in Lamming (1984, pp. 211ff.).

75. The remarks were made on the BBC Radio 4 series 'Caribbean Connections' which was recorded in the summer of 1983 and transmitted in the spring of 1984. The series producer was Joan Griffiths who also edited the booklet based on the programmes, *Caribbean Connections*.

76. Black bus conductors and drivers because of the close and intense interaction with the wider public that their work entailed had a particularly rough time during those early and dark years. One conductor recalled meeting on average 800 people per day and remembered having had to fight 'many verbal battles' (Hinds 1966: 73–4). Another, having insisted that a passenger paid the correct fare, was told: 'You coloured people are all the same. Give you a little authority and you lose your sense of humour. Give you a country to run and you turn it into a God damn "dictatorship"' (Ibid.: 26). 'You get insults left, right and centre,' said one Caribbean conductor, 'I'm not bothered now – "bastard" is just a national name' (Brooks 1975: 111). Data from London Transport's legal department showed that the assaults were not exclusively verbal: 'In 1968, roundly 60% of reported assaults were on coloured staff. Most of these were assaults on Central Bus conductors. As only about one-third of Central Bus conductors were coloured and they experienced about three-fifths of the assaults, the coloured conductor was roughly three times as likely as his white colleague to be assaulted. The trend of assaults on public transport staff in London is rising. In 1966, 727 cases were reported. By 1969, the figure had risen to 1,120' (Ibid.: 114–15). It was therefore not surprising that 'On one occasion a Jamaican driver, incensed by the racialism around him, just left his bus in the High Street and walked off' (Sivanandan 1982: 5). If his autobiographical short story is anything to go by, Donald Hinds himself seems to have had an easier time than many of his fellow Caribbeans of being a conductor. See Hinds (1972b).

Bibliography

AFFOR (All Faiths for One Race) (1981), *Elders of Minority Ethnic Groups*, Birmingham.
African Women (1988–89), *African Woman*: Quarterly Development Journal, Issues 1–3.
Ahmed, Shama, J. Cheetham & J. Small, eds (1986), *Social Work with Black Children and Their Families*, London: Batsford Ltd.
Allen, S. (1970), 'Immigrants and Workers', in S. Zubaida, ed., *Race and Racialism*, Tavistock/BSA.
Alleyne, M. (1988), *Roots of Jamaican Culture*, London: Pluto Press.
Amin, Samir and Kostas Vergopoulos (1975), *La Question Paysanne et le Capitalisme*, Paris: Editions Anthropos.
Anderson, Benedict (1983), *Imagined Communities: Reflections on the Origins and Spread of Nationalism*, London: Verso.
Anderson, J. S. Duncan and R. Hudson, eds (1983), *Redundant Spaces in Cities and Regions*, London: Academic Press.
Andrews, Norma (1975), 'Trinidad and Tobago', in A. L. Segal, ed., *Population Policies in the Caribbean*, Lexington (MA): Lexington Press, pp. 73–87.
Aptheker, Herbert (1971), *Afro-American History: the Modern Era*, New York: Citadel Press.
Banks, M. (1981), *Young People Starting Work*, Sheffield University: Department of Psychology.
Barker, J. and H. Downing (1980), 'Word Processing and the Transformation of the Patriarchal Relations of Control and the Office', *Capital and Class*, no. 10.
Barker, Martin (1981), *The New Racism*, London: Junction Books.
Barrett, David B. ed. (1982), *World Christian Encyclopedia*, Oxford: Oxford University Press.
Barrett, M. and M. MacIntosh (1982), *The Anti-Social Family*, London: Verso.
Barrett, Michele (1981), *Women's Oppression Today*, London: Verso.
Basaglia, F. (1980), 'Problems of Law and Psychiatry: The Italian Experience', *International Journal of Law and Psychiatry* vol. 3: 17–37.
Bastide, Roger (1971), *African Civilisations in the New World*, London: C. Hurst.
Bastide, Roger (1974), 'The Present Status of Afro-American Research in Latin America', in Sidney Mintz, ed., *Slavery, Colonialism, and Racism*, New York: W. W. Norton and Co.
Bastide, Roger (1978), *The African Religions of Brazil: Toward a Sociology of the Interpretation of Civilizations*, Baltimore: Johns Hopkins University Press.
Bauman, Zygmunt (1991), *Modernity and Ambivalence*, Cambridge: Polity Press.

Beckles, Hilary (1984a), 'On the Backs of Blacks: The Barbados Free-Coloureds Pursuit of Civil Rights and the 1816 Slave Rebellion', *Immigrants and Minorities*, 3(2), July 1984.

Beckles, Hilary (1984b), *Black Rebellion in Barbados: The Struggle Against Slavery 1627–1838*, Bridgetown: Antilles Publications.

Beckles, Hilary (1989), *Natural Rebels: A Social History of Enslaved Black Women in Barbados*, London: Zed Press.

Behar, I. (1974), 'Surpopulation rélative et réproduction de la force de travail', *La Pensée*, no. 176 (Juillet–Août).

Ben-Tovim, G. and Gabriel (1979), *The Politics of Race in Britain*, no. 44, Sage Race Relations Abstracts.

Benson, S. (1981), *Ambiguous Ethnicity: Inter-racial Families in London*, Cambridge: Cambridge University Press.

Bernal, Martin, (1987), *Black Athena: The Afroasiatic Roots of Classical Civilization, vol. 1 – The Fabrication of Ancient Greece 1785–1985*, London: Free Association Books.

Bolton, F. and S. Bolton (1987), *Working with Violent Families*, London: Sage.

Boodhoo, Martin J. and Ahamad Baksh (1981), *The Impact of Brain Drain on Development: A Case Study of Guyana*, Georgetown: University of Guyana.

Borkowski, M., M. Murch and V. Walker (1982), *Marital Violence: The Community Response*, London: Tavistock.

Bousquet, Ben and Colin Douglas (1991), *West Indian Women at War*, London: Lawrence & Wishart.

Brackx, A. and C. Grinshaw, eds (1989), *Mental Health Care in Crisis*, London: Pluto Press.

Braithwaite, L. (1975), *Social Stratification in Trinidad*, Kingston: Institute of Social and Economic Research.

Brathwaite, Edward (1971), *The Development of Creole Society in Jamaica 1770–1820*, Oxford: Clarendon Press.

Brathwaite, Edward (1984), 'Caribbean Women During the Period of Slavery', *Caribbean Contact*, vol. 11, no. 12, May 1984.

Brereton, Bridget (1979), *Race Relations in Colonial Trinidad: 1870–1900*, Cambridge: Cambridge University Press.

Breugal, Irene (1979), 'Women as a Reserve Army of Labour: A Note on Recent British Experience', *Feminist Review*, no. 3: 12–23.

Brixton Black Women's Group (1983, 1984), *Speak Out*, nos. 4 and 5.

Brooks, A.D. (1984), 'Defining the Dangerousness of the Mentally Ill', in M. Craft and A. Craft, eds, *Mentally Abnormal Offenders*, London: Ballière Tindall.

Brooks, Dennis (1975), *Race and Labour in London Transport*, Oxford University Press for Institute of Race Relations.

Brown, Colin (1984), *Black and White Britain: The Third PSI Survey*, The Policy Studies Institute.

Bryan, Beverly, Stella Dadzie and Suzanne Scafe (1985), *The Heart of the Race: Black Women's Lives in Britain*, London: Virago Press.

Bush, Barbara (1982), 'Defiance or Submission? The Role of the Slave Woman in Slave Resistance in the British Caribbean', *Immigrants and Minorities*, 1(1), March 1982.

Bush, Barbara (1990), *Slave Women in Caribbean Society, 1650–1838*, London: James Currey.

Byrne, D. and D. Parson (1983), 'The State and the Reserve Army: the Management of Class Relations in Space,' in J. Anderson et al.

Cambridge Economic Policy Review (1982), *Employment Problems in the Cities and Regions of the United Kingdom: Prospects for the 1980s*, vol. 8(2), December 1982, Cambridge University Press, Cambridge.

Camden & Islington Black Sisters Group (1983), *Newsletter*, March 1983.

Campbell, Mavis (1976), *The Dynamics of Change in a Slave Society: A Socio-Political History of the Free Coloureds of Jamaica 1800–1865*, London: Associated Universities Press.

Campbell, Mavis (1988), *The Maroons of Jamaica, 1655–1796*, London: Bergin and Garvey.

Caribbean Teachers' Association, ed. (1984), *Black Youth Speak Out* (Report of the CTA Youth Conference, 1984), London.

Carlen, P. (1983), *Women's Imprisonment: A Study in Social Control*, London: Routledge and Kegan Paul.

Carlen, P. et al. (1985), *Criminal Women, Autobiographical Accounts*, Cambridge: Polity Press.

Carney, M. W. and L. Bacelle (1984), 'Psychosis After Cannabis Abuse,' *British Medical Journal*, 7 April 1984.

Carothers, J. C. (1954), *The Psychology of the Mau Mau*, Colony and Protectorate of Kenya, Nairobi.

Carter, Bob and Shirley Joshi (1984), 'The Role of Labour in Creating a Racist Britain', *Race and Class*, vol. XXV (winter): 53–70.

Carter, Bob, Clive Harris and Shirley Joshi (forthcoming 1993), *No Blacks Please, We're British!*, London: Routledge.

Carter, T. (1986), *Shattering Illusions: West Indians in British Politics*, London: Lawrence & Wishart.

Cashmore, E. and B. Troyna (1982) *Black Youth in Crisis*, London: George Allen & Unwin.

Cassidy, F. (1971), *Jamaica Talk*, London: Macmillan.

Cassidy, F. and R. LePage (1980), *Dictionary of Jamaican English*, Cambridge: Cambridge University Press.

Castells, Manuel (1975), 'Immigrant Workers and Class Struggle in Advanced Capitalism', *Politics and Society*, vol. 5.

Castles, Steven and Godula Kosack (1973), *Immigrant Workers and Class Structure in Western Europe*, London: Oxford University Press.

Centre for Contemporary Cultural Studies, ed. (1992), *The Empire Strikes Back: Race and Racism in 70s Britain*, London: Hutchinson.

Césaire, Aimé (1969), *Return to My Native Land*, Harmondsworth: Penguin.

Césaire, Aimé (1972), *Discourse on Colonialism*, New York: Monthly Review Press

Chief Inspector of Prisons (1985), *The Report of Her Majesty's Chief Inspector of Prisons*, London: HMSO.

Christian, L. (1983), *Policing by Coercion*, London: GLC Committee Suppport Unit.

Christopherson, Susan (1986), 'Peak Time, Slack Time: The Origins of Contingent Labour Demand', Unpublished Paper.

Clark, David (1982), 'Production Workers on Shifts: Choice or Constraint?', *New Community*, vol. X(1), summer 1982.

Cleaver, E. (1968), *Soul on Ice*, New York: Dell.

Cleaver, H. (1979), *Reading Capital Politically*, Hassocks: Harvester Press.

Clough, Elizabeth and David Drew (1985), *Futures in Black and White*, Sheffield: Pavic Publications.

Coard, B. (1971), *How the West Indian Child is Made Educationally Sub-normal in the British School System*, London: New Beacon Books.

Cochrane, R. (1977), 'Mental Illness in Immigrants to England and Wales: An Analysis of Mental Hospital Admissions', *International Journal of Social Psychiatry*, no. 12, pp. 25–35.

Cockburn, Cynthia (1977), *The Local State*, London: Pluto Press.

Cohen, B. and P. Jenner (1968), 'The Employment of Immigrants: A Case Study within the Wool Industry', *Race*, vol. X(1).

Cohen, David and J. Greene, eds (1972), *Neither Slave Nor Free: The Freedmen of African Descent in the Slave Societies of the New World*, Baltimore: Johns Hopkins University Press.

Cohen, Robin (1982), 'Althusser meets Anancy', *Sociological Review*, vol. 30, no. 2, May 1982.

Collins, Jock (1978), 'Fragmentation of the Working Class', in Wheelwright, E. and K. Buckley, eds.

Cook, Ann (1970), 'Black Pride? Some Contradictions', in Toni Cade, ed., *The Black Woman: An Anthology*, New York: New American Library Inc.

Cooper, Jo (1979), 'West Indian Elderly in Leicester: A Case Study', in F. Glendenning, ed., *The Elders in Ethnic Minorities*, Stoke-on-Trent: Beth Johnson Foundation Publications for Commission for Racial Equality.

Cottle, T. (1978) *Black Testimony: The Voices of Britain's West Indians*, London: Wildwood House.

Counter Information Services (1981), *Women in the '80s*, London: CIS Publications.

Craton, M. (1982), *Testing the Chains: Resistance to Slavery in the British West Indies*, New York: Ithaca.

Cross, Malcolm (1973), *The East Indians of Guyana and Trinidad*, London: Minority Rights Group.

Cross, Malcolm (1978), 'Colonialism and Ethnicity: A Theory and Comparative Study', *Ethnic and Racial Studies*, 1: 37–59.

Cross, Malcolm (1983), *Migrant Workers in European Cities: Concentration, Conflict and Social Policy*, Working Papers on Ethnic Relations, no. 19, SSRC Research Unit on Ethnic Relations, University of Aston in Birmingham.

Cross, Malcolm and Allen M. Schwartsbaum (1969), 'Social Mobility and Secondary School Selection in Trinidad', *Social and Economic Studies*, 18: 189–207.

Cross, Malcolm and Douglas Smith (1987), *Black Youth Futures – Ethnic Minorities and the Youth Training Scheme*, National Youth Bureau.

Dabydeen, David (1987), 'Preface', in D. Dabydeen and B. Samaroo, eds, *India in the Caribbean*, London: Hansib, pp. 9–12.

Davidson, Betty (1968), 'No Place Back Home', *Race*, vol. IX, No. 4.

Davis, A. (1981), *Women, Race and Class*, London: The Women's Press.

Davison, R. (1962), *West Indian Migrants*, Oxford University Press for Institute of Race Relations.

Davison, R. (1963), 'Immigration and Unemployment in the United Kingdom, 1955–1962', *British Journal of Industrial Relations*, vol. 1(1–3), pp. 42–61.

Debray, R. (1983), *Critique of Political Reason*, London: Verso.

Dennis, Ferdinand (1988), *Behind the Frontlines: Journey into Afro-Britain*, London: Victor Gollancz.

Department of Employment/Unit for Manpower Studies (DE/UMS) (1977), *The Role of Immigrants in the Labour Market*, DES.

DES (Department of Education and Science) (1981), *West Indian Children in Our Schools*, London: HMSO (London).

DES (1985), *Education for All*, London: HMSO.

Despres, Leo (1967), *Cultural Pluralism and Nationalist Politics in British Guiana*, Chicago: Rand McNally.

Dickson, James (1983), 'Race, Custom and Incorporation in the Trade Union Response to Immigration Between 1945 and 1962', draft paper, University of Glasgow.

Diop, C.A. (1974), *The African Origin of Civilization*, New York: Lawrence Hill.

Dobash, R.E and R. Dobash (1979), 'Wifebeating: The Victim Speaks,' *Victimology*, 2(3–4).

Dobash, R.E. & R. Dobash (1980), *Violence Against Wives*, Shepton Mallet: Open Books.

Dodgson, Elyse (1984), *Motherland: West Indian Women to Britain in the 1950s*, London: Heinemann Educational Books Ltd.

D'Orey, S. (1984), *Immigration Prisoners: A Forgotten Minority*, London: Runnymede Trust.

Doyal, Leslie (1979), *The Political Economy of Health*, London: Pluto Press.

Doyal, Leslie et al. (1980), *Migrant Workers and the National Health Service*, Polytechnic of North London: Department of Sociology.

Duffield, Mark (1988), *Black Radicalism and the Politics of Deindustrialisation*, Avebury.

Durbin, Mridula Adenwala (1973), 'Formal Changes in Trinidad Hindi as a Result of Language Adaptation', *American Anthropologist*, 75: 1290–1304.

Dyer, Richard (1988), 'White', *Screen*, vol. 29(4): 44–64.

Edwards, S. (1981), *Female Sexuality and the Law*, Oxford: Martin Robertson.

Edwards, S. (1984), *Women on Trial*, Manchester University Press.

Edwards, S. (1985), 'A Socio-legal Evaluation of Gender Ideologies in Domestic Violence Assault and Spousal Homicides', *Victimology*, 10(4): 186–205.

Edwards, S. (1986a), 'Police Attitudes and Dispositions in Domestic Disputes: The London Study', *Police Journal*, vol. LVIX(3), July–September 1986.

Edwards, S. (1986b), *The Police Response to Domestic Violence in London*, Polytechnic of Central London.

Edwards, S., ed. (1986), *Gender, Sex and the Law*, Croom Helm.

Edwards, S. (1989), *Policing 'Domestic Violence', Women, the Law and the State*, London: Sage.

Egbuna, Obi (1971), *Destroy This Temple: The Voice of Black Power in Britain*, London: MacGibbon & Kee.

Ehrlich, Allen S. (1971), 'History, Ecology and Demography in the British Caribbean: An Analysis of East Indian Identity', *Southwestern Journal of Anthropology*, 27: 166–180.

Ehrlich, Allen S. (1976), 'Race and Ethnic Identity in Rural Jamaica: The East Indian Case', *Caribbean Quarterly*, 22: 19–27.

Enloe, Cynthia (1982), 'Guyanese Response to Migration,' *Revista Interamericana*, 4: 492–500.

Erickson, Edgar (1934), 'The Introduction of East Indian Coolies into the British West Indies', *Journal of Modern History*, 6: 127–46.

Fanon, Frantz (1965), *A Dying Colonialism*, New York: Monthly Review Press.

Fanon, Frantz (1967), *The Wretched of the Earth*, Harmondsworth: Penguin.

Fanon, Frantz (1970), *Black Skin, White Mask*, London: Paladin.

Fanon, Frantz (1970), *Toward the African Revolution*, Harmondsworth: Penguin.

Feminist Review (1984) 'Many Voices One Chant – Black Feminist Perspective', no. 17 (autumn 1984).

Fenton, Steve et al. (1984), *Ethnic Minorities and the Youth Training Scheme*, Manpower Services Commission.

Feuchtwang, Stephan (1982), 'Occupational Ghettoes', *Economy of Society*, 11(3): 252–91, August 1982.

Fevre, Ralph (1984), *Cheap Labour and Racial Discrimination*, London: Gower.

Fick, Carolyn (1990), *The Making of Haiti: The Saint Domingue Revolution from Below*, Knoxville: University of Tennessee Press.

Field, F. and P. Haikin (1971), *Black Britons*, London: Oxford University Press.

Fitzgerald, M. (1984), *Political Parties and Black People*, London: Runnymede Trust.

Flett, H. (1979), *Black Council Tenants in Birmingham*, Working Papers in Ethnic Relations, No. 12, SSRC Research Unit in Ethnic Relations, University of Bristol.

Flett, H. (1981), *The Policing of Dispersal in Birmingham*, Working Papers on Ethnic Relations, No. 14, SSRC Research Unit in Ethnic Relations, University of Aston in Birmingham.

Foner, Nancy (1973), *Status and Power in Rural Jamaica*, New York.

Foner, Nancy (1975), 'The Meaning of Education to Jamaicans at Home and in London', *New Community*, vol. IV, no. 2 (summer 1975).

Foner, Nancy (1977), 'The Jamaicans: Cultural and Social Change Among Migrants in Britain', in J. Watson (ed.).

Foner, Nancy (1979), *Jamaica Farewell: Jamaican Migrants in London*, London: Routledge & Kegan Paul.

Foot, Paul (1965), *Immigration and Race in British Politics*, Harmondsworth: Penguin Books Ltd.

Foucault, M. (1978), 'About the Concept of the Dangerous Individual in Nineteenth Century Legal Psychiatry', *International Journal of Law and Psychiatry*, vol. 1 pp. 1–18.

Foucault, M. (1980), *Discipline and Punish*, London: Allen Lane.

Fouchard, Jean (1981), *The Haitian Maroons: Liberty or Death?* New York: Edward W. Blyden Press.

Francis, E. (1985), 'How Did Michael Dean Martin Die?', *OpenMind*, no. 13 February/March 1985.

Frazier, E.F. (1957), *Black Bourgeoisie*, New York: Collier Books.

Freeman, G. (1975) *Immigrant Labour and Racial Conflict in Industrial Societies: The French and British Experience 1945–1975*, Princeton University Press.

Friend A. and A. Metcalfe (1981), *Slump City: The Politics of Mass Unemployment*, London: Pluto.

Fryer, P. (1984) *Staying Power: The History of Black People in Britain*, London: Pluto.

Fuller, Ken (1985), *Radical Aristocrats: London Busworkers from the 1880s to the 1980s*, London: Lawrence & Wishart.

Gambhir, Surendra (1988), 'Structural Development of Guyanese Bhojpuri,' in R.K. Barz and J. Siegel, eds, *The Development of Overseas Hindi*, Wiesbaden: Otto Harrassovitz, pp. 69–94.

Gans, H. (1979), 'Symbolic Ethnicity: The Future of Ethnic Groups and Cultures in America', *Ethnic and Racial Studies*, vol. 2, no. 1.

Garrison, L. (1977), *Towards a Positive Approach to Multi-cultural Education*, London: Centre for Urban Educational Studies.

Garrison, L. (1983), *Black Youth, Rastafarianism and the Identity Crisis in Britain*, London: ACER.

Genovese, Eugene (1979), *From Rebellion to Revolution: Afro-American Slave Revolts in the Making in the New World*, Baton Rouge: Louisiana State University Press.

Giddens, Anthony (1991), *Modernity and Self-Identity: Self and Society in the Late Modern Age*, Cambridge: Polity Press.

Gilroy, P. (1987), *There Ain't No Black in the Union Jack*, London: Hutchinson.

Gimenez, Martha (1977), 'Population and Capitalism', *Latin American Perspectives*, vol. IV(4).

Glass, Ruth (1960), *Newcomers: The West Indians in London*, London: Centre for Urban Studies and Allen & Unwin.

Gomes, A.M. (1973), 'I am an Immigrant', in A. Salkey, ed.

Gordon, P. (1986), *Racial Violence and Harassment*, London: Runnymede Trust.

Gordon, Paul (1981), *Passport Roads and Checks*, London: Runnymede Trust.

Gordon, Paul (1983), *White Law, Racism in the Police, Courts and Prisons*, London: Pluto Press.

Gordon, P. and A. Newnham (1985), *Passports to Benefits? Racism in Social Security*, London: Child Poverty Action Group & Runnymede Trust.

Graham, Sara and Derek Gordon (1977), *The Stratification System and Occupational Mobility in Guyana*, Mona: Institute of Social and Economic Research.

Greater London Council, IEB (1985), *London Industrial Strategy*.

Grewal, S. et al. (1988), *Charting the Journey: Writings by Black and Third World Women*, London: Sheba.

Griffiths, Joan, ed. (1984), *Caribbean Connections*, London: Commission for Racial Equality by special arrangement with BBC Continuing Education, Radio.

Gunter, Harold (1955), *A Man's a Man: A Study of the Colour Bar in Birmingham*, The Communist Party.

Gupta, Partha (1975), *Imperialism and the British Labour Movement, 1914–1964*, London: Macmillan.

Gutzmore, Cecil (1975–76), 'Imperialism and Racism: The Crisis of the British Capitalist Economy and the Black Masses in Britain', *The Black Liberator*, vol. 2(4).

Gutzmore, Cecil (1978), 'Carnival, the State and the Black Masses in the United Kingdom', *Black Liberator*, December 1978.

Gutzmore, Cecil (1983a), ' "Black Youth", the Crisis of Accumulation of British Domestic Capital and the "Criminalization" of the Black Community', paper presented at the International Conference, *Legacies of West Indian Slavery*, University of Hull, 26–30 July 1983.

Gutzmore, Cecil (1983b), 'Capital, Black Youth and "Crime"', *Race and Class*, vol. XXV, no. 2 (autumn 1983).

Gutzmore, Cecil and A.X. Cambridge (1974–75), 'The Industrial Action of the Black Masses and the Class Struggle in Britain', *The Black Liberator*, vol. 2(3).

Hall, Douglas (1972), 'Jamaica' in Cohen and Greene eds.

Hall, Douglas (1978), 'The Flight from the Estates Reconsidered: The British West Indies, 1838–42', *Journal of Caribbean History*, 10/11: 7–24.

Hall, Stuart (1980), 'Race, Articulation and Societies Structured in Dominance,' in UNESCO, ed., *Sociological Theories: Race and Colonialism*, Paris: UNESCO.

Hall, Stuart (1988), *The Hard Road to Renewal: Thatcherism and the Crisis of the Left*, London: Verso.

Hall, Stuart (1989), 'Ethnicity: Identity and Difference', *Radical America*, 23(4), October–December 1989.

Hall, Stuart (1990), in J. Rutherford, ed., *Identity: Community, Culture, Difference*.

Hall, Stuart (1991), 'The Local and the Global: Globalization and Ethnicity', and 'Old and New Identities, Old and New Ethnicities', in Anthony King, ed., *Culture, Globalization and the World System*, London: Macmillan.

Hall, Stuart et al. (1978), *Policing the Crisis: Mugging, the State and Law and Order*, London: Macmillan.

Haller, J. S. (1970), 'Race Inferiority in Nineteenth Century Anthropology', *Bulletin of the History of Medicine*, no. 25 pp. 40–51.

Haller, J. S. (1970), 'The Physician Versus the Negro: Medical Concepts of Race in the Late Nineteenth Century', *Bulletin of the History of Medicine*, no. 44, pp. 154–67.

Handler, J. (1974), *The Unappropriated People: Freedom in the Slave Society of Barbados*, Baltimore: Johns Hopkins University Press.

Harewood, Jack (1971), 'Racial Discrimination in Employment in Trinidad and Tobago', *Social and Economic Studies*, 20: 267–93.

Harris, Clive (1981), *Primitive Accumulation and the State or Formal Capitalism in Jamaica*; Ph.D. Thesis, University of Birmingham.

Harris, Clive (1984), 'Not a Doctrine but a Method', unpublished paper.

Harris, Clive (1987), 'British Capitalism, Migration and Relative Surplus-Population', Paper presented at the conference on the Caribbean Diaspora, Centre for Caribbean Studies, Goldsmith's College, University of London, November 1984. Also printed in *Migration*, Band 1, Heft 1 (Jahrgang 1987), pp. 47–90.

Harris, Clive (1987), *Racism, Sexism and the Industrial Reserve Army*, Paper presented at PEWS Annual Conference, State University of New York, Binghamton.

Harris, Clive (1988), 'Images of Blacks in Britain: 1930–1960', in S. Allen and M. Macey, eds, *Race and Social Policy*, ESRC.

Harris, Clive (1991a), 'Configurations of Racism: The Civil Service, 1945–60', *Race and Class*, vol. 33(1), July–September 1991.

Harris, Clive (1991b), 'Researching Racism', Paper presented at *Racism and Migration in Europe in the 1990s* Conference, University of Warwick, 20–22 September 1991.

Harris, Marvin (1970), 'Referential Ambiguity in the Calculus of Brazilian Racial Identity,' in Norman Whitten and J.F. Szwed, eds, *Afro-American Anthology*, New York: The Free Press.

Harris Research Centre (1987), *Political Attitudes Survey*, JN (98746), Conducted 25–29 May 1987).

Harrison, P. (1983), *Inside the Inner City*, Harmondsworth: Penguin.

Hart, Richard (1985), *Slaves Who Abolished Slavery*, vol. 2, Blacks in Rebellion, Kingston: Institute of Social and Economic Research.

Hartmann, Heidi (1979), 'The Unhappy Marriage of Marxism and Feminism', *Capital and Class*, no. 8.

Henriques, F. (1968), *Family and Colour in Jamaica*, London: MacGibbon & Kee.

Henriques, F. and J. Manyoni (1977), 'Ethnic Group Relations in Barbados and Grenada', in UNESCO, *Race and Class in Post-Colonial Society: A Study of Ethnic Group Relations in the English-Speaking Caribbean, Bolivia, Chile and Mexico*, Paris: UNESCO.

Herskovits, M. (1958), *The Myth of the Negro Past*, Boston: Beacon Press.

Heuman, Gad (1981), *Between Black and White: Race, Politics and the Free Coloureds in Jamaica, 1792–1865*, Oxford: Clio Press.

Heuman, Gad (1986), *Out of the House of Bondage: Runaways, Resistance and Marronage in Africa and the New World*, London: Frank Cass.

Higman, B. (1976), *Slave Population and Economy in Jamaica 1807–1834*, Cambridge: Cambridge University Press.

Hill, Errol (1972), *The Trinidad Carnival*, Austin: Texas University Press.

Hill, Robert (1983), 'Leonard P. Howell and Millenarian Visions in Early Rastafari', *Jamaica Journal* (Quarterly of the Institute of Jamaica), vol. 16, no. 1, February 1983.

Hinds, D. (1966), *Journey to an Illusion: The West Indian in Britain*, London: Heinemann.

Hinds, D. (1972a) 'Small Islan' Complex', (1972b) 'Busman's Blues', in A. Salkey, ed.

Hintzen, Percy (1985), 'Bases of Elite Support for a Regime: Race, Ideology and Clientelism as Bases for Leaders in Guyana and Trinidad', *Comparative Political Studies*, 16: 363–91.

Hintzen, Percy (1989), *The Cost of Regime Survival: Racial Mobilization, Elite Domination and Control of the State in Guyana and Trinidad*, Cambridge: Cambridge University Press.

Hiro, Dilip (1973), *Black British, White British*, Harmondsworth: Penguin Books Ltd.

Hoel, B. (1982), 'Contemporary Clothing "Sweatshops": Asian Female Labour and Collective Organisation', in J. West ed.

hooks, bell (1991), 'Representing Whiteness', in *Yearning, Race, Gender and Cultural Politics*, Boston: South End Press.

hooks, bell (1992), 'Representing Whiteness in the Black Imagination', in L. Grossberg, C. Nelson and P. Treichler, eds, *Cultural Studies*, London: Routledge.

House of Commons Social Services Committee (1985–86), Report 3 on the Prison Medical Service, House of Commons, no. 72.

Howe, Darcus, ed. (1977), *The Road Made to Walk on Carnival Day*, a *Race Today* Publication.

Humphrey, Derek (1972), *Police Power and Black People*, London: Panther Books.

ILEA (Inner London Education Authority) (1981) *Ethnic Census of School Support Centres and Educational Guidance Centres* (RS 784/81) ILEA Research and Statistics Branch.

ILEA (Inner London Education Authority) (1985a), *Educational Opportunities for All*, London: ILEA Research Studies.

ILEA (Inner London Education Authority) (1985b), *School Support Programme: The Re-Integration of Pupils into Mainstream Schools* (RS 968/85) ILEA Research and Statistics Branch.

Institute of Contemporary Arts, ed. (1987), *Identity: The Real Me* (ICA Documents, no. 6), London: ICA.

Institute of Contemporary Arts, ed. (1988), *Black Film, British Cinema* (ICA Documents, no. 7), London: ICA.

Institute of Race Relations (1987), *Policing Against Black People*, London: IRR.

James, C.L.R. (1963), *The Black Jacobins* (orig. 1938), New York: Vintage Books.

James, C.L.R. (1980), 'The West Indian Middle Classes', *Spheres of Existence: Selected Writings*, London: Allison & Busby.

James, G. (1954), *Stolen Legacy*, New York: Philosophical Library.

James, Winston (1983a), 'The Decline and Fall of Michael Manley: Jamaica 1972–80', *Capital and Class*, no. 19, spring 1983.

James, Winston (1983b), 'The IMF and "Democratic Socialism" in Jamaica', in Latin American Bureau (ed.), *The Poverty Brokers: The IMF and Latin America*, London: Latin America Bureau.

James, Winston (1983c), 'The Hurricane that Shook the Caribbean', *New Left Review*, no. 138, March–April 1983.

James, Winston (1983d), 'States of the Nation', review of Benedict Anderson (1983), *City Limits*, 9–15 September 1983.

James, Winston (1983), 'The Decline and Fall of Michael Manley: Jamaica 1972–80', *Capital and Class*, no. 19, spring 1983.

James, W. (1984), 'On Black Identity and Nationalism in Britain', paper presented on March 11 to History Workshop Conference on Patriotism: Myth and Ideology in the Making of English National Identity.

James, Winston (1986), 'A Long Way from Home: On Black Identity in Britain', *Immigrants and Minorities*, 5(3), November 1986.

James, Winston (1989), 'The Making of Black Identities', in Raphael Samuel, ed.

Jiminez (1987), 'Population and Capitalism', *Latin American Perspectives*, vol. 4, no. 4.

Johnson, B. (1983), 'Claudia Jones: Freedom Fighter', *Dragons Teeth*, no. 16, winter 1983.

Johnson, B. (1985), *I Think of My Mother: Notes on the Life and Times of Claudia Jones*, Karia Press.

Jones, Claudia (1964), 'The Caribbean Community in Britain', *Freedomways*, summer 1964.

Jones, P. (1981), 'Ins and Outs of the Home Office and IPS Migration Data: A Reply', *New Community*, vol. IX, no. 2.

Jung, C. G. (1970), 'Your Negroid and Indian Behaviour', *Forum*, vol. 83(4), April 1970.

Jung, C. G. (1928), *Contributions to Analytical Psychology*, New York: Harcourt Brace Jovanovich.

Kapo, R. (1982), *A Savage Culture – Racism, a Black British View*, London: Quartet.

Katznelson, Ira (1976), *Black Men, White Cities*, London: Oxford University Press for Institute of Race Relations.

Kay, Geoffrey and James Mott (1982), *Political Order and the Law of Labour*, London: Macmillan.

Kasinitz, P. (1992),*Caribbean New York: Black Immigrants and the Politics of Race*, Ithaca: Cornell University Press.

Kellman, T., 'Black Moods in Britain', *Caribbean Contact* May 1984.

Kennedy, Lisa, Cornell West, Joan Morgan, Joe Wood, Julius Lester, Greg Tate, Michelle Wallace, bell hooks (1991), 'Black Like Who? Notes on African American Identity', *The Village Voice*, 17 September 1991.

Khan, Naseem (1984), 'Work in Progress', *New Statesman*, September 1984.

Knight, F. (1970), *Slave Society in Cuba During the Nineteenth Century*, London: University of Wisconsin Press.

Kruijer, G. J. (1969), *A Sociological Report on the Christiana Area*, Kingston: Ministry of Agriculture.

La Guerre, J. ed. (1974), *Calcutta to Caroni: The East Indians of Trinidad*, London: Longman.

Lambert, J. (1970), *Crime, Police, and Race Relations*, London: Oxford University Press for Institute of Race Relations.

Lamming, George (1980) [1954], *The Emigrants*, London: Allison & Busby.

Lamming, George (1984) [1960], *The Pleasures of Exile*, London: Allison & Busby.

Latin America Bureau (1984), *Guyana: Fraudulent Revolution*, London: Latin America Bureau.

Laubscher, B. J. F. (1937), *Sex, Custom and Psychopathology: A Study of South African Pagan Natives*, London: George Routledge & Sons.

Laurence, K. (1971), *Immigration into the West Indies in the Nineteenth Century*, Aylesbury: Ginn & Co.

Lawrence, D. (1974), *Black Migrants: White Natives*, London: Cambridge University Press.

Lawrence, E. (1982), 'In the Abundance of Water the Fool is Thirsty: Sociology and Black "Pathology" ', in Centre for Contemporary Cultural Studies, ed.

Layton-Henry, Zig (1984), *The Politics of Race in Britain*, London: Allen & Unwin.

Lerner, Gerda, ed. (1973), *Black Women in White America: a Documentary History*, New York: Vintage Books.

Lever-Tracy, Constance (1983), 'Immigrant Workers and Post-war Capitalism: In Reserve or Core Troops in the Front Line?', *Politics and Society*, 13(1): 127–57.

Lewis, G. (1969), 'Race Relations in Britain: A View from the Caribbean', *Race Today*, vol. 1, No. 3, July 1969.

Lewis, G. (1978), *Slavery, Imperialism and Freedom*, New York: Monthly Review Press.

Lewis, G. (1983), *Main Currents in the Caribbean Thought*, Baltimore: Johns Hopkins University Press.

Little, Ken (1947), *Negroes in Britain*, London: K. Paul, Trench, Trubner.

Littlewood, R. and M. Lipsedge (1981a), 'Acute Psychotic Reactions in Caribbean Born Patients', *Psychological Medicine*, vol. 11, pp. 289–302.

Littlewood, R. and M. Lipsedge (1981b), *Aliens and Alienists – Ethnic Minorities and Psychiatry*, London: Penguin.

Long, Edward (1970) [1774], *The History of Jamaica* (2 vols), London: Frank Cass.

Lowenthal (1972), *West Indian Societies*, London: Oxford University Press for Institute of Race Relations.

Lowenthal, D. (1978), 'West Indian Emigrants Overseas,' in C. Clarke, ed., *Caribbean Social Relations*, Centre for Latin-American Studies, University of Liverpool, Monograph no. 8, Liverpool.

McCollester, Charles (1973), 'The Political Thought of Amilcar Cabral', *Monthly Review*, vol. 24(10).

Macdonald, Ian, Reena Bhavnani, Gus John, Lily Khan (1989), *Murder in the Playground: The Report of the Macdonald Inquiry into Racism and Racial Violence in Manchester Schools*, London: Longsight Press.

McGuire, S. (1988), ' "Sorry Love" – Violence Against Women and the State Response', Critical Social Policy.

McKay, J. and Lewins, F. (1978), 'Ethnicity and the Ethnic Group: A Conceptual Analysis and Reformulation', *Ethnic and Racial Studies*, vol. 1, no. 4, October.

Mackenzie, S. and D. Rose (1983), 'Industrial Change, the Domestic Economy and Home Life,' in J. Anderson et al.

Mackintosh N. J. and C. G. N. Mascie-Taylor (1985), 'The IQ Question', in DES, 1985.

Madoo, P. (1965), 'The Transition from "Light Skinned" to "Coloured" ', in Tajfel and Dawson, eds.

Mama, A., A. Mars and P. Stevens (1986), *Breaking the Silence: Women's Imprisonment*, Women's Equality Group/London Strategic Policy Unit.

Mangru, Basdeo (1987), *Benevolent Neutrality: Indian Government Policy and Labor Migration to British Guiana 1854–1884*, London: Hansib.

Mannheim, Karl (1952), Essays *on the Sociology of Knowledge*, London: Routledge & Kegan Paul.

Marx, Karl (1973), 'The Eighteenth Brumaire of Louis Bonaparte', in Karl Marx, *Surveys from Exile*, ed. D. Fernbach, Harmondsworth: Penguin.

Marx, Karl (1974), *Capital* vol. 1, London: Lawrence & Wishart.

Massey, D. (1983), 'Industrial Restructuring as Class Restructuring: Production Decentralisation and Local Uniqueness', *Regional Studies*, vol. 17, no. 2.

Massey, D. (1985), *Spatial Divisions of Labour*, London: Macmillan.

Mercer. K./Black Health Workers & Patients Group (1984), 'Black Communities Experience of Psychiatric Services', *International Journal of Social Psychiatry*, vol. 30(1&2).

Miles, Robert (1982), *Racism and Migrant Labour*, London: Routledge & Kegan Paul.

Milkman, Ruth (1975), 'Women's Work and Economic Crisis: Some Lessons from the Great Depression', *Review of Radical Political Economics*, 8(1), spring 1975.

Milne, R.S. (1981), *Politics in Ethnically Bi-Polar States: Guyana, Malaysia and Fiji*, Vancouver: University of British Columbia Press.

Ministry of Labour (1964), *Report of the Committee of Inquiry to Review the Pay and Conditions of Employment of the Drivers and Conductors of the London Transport Board's Road Services*, London: HMSO.

Mitter, Swasti (1986), 'Industrial Restructuring and Manufacturing Homework: Immigrant Women in the UK Clothing Industry', *Capital and Class*, no. 27, winter 1986: 37–80.

Moore, Brian (1977), 'The Retention of Caste Notions Among the Indian Immigrants in British Guiana During the Nineteenth Century', *Comparative Studies in Society and History*, 19: 96–107.

Moore, Robert (1975), *Racism and Black Resistance in Britain*, London: Pluto Press.

Mörner, M. (1967), *Race Mixture in the History of Latin America*, Boston: Little Brown.

Morrison, Lionel (1987), 'Roy Sawh: A Profile', in Roy Sawh, *From Where I Stand*, London: Hansib Publishing Limited.

Morrison, Toni (1992), *Playing in the Dark: Whiteness and the Literary Imagination*, Cambridge, MA: Harvard University Press.

Morrissey, Marietta (1989), *Slave Women in the New World: Gender Stratification in the Caribbean*, Lawrence: University Press of Kansas.

Multiple Image Productions (for Channel 4 Television) (1986), *We're Not Mad, We're Angry*, 17 November 1986.

Naipaul, V.S. (1969), *The Middle Passage*, Harmondsworth: Penguin Books.

Naipaul, V.S. (1972), *The Overcrowded Barracoon and Other Articles*, London: André Deutsch.

Nath, Dwarka (1950), *A History of Indians in Guyana*, London: published by the author.

Nettleford, Rex (1970), *Mirror, Mirror: Race, Identity and Protest in Jamaica*, Kingston: William Collins & Sangster.

Nevadomsky, Joseph (1983), 'Economic Organization, Social Mobility and Changing Social Status Among East Indians in Rural Trinidad', *Ethnology*, 22: 63–79.

Newnhan, Anne (1986), *Employment, Unemployment and Black People*, London: Runnymede Trust.

Nikolinakos, M. (1975), 'Notes Towards a General Theory of Migration', *Race and Class*, 17(1).

Office of Population Census and Surveys (OPCS) (1982), *Labour Force Survey, 1981*, London: HMSO.

OPCS (1984), *International Migration: Migrants Entering and Leaving the United Kingdom and England and Wales*, 1982 (Series MN no. 9), London: HMSO.

OPCS (1988), *Labour Force Survey, 1986*, London: HMSO.

OPCS (1989), *Labour Force Survey, 1987*, London: HMSO.

OPCS Monitor (1984), *International Migration, 1983*, London: HMSO.

Owens, Joseph (1976), *Dread: The Rastafarians of Jamaica*, Kingston: Sangster.

Pahl, J. (1982), 'Police response to battered women', *Journal of Social Welfare Law*, no. 337.

Pahl, J., ed. (1985), *Private Violence and Public Policy*, Routledge & Kegan Paul.

Parmar, P (1982), 'Gender, Race and Class: Asian Women in Resistance', in Centre for Contemporary Cultural Studies, ed.

Pasquino, P. (1978), 'Theatricum Politicum. The Genealogy of Capital – Police and the State of Prosperity', *Ideology and Consciousness*, no .4, autumn 1978.

Patterson, O. (1967), *The Sociology of Slavery*, London: MacGibbon & Kee.

Patterson, H. Orlando (1968), 'West Indian Migrants Returning Home', *Race*, vol. X, no. 1.

Patterson, O. (1987), 'The Emerging West Atlantic System: Migration, Culture and Underdevelopment in the United States and the circum-Caribbean Region', in W. Alonso, ed., *Population in an Interacting World*, Cambridge, Mass.: Harvard University Press.

Patterson, S. (1965), *Dark Strangers: A Study of West Indians in London*: Harmondsworth: Penguin Books.

Peach, Ceri (1968), *West Migration to Britain*, London: Oxford University Press.

Peach, Ceri (1968), 'The Force of West Indian Island Identity in Britain', in C. Clarke, D. Ley and C. Peach, eds, *Geography and Ethnic Pluralism*, London: Allen & Unwin.

Peach, Ceri (1981a), 'Ins and Outs of Home Office and IPS Migration Data', *New Community*, vol. IX, no .1.

Peach, Ceri (1981b), 'Straining at Gnats and Swallowing Camels', *New Community*, vol. IX, no. 2.

Pearson, D. (1977), 'West Indian Communal Associations in Britain: Some Observations', *New Community*, vol. V, no. 4, spring–summer 1977.

Pearson, D. (1981), *Race Class and Political Activism: A Study of West Indians in Britain*, Farnborough: Gower.

Perlo, Victor (1975), *Economics of Racism U.S.A.: Roots of Black Inequality*, New York: International Publishers.

Philipson, Ilene (1991), 'What's the Big I.D.? The Politics of the Authentic Self', with responses from Henry Gates, Ellen Willis, David Biale, and Arthur Waskow, *Tikkun*, November–December 1991.

Phillips, Ron (1975–76), 'The Black Masses and the Political Economy of Manchester', *The Black Liberator*, vol. 2(4).

Pilkington, E. (1988), *Beyond the Mother Country: West Indians and Notting Hill White Riots*, London: I. B. Tauris.

Philpott, S. (1977), 'The Montserratans: Migration, Dependency and the Maintenance of Island Ties in England', in J. Watson ed.

Phizacklea, A. (1982), 'Migrant Women and Wage Labour: The Case of West Indian Women in Britain', in J. West, ed.

Portman, M.V. (c.1895), Ethnographic Studies of the Andamaneses Islands. Photographs nos. 188/1–7 & 10–11; Notes vols 8–9 & 12–13. India Office Library (London).

Post, Ken (1970), 'The Bible as Ideology: Ethiopianism in Jamaica 1930–38', in C.H. Allen and R. W. Johnson (eds), *African Perspectives: Papers in the History, Politics and Economics of Africa Presented to Thomas Hodgkin*, Cambridge: Cambridge University Press.

Post, Ken (1978), *Arise Ye Starvelings: The Jamaican Labour Rebellion of 1938 and Its Aftermath*, The Hague: Martinus Nijhoff.

Post, Ken (1981), *Strike the Iron: A Colony at War*, 2 vols, New Jersey and The Hague: Martinus Nijhoff.

Post, Ken (1984), 'Class, Race and Culture in the Caribbean: Some Speculations on Theory', mimeo.

Premdas, Ralph (1972–3), *Party Politics and Racial Division in Guyana*, Studies in Race and Nations, vol. 4, Denver: University of Denver Center on International Race Relations.

Price, R., ed. (1973), *Maroon Societies: Rebel Slave Communities in the Americas*, New York: Anchor Books.

Prins, H.A. (1980), *Offenders, Deviants or Patients?*, London: Tavistock.

Pryce, K. (1979), *Endless Pressure: A Study of West Indian Lifestyles in London*, Harmondsworth: Penguin.

Pulle, Stanislaus (1972), *Employment Policies in the Hosiery Industry*, Runnymede Industrial Unit.

Ramchand, K. (1965), 'The Colour Problem at the University: A West Indian's Changing Attitudes', in H. Tajfel and J. Dawson, eds.

Ramdin, R. (1987), *The Making of the Black Working Class in Britain*, Aldershot: Wildwood House.

Ratcliffe, Peter (1981), *Racism and Reaction: A Profile of Handsworth*, London: Routledge & Kegan Paul.

Rex, J. and S. Tomlinson (1979), *Colonial Immigrants in a British City: A Class Analysis*, London: Routledge & Kegan Paul.

Rex, John (1983), *Race Relations in Sociological Theory*, 2nd edn, London: Routledge & Kegan Paul.

Ritchie, S. S., Q.C. (for the Department of Health and Social Security) (1985), *Inquiry Concerning the Death of Michael Martin at Broadmoor Hospital on July 6 1984*, London: DHSS (London).

Roach Family Support Committee (1989), *Policing in Hackney, 1945–1984*, London: Karia Press.

Roberts, G.W. and J. Byrne (1966), 'Summary Statistics on Indenture and Associated Migration Affecting the West Indies 1834–1918', *Population Studies*, 20: 125–34.

Rodney, Walter (1975), *The Groundings with My Brothers*, London: Bogle L'Ouverture Publications.

Rodney, Walter (1981), *A History of the Guyanese Working People, 1881–1905*, London: Heinemann Educational.

Rohlehr, Gordon (1981), *Pathfinder: Black Awakening in the Arrivants of Edward Kamau Brathwaite*, Tunapuna: Gordon Rohlehr.

Roosens, Eugeen (1989), *Creating Ethnicity: The Process of Ethnogenesis*, Newbury Park: Sage Publications.

Rose, E.J. et al. (1969), *Colour and Citizenship*, London: IRR/OUP.

Rout, L.B. (1976), *The African Experience in Spanish America, 1502 to the Present Day*, Cambridge: Cambridge University Press.

Rubenstein, H. (1982), 'Return Migration to the English-Speaking Caribbean: Review and Commentary', in Skinner, W. et al., eds, *Return Migration and Remittances: Developing a Caribbean Perspective*, Washington DC: Smithsonian Institution.

Runnymede Trust (1983), Bulletin no. 158, August 1983.

Runnymede Trust and the Radical Statistics Race Group (1980), *Britain's Black Population*, London: Heinemann.

Rutherford, J., ed. (1990), *Identity: Community, Culture, Difference*, London: Lawrence & Wishart.

Ryan, Selwyn (1972), *Race and Nationalism in Trinidad and Tobago*, Toronto: University of Toronto Press.

Salaman, Graeme (1984), *Class at Work*, London: Batsford Academic and Educational Ltd.

Salkey, A., ed. (1972), *Stories from the Caribbean: An Anthology*, 2nd edn., London: Paul Elek Books.

Salkey, A., ed. (1973), *Caribbean Essays: An Anthology*, London: Evans.

Samuel, Raphael, ed. (1989), *Patriotism: The Making and Unmaking of British National Identity*, vol. 1 (1989a); *History and Politics*, vol. 2 (1989b); *Minorities and Outsiders*, vol. 3 (1989c): National Fictions, London: Routledge.

Sartre, Jean-Paul (1976), *Black Orpheus*, Paris: Présence Africaine.

Sawh, R. (1987), *From Where I Stand*, London: Hansib Publishing.
Scarman, Lord (1981), *The Brixton Disorders 10–12 April 1981*, cmnd 8427, London: HMSO.
Schwartz, Barton, ed. (1967), *Caste in Overseas Indian Communities*, San Francisco: Chandler.
Schweitzer, P., ed. (1984), *A Place to Stay: Memories of Pensioners from Many Lands*, London: Age Exchange Theatre.
Scull, A. T. (1980), *Museums of Madness: The Social Organisation of Insanity in Nineteenth Century England*, London: Allen Lane.
Searle, Chris, ed. (1984), *Words Unchained*, London: Zed Books.
Selbourne, David (1983a), 'I'm Getting Out Before It Fall on Me', *New Society*, 23 May 1983.
Selbourne, David (1983b), 'The New Black Exodus: Blacks Who Have Their Eyes Set on Home', *New Society*, 19 May 1983.
Selvon, Sam (1986), 'Three into One Can't Go: East Indian, Trinidadian or West Indian?' *Wasafiri*, no. 5, autumn 1986.
Senior, Clarence and Douglas Manley (1956), *The West Indian in Britain*, London: Fabian Colonial Bureau.
Sennett, Richard and Jonathan Cobb (1977), *The Hidden Injuries of Class*, Cambridge: Cambridge University Press.
Shepherd, Verene (1988), 'Indians and Blacks in Jamaica in the Nineteenth and Early Twentieth Centuries: A Micro-study of the Foundations of Race Antagonisms', *Immigrants and Minorities*, 7:95–112.
Sherwood, Marika (1985), *Many Struggles*, London: Karia Press.
Sherwood, R. (1980), *The Psycho-dynamics of Race: Vicious and Benign Spirals*, Brighton: Harvester Press.
Shyllon, Folarin (1981), 'Folarin Shyllon Talks to Imruh Caesar', *Frontline*, pp. 109–11.
Simeral, Margaret (1978), 'Women and the Reserve Army of Labour', *Insurgent Sociologist*, vol. VIII (2–3), fall 1978.
Simpson, K. (1980), 'Intermediate Treatment in an Age of Short Sharp Shocks', *Community Education*, no. 1.
Singaravelou (1987), *Les Indiens de la Caraibe*, 3 vols, Paris: l'Harmattan.
Singleman, J. and Tienda (1985), 'The Process of Occupational Change in a Service Society: The Case of the United States', in B. Roberts et al., *New Approaches to Economic Life*, Manchester: Manchester University Press.
Sivanandan, A (1982), *A Different Hunger: Writings on Black Resistance*, London: Pluto Press.
Smart, B. and C. Smart (1978), *Women, Sexuality and Social Control*, London: Routledge & Kegan Paul.
Smart, C. (1976), *Women, Crime and Criminology: A Feminist Critique*, London: Routledge & Kegan Paul.
Smith, B., ed. (1983), *Home Girls: A Black Feminist Anthology*, New York: Women of Color Press.
Smith, D. (1976), *The Facts of Racial Disadvantage*, London: PEP.
Smith, D. (1977), *Racial Disadvantage in Britain*, Harmondsworth: Penguin Books Ltd.
Smith, David (1981), *Unemployment and Racial Minorities*, Policy Studies Institute.
Smith, Graham (1987), *When Jim Crow Met John Bull*, London: I.B. Tauris & Co. Ltd.
Smith, M.G. et al. (1960), *The Report on the Ras Tafari in Kingston, Kingston*: University College of the West Indies.

Smith, Susan (1989), *The Politics of 'Race' and Residence: Citizenship, Segregation and White Supremacy in Britain*, Cambridge: Polity Press.

SNHDC (Stoke Newington & Hackney Defence Campaign), (c.1985), Bulletin, no. 30.

Snowden, Frank (1970), *Blacks in Antiquity: Ethiopians in the Greco-Roman Experience*, Cambridge, MA: Harvard University Press.

Solomos, John (1989), *Race and Racism in Contemporary Britain*, London: Macmillan.

Staples, R. (1982), *Black Masculinity: The Black Male's Role in American Society*, Black Scholar Press.

Steele, Beverly (1976), 'East Indian Indenture and the Work of the Presbyterian Church Among Indians in Grenada', *Caribbean Quarterly*, 22: 28–39.

Sutton, Constance (1987), 'The Caribbeanization of New York City and the Emergence of a Transnational Socio-Cultural System', in C. Sutton and Elsa Chaney, eds, *Caribbean Life in New York City: Sociocultural Dimensions*, New York Center for Migration Studies of New York, Inc.

Tajfel, H. and J. Dawson, eds (1965), *Disappointed Guest by African, Asian and West Indian Students*, London: Oxford University Press.

Taylor, E. (1976), 'The Social Adjustment of Returned Migrants to Jamaica', in Henry, F., ed, *Ethnicity in the Americas*, The Hague: Mouton.

Tewfik, G. I. and A. Okasha (1965), 'Psychosis and Immigration', *Postgraduate Medical Journal*, vol. 44, pp. 603–11.

Thakur, Manab (1970), *Industry as Seen by Immigrant Workers*, London: Runnymede Industrial Unit.

The Imperial Gazetteer of India (1908), vol. V, Oxford: Clarendon Press.

Thiam, Awa (1986), *Black Sisters Speak Out: Feminism and Oppression in Black Africa*, London: Pluto Press.

Thomas, A. and S. Sillen (1979), *Racism and Psychiatry*, New Jersey: The Citadel Press.

Thomas-Hope, E. (1985), 'Return Migration and its Implications for Caribbean Development', in R. Pastor, ed., *Migration and Development in the Caribbean: The Unexplored Connection*, Boulder: Westview Press.

Tinker, H. (1974), *A New System of Slavery: The Export of Indian Labour Overseas 1830–1920*, London: Oxford University Press for Institute of Race Relations.

Tomlinson, S. (1981), *Educational Sub-normality – A Study in Decision-making*, London: RKP.

Toney, J. (1989), 'The Perpetuation of a Culture of Migration: West Indian American Ties with Home, 1900–1979', *Afro-Americans in New York Life and History*, vol. 13, no. 1.

Troyna, Barry (1979), 'Differential Commitment of Ethnic Identity by Black Youths in Britain', *New Community*, vol. VII, no. 3, winter 1979.

Turner, Louis and Joan Ash (1975), *The Golden Hordes: International Tourism and the Pleasure Periphery*, London: Constable.

van der Meer, Peter and Steven Vertovec (1991), 'Brahmanism Abroad: on Caribbean Hinduism as an Ethnic Religion', *Ethnology*, 30: 149–66.

Vernon, P.E. (1969), *Intelligence and Cultural Environment*, London: Methuen.

Vertovec, Steven (1990), 'Oil Boom and Recession in Trinidad Indian Villages', in C. Clarke, C. Peach, S. Vertovec, eds, *South Asians Overseas: Migration and Ethnicity*, Cambridge: Cambridge University Press.

Vertovec, Steven (1992a), *Hindu Trinidad: Religion, Ethnicity and Socio-Economic Change*, London: Macmillan.

Vertovec, Steven (1992b), 'Community and Congregation in London Hindu Temples: Divergent Trends', *New Community*, 18(2), January 1992.

Vertovec, Steven (n.d.), 'Official and Popular Hinduism in Diaspora: Historical and Contemporary Trends in Surinam, Trinidad and Guyana', forthcoming.

Vertovec, Steven (forthcoming), 'Caught in an Ethnic Quandary: Indo-Caribbean Hindus in London', in Roger Ballard, ed., *Desh Pardesh: The South Asian Presence in Britain*, London: C. Hurst & Co.

Vint, A. (1932), 'A Preliminary Note on the Pre-frontal Cortex of the East African Native', *East African Medical Journal*, no. 9, pp. 30–55.

Walker, A. (1983), *The Color Purple*, London: Women's Press.

Walker, A. (1983), *In Search of Our Mothers' Gardens: Womanist Prose*, New York: Harcourt Brace Jovanovich.

Walmsley, Anne (1986), 'The Caribbean Artists Movement', *Wasafiri*, no. 5, autumn 1986.

Watson, James L. ed. (1977), *Between Two Cultures: Migrants and Minorities in Britain*, Oxford: Basil Blackwell.

West, J., ed. (1982), *Work, Women and the Labour Market*, London: Routledge & Kegan Paul.

West Indian Standing Conference (1967), *The Unsquare Deal: London's Bus Colour Bar*, WISC.

Wheelwright, E. and K. Buckley, eds (1978), *Essays in the Political Economy of Australian Captialism*, vol. 3, Sydney: ANZ Books.

Williams, Eric (1969), *The Negro in the Caribbean*, Westport (Connecticut): Greenwood Press.

Wilson, E. (1977), *Women and the Welfare State*, London: Tavistock.

Women's Aid Federation England (1988), *You Can't Beat a Woman: Women and Children in Refuges*, WAFE, PO Box 391, Bristol.

Women's National Commission (1984), *Violence Against Women*, Report of an Ad Hoc Working Group, London: Cabinet Office.

Wood, Donald (1968), *Trinidad in Transition: The Years After Slavery*, London: Oxford University Press.

Yllo, K. and M. Bograd (1988), *Feminist Perspectives on Wife Abuse*, Newbury Park: Sage.

List of Contributors

Bob Carter is co-author of *No Blacks Please, We're British!* (Routledge, forthcoming). He has written on issues concerning education, anti-racism and national identity. Currently, he is a senior lecturer in sociology at Worcester College of Higher Education.

Errol Francis, a pioneer campaigner against racism in psychiatry, was for many years the Director of the Afro-Caribbean Mental Health Association. Until recently he was a fellow of the Cambridge Institute of Criminology, University of Cambridge. He has researched and written extensively on black people and psychiatric services in Britain.

Cecil Gutzmore was born in Jamaica. He studied at the University of Leicester and at the School of Oriental and African Studies, University of London. He co-edited the *Black Liberator* journal and is widely published. He has been at the forefront of grassroots black politics in Britain for many years. He currently works as a training consultant and researcher.

Clive Harris is co-author of *No Blacks Please, We're British!* (Routledge, forthcoming). He has written on Caribbean history and underdevelopment, post-war migration, and racism and identity. He currently lectures in race and ethnic studies in the Centre for Research in Ethnic Relations, Warwick University.

Winston James studied at the University of Leeds and at the London School of Economics and Political Science, University of London. He has written on the Caribbean diaspora and on Caribbean history, politics and political economy. He has taught at Goldsmiths' College, University of London and at the University of Reading. He was, until recently, the Director of Caribbean Studies at the University of North London, and currently teaches History and Sociology at Columbia University, New York.

Shirley Joshi is co-author of *No Blacks Please, We're British!* (Routledge, forthcoming). She lectures in sociology at the University of Central England in Birmingham.

Gail Lewis has written extensively on women and the labour market. She studied at the London School of Economics and the Institute for Development Studies at Sussex University. She currently teaches part-time at the Open University.

307

Amina Mama is Nigerian. She studied at the University of St. Andrews and at Birkbeck College, University of London. She is widely published and is the author of *The Hidden Struggle: Statutory and Voluntary Sector Responses to Violence Against Black Women in the Home*, (London: Runnymede Trust 1989). She has for many years been involved in black women's politics in Britain and Africa. Until recently she taught at the Institute of Social Studies in The Hague.

Steven Vertovec is author of *Hindu Trinidad: Religion, Ethnicity and Socio-Economic Change* (Macmillan, 1992), editor of *Aspects of South Asian Diaspora* (Oxford University Press, 1991) and co-editor of *South Asians Overseas: Migration and Ethnicity* (Cambridge University Press, 1990). He is currently research fellow at the School of Geography, Oxford University.

Claudette Williams studied at Goldsmiths' College, University of London. She has for many years been involved in black women's politics and in anti-racist educational campaigns in Britain. She has written on black women and on education. She is currently Senior Lecturer in education at the University of North London.

Index